MICROSOFT®
SMS 1.2
ADMINISTRATOR'S
SURVIVAL GUIDE

Ric Anderson, Rob Cryan, James Farhat, Teri Guendling,
Blake Hall, Gary Hughes, Lance Mortensen, David
Mosier, Jeff Sparks, Paul Thomsen, Doug Walcutt

SAMS
PUBLISHING

201 West 103rd Street
Indianapolis, Indiana 46290

PUBLISHER AND PRESIDENT	Richard K. Swadley
PUBLISHING MANAGER	Rosemarie Graham
DIRECTOR OF EDITORIAL SERVICES	Cindy Morrow
MANAGING EDITOR	Mary Inderstrodt
ASSISTANT MARKETING MANAGERS	Kristina Perry
	Rachel Wolfe

ACQUISITIONS EDITOR
Corrine M. Wire

DEVELOPMENT EDITOR
Todd Bumbalough

SOFTWARE DEVELOPMENT SPECIALIST
John Warriner

PRODUCTION EDITOR
Brice P. Gosnell

COPY EDITORS
Margaret Berson
Kris Simmons

INDEXER
Christine Nelsen

TECHNICAL REVIEWER
Blake Hall

EDITORIAL COORDINATOR
Katie Wise

TECHNICAL EDIT COORDINATOR
Lorraine Schaffer

RESOURCE COORDINATOR
Deborah Frisby

Editorial Assistants
Carol Ackerman
Andi Richter
Rhonda Tinch-Mize

COVER DESIGNER
Jay Corpus

BOOK DESIGNER
Alyssa Yesh

COPY WRITER
Peter Fuller

PRODUCTION TEAM SUPERVISORS
Brad Chinn
Charlotte Clapp

PRODUCTION
Carol Bowers
Jeanne Clark
Cyndi Davis
Gene Redding

Overview

Contents

PART III   IMPLEMENTING SMS—SETTING UP SHOP

8   Installing and Upgrading Your NT Servers   159

Acknowledgments

From Ric Anderson: I'd like to thank my wife, Sharon, for her patience and support. To my children, Derrick, Justin, Heather, and Michael, for sacrificing quality time so Dad could "work on the book." To my parents, Darlene and Jim, for always believing in me. To Steph, Jamie, and Russ, as well as my other good friends and coworkers at Stream International, for their support. Tom, Michael, and the rest of the Bell Atlantic gang were also a big help. Finally, to Corrine Wire and Todd Bumbalough for their patience and guiding hand.

From Rob Cryan: I would like to extend special thanks to my wonderful wife, Melissa, for her patience when I work late, encouragement to pursue this writing, and every other technology-related endeavor that takes me away from home, and support when the computer industry's stress reaches critical mass. Without her I would not be where I am today. I also would like to thank my mom, dad, and sister for always being there.

From James Farhat: There are many people that I want to thank. I especially want to thank my family for their support while writing the book. I thank C.J. for the wisdom and strength to take on this project, as well as for her insight and advice from which I have benefited greatly. C.J., you're wonderful. Thanks to Devry and John for their knowledge and advice, which teaches me what to expect. To Jason Rader, for the help and understanding when I am in need. To Lenette, for dealing with me in time of difficulty. For Kimmer, who supports me in my endeavors. To Rhonda, who pushes me to keep grasping. To Roomie Mike, for the mess in the living room and the many times he dealt with a cranky James. Gina, for your tired hands and your sweet nature, which made you a very understanding person. To all the people at PPI that helped me during the time I wrote the book. To Corrine, for her assistance and her understanding while working to finish. And to my father, a person who pushed me and encouraged me to work hard and smart in improving myself to do the right thing.

From Gary Hughes: I would like to thank my wife and daughters for their loyal support and patience during the writing of this manuscript. I have once again spent far too many hours in front of a computer instead of with them. And though it is hard to justify all of the long hours that work and professional endeavors consume, I would like the world to know that everything I do, I do for my family. Without them, it would all mean nothing.

From Lance Mortensen: For my wife, Luann, who has always supported me throughout my sometimes difficult career, and to my children, Bryce, Jessany, and Devin, who were always understanding when Daddy had to work instead of play.

From David Mosier: I would like to thank my family for their support and guidance, and my wife, a computer widow, whose patience is greatly appreciated and significantly responsible for my experiences with and knowledge of the computer industry.

About the Authors

Ric Anderson is a marketing and technical consultant with Stream International, Inc. and a trainer with Learning Tree International. Ric has over 11 years of experience in the computer industry, focusing on desktop and LAN/WAN implementations. Ric currently holds Microsoft's Certified Professional (MCP), Microsoft Certified Systems Engineer (MCSE), Microsoft Certified Trainer (MCT), Novell Certified NetWare Engineer (CNE), and NetWare 4.1 Certified Network Administrator (CNA) certifications. In addition to his certifications, Ric has helped several Fortune 500 and 1000 companies implement Windows NT, Windows 95, NetWare 3.x-4.x, SQL Server, and SMS. Ric has been involved with SMS since it was Hermes, Windows since version 1.0, DOS since 2.0, OS/2 since 1.1, Windows NT since Beta 3.1, and NetWare 2.x since it required keycards. Ric has also worked closely with Microsoft for development. Ric can be reached at Ric_Anderson@Stream.com.

Rob Cryan is a Senior Engineer with USConnect Baltimore in the Microsoft in the BackOffice Practice Group. He is a Microsoft Certified Systems Engineer and a Certified NetWare Engineer, focusing on providing solutions via Microsoft products ranging from design and consultation services to integration. He specializes in capacity planning, the upper echelon of server and storage products, SMS design and implementation, and remote communications design and implementation. He is also involved with Internet/intranet and firewall solutions.

Rob has six years of experience in the computer industry providing support and solutions to a variety of clients. He prefers the quiet of the mountains, but the challenge of fast-paced technology in the Baltimore/Washington area has some appeal. He can be reached via the Internet at Rob_Cryan@wash-balt.usconnect.com.

James Farhat's ongoing passion for all areas of computer technology and telephony were sparked in 1979 when, at age 5, he received his first computer, a TRS 80 Model 3. At age 17, James was providing network installation, integration, and consulting services. At age 19, he was the network administrator for Gates Energy Corporation. James achieved Certified NetWare Engineer (CNE) certification at 19, Certified NetWare Instructor (CNI) and Master CNE certifications at age 20, and Microsoft Certified Systems Engineer (MCSE) certification at age 21.

James continues to share his technical expertise and vision of technology through various venues, including hosting a call-in radio talk show, *Tech Chat with Farhat*, authoring technical manuals, and speaking engagements with organizations such as the International Technical Training Association (ITTA) on topics including *Business Opportunities in Multi-media Training over High Speed Networks*. James also attends the *Windows NT Magazine* Professional Conference, speaking on his favorite topics.

James is employed as a technical trainer for Productivity Point International, located in Jacksonville, Florida, and enjoys reading, music, snowboarding, and speculating in high technology stocks. James can be reached at JFarhat@ProPoint.com.

Teri Guendling launched her career over twenty years ago and has successfully managed a dual career of teaching and corporate consulting. Taking advantage of a solid educational foundation, she has been able to play a leading role in corporate projects, including business modeling, systems analysis and design, expert systems development, and enterprise-level networking systems.

Teri holds an undergraduate degree in Computer Science and a master of science degree in Management Information Systems. Studying as a doctoral candidate, she was able to develop graduate-level courses in the design and implementation of corporate expert systems. She is presently involved in a project focusing on using expert systems technology with Microsoft BackOffice systems. Teri was a tenured instructor of Computer Science and taught undergraduate as well as graduate level courses. She is also a Microsoft Certified Professional, concentrating on the BackOffice products, and she is experienced with Novell NetWare operating systems. Teri can be reached at 102415.3262@compuserve.com.

Teri began her career working on large-scale mainframe systems. Her career progression has paralleled technological advances, positioning her for enterprise networking consulting and technical training. Her special areas of interest are Microsoft Windows NT, Windows 95, and Systems Management Server. She has edited several books on these topics and has developed, authored, and taught courses for an international training organization. Her consulting roles are typically for special projects needing a combination of technical acumen with a broad strategic management perspective.

Teri resides in the Chicagoland area with Bill, her husband of over thirty years. As founder and owner of TMG & Associates, she has developed a widespread reputation within the computer industry and is recognized as an industry expert.

Blake Benet Hall is a freelance consultant for his own firm, Benet Systems. His broad background began with a bachelor of science in Computer Science from the University of Mississippi. Since then, he has developed and implemented various software systems on many operating systems using various programming languages/tools, and has been involved in several real-time network programming projects.

Those experiences helped him transition into server and network administration several years ago.

Currently, he designs and implements custom applications, stays abreast of evolving technologies, and expands his personal interest in 3D animation/video techniques.

He can be reached at 76400,543@CompuServe.com.

Gary Hughes has over twenty years of professional experience in the computer industry, including both software development and networking disciplines. He is currently a Technical Manager with USConnect Baltimore, where he manages a team of highly skilled consulting engineers to deliver network and systems integration services. His team is devoted to designing and implementing solutions based on Microsoft BackOffice products.

Gary has worked with NT since its first release and has led several large-scale initiatives involving NT and SMS. Before joining USConnect, Gary served a key role within the IT organization for a large Regional Bell Operating Company on the East Coast. He was instrumental in introducing NT into that company as the chief architect of a new and innovative client/server application that was based on a distributed NT architecture. As program manager for that same project, Gary also successfully introduced SMS into the corporation as their primary software distribution and asset inventory vehicle. Based on Gary's early successes with NT, he was subsequently ask to spearhead a project to design a corporate-wide NT infrastructure and to lead a multi-disciplined team in developing a migration strategy. In his current role at USConnect, Gary remains focused on developing enterprise-scale IT strategies involving NT and other Microsoft BackOffice products for a number of major corporations.

Gary holds an MBA/Decision Sciences degree from Loyola College of Maryland and a BS in Management Studies from the University of Maryland, where he concentrated in Technology Management. Gary is also a Microsoft Certified Systems Engineer (MCSE) and an ICCP Certified Computing Professional (CCP). You may contact Gary via e-mail at Gary_Hughes@Wash-Balt.USConnect.com.

Lance Mortensen is both a Microsoft Certified Engineer and a Microsoft Certified Trainer, and consults and teaches on NT and BackOffice. He has a Master's degree in Business Information Systems, and has over 10 years of experience in the PC and networking environment.

David Mosier is a Consulting Engineer with the BackOffice Group of USConnect Baltimore. His areas of focus include NT domain architecture, SMS design strategy, and Exchange enterprise architecture. He has worked with NT since 1992 and with

SMS since 1993. David has been involved with Microsoft networking since the release of LAN Manager 2.0 on the OS/2 platform. Other areas of experience include various flavors of UNIX, network design, wireless LANs, as well as several releases of AT&T's StarGroup network operating system, the official port of Microsoft's LAN Manager to the UNIX operating system.

David has over twelve years of professional experience in the computer industry and is a graduate of the College of Business Administration at Towson State University in Baltimore, Maryland. Although he prefers the Baltimore/Washington area, supporting customers has taken him to locations throughout the United States, and as far away as Warsaw, Poland. David contributed to *Microsoft Exchange Server Survival Guide*, also by Sams Publishing. He can be reached on the Internet at David_Mosier@Wash-Balt.USConnect.com.

Jeff Sparks has been able to combine over 15 years of experience with mainframe systems and enterprise network consulting. Authoring, training, and courseware development have been an integral component of Jeff's work, in addition to network consulting.

Jeff's efforts with mainframes have focused on supporting systems ranging from small-scale systems to water-cooled super scale systems. This highly technical background has provided a foundation for progression to consulting projects in the enterprise network world. Jeff's consulting typically has involved projects in a heterogeneous, multi-vendor networking environment.

Jeff's credentials include a degree in Electronics Engineering and Business Administration. This has given Jeff the balance in perspective necessary for corporate enterprise projects. Other credentials include Microsoft Certifications of MCSE and MCT. Jeff can be reached at ATS1@MSN.COM.

Paul Thomsen, MCSE, MCT, is the SMS Columnist for *BackOffice Magazine* and a frequent contributor of SMS-related articles. He has also contributed to *Microsoft BackOffice 2 Unleashed*, by Sams Publishing, and reviewed Que Publishing's *Using Microsoft SMS 1.2, Special Edition*. Paul is a Personal Computing Integration Specialist for a large governmental organization in Ontario, Canada, and teaches Microsoft and Digital courses in Southeast Asia for Global Consulting Networks. Previously, Paul was a technical specialist and programmer for 15 years, 10 of those in large end-user organizations in government and the health industry. Paul lives at his home, fronting Chemong Lake, in Peterborough, Ontario, with his wife, Janet, and golden retriever, Kaila. He can be contacted at thomsenp@gov.on.ca.

TELL US WHAT YOU THINK!

As a reader, you are the most important critic and commentator of our books. We value your opinion and want to know what we're doing right, what we could do better, what areas you'd like to see us publish in, and any other words of wisdom you're willing to pass our way. You can help us make strong books that meet your needs and give you the computer guidance you require.

Do you have access to CompuServe or the World Wide Web? Then check out our CompuServe forum by typing GO SAMS at any prompt. If you prefer the World Wide Web, check out our site at http://www.mcp.com.

> **Note**
>
> If you have a technical question about this book, call the technical support line at (800) 571-5840, ext. 3668.

As the publishing manager of the group that created this book, I welcome your comments. You can fax, e-mail, or write me directly to let me know what you did or didn't like about this book—as well as what we can do to make our books stronger. Here's the information:

Fax: 317/581-4669

E-mail: enterprise_mgr@sams.mcp.com

Mail: Rosemarie Graham
           Sams Publishing
           201 W. 103rd Street
           Indianapolis, IN 46290

Introduction

What exactly can Microsoft Systems Management Server do for you? Is it one of those Swiss army knives that are good for everything? No, it's not. If you are looking for a product that can handle your LANs, your WANs, and your desktops, this product is not all-inclusive. If you are looking for a product that handles the desktop well and can help you with some of your server functions, you have definitely chosen the right package. With Microsoft Systems Management Server, you can do the following:

Access every computer, whether at local or remote sites, without leaving your desk

Conduct inventory of both hardware and desktop software

Update every workstation with the latest version of software

Conduct diagnostic tests to find and resolve network problems

Monitor the network traffic on various segments to determine why network latency has increased

What can *Microsoft® SMS 1.2 System Administrator's Survival Guide* do for you? This book is not the definitive resource for Microsoft SMS. Our goal is to give you a book to help you become an effective SMS administrator, and help you maneuver through the day-to-day tasks associated with that job. This book is both a hands-on guide to walk you through various tasks and a resource you will reference time and again. Those of you new to SMS will learn the essentials and gain insights from the experience of others. Those of you with strong backgrounds in SMS and administration will benefit from the real-world examples, tips, tricks, and workarounds from the authors. This book is organized by the various components of SMS and the tasks each administrator works through. The following outline the structure of this book:

Fundamentals of Systems Management Server and the Role of the SMS Administrator

Concepts and Planning of the System

Implementing SMS—Setting up Shop

Operating SMS—Running the Shop

Performance Tuning and Optimization

Hopefully, each of you will gain something from this book: a deeper understanding of a particular task, routines to help your job go smoother, and workarounds that fix particular headaches.

WHO SHOULD READ THIS BOOK?

This book covers all aspects of Systems Management Server. It acts as a great reference guide for the administrator in the trenches, covering operation from planning to implementing and maintaining. Anyone that is preparing for or in the middle of implementing and maintaining an SMS environment will benefit greatly from this book. It gives real-life examples that can be followed to provide meaningful information to an administrator.

It is important to make sure that you have a good deal of Windows NT Server experience prior to utilizing this book. Windows NT Server is the foundation of this product and provides some of its functionality. There also needs to be some knowledge and experience dealing with the client operating systems. The client operating systems are going to be where SMS will truly affect your environment.

CONVENTIONS USED IN THIS BOOK

The following are conventions that will be used throughout this book:

Note

A Note box presents interesting pieces of information related to the surrounding discussion.

Tip

A Tip box offers advice or teaches an easier way to do something.

STRANGER THAN FICTION

Some say truth is stranger than fiction. These boxes offer fun facts to know and tell that *are* stranger than fiction.

REAL-LIFE EXPERIENCE

This box highlights experiences that have happened to the authors and that might happen to you as well. Their experiences might help you with some of yours.

◆ Menu names are separated from menu options by a vertical bar (|). For example, "File | Open" means "Select the File menu and choose the Open option."

◆ All code appears in `monospace`.

◆ When a line of code is too long to fit on only one line of this book, it is broken at a convenient place and continued to the next line. The continuation of the line is preceded by a code continuation character (➡). You should type a line of code that has this character as one long line without breaking it.

◆ A **`boldfaced computer font`** indicates text you type.

- Introduction to Distributed Systems Management

- The Evolution of Microsoft SMS Server

- Role of the Systems Management Server Administrator

PART I

Introduction to SMS

- The History of
  Systems Management

- Distributed Software
  Management

- Operational Perfor-
  mance Management
  and SNMP

- Capacity Planning in
  the Client/Server Era

- Microsoft Systems
  Management Server

CHAPTER 1

Introduction to
Distributed Systems
Management

The various technologies involved in computers have evolved from very simple forms from several decades ago, to powerful, flexible, and complex machines today. Through this evolution, networking has emerged as the central technology, bringing all the components together, and making many invaluable solutions possible.

Now, in the late nineties, computers and their respective operating systems are designed with networking in mind. The personal computer has achieved the status of a full network citizen. Networking allows you to combine the power of the desktop computer with the enormous computing power and storage capabilities of centralized systems, allowing for quick and efficient delivery of information. Because the information being passed and manipulated has become critical to organizations, organizations now demand that each component of the network remain operational as much as possible. Mainframe computer systems have always been well-managed (one system, clear methodologies, and dedicated personnel to perform critical functions) to ensure the maximum system availability. This systems management paradigm must now be moved from the traditional glass house data center to network operations personnel and LAN administrators. Systems management is critical to ensure maximum availability for all types of systems.

Personal computers were designed to be simple and inexpensive, and as a result, have achieved high deployment and reduced the need for centralized computing resources. Given the relatively small number of components involved, it has been fairly easy for centralized systems to be well-managed and maintained so that they reliably deliver mission-critical services in a consistent and reliable manner. Personal computers didn't utilize this expertise or didn't require dedicated operations personnel until the two worlds of computing, personal and centralized systems, became interconnected through the use of networking. With the large number of personal computers deployed, and the dependence now on them, it has become very important to use professional system management techniques with personal computers.

The History of Systems Management

Systems management is classically defined as the management of resources for maximum efficiency and availability; however, this management has focused on disparate but interconnected subsystems.

Host Systems Management

Mainframe and minicomputer systems (often called "host" systems because they accommodate users and applications) cost millions of dollars to own and operate. Strict systems management methodologies were implemented in order to control these high operating costs. These systems were maintained in environmentally controlled rooms. Disk utilization was closely monitored and maintenance was performed on a regular basis. Access to these machines was accomplished through the use of terminals and was under the strict control of the Data Center operations staff. This environment was often referred to as the "glass house," because the systems were located in a secured computer room, with walls that had large windows so that everyone could view this significant investment.

Figure 1.1 gives a conceptual view of a host system environment. The large, central computer (in this case, an IBM System 370), is connected to terminals (sometimes called "monitors") via simple cables and a centralized connection subsystem (in this case, an IBM 7171). The user accesses the system via the terminals, but all data and applications are kept at the System 370, which does all the computing.

Figure 1.1.
Host-based
computing.

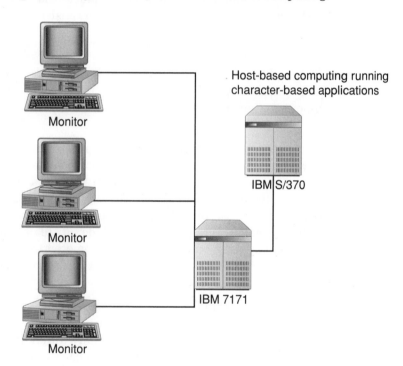

Host-based computing running
character-based applications

Monitor

IBM S/370

Monitor

IBM 7171

Monitor

Programs were tested and tuned in terms of size and execution time, and were given priorities based on the urgency of the program's results. Operating systems improved to allow multiple programs to run at the same time, with each sharing instruction cycles. Systems management utilities emerged, reducing the amount of time to perform user account management, access security, job prioritization, and print jobs. These system management utilities were character-based commands. A system manager's job was to ensure the orderly use of these precious and expensive resources. Asset management was easily accomplished because of the limited number of devices. Software was maintained as a single installation, and typically was leased under an annual license agreement. Support was provided by the application developers who knew the system from the code to the business logic.

NETWORK EQUIPMENT AND THE SNMP STANDARD

As the communications subsystems of host systems began to include communications between multiple host systems, the equipment that allowed the interconnections became critical to the operation of business. New staffing resources were dedicated to ensure the operational readiness of these network subsystems. Because of the growing complexity of the various communications devices and the need to interconnect hosts spanning multiple, geographically isolated sites, the industry recognized the need to manage these devices in a consistent manner.

Note

When multiple computers communicate with each other, this system is referred to as a network; networking devices make this kind of communication possible.

Necessity is the seed for invention. Network administrators were tasked to perform rudimentary diagnostics on a regular basis. Technical personnel who performed these rudimentary tasks found that they could automate some of these functions by utilizing scripting techniques. The simple TCP/IP utility PING was used to perform a basic device presence test. Industry proponents also recognized that great minds (and their hourly wage) were going to waste doing this simple work, and that businesses would pay for good utilities that automated these tasks. The problem was that each device typically could respond to a simple ping; their internal code for management and configuration was different.

Administrators would create terminal sessions over the network, to the network devices, and then utilize built-in configuration utilities to set, reset, and list configuration parameters. Each manufacturer had a different means of performing these tasks. Network managers now had to learn each vendor's specific diagnostic and configuration program.

The Internet community had a means for identifying needs and formulating specifications for modifications to the Internet's fundamental networking protocols of TCP and IP (usually referred to jointly as TCP/IP). In August of 1988, an ad hoc group presented to the Internet community an initial specification for the Internet Network Management Framework. In April 1989, the Internet Activities Board elevated the framework to a status of "recommended." The framework consisted of the following three components:

◆ Structure of Management Information (SMI). A definition for the schema and structure of management information; specifies how to define managed components and their attributes.

◆ Management Information Base (MIB). A standard implementation of the definition; defines a standard baseline of managed devices and their attributes.

◆ Simple Network Management Protocol (SNMP). The protocol defined to carry management information within the Internet Management framework.

This was clearly a huge success for the Internet, as it offered a consistent means of setting and receiving network device information across a TCP/IP network. The SNMP management paradigm focused on the following three components:

◆ SNMP Agent. A process running on the IP device that executes on instructions received from a management station.

◆ Network Management Station (NMS). Typically, the management station provides a GUI (graphical user interface)-based means of issuing instructions to a network device that allows setting its operational parameters. The management station can also get device characteristics and dynamic operating statistics. This is done through an intermediate information store called the MIB.

◆ Management Information Base (MIB). This is the critical element that allows for the multivendor management of IP devices. The MIB is the common information base that can be accessed by both the network device (via the SNMP Agent) and the management station. The MIB provides an application programming interface (API).

SNMP management of network devices has been typically accomplished using a vendor-supplied NMS. Because network equipment vendors have made private MIB extensions to manage special features of their devices, a competing NMS can only manage the general MIB elements, which is a less than ideal situation. Additionally, because a MIB does not contain qualifying information, such as what a returned status value 7 means, the NMS must possess the logic necessary to interpret this value. This logic is only known across vendor-specific devices if the vendors publish their uncompiled MIBs. Because a vendor would be reluctant to publish the private (read, competitive advantage) portion of their MIB, only generic characteristics of their devices could be managed from an alternative SNMP console. Typically, this type of NMS is only used as a means of monitoring the network for operational readiness and for high-level diagnostics in determining the location of a network fault. The vendor-specific NMS is used to perform more advanced functions.

Typically, the NMS uses a polling architecture to determine operational readiness and statistics. This methodology is good when assessing semi-static information, but does not lend itself well to proactive measurements in failure situations. SNMP traps are used to forward information about activities that exceed pre-set thresholds to the NMS. This is program logic executed by the SNMP agent that sends an alarm to the NMS when certain conditions are encountered. It is then up to the NMS to perform the necessary actions to resolve the event.

SNMP systems utilize polling to effectively provide management of the network devices, meaning that the systems routinely check on devices, even if there is no reason to suspect any problems. The systems also use interrupts (also known as events), meaning that when something unusual occurs, the device will initiate a warning about the activity. The interval of polling and the type and nature of device events must be managed in order to minimize the administrative overhead on network bandwidth. Given the relatively limited and, therefore, understandable number of network devices and critical events that could happen, SNMP is a good management framework for these devices.

LAN SERVERS AND THE SNMP STANDARD

Local Area Network (LAN) servers can be configured and viewed as both network communications devices and as host systems. The network interface card in the server, as well as the system as a whole, are properly managed by SNMP. Additionally, SNMP agents can effectively translate server events to SNMP traps for the NMS to receive. In this case, the number of devices and elements are limited and well defined.

DESKTOP SYSTEMS MANAGEMENT AND THE DMI STANDARD

Desktop systems can be built from a seemingly infinite amount of configurable components. These systems can also have a comparable number of software parameters and possible events that can happen to them. Because of these factors, the static nature and known structure of the SNMP MIB does not lend itself well towards being managed by SNMP.

For example, consider cars on the highway as analogous to the network infrastructure. In order to effectively manage the enterprise using SNMP, each car would need to be registered as it enters the highway toll booth, noting its make, model, the vehicle identification number (VIN), and the operating condition of the car. Additionally, progress of each car's operating characteristics would be monitored by installing toll booths at intermediate points. Finally, an event notification would be required on changes made in each car (such as, sounding of the horn). This might be acceptable on a seldom used highway, but when many cars are involved, the combination of the traffic jams at the booths and car noise level on the highway would make travel on the highway unacceptable.

What makes the desktop appealing is its open nature and versatility to be configured to meet the needs of the individual. Corporate Information Systems departments struggle with the balance of meeting individual needs, while ensuring that this desktop system can perform in its role as a network citizen delivering mission-critical objectives. The costs of doing this are becoming increasingly prohibitive, and this is why management of the desktop is becoming more of a priority of the corporate Chief Information Officer. Gartner Group estimates that the five-year life cycle cost of operating a network-attached personal computer is at $40,000. That's approximately $8,000 per user, per annum, and most of the cost is in the support of these devices. LAN and host management account for approximately 13% of this cost.

The industry has recognized that what has been a cash cow is now threatening to ruin the farm. The industry is now taking steps to correct some of the inherent difficulties of desktop management as a full network citizen.

The Desktop Management Task Force (formed by vendors) has taken the lead in the development of standards for proper management of the distributed client. Similar to the Internet Network Management Framework's standard, SNMP, the DMTF's DMI specification provides for delivery of information to a common store. DMI utilizes the management, agent, and information store paradigm, but improves on SNMP in areas of qualitative parameters passed to the centralized information store. Additionally, only changed data is passed, reducing the administrative overhead. The DMI is constructed of the following four basic components:

- ◆ Component Interface (CI). The CI registers itself with the service layer, defining where the management information can be found. It could even define an executable that allows for actions to occur on the component.

- ◆ Management Interface (MI). An interface by which a DMI-compliant application can query a component and the result would be fully qualified (such as HP Laserjet 5p, status is jammed).

- ◆ Service Layer. The service layer provides the services so that the MI can access the components. It collects the information from the CI, including location of the MIF file and any executable that might be launched.

- ◆ Management Information File (MIF). The MIF defines the component, the attributes, and actions that can be performed on the component.

An example of the implementation of the DMI standard is provided in Figure 1.2, where the Windows 95 implementation is diagrammed.

Figure 1.2.
DMI as imple-
mented in
Windows 95.

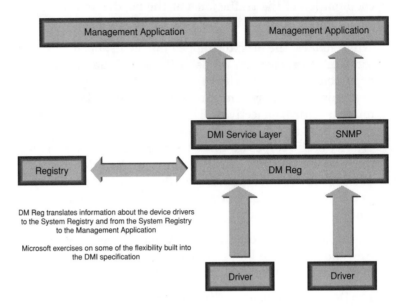

Although any type of MIF can be defined, three working groups have provided standards for MIFs: LAN adapters, printers, and systems. Modem MIFs are being developed as well as video subsystems. But, why is all this important? Asset management is very important in the desktop environment. Because of these three working groups, the management of these kinds of assets is much more vendor-independent than for other computer assets. Coupled with their inherently distributed nature and the sheer number of assets involved, tracking and quantifying the costs for upgrades and enhancements are difficult. Knowing what you have goes a long way towards quantifying project costs. Vendors now have a standard way of defining their products, and DMI application vendors have a means of getting that information. Listing 1.1 demonstrates how Microsoft uses a MIF standard to report the status of a workstation installation.

LISTING 1.1. SAMPLE SOFTWARE COMPONENT MIF.

```
Start Component
Name = "Workstation"
Start Group
Name = "InstallStatus"
ID = 1
Class = "MICROSOFT¦JOBSTATUS¦1.0"
Start Attribute
Name = "Status"
```

```
ID = 1
Type = String(16)
Value = "SUCCESS"
End Attribute
Start Attribute
Name = "Description"
ID = 2
Type = String(128)
Value = "Audit job ran successfully."
End Attribute
End Group
End Component
```

DISTRIBUTED SOFTWARE MANAGEMENT

Because the desktop provides for many configuration variables, installation and validation of software components represent a significant portion of the full life cycle costs of maintaining the desktop. The average application can expect to see as many as five major revisions and fifteen minor revisions, per application, during the desktop life cycle. Multiply this by the average of seven applications and OS changes, and you could expect to see up to 160 desktop system configuration changes during the life cycle of the asset. Keeping software at its current supportable version is a major undertaking.

If a network administrator had to support at least 100 desktops, and he or she spent just 15 minutes performing these updates, it would represent approximately 40% of the administrator's time. LAN administration (such as new user accounts, security, and system management) accounts for approximately 10–13% percent of the time spent. This then raises the aggregate use of time to 53%. If 25% of staff time is spent on administrative functions (such as sick leave, training, vacation time, meetings, and reporting), this means approximately 22% of time is left (4.4 hours per year per client) performing support, new projects, move or add changes, repairs, and maintenance.

This situation clearly does not lend itself to having a well-managed computing environment, and the average number of applications per desktop is increasing. Reducing the amount of effort required to maintain the desktop is necessary to ensure that staff productivity and business competitiveness are maintained. The desktop resembles a low-cost architecture, one where error correcting memory and error-free disk subsystems are just a dream. This inability to handle errors also demonstrates why these systems are error-prone.

The operating system cannot prevent file corruption from occurring on the disk. Software application installation is also a source of desktop instability. Install code seldom checks for the existence of newer files before it lays down dated system components. Nearly 25% of all non-functional software-related support calls are resolved by reinstallation. Significant reductions on basic calls can be achieved with automated software distribution procedures. The way to provide better overall customer service is to use tools.

OPERATIONAL PERFORMANCE MANAGEMENT AND SNMP

Monitoring your system is very important. Things will sometimes go wrong without any obvious warning. For example, your customers would probably much rather be told that access would be restricted at 4:00 pm than have an unscheduled outage at 9:00 am the next morning. You need to catch the problem while it is occurring in order to be proactive. In order to be proactive, you need to spend time in advance to review the systems. SNMP will provide you with a proactive knowledge of information (polling) and real-time knowledge of events (traps) for some computer devices. Microsoft Systems Management Server (SMS) will provide similar facilities for others. You need to spend time setting up such management applications and learning the applications' tools before you actually use them. Microsoft Systems Management Server is definitely a set of tools you'll want to learn in advance. Spend the time; the rewards are huge.

CAPACITY PLANNING IN THE CLIENT/SERVER ERA

In the era of client/server computing, mission-critical systems logic, and the need for delivery of timely information, it is necessary that each desktop system be as well managed as the network infrastructure and the back office system it runs on (LAN servers and midrange to mainframe hosts). This requires that system architects, analysts, programmers, and support personnel be aware of the performance aspects of each of the client/server components: host configuration and performance, network topology and bandwidth, and client configuration and performance. Host and network parameters are easily quantifiable with existing tools. What is more difficult is determining the client computer constraints and determining how to deploy applications. Deploying an application might not be possible without expending considerable man hours towards the required group of target workstations. This could cause considerable risk to the success of a project.

Is it any wonder that most Chief Information Officers are hesitant to endorse a major client/server project with so many unknown variables? In order to design a reliable and robust client/server system, you need to know what you have and what you have to work with. This will help you to be able to determine what the necessary steps are that need to take place to roll out your application into production. Host system planning and management tools are readily available and are typically utilized today. Network parameters can also be easily quantified. The most critical question for the nineties revolves around the desktop system and its configuration.

Some basic project planning questions might be the following:

> Is each client running a compatible operating system?
>
> What is the performance level of the desktop?
>
> Is there sufficient disk capacity for the client installation?
>
> What are the costs that might be encountered in client upgrades?
>
> What costs might be involved in the distribution of the client application to the desktop?
>
> Are there any existing applications that might be incompatible with the client/server system?
>
> What is the capacity of the network related to my target audience?
>
> Do I build a client/server system with simple or complex clients?

These are some tough questions that have variable answers. Questions posed at the desktop are like those asked of a politician: You'll never get a straight answer and it will change before you are ready to implement your change. But there are answers that you can get, real-time answers. Microsoft Systems Management Server can help you answer your questions. These answers might not always come easy, but with some quantifying numbers to back your decisions, life is better.

Microsoft Systems Management Server

What are the odds that system managers can keep control of the costs and assist in the management of the desktop so that real gains can be made in the client/server era? Do you think the odds slim to none? If so, you must not be using the right set of tools. Stop doing things the old way. Use Microsoft Systems Management Server as one of your tool sets.

In order to manage your environment, you need to manage your desktop effectively. The only way that can be accomplished, short of adding an army of technical foot soldiers, is to implement tools that assist in this endeavor. This is where SMS enters.

LAN servers provide utilities and tools for user account management, and disk monitoring utilities are also available. But these tools can only reduce part of the 13% you spend on system administration. Look closely at how you spend your time. If my shop is a good barometer of the industry, then 65% is spent on desktop support. The real gain can be made at the desktop and its interaction with the network. Microsoft Systems Management Server is directly aimed with this goal in mind, thus reducing the time spent at the desktop, the time spent traveling to get to the desktop, and the visits at the desktop. (I know what you're thinking: It is very important that you maintain a very good relationship with your customers. Direct contact with users goes a long way to maintaining that relationship. But with the time SMS saves, you can afford to give them a call to say hello every now and again.)

What exactly can Microsoft Systems Management Server do? Is it one of those Swiss army knives that is good for everything? No, it's not. If you are looking for a product that can handle your LANS, your WANS, and your desktops, this product is not all inclusive. If you are looking for a product that handles the desktop well, and can help you with some of your server functions, you have definitely chosen the right package. Microsoft Systems Management Server can do the following:

> First, you need to know what you have. SMS provides for both the hardware and software inventory of the desktop. You know those reports your boss always requests at 6:00 p.m. as you're getting ready to leave? Well, they can be quickly prepared and delivered so that you're out of the office by 6:10.

> Secondly, you'll need to be able to update every workstation with the latest version of the software. This week it's the Internet browser. Lately, it has been a weekly update to the browser, but you get my point—change is constant. Microsoft helps you handle the load and reduce the walking around.

> You'll also need to access every computer, without leaving your desk. SMS provides a means for remote desktop support.

> And finally, you'll need a network diagnostic program. Why? Because the network comes to a crawl at 10:00 a.m. and the Chief Financial Officer is going to choke you if he can't get his work done and get to the bank by 12:00 p.m. SMS provide a means of monitoring the network traffic on various segments to determine why network latency has increased. (His assistant was downloading news from the Internet!)

SUMMARY

In this chapter you have learned about the following:

- The history of computers indicates continual change in both the number of systems used and the manner in which they are used.
- Tools are essential for the proper management of computers.
- Network equipment uses the Internet-standard management framework and the SNMP protocol to effectively manage the network devices.
- The Internet-standard management framework and SNMP do not provide an effective way to manage the desktop.
- The Desktop Management Task Force (DMI) is a better means of handling distributed systems management for configuration and inventory. Microsoft has endorsed this technology and is implementing it in both SMS and its other products (such as Windows 95).
- Software distribution is important in the management of the desktop. Tools are necessary in order to meet the demands in a timely and efficient manner.
- Network monitoring and the use of other tools to proactively manage the computer systems are important in meeting the demands of your job.
- Major projects such as client/server application development, or other application deployments, require valid up-to-date information for proper planning and decision making. The success of the projects demands an efficient means of software distribution.
- Microsoft Systems Management Server provides hardware and software inventory, software distribution, help desk utilities, and network monitoring.
- Microsoft Systems Management Server is targeted at maintaining the most difficult and numerous network device there is, the desktop workstation.

The next chapter discusses Microsoft Systems Management Server capabilities in depth.

CHAPTER 2

The Evolution of Microsoft
SMS Server

To show the evolution of SMS, this chapter reviews the changes that were made in each product release. These changes are generally benefits to the product, according to certain feedback given by customers. This chapter discusses the evolution of SMS and how SMS has changed over the revisions that have been made from SMS version 1.0 to SMS version 1.2. The benefits of these changes and how they work in an organization's environment are also covered.

THE PROBLEMS OF SYSTEMS MANAGEMENT

Systems management is not the new buzzword on the street; it has been around since the days of mainframes. Even though systems management is nothing new, it has not been used to the greatest possible advantage of the organization. This is largely due to the lack of management tools for the system administrator in the past. The system administrator generally had to use several different tools in order to do many functions, and he had to manually retrieve inventory. Also, in the past, there were many different types of systems to choose from. First, there were mainframes, which came with relatively simple management tools that were used to manage the mainframe. However, the industry's focus has shifted from mainframes to local area networks, and many different tools were used to do several different tasks. These included different administration tools for each operating system, network administration tools, and various approaches to setting up applications. This made things cumbersome and difficult to control because the system administrator would have to deal with several different tools, learn how to use those tools, and then actually have to use those tools. This became a nightmare for the administrator.

Because there were many problems as a result of not having complete single-tool control of the system, the cost and difficulty of administering systems were extremely high. As systems management has developed, several different key areas of focus, such as network management, desktop management, server management, application management, and user management, have proven to be fundamental.

One of the key problems in the past was being able to provide systems management over long distances. If there were two sites, the maintenance of a remote site was extremely difficult and sometimes impossible. Many times, a second system administrator needed to be hired for the remote site, or the administrator from the first site needed to travel to the site to manage the system. Thus, managing more than one system took longer and was very costly.

SEARCHING FOR THE ANSWER

During the early 1980s, a revolution began with the widespread use of personal computers. The trend towards the use of personal computers began in organizations all over the United States because these computers were relatively cost-efficient, could be controlled by the user, and had important new functions (such as spread-sheets). All corporations, large to small, now use personal computers in almost every facet of their businesses. The use of terminals has become almost non-existent. Now, a personal computer can not only be an assistant for someone, but at the same time, operate as a terminal. The actual maintenance of personal computers is now a large part of what has to be done by a system administrator. This can be very expensive and also cumbersome, depending on how desktops are actually managed.

Imagine being in an organization and within four or five years going from having very few or no personal computers to having 2,000 to 5,000 computers. This is what many corporations have had to face coming into this huge personal computer revolution. Microsoft has created a world of products, from operating systems to applications, that deliver solutions for the personal computer. In looking at their solutions to other problems, Microsoft saw a need for a tool to facilitate desktop management and network. Microsoft products all integrate nicely with each other, so it seemed that Microsoft was the perfect company to create some type of solution for this problem. In creating a solution, they saw that they needed to make things easier for customers when upgrading operating systems and deploying applications, while also being able to gather information about the systems and remotely manage them.

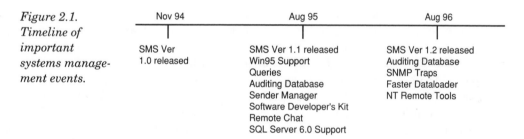

Figure 2.1. Timeline of important systems management events.

Nov 94
SMS Ver 1.0 released

Aug 95
SMS Ver 1.1 released
Win95 Support
Queries
Auditing Database
Sender Manager
Software Developer's Kit
Remote Chat
SQL Server 6.0 Support

Aug 96
SMS Ver 1.2 released
Auditing Database
SNMP Traps
Faster Dataloader
NT Remote Tools

FINALLY, THE ANSWER

The answer has been anticipated for many years and it has finally arrived, at the right time. The new product, called Systems Management Server (SMS), makes management easier for the system administrator by putting the administration directly in his or her hands. As organizations now upgrade to the new Windows 95 or Windows NT Workstation desktops, new Office 95–97 packages, and other new application variants, they are upgrading their administration tools to SMS as well.

Systems Management Server answers the question of how to manage desktops more effectively and efficiently by offering inventory management, application management, auditing what applications are on the desktop, troubleshooting, and diagnostics. SMS is a robust scaleable solution that allows any size organization to take advantage of these services. It also offers solutions for network management by using a separate product that is included with SMS called Network Monitor, and by being able to communicate with other network systems management products to facilitate information gathering. These products include Netview, HP Openview, and many other Simple Network Management Protocol (SNMP)–aware products.

Another benefit of SMS is that it uses another Microsoft product called SQL Server. SQL Server is a database server that allows a Windows NT server to maintain, index, and search through large amounts of data. SMS uses SQL Server as its back end to organize information that has been gathered about the desktops. Microsoft has created a seamless integration between SMS and SQL Server. Like all Microsoft products, SMS is also able to integrate with several of the programming languages. It can use Visual Basic and Visual C++, and it offers integration with applications such as Excel and Word. Some of the services SMS offers are

◆ Inventory management

◆ Application management

◆ Troubleshooting and remote control tools

◆ Network monitor

INVENTORY MANAGEMENT

Inventory management can be the bloodline of an information systems department. It provides the capability to collect software and hardware inventory and to maintain it. This inventory is gathered by SMS and stored by SQL Server. The SQL Server acts as a depository for this information so that it can later be retrieved and used. SMS uses a login script or similar procedure to gather information from the desktops. It brings the information to the SMS servers by using a MIF (Management Information File), which actually puts the data into the SQL Server. MIF files use a format similar to that developed by the DMTF (Desktop Management Task Force).

Note

Desktop Management Task Force is an organization that created a standard called DMI (Desktop Management Interface) to gather specific hardware information and additional inventory information specific to the computer. It facilitates asset management, configuration management, real-time monitoring, and control capabilities to help desktop management.

> **RESOURCE**
>
> www.dmtf.org is the Web site for the Desktop Management Task Force organization.

APPLICATION MANAGEMENT

Application management is probably one of the most powerful tools of SMS. It allows software distribution and has an unattended installation feature for individual personal computers or a group of machines. There is also a feature for distributing program groups and sharing them. It allows the administrator to install applications and program groups in remote sites over WAN connections so that if there is no administrator in the remote site, the administrator can still maintain and update the software in that site. It also enables the administrator to define a standard for the desktops in his or her environment.

TROUBLESHOOTING AND REMOTE CONTROL TOOLS

Remote control is the capability to control the desktop remotely. SMS provides remote control features for MS-DOS, Windows 3.1, Windows for Workgroups, Windows 95, Windows NT Workstation, and Windows NT Server. Remote control enables help desk people or system administrators to take control of the desktop and user's actions. This helps in working with the users and assisting them with problems or questions. This tool is important because, in the past, many help desks had problems being able to communicate over the telephone with users on how to do things, generally making the help desk person get up and go to the user's personal computer.

Troubleshooting is very important. SMS enables you to go in and troubleshoot the desktop by looking at certain valuable information about how the desktop is performing. This tool is much like running Microsoft Diagnostics on the machines. There is also the functionality of being able to remotely execute programs and remotely reboot MS-DOS and Windows-based machines. You can also monitor performance, events, and certain other factors of Windows NT Servers and Windows NT Workstations.

NETWORK MONITOR

The Network Monitor is an additional tool that comes with SMS. It enables you to decode the packets that go across the wire. It supports all of the major protocols, such as TCP/IP, IPX/SPX, NetBIOS, AppleTalk, NCP, and SMBs. This tool helps provide the administrator with information that is very useful for network management. The amount of traffic on the network can also provide information on possible hardware failures.

HOW FLEXIBLE IS THE SYSTEMS MANAGEMENT SERVER?

One of the greatest features of SMS is its flexibility. It will run with virtually all networks and almost any desktop. The network operating systems supported by SMS are Windows NT Server 3.1, 3.5, 3.51, and 4.0; NetWare 3.1x and 4.x; LAN Manager 2.1 or later; and LAN Server 3.0 and 3.1. The clients supported by SMS are MS-DOS 5.0 or later; Windows 3.1; Windows for Workgroups 3.11; Windows NT Workstation 3.1, 3.5, 3.51, and 4.0; and Macintosh Systems 7.x.

SMS can also take advantage of multiprocessors. It is, by far, one of the most flexible systems management products on the market today. It allows communication with other network management systems. It will communicate with products such as Digital Polycenter Manager, Hewlett-Packard's Openview, IBM Netview 6000, Network Managers, and MC Vision. It has support for Simple Network Management Protocol (SNMP) to provide information about network components. SMS also provides support for ODBC, so applications that support ODBC can view the SMS database and offer support for the desktop management interface.

THE EARLY YEARS OF SYSTEMS MANAGEMENT SERVER

Microsoft released SMS version 1.0 in November of 1994. Because Microsoft wanted to come out with the BackOffice product, they accelerated the release of SMS Version 1.0 without incorporating enough documentation and resources for the customer. It was not well received by many of Microsoft's customers, in large part due to poor documentation, many bugs, and multiple site communication problems, all of which made the product incomplete. It seemed to be ignored by all; it did not have the success of many of the other BackOffice products. However, many customers indicated that Microsoft should continue to work with the product and develop it into something spectacular.

When Microsoft Windows NT 3.1 Advanced Server came out, it left much to be desired. But looking back and seeing the movement and progress that Microsoft made to where they are today with NT Server 4.0, customers are pleased. Many saw the vision of where Microsoft was heading with all of its products. With SMS version 1.0, Microsoft had developed a product to allow system administrators to not only manage, but also distribute the operating system and applications Microsoft developed. It all looked like a nice neat package, even though the actual application itself did not work as well as most expected. For this reason, SMS version 1.0 was not used very often in large-scale production environments.

Systems Management Server Version 1.1

Microsoft then developed a product that gained serious momentum. SMS version 1.1 was a much improved product from 1.0. It was very much like the change between Windows NT 3.1 Advanced Server and Windows NT 3.5 Server. Much of the functionality of SMS version 1.1 was adjusted. There were many added features and enhancements that allowed system administrators to find information more readily and to be able to work with it much more effectively. Most of the feature changes were made because of customer feedback, because SMS version 1.0 did not meet the customers' needs.

Many of the problems that SMS version 1.0 presented to system administrators were resolved in SMS 1.1. Because of these changes, SMS version 1.1 was a greater success. Many companies adopted this as a new desktop management package that allowed the system administrators to manage their desktops. However, SMS still wasn't a product that many people put a great deal of faith in. There were still non-believers. Many of the people who had tried to use SMS version 1.0 still doubted version 1.1, due to bugs and some new problems that were discovered, such as those with Windows 95.

SMS version 1.1 was released with many new features that provided easier operation, improved control, and better interoperability of the desktops that existed in the organization's environment. One of the reasons SMS version 1.1 was released was to help manage the upgrades to Windows 95 and to reduce the cost of upgrading. SMS version 1.1 played an important role in being able to migrate to Windows 95. It did Windows 95 upgrades automatically without anyone having to visit the computer. It worked much more reliably than SMS 1.0. Some of the areas that were enhanced are as follows:

◆ Queries

◆ Auditing

◆ Support for new operating systems

◆ Software developer's kit

◆ Help desk improvements

◆ Communication and miscellaneous improvements

QUERIES

Queries enable administrators to spend less time searching for information and conditions about machines, generally reducing setup time and making work much easier. SMS version 1.1 was the first version to include predefined queries. Prompted queries were another feature put into the SMS version 1.1. This feature allows the administrator to add an extra condition after the query has already run. It runs much like a wizard. "Negative-condition" queries have been added to SMS version 1.1 functionality. You can specify something that does not meet a condition of the query made. The final improvement to the query engine was that it operated much faster through many enhancements.

AUDITING

SMS version 1.1 was much better in doing audits than its predecessor. In 1.0, you had to actually create a Package Definition File (PDF). In 1.1, there was an audit database of up to 2500 software packages from the leading software vendors. You could audit on several different properties, not just the filename. You could use time, date, size, checksum, and CRC (cyclic redundancy check). This feature also allowed the inventory of system-critical files such as CONFIG.SYS, AUTOEXEC.BAT, WIN.INI, and SYSTEM.INI.

SUPPORT FOR NEW OPERATING SYSTEMS

SMS version 1.1 had support for Microsoft Windows NT Server 3.51 and Workstation 3.51. This support for NT Server 3.51 could allow NT Server 3.51 to act as a client or as a server. Microsoft Windows NT Workstation 3.51 could act as a client. Also, there was support for the new OS/2 Warp and LAN Server 4.0. These products came out after SMS version 1.0.

SOFTWARE DEVELOPER'S KIT

SMS version 1.1 came with a software developer's kit that gave you the flexibility of enhancing some of SMS's 1.1 features and processes. These things include the following:

◆ More sophisticated options for the distribution of applications

◆ Extending the user interface

◆ Adding details to the inventory database so you can extend the database by customizing what information you are going to gather

◆ APIs to enable you to work with the core processes of the Systems Management Server

♦ New reporting tools so that you could more readily gain access to the inventory data and report it in a better manner

♦ The capability to extend the Network Monitor

You can write your own specific protocol parsing tools. The software developer's kit is just a collection of tools that enable the administrator to customize the way SMS will run in his or her environment. You can use SMS APIs to allow you to integrate with existing management packages. It opens up the possibility to operate the core processes that SMS does, such as the help desk. You can use these with Visual C++ and Visual Basic to view and adjust information.

HELP DESK IMPROVEMENTS

Many new features were added to the remote help desk feature of SMS version 1.1. version 1.1 added remote chat so you could chat with the client at the workstation. Another feature added was the capability to run remote control over TCP/IP. There were several new help desk options, including support for Windows 95, DHCP and WINS, MS-DOS diagnostics (Windows Memory, Windows Modules, GDI Heaps, and Global Heaps), drivers, ROM information memory, and CMOS. You could use ping tests to see if you are capable of sending and receiving information. There was also a security option that allows the client to deny the administrator from using remote control. You could customize the SMS Administrator fields and the Site window to view things the way you want to view them.

COMMUNICATION AND MISCELLANEOUS IMPROVEMENTS

The bandwidth control mechanism for the senders was also improved. You could allow concurrent senders to be connected and balance the load between the senders, which allows you to adjust the percentage of bandwidth being used. Some real-time information could be collected for Windows NT machines, and some new built-in database cleanup mechanisms in SMS version 1.1 provided some maintenance needed for large databases. Support for SQL Server 6.0 was also provided.

SYSTEMS MANAGEMENT SERVER 1.2

SMS version 1.2 is looked at as a more sound desktop management product. It has been adopted and looked upon by customers as a capable solution for their organizations. Many called SMS "Slow Moving Software," but now, because of its enhancements, that name is starting to fade away.

The change between SMS 1.2 and SMS 1.1 is not as great as the change between versions 1.0 and 1.1, although it is the type of change that has persuaded many customers to adopt version 1.2 for their desktop management needs. One of the things that was promised was SNMP integration. This has now been added to the SMS product. SMS version 1.2 also has greater support for many more applications and has even doubled its software inventory database to 5000 applications. The remote control features have been adjusted to support Windows NT Workstation, and enable NT Server to be remotely controlled. Also, WinSock is now supported as a remote control protocol. The data loader is multithreaded and allows access to the database at a much faster rate. These changes make SMS 1.2 a much more sound product. This product will be adopted by large companies and used in an enterprise-wide environment with more stability and confidence.

Note

SMS versions 1.1 and 1.2 both support SQL Server 6.5 and SQL Server 6.0 as well.

SUMMARY

At last, Microsoft has created a solution to the problems of systems management, called the Systems Management Server. Although it took several versions to get it where it is today, the evolution of SMS has proven to be a successful one. From the days of mainframes to LANs, there have been many problems in moving toward a complete systems management solution. SMS is now the complete solution. It not only provides a means of being able to control all of your desktops, but it also helps with the network and allows the system administrator to gather information and organize it in a manner that can be used to do things such as capacity planning, trend analysis, or even an accounting audit. As discussed, the SMS 1.2 product has the tools and mechanisms needed for an enterprise-wide solution to allow any size enterprise to perform the tasks necessary to manage its environment, including desktops, networks, and servers.

CHAPTER 3

Role of the Systems Management Server Administrator

This chapter's main emphasis is the role of the Information Services (IS) department in a systems management environment. This chapter discusses general roles such as the network administrator, systems LAN administrator, database administrator, and desktop specialist. The Systems Management Server (SMS) is a large animal, which needs to be tended by experienced system administrators. The chapter also covers the roles that many other players will perform in the SMS environment. All these roles have specific tasks and functions that are linked to their jobs. The roles help cover the main categories of SMS's operations, and they play an important part in what happens in an SMS environment.

HUMAN RESOURCES IN THE IS DEPARTMENT

Many variables come into play when you are dealing with the network and system issues of the IS department. These variables can consist of what type of network operating system is being used, what your desktop platform is, whether there are mainframes in the environment, whether midframes are involved, what kind of database servers exist in your environment, how many users you have, and whether your sites are centralized or spread out. Many such questions come to mind. These questions will generally form and shape what your IS department will look like. This section discusses several roles in the IS department and deals with some of the basic operations and tables associated with these roles.

NETWORK ADMINISTRATOR

In this day and age, the responsibilities of a network administrator can be broken down into two areas, the networks (local to each site, usually called Local Area Networks) and the internetwork connecting them (covering the entire organization, usually called the Wide Area Network). Many companies have grown so much that they have exceeded their original sites and stretched their boundaries. They have moved into other locations, and their IS departments have grown immensely. Because of this, you need two categories for a network administrator. Sometimes, one person can fill both of these roles. One of the main jobs for the network administrator is to provide information to other people in the organization on the amount of bandwidth being used and what kind of capacity the system's network infrastructure can handle. Other tasks can include making sure that the network stays up and that the infrastructure of the network grows as the organization grows. The network administrator's role is a key role in systems management.

NETWORK

An administrator who controls the network itself generally has to be familiar with several different things. A set of infrastructure rules is one of these things. The administrator needs to understand the topology of the local area network and know what the device limitations in the network are and the limitations of the technology itself. For example, if you had an EtherNet network in your environment, you would expect that the network administrator (the person in charge of the local area network) would be very familiar with EtherNet standards. He or she would need to be familiar with speeds, limitations, hardware configurations, and management of the particular EtherNet network. A person in charge of the network also needs to be familiar with several different types of protocols. In the Microsoft environment, there are some specific protocols that should be known. If running specific transport protocols such as NetBEUI, TCP/IP, or IPX/SPX, the network person should be familiar with the transport protocol running in his environment. He should also be familiar with other things such as SMB (Server Message Blocks), RPC (Remote Procedure Calls), DHCP (Dynamic Host Configuration Protocol), and WINS (Windows Internet Naming Service). These things are generally run in almost every environment, so the network person needs to understand how they work and what role they play. The SMS environment uses these things to be able to communicate between sites and with its clients.

INTERNETWORK

The internetwork expert needs to be familiar with much more than just the local area network. These items include site-to-site communication and communicating to other geographical locations by using things such as frame relay, ISDN (Integrated Services Digital Network), T1s, DDS (Dedicated Digital Service), and any other appropriate transport mechanisms serviced by a telecommunications carrier. An internetwork expert also needs to be familiar with the amount of bandwidth used over these channels and to monitor these connections to measure the amount of traffic across these connections. The internetwork expert should also be somewhat familiar with site-to-site communication issues when using the SMS itself. One of these issues is the senders, which are the foundation of the SMS site communication. In some companies, the telecommunications department plays the role of the internetwork administrator. If this is the case, there generally has to be some communication by the person controlling the network and the telecommunications department. This becomes the key in being able to monitor what SMS is doing because telecommunications departments are not always aware of systems applications.

Note

The network administrator is not always a single person; sometimes this role is shared with someone who is also the systems/LAN administrator.

SYSTEMS/LAN ADMINISTRATOR ROLE

The systems/LAN administrator deals with many things that involve the network operating system. This role varies, depending upon which network operating system is being used. At one time, the predominant network operating system was Novell NetWare. However, with the rapid growth of Windows NT Server, this is changing. The approach to managing NetWare is much different than the approach to managing a Windows NT Server domain. So, the administrator's role would change, of course, between these two systems. These two systems are not the only two systems that work with the SMS, although they are the only two that seamlessly integrate with it. For these reasons, the two main points covered here and throughout the book will be Windows NT domains and NetWare servers.

WINDOWS NT DOMAIN

You have a key advantage if you are running a Windows NT domain. The reason for this advantage is that both Windows NT and SMS were created by Microsoft. As time goes on, you will find that a Windows NT domain and SMS environment will be easier to operate than an environment that also includes NetWare. The administrator who is going to be managing the NT environment needs to be familiar with several key issues. These issues include user management, Net logon service, directory replicator service, login scripts, domain management, security, and server management. There is a lot more to being a Windows NT domain administrator than those key issues, however. One of the key advantages of your SMS environment being specifically just an NT domain environment is that you automatically reduce the amount of personnel needed. If you were in a NetWare environment, you would need Windows NT domain management at the same time as you would need NetWare management.

NETWARE

NetWare administrators have, in the past, found countless numbers of ways to manage desktops. From using login scripts to using the Novell Navigator and WSUpdate, this has been a key issue for NetWare administrators. SMS now gives the administrator the ability to do this. A NetWare administrator will still need to understand the functionality of an NT domain environment, due to the fact that SMS doesn't rely completely on NetWare. SMS requires Windows NT, so the NetWare administrator needs to be familiar with several key issues in NetWare administration. These key issues include user management, login scripts, server management, NLMs, VLMs, and security.

Note

If the NetWare environment is NetWare 4.1, the administrator will have to be aware of certain NDS issues such as bindery services.

DATABASE ADMINISTRATOR

A database administrator (DBA) is one of the key roles in an IS department. Generally, an IS department's main job is to protect data and allow communication of data throughout the company. The DBA is generally responsible for databases that contain this data. This responsibility is an important one and generally requires the database administrator to install and maintain a database server of some sort.

In the SMS environment, the database administrator needs to be familiar with Microsoft SQL Server. The database administrator needs to be aware of issues such as creating views, providing security, and backing up and restoring the database. Some environments actually put the SMS database on the same database server as some of the other databases in their environment. This practice is sometimes not accepted by a database administrator, although it is widely used. Database administrators are involved and more aware of things dealing with database operations than network and system operations. Those issues are managed by the system administrator and the network administrator. The database administrator's key responsibilities are the database server and protecting the database.

In the SMS environment, a DBA needs to be able to understand Windows NT, have some knowledge of SQL (Structured Query Language), and understand database design. A database administrator has many responsibilities. These include, of course, providing security, backing up and restoring, monitoring storage space, moving data, and enforcing standards. The DBA constantly works with the systems and network administrator while maintaining his database. This interaction can include discussions of network protocols and bandwidth control with the network administrator and with the system administrator regarding server management, storage space requirements, and services.

DESKTOP SPECIALIST ROLE

Desktop specialists generally work at a help desk. The help desk provides information on a continuous basis for users in the environment. They provide help when the user gets stuck in an application or his computer is not operating as it should. The biggest role of the desktop specialist is troubleshooting. He or she must make sure that the user operates in a seamless manner and that the user's system will run with as few problems as possible. Most desktop specialists have to become familiar with the desktops and client applications that the organization is running.

Some of the issues about the client are, of course, performance mechanisms, being able to change configuration files, interaction with applications to make sure that there is no conflict, memory requirements, and resource accessibility for certain applications to run. The overall goal is to enable the desktop to run to the best of its ability with little or no downtime.

Administration of desktop systems is one of the roles that will benefit the most from SMS. Many of the functions in SMS will enable desktop specialists to troubleshoot and diagnose the workstations and to manage them more easily. Other SMS functions will allow the specialists to remotely control, remotely execute, and reboot machines at any time.

Note

Many of these roles can be filled by one person, depending on the size of the organization. In a smaller organization, one person might be assigned several of these roles, whereas in a larger organization, these roles could be distributed among many people.

WHAT IS AN SMS ADMINISTRATOR?

Unfortunately, an SMS administrator is not just a representation of one task or one operation. It deals with several different tasks and operations that provide full support for the SMS environment. These roles deal with every facet of SMS, from inventory management, application management, troubleshooting and diagnostics, to database administration. There are even roles to set standards, to help plan and roll out the SMS environment, and to keep it maintained so that the infrastructure remains stable and reliable. In a small environment, one person might take on many roles. In a larger environment, though, you could actually see one role per person. These roles are described in the following sections:

◆ Technical architect

◆ Project manager

◆ Site administrator

◆ Site operator

◆ SQL Server administrator

◆ Site communications manager

◆ Job automation developer

◆ Support staff

TECHNICAL ARCHITECT

When an architect designs a building, he or she needs to know about all aspects of the infrastructure of that building. The architect of the SMS site has to be aware of all aspects of SMS from a technical to a general planning perspective. The technical architect has to be able to provide concepts on planning, implementation, and management for all other roles to follow. The architect sets standards for how the infrastructure for the SMS environment will be laid out, and makes sure that no problems will arise in the implementation and management of the environment. All other roles use this information to help them do their tasks and operations. The technical architect is generally a person who has a great deal of knowledge and experience in and about the SMS product and understands all of the technical aspects of how SMS works inside and out.

PROJECT MANAGER

Many of you have worked on projects before. Generally, when a project gets started, a manager is assigned to help dictate and manage all aspects of the project. The manager deals with the key points of tasks and operations that all members of the team or the project have to follow. The project manager of an SMS environment has to deal with other operations also, such as being the MS director or associated with the MIS director in some integrated position. Because of this, the project manager doesn't necessarily have to have complete technical expertise in the SMS product itself, although he or she needs to understand the underlying concepts and planning of an SMS environment. The project manager sets tasks and deadlines for the people in the environment to follow so that all roles and the tasks that correspond to them are followed up and are completed.

SITE ADMINISTRATOR

This role corresponds greatly to the systems administrator role. It deals with site creation, maintenance of a site, performance, and administration. The site administrator should not only be familiar with SMS but also have a great deal of knowledge of the Windows NT operating system. The reason for this is that the site administrator is going to have to deal with SMS on a daily basis and with the SMS Administrator program, making sure that the site is maintained. While making sure the site is maintained, the site administrator also has to deal with issues such as system capacity planning, resource allocation, and many other factors that could affect a Windows NT server. Many times, the site administrator shares the same role as the system administrator for the network. The site administrator should also always be aware of the size and growth of the SMS system. Other things the site administrator is somewhat responsible for include SMS configuration and troubleshooting on the client platforms, troubleshooting any problems dealing with the

SMS Administrator program, and monitoring events and alerts that either SMS or NT provides.

SITE OPERATOR

The site operator works much like an assistant to the site administrator. His role is an important one. This role deals with the day-to-day operations of doing certain tasks outside of managing the SMS site. Many of these tasks include being able to work with the desktops in several different ways. The site operator has to have the same or even greater knowledge of Windows NT than the site administrator. This is because the site operator deals with a lot more tasks on the NT domain. The site administrator deals with creating and maintaining users, creating packages and jobs for distribution of applications to the desktop, running reports and queries, and monitoring and reporting any problems or events to the site administrator. The type of person needed to be a successful site operator is someone who has extensive knowledge of the SMS Administrator program and Windows NT and can trouble-shoot situations that involve the SMS site.

Note

> Many times the site operator acts as the site administrator. These two roles are generally synonymous. At times, in large environments, you will seek separate individuals; one will be a site operator, and the other will be a site administrator.

SQL SERVER ADMINISTRATOR

As discussed earlier regarding the DBA, the SQL Server administrator plays the same role. This role is a little different than the actual DBA of most organizations. This DBA has an additional role of being able to communicate with the site administrator and other players such as the technical architect and project manager of the SMS site. The SQL Server administrator now has an added responsibility other than the DBA jobs that were given before. Now he has to deal with a database that handles the management of the systems that the DBA uses. It's good for a SQL Server administrator who is dealing with the SMS site to be very familiar with SMS terminology. Generally, the DBA that you have had for all of your other databases will function as your SMS SQL Server administrator in smaller environments. In a large environment, some organizations will hire a separate SMS SQL Server administrator because the database is so large, and is probably replicated to many sites. Some of the DBA responsibilities include maintaining and managing the database and, at the same time, offering security and protection by using backup and recovery.

SITE COMMUNICATIONS MANAGER

This role can be synonymous with the network administrator role discussed earlier. A site communications manager will interact with a network administrator most of the time. The site communications manager deals with the site-to-site communication using senders. The site communications manager needs to be familiar with the same issues the system, network, and internetwork administrator is familiar with. Because site communications manager means site-to-site communication, this means that you are dealing with internetwork issues. In dealing with an internetwork, a site communications manager needs to be familiar with things such as routers, several transport protocols such as TCP/IP and IPX/SPX, and such things as RAS (Remote Access Service), SNA (Systems Network Architecture), and LAN Senders. The responsibility of the site communications manager is to maintain the senders and to make sure the site-to-site communication works as seamlessly as possible. He or she also needs to offer troubleshooting and bandwidth control mechanisms so that sites can communicate at the fastest rate possible.

JOB AUTOMATION DEVELOPER

This, by all means, is the most difficult role ever given to anyone dealing with an SMS environment. This person has to deal with being able to automate the jobs. This might seem like an easy process; however, many things are required in being able to automate a job. Because several circumstances might arise on the desktop, many variants have to be considered when creating a package/job pair. In creating a package/job pair, a job automation developer at times has to create a script and a PDF file. A script is a programming tool that allows the application to be installed seamlessly. PDF files are Package Definition Files, which define what the package is so that you can give different types of installation. All of these processes have to be created by the job automation developer. The processes are very time consuming. At the best times, to create a job from scratch to meet most of the circumstances in your environment can take a minimum of three hours. This amount of time can range all the way up to 10 to 12 hours, depending upon the complexity and the number of circumstances in your environment. This makes the job automation developer role a good fit for someone who is extremely patient and has a lot of time. The job automation developer requires a person who is very knowledgeable about different scripting tools and is able to understand different PC configurations so he can write for variances that are in the environment.

SUPPORT STAFF

The support staff role is associated with the desktop specialist. These are the people who generally work the help desk to help the users troubleshoot and diagnose their workstations. At times, users get stuck or have problems being able to do certain operations and tasks at their desks. Help desk people are generally there to help them out. These people have different roles in the environment to make sure that any problems that occur in an SMS operation or task are reported to the site administrator and to additional roles so that things can be accomplished. A support staff person's main job is to be able to work with client problems. Some of the requirements for a support staff person are definitely SMS troubleshooting knowledge and being able to understand the client platforms. He or she also needs to have very sharp support skills and good familiarity with hardware.

SUMMARY

As you have seen, many roles can be played in an SMS environment. To define the job of an SMS administrator, you are actually defining several different operations and tasks that are given to several different roles to make your environment run as seamlessly as possible. SMS is not a complete solution. If you use these roles effectively and efficiently, you can assign tasks and operations to people in your environment so that they have a clear understanding of what their job is. In a small environment, the roles of SMS are shared with the human resource roles. In a larger environment, you might hire an entire SMS staff. Much of how you are going to appoint these roles will be according to the knowledge and expertise the person has. As you see, to be an SMS administrator covers many different aspects of what networking systems is about.

PART II

Concepts and Planning
of the System

- SMS Architecture

- NT Integration

- Administration of
  SMS

CHAPTER 4

SMS Server: Under
the Hood

This chapter takes a close look at SMS and exactly what it is composed of. The SMS services will be covered, as well as how SMS interacts with NT and SQL Server.

SMS ARCHITECTURE

SMS may seem initially overwhelming because of its many functions, its required integration with both NT and SQL Server, and because, for many of the people who install SMS, it will be their first enterprise management package. There is hope, however, because SMS is by nature very modular, and its functions are easily broken down into individual services and processes. Taken individually, the SMS functions and services are a lot easier to understand, install, maintain, and troubleshoot than when taken as a whole.

There are six basic functions of SMS, and making up those functions are 17 services. The six functions are inventory (covered in Chapter 14, "Inventory: Knowledge Is Power;" Chapter 16, "Queries;" and Chapter 17, "Machine and Site Groups"), software distribution and network application management (covered in Chapter 18, "Packages;" Chapter 19, "Jobs;" and Chapter 20, "Making the Software Distribution"), troubleshooting , client services (covered in Chapter 13, "Installation of SMS Clients") and administrative functions (covered in Chapter 10, "Installation or Upgrading Primary Site Servers," and Chapter 11, "Installation of Additional Site Servers"). The NT services that perform client functions are present on NT workstation clients and also on the SMS servers themselves, as they are also SMS clients. Table 4.1 shows which services contribute to which functions. An X signifies a service contained within the SMS Executive Service.

TABLE 4.1. SMS SERVICES AS COMPARED TO SMS FUNCTIONS.

	Inventory	Software Distribution	Network Apps	Trouble-shooting	Client	Administration
SMS_Hierarchy_Manager						X
SMS_Site_Config_Manager						X
SMS_Executive						X
*Scheduler		X	X			
*Despooler		X	X			
*Senders		X	X			
*Maintenance Manager	X	X	X			
*Inventory Processor	X					

	Inventory	Software Distribution	Network Apps	Trouble-shooting	Client	Administration
*Inventory Data Loader	X					
*Alerter	X			X		
*Applications Manager	X		X			
*Site Reporter						X
*SMS_Trap_Filter						X
SMS_Inventory _Agent					X	
SMS_Package_Command_ Manager_NT		X			X	
SMS_Client_Config_Manager					X	X
SMS Remote Control Agent				X	X	

SMS COMPARED TO A FACTORY

The functions and services of SMS can be more easily understood if compared to factory workers with their functions and responsibilities. Just as a factory can be asked to produce different things simultaneously, SMS can also do different functions at the same time. Factories have procedures and processes in place to ensure high quality and efficient organization. SMS also has procedures, processes, and flowcharts that it follows to produce the desired output, whether it be an inventory list of all personal computers in the company, or a job that installs MS Office 97 to the local workstations.

Sometimes in a factory, procedures can be bypassed for one reason or another. For better or worse, SMS is very rigid and acts similarly, whether it resides on a single server with only five clients, or is spread out over 20 servers with thousands of clients. This inflexibility of SMS can seem frustrating at first, but it soon becomes an asset, both for understanding SMS and for troubleshooting components if something doesn't work as expected.

In a factory, work is going on constantly. SMS has the unique characteristic of being able to control how often work is done. There is a generic response mode setting for SMS that controls how often the services wake up and look for things to do. The response time can be set to Very Fast, Fast, Medium, or Slow, which correspond to the services waking up every 1, 5, 15, or 30 minutes, respectively. If set to a faster response time, SMS responds to requests more quickly, but the computer that SMS is running on will be slower for anything else. You can set the response time by going to the properties of your site in SMS Administrator, as seen in Figure 4.1.

Figure 4.1.
Adjusting the
response time of
SMS.

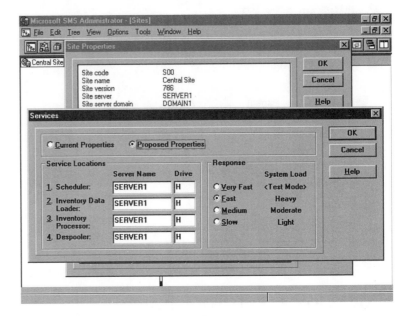

Companies may want to dedicate a server to SMS because of these performance issues. Chapter 7, "System Planning with SMS," provides more specifics on system planning. Response time affects every SMS service with the exception of the client services.

The frequency with which the service checks for proposed changes from the administrator and for status reports from lower services is one of the key parameters that control the responsiveness of SMS.

TIME FOR COFFEE

One of the frustrations in administering SMS is that it is not real-time like most applications. For example, if this was an Excel book and you were doing examples along with the book, a mistyped step would give you immediate feedback that it didn't work. It would be relatively easy to see what was done wrong and fix it. SMS not only works in the background, but its response mode may be set so slow that feedback may be five minutes or more in coming. After identifying and fixing the mistake, it may take another five minutes or more before new feedback assures the administrator that the problem was found and corrected. Many times, the administrator looks for problems and changes things too soon, only to find that SMS actually did do the task correctly. When waiting for SMS to work, just remember the old saying that a watched pot never boils. Sometimes a coffee break for the administrator can do wonders for SMS because it gives SMS enough time to catch up to all the changes it has been given to process. SMS Trace can be invaluable in determining exactly what SMS is doing. See Chapter 5, "Understanding the SMS System," on how to install and use SMS Trace.

SMS SERVICES

There are several ways to see the SMS services. From Control Panel, the Services icon will list only the major SMS services, as shown in Figure 4.2.

To see all of the SMS services, you will need to use the SMS Service Manager as seen in Figure 4.3. Not all services can be seen without scrolling the window.

Figure 4.2.
SMS services
when viewed from
Control Panel /
Services.

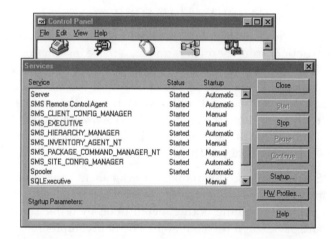

Figure 4.3.
SMS services
when viewed from
SMS Service
Manager.

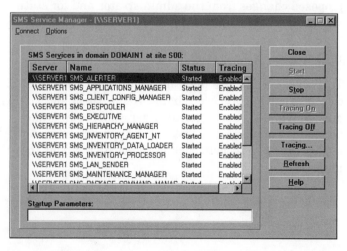

The services can be compared to workers in a factory and are explained in the following sections:

◆ SMS_Hierarchy_Manager

◆ SMS_Site_Config_Manager

◆ SMS_Client_Config_Manager

◆ SMS_Executive

Note

SMS 1.1 has fewer services than SMS 1.2 because the SMS Remote Control Agent, SMS_Trap_Filter, and SMS_Client_Config_Manager_NT Services are not present until SMS 1.2.

SMS_HIERARCHY_MANAGER

This service acts like vice president of production. In a factory, it would get its instructions from the owners and pass those instructions down the factory hierarchy for ultimate action. It would meet regularly with the owners to report the status of past recommendations and to ask for new recommendations. It would also have a method of communication between it and the people in the factory that would actually be making the change. The vice president has to check in with the owners and subordinates on a regular schedule (at least in this example). The owner gets to set the frequency of the meetings.

In SMS, the hierarchy manager works about the same way. It gets its instructions from the SMS administrator and writes a file with the proposed changes. The proposed change file is then acted upon by other services, which will eventually report back when the change has been accomplished. The service checks for both proposed changes from the administrator and for status updates from other SMS services. The frequency is based on the SMS response mode.

SMS_SITE_CONFIG_MANAGER

This service acts like a plant manager. In a factory, the plant manager would be in charge of getting proposed changes done. He or she would get a memo from the vice president and act on it. The manager would either take care of the recommendation themselves or assign the task to the appropriate person. After the change has been made, he or she reports back to the vice-president that the task has been accomplished.

The SMS_Site_Config_Manager looks for proposed changes from the hierarchy manager and acts on those changes. It either makes the change itself or assigns it. It then reports back to the SMS_Hierarchy_Manager.

SMS_CLIENT_CONFIG_MANAGER

This service is like the human resources department, which is in charge of orientation for all new employees, and informing existing employees of any changes in employee policies.

This service installs new clients in the site and responds to instructions from the administrator to change configurations for existing clients.

SMS_EXECUTIVE

This service acts like a plant foreman. In a factory, he or she has direct supervision over the workers. The foreman gets detailed instructions from the plant manager and makes sure the workers know what to do. He or she closely supervises the workers and reports back when the work is done.

The SMS_Executive service is unique in that it contains 10 or more subservices or processes. When the services are viewed from Control Panel, only the SMS_Executive shows up. When the SMS Service Manager is run from the SMS program group, all of the services appear.

The executive service gets instructions from the SMS_Site_Config_Manager and assigns one of its subservices or processes to the task. This service contains the subservices or processes discussed in the following sections:

- SMS_Scheduler
- SMS_Despooler
- The Senders
- SMS_Maintenance_Manager
- SMS_Inventory_Data_Processor
- SMS_Inventory_Data_Loader
- SMS_Alerter
- SMS_Applications_Manager
- SMS_Site_Reporter
- SMS_Trap_Filter

SMS_SCHEDULER

This service acts like a shipping clerk. In a factory, the clerk would accept mail or products from other workers, package it up, and put a label on it. The clerk would check to see if the package had to be sent overnight or could go in regular mail, and he or she would contact the appropriate shipper. The clerk is also in charge of monitoring the shippers to make sure the package actually arrived.

The scheduler service acts just like its factory twin. It prepares packages that have been designed by the administrator, determines their priority, and picks the appropriate senders. It prepares the package by compressing the files that are to be sent out. It also makes instructions for where and when to deliver the package. It monitors the senders to make sure the package is delivered.

SMS_DESPOOLER

This service acts like a receiving clerk. The clerk would watch for incoming packages, open boxes to get what was inside, and route the package to the appropriate person.

The despooler watches for incoming jobs and packages, decompresses them and their instructions, and puts them on the distribution/application servers.

THE SENDERS

These services act like the carrier that transports the package from the shipping dock to the receiving dock. Different factories may have preferred carriers, or different carriers for different types of packages, or different days one carrier might be preferred over another.

If a package has to be delivered within the same plant, some kind of interoffice mail or local transport system is probably used. It would be very inefficient to have Federal Express pick up a package at the shipping dock and deliver it 100 yards away to the receiving dock, but this is exactly what SMS does. It doesn't matter if SMS is installed on one server or 20 servers; SMS copies the compressed package from the sending site to the receiving site using its own sender services rather than NT's copy command. This may seem inefficient if there is only one server, but the modularity and consistency make SMS easy to expand and modify as your network grows.

There are six possible senders that SMS can use, although there is only one installed by default. The default sender is the SMS_LAN_SENDER, which will copy packages using the TCP/IP, NWLink, or NetBEUI protocols. Other senders include those designed for RAS for X.25, ISDN or Async (modem), as well as SNA batch or SNA interactive. Senders are covered in detail in Chapter 5.

SMS_MAINTENANCE_MANAGER

This service acts like the janitor in the factory. The janitor has to clean up after everyone and put things in their place.

The maintenance manager is constantly working, making sure things are where they are supposed to be. It does most of the minute-to-minute routine maintenance and updating of SMS. It copies client configuration files from SMS to the logon servers, and it copies collected inventory from the logon servers back up to SMS.

SMS_INVENTORY_DATA_PROCESSOR

This service acts like the reporting clerk at the plant. The reporting clerk has to sort through the daily reports from every worker in the plant. He or she throws out everything that was in earlier reports and organizes what is left into a condensed report. The report will contain the complete status of any new workers and updated status of existing workers. The report is then forwarded to the boss's administrative assistant.

The frequency of the reports determines how up-to-date the data is. If reports are requested on a monthly basis, vital data could be out of date by the time it is reported. Conversely, if daily or even hourly reports are requested, a lot more paperwork (or, in this case, e-mail) is generated and the clerk has a lot more to sort through, but the data is considerably more up-to-date.

The inventory data processor sorts through all the raw inventory data that has been brought back by the maintenance manager in order to find changes to existing inventory. If a client has reported inventory for the first time, the entire inventory is included, or else it makes a `Delta.Mif` file, which contains just the inventory that has changed since the last inventory. It then passes the `Delta.Mif` to the inventory data loader. By creating a `Delta.Mif` file with only the changes from the last inventory, SMS conserves database space and can keep an inventory history of the SMS clients.

SMS_INVENTORY_DATA_LOADER

This service acts like the administrative assistant who takes the condensed status report to the boss. He or she makes a full report on any new workers and gives an updated status on existing workers.

The inventory data loader is the one that makes a SQL connection and either adds a new record for a new computer or adds updated data to the record for an existing computer. After a baseline inventory is taken, only changes are loaded in SQL.

4

SMS_ALERTER

This service acts like the person who fills vending machines at the factory. He or she comes calling at regular intervals and has a list of what to check for and what to do if the machines need filling. Even if no one ever uses the machine, the person still comes at regular intervals and checks it against his list.

The alerter checks for alerts the administrator has defined. An alert consists of a predefined query that runs against the SMS database, how often to run the query, and an assigned action to perform if the query finds anything. If the query is successful, the alert service performs the predefined action; otherwise, the service goes inactive until the next interval. The frequency of the alert service is determined by the SMS response frequency. Queries and alerts are covered in more detail in Chapters 16, "Queries," and 23, "Housecleaning in SMS," respectively.

SMS_APPLICATIONS_MANAGER

This service acts like a secretary who takes dictation from the vice president about current requests and translates it into the actual instructions required to carry out the request.

The applications manager makes the client configuration files that the maintenance manager copies to the logon servers.

SMS_SITE_REPORTER

This service acts like the cub reporter who takes everything this factory is doing, makes a newsletter, and passes it to the factory higher in the company hierarchy.

The site reporter is in charge of seeing that child sites report correctly to their parent sites.

SMS_TRAP_FILTER

This service acts like the person who is the major grapevine connection in the company. He or she decides what to pass around or what to keep to himself.

The trap filter can selectively filter the SNMP traps that can be added to the SMS database.

THE SMS CLIENT SERVICES

The following services give the SMS client its functionality. On NT machines, the client functions are implemented as services, while on other clients they are implemented as applications.

- ◆ SMS_Inventory_Agent
- ◆ SMS_Package_Command_Manager_NT
- ◆ SMS Remote Control Agent

SMS_Inventory_Agent

Normally, inventory is run on a computer during the logon process through the logon script. Servers can't be assured of having a user log into them at any regular interval, so this service installs on all servers in the SMS site. This service will automatically take inventory of NT servers every 24 hours.

SMS_Package_Command_Manager_NT

When a package is sent, it needs something on the client side to trigger the operation of the package. For normal workstations, the client programs are run when the workstation is booted. Under NT, processes are implemented as services, which gives them the advantage of being able to run before a person is logged in. This service reads the instructions of packages that have been sent to that computer and manages the running of the packages.

SMS Remote Control Agent

This service is required on NT clients that want to allow real-time help desk functions, which include file transfer, chat, remote execute, remote control, and remote reboot.

NT Integration

SMS is tightly integrated with NT and makes quite a few changes to NT during the installation. SMS requires that an NT user be created. SMS will create directories, shares, services, and registry entries. Also, SMS automatically installs the client software to any and all servers that are running SMS.

The SMS Administrator Account

NT server breaks up its functions into services. Various services include the Browser service, which provides a listing of shared resources; the Server service, which fulfills requests from the network; and the Workstation service, which allows the computer to access resources on the network. A service can be set in one of two ways—either it can act using a generic system account, or it can have an NT user account assigned to it and can act like that user. Services that only act on the local computer usually work best when left at the default setting that uses the system account, or, in other words, acts as part of the NT system. Services that communicate with other computers directly usually need an NT user assigned to them. An example of a service that needs a user assigned to it is the Directory Replicator service, which synchronizes files between servers. This service is literally connecting across the network to other servers, and it needs an NT user to connect with.

The SMS services connect all over the network to collect inventory, update software scanning rules, search and install new logon servers, and so on. SMS needs a user assigned to it in order to function correctly. The user needs to be created in User Manager and be made a member of the Domain Admins global group before SMS is installed. The user also needs to have the Logon as a Service right assigned to it. For this example, we will use the name SMSAdmin, although for security reasons you may want to use another name. See Chapter 7 for more details on security.

DIRECTORY CHANGES

SMS will, by default, install to the NTFS partition with the most free hard drive space. SMS is one of the few programs that require an NTFS partition to install to. By default, a directory called SMS will be created off the root of the drive SMS installs to. Under the SMS directory, there are four subdirectories roughly corresponding to different roles a server can play in an SMS site as well as a directory for the network monitor software.

THE Logon.Srv DIRECTORY STRUCTURE

The directory structure that starts with logon.srv has to do with client files. In this directory structure, the client inventory executables and instructions for what the inventory scans will look for are stored. Also in this directory are batch files that will install the client software to various platforms. Figure 4.4 shows the directory and subdirectories.

THE Helper.Srv DIRECTORY STRUCTURE

This directory structure appears on servers that have been designated as helper servers in the SMS hierarchy. On SMS primary servers, the directory structure is in place, although it is pretty much empty. The Helper.Srv directory can also be seen in Figure 4.4.

Figure 4.4.
The Helper.Srv
and Logon.Srv
*directory struc-
ture.*

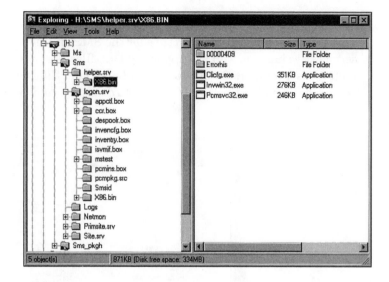

THE Primsite.Srv DIRECTORY STRUCTURE

This directory structure holds configuration and script files that can later be used to create automated installation or deinstallation packages. Figure 4.5 shows the directory structure.

The Audit directory holds the configurations for software auditing, and the Import.src directory holds the scripts under the ENU (English) directory. If another language is being used with SMS, the scripts for that particular language would be found under its respective language directory.

Figure 4.5.
The Primsite.Srv
*directory struc-
ture.*

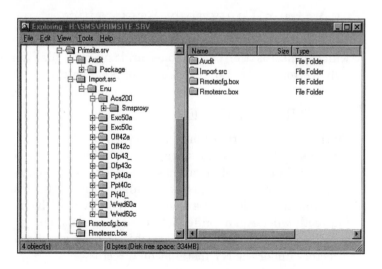

THE Site.Srv DIRECTORY STRUCTURE

This is the main directory structure for the SMS site. The executables for the SMS services are here, as well as supporting DLL files. As shown in Figure 4.6, for Intel platform servers, an X86 directory will be created that holds the executables. For DEC Alpha servers, there will be an Alpha directory, and for Mips servers, there will be a Mips directory.

Figure 4.6.
The Site.Srv
directory struc-
ture.

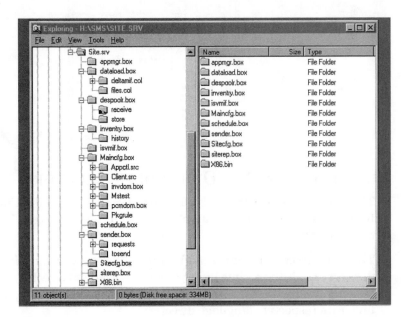

THE Netmon DIRECTORY STRUCTURE

Installing Network Monitor during the SMS installation will create this directory, which contains the executables and support files for the network monitor. Subdirectories are also included for packet captures.

REGISTRY CHANGES

The Registry in NT takes the place of the .INI files (used by applications in previous versions of Windows) to store their configurations. The Registry is a central database that has configuration settings for both the server side of NT and the client side. The Registry can also track configurations by the user, which allows different and unique profiles to be kept on an individual basis. The Registry is edited indirectly whenever a configuration is changed for a program. The Registry can also be edited directly using the Regedit32.exe program that is found in the System32 directory under the NT installation directory.

Five folders or keys are present in the Registry. (See Figure 4.7.) SMS will add keys corresponding to the main SMS services to the HKEY_LOCAL_MACHINE Registry, under the CurrentControlSet/Services key, as seen in Figure 4.8. SMS will also create a new key called SMS under the Software/Microsoft section, as seen in Figure 4.9. This key holds the many subkeys that hold the bulk of the configurations for SMS.

Figure 4.7.
The NT 4.0
Registry.

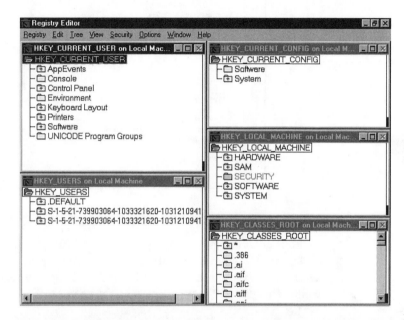

Figure 4.8.
The SMS subkeys
in the Current-
ControlSet /
Services key.

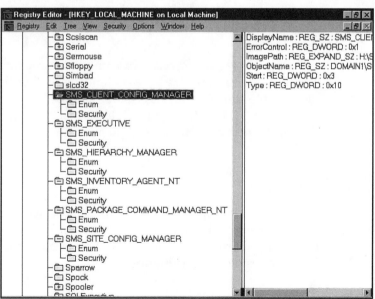

Figure 4.9.
The SMS subkeys
in the Software /
Microsoft key.

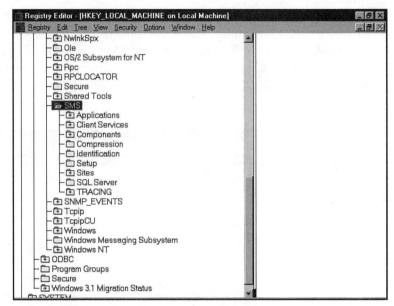

Note

The keys of the Registry represent general categories of information. NT 3.51 and earlier have only four keys. The HKEY_CURRENT_ CONFIG key is unique to NT 4.0 and represents different hardware profiles that NT 4.0 can track and boot with. SMS doesn't affect this new key.

Caution

Editing the Registry directly can have catastrophic results. Edits made to the Registry take place immediately, but they may not take effect until the next time the server is booted. If you are curious about what is in the Registry, you should turn on the read-only toggle—it can be found under the Options menu.

SHARE CHANGES

After SMS installs, it will create shares on some of its directories. Although My Computer or Explorer will show when a directory is shared, the easiest way to both view and manage shared directories is with Server Manager using the Computer | Shared Directories menu. (See Figure 4.10.)

SMS shares the Logon.srv directory with the name of SMS_SHR. The permissions are set with both the administrator and everyone groups having full control. This directory is shared so clients can connect and install from here if automatic installation is turned off.

The SMS root directory is shared as SMS_SHR*x* with *x* standing for the drive where SMS was installed. The permissions on the SMS_SHR*x* share are the administrator group with full control, and everyone with read access. This directory is shared so that applications and processes that need to add to the SMS installation can connect to it, no matter where SMS was installed.

The SMS\SITE.SRV\despoolr.box\receive directory is shared as SMS_SITE, with only the administrator group having full control. This share acts like an inbox for the despooler service.

SMS will also create a directory and a share based on that directory after the first package is sent. The directory will be called SMS_PKG*x* with *x* being the drive letter where it is installed. The directory will be shared as SMS_PKG*x*, with the everyone group having full control.

Figure 4.10.
Server Manager
managing shared
directories.

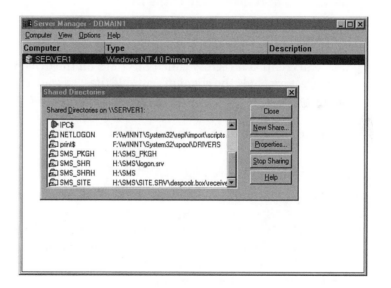

NT Replication Interaction

Although not technically required for SMS to operate, NT's directory replication service has to be enabled in order to take advantage of SMS's ability to automatically install SMS clients.

SMS can be set to automatically edit logon scripts so that client software will be installed, and computers will be inventoried when users log on.

WHY USE NT'S REPLICATION?

In an NT domain, there is one Primary Domain Controller (PDC) that contains the database of users, groups, and passwords. Other servers can be installed as Backup Domain Controllers (BDC) that have a backup copy of the database on them. When users log into the domain, their computer finds the closest copy of the database so the user can get authenticated more quickly. NT automatically keeps the databases in sync between the PDC and the BDCs. Logon scripts must be run from the controller that authenticates the user, but NT does not automatically keep the logon scripts in sync between servers.

By enabling directory replication, an export or master directory is specified that holds the master copy of the logon script. This directory is then synchronized with the logon script directories on other controllers. When a change is made to the master copy of someone's logon script, the change will be reflected in every copy of the script that resides on all of the BDCs.

CLIENT CHANGES

SMS will create a directory called MS/SMS on the drive with the most free space. This directory holds the client executable files, as well as blank and completed .MIF files. The configurations for the client are held in the SMS.INI file, which is located in the root directory of the C drive. The file is marked as a hidden file and is created when the client files are installed on that workstation or server.

SQL SERVER INTEGRATION

The designers of SMS had two basic choices on how to store the inventory and system data that SMS generates. They could build a new database engine for SMS to use, or they could use an existing database standard and engine. Many programs write a whole new engine for the database part, but it is a time consuming and complex undertaking. However, Microsoft already had a world-class database engine in SQL Server that was part of BackOffice.

The designers of SMS decided to store its data in an existing standard format using SQL Server. The SQL database language is a mature, open standard that has gained in popularity over the years. SQL stands for Structured Query Language, which is a database definition and query language. The advantages of using SQL Server are many. First, SQL running on NT currently holds the record for cost efficiency for any SQL database engine. Second, MS SQL Server is an integral part of BackOffice, and sites that already had SQL in place would incur little or no additional dollar cost for the SMS usage (although there may be a performance cost). Capacity planning for the SQL server is covered in Chapter 7. Third, by using an open database standard like SQL Server, other applications can easily get at the SMS data for further analysis, Web publishing of inventory, or any other added functionality that SMS may not support. In fact, SMS includes Crystal Reports, a third-party reporting program that can create professional reports from the SMS database in minutes.

SMS tightly integrates with SQL in that most of the SMS services are either adding to or editing data in the database, or are running queries against it. SMS keeps no data outside of SQL except for that in the Registry. The only exceptions are the SMS client services, which keep their configurations in an .INI file.

SQL SERVER BASICS

Microsoft's SQL Server application is a relational database engine. One of the things to remember when dealing with SQL Server is that it is designed to be fast, not efficient. For example, SQL Server preallocates memory for connections from clients. The memory is used even if no one ever connects. This makes SQL very fast, but very RAM-consuming as well. SQL Server also preallocates hard drive space for databases, even if there is little or no data in the database.

SQL Server can be finely adjusted in order to ensure the fastest responses with the databases and applications being used. SQL Server has over 50 parameters to set, and several of these are so critical that incorrect settings can slow down the server by a factor of 10 or even greater! SMS administrators who don't have someone skilled in SQL Server are encouraged to either find someone to help if things go wrong with SQL, or dive into SQL Server as well as SMS.

RELATIONAL DATABASE BASICS

Two of the most common database formats are the flat-file database and the relational database. A flat-file database can be thought of as a large spreadsheet, with one row corresponding to a complete entry. The advantage of a flat-file database is its simplicity. The disadvantage is that redundant data is often entered, and it may be difficult to update all occurrences when something changes (like someone's phone number). See Figure 4.11 for an example of a simple database to track people checking out books from a local library. Reports and queries are relatively easy to run because all of the columns are in one table.

Figure 4.11.
A simple flat-file
database.

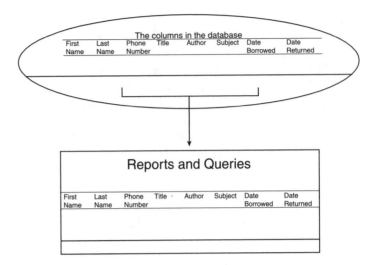

A relational database differs from a flat-file database in that the data is broken down into tables of like data. When reports are run or data needs to be looked up, the tables are related back to each other using keys. Relational databases are much more complex to set up than flat-file databases, but they are more efficient in the long run from both a data storage as well as a maintenance point of view. Figure 4.12 shows the tables within a relational database and how they would be recombined for reports or queries.

Figure 4.12.
An example of
a relational
database.

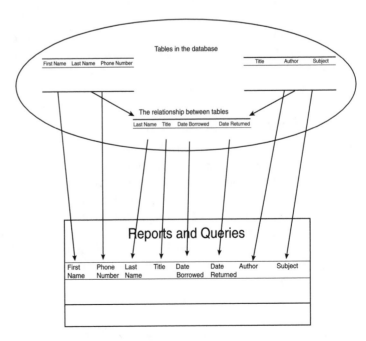

SMS supports the relational database model. In fact, SMS creates over 70 different tables within the database to try to efficiently store the data, as shown in Figure 4.13.

Figure 4.13.
Some of the tables
that comprise the
SMS database.

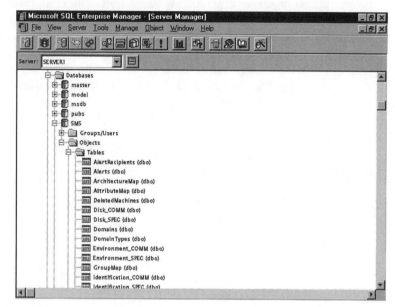

Administrators can also add new customized tables to the SMS database. See Appendix D, "Extending Inventory Collection," for more details.

SQL DEVICES AND DATABASES

The creation of a database is a two-step process. First, the preallocation of hard drive space is done by creating a database device, which is just a file with a name and size. The database is then created by assigning space from one or more devices to the database.

Although there may be wasted space because the database is much larger than the data actually in it, speed is considered more important than system resources from a SQL Server point of view.

During installation, SMS deals with SQL differently, depending on whether SMS is being installed on the same server as SQL. If it is being installed on the same computer, SMS can create both the SQL devices and databases. If SMS is being installed on a server that will not contain the database, the SQL administrator has to create the devices by hand before SMS can be installed. SMS will then create the database during installation.

THE TRANSACTION LOG

SQL caches data going into and out of the database. Using a RAM cache speeds operations up tremendously, but it makes the data susceptible to loss due to power interruptions or server crashes. SQL also writes all changes made to the database to a part of the database called the transaction log. The log can be stored on the same device as the database, but for performance and reliability reasons, it is usually best to put it on a separate device. SMS will make a subdirectory called SMSDATA and will create a 45MB device called smsdata.dat for the database and a 10MB device called smslog.dat for the transaction log by default. SMS will then create a database called SMS using those two devices.

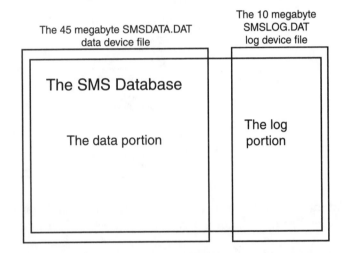

Figure 4.14.
The devices and
databases created
by SMS.

The 45 megabyte SMSDATA.DAT
data device file

The 10 megabyte
SMSLOG.DAT
log device file

The SMS Database

The data portion

The log
portion

> ## Note
>
> SMS 1.1, by default, creates a 45MB database and an 8MB log. If you are installing SMS 1.1, you can change the default from 8 to 10 megabytes for the log to match SMS 1.2.

ADMINISTRATION OF SMS

Once SMS is installed correctly, it requires little maintenance for the server itself. Administration tasks usually consist of tuning inventory collection, adding packages and jobs, running queries against the inventory, and occasionally cleaning and backing up the database. Administration of SMS is covered in Part IV, "Operating SMS—Running the Shop." Backing up the database is covered in Chapter 23.

How to Make Changes to SMS

Most changes are made using SMS Administrator. By examining the properties of the site and using the appropriate button, you can change the characteristics of SMS. Other tools that you can use to control the way SMS works are the Sender Manager and the Registry Editor. Chapter 6, "SMS Site Components," has more details on the SMS tools and how to use them.

SMS Administrator

Because all of the SMS data is stored in a SQL database, SMS Administrator needs a valid SQL logon user and password before it can connect to the SQL server and display the data. By highlighting the site and choosing the Properties icon, you can see and modify the characteristics of the site. Figure 4.15 shows what the site properties buttons look like.

Figure 4.15.
Properties of an
SMS site.

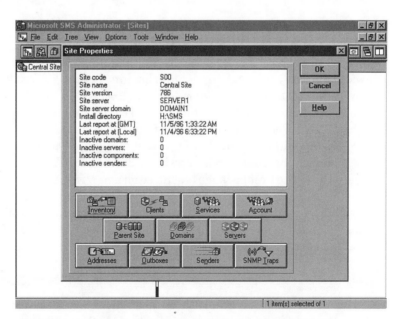

> ## Note
>
> The properties of a site will look different in SMS 1.1 because it has one less button—SNMP Traps is new for SMS 1.2. The buttons are also in a different order in SMS 1.1.

CONTROLLING THE WAY SMS USES NETWORK BANDWIDTH

By default, SMS will copy files around the network in the fastest way possible. This might lead to slowdowns for other applications because SMS could occupy the entire bandwidth if large packages are sent during peak hours. Bandwidth restrictions can be imposed using the SMS Sender Manager, which will be covered in more depth in Chapter 5.

Note

In SMS 1.1, the Sender Manager does not get installed by default. It must be copied from the PSS tools directory on the CD-ROM to the `Site.srv\x86` directory (for Intel platforms) in order to use it. For DEC Alpha or Mips servers, copy the appropriate version to the `Site.srv\alpha` or `Site.Srv\Mips` directory.

CHANGING SMS THROUGH THE REGISTRY

Direct editing of the Registry is not usually required with SMS, with the exception of altering the compression levels of packages. The key is `HKEY_LOCAL_MACHINE\SOFTWARE\Microsoft\SMS\Compression`. Levels range from 1 to 7, with 1 being the fastest and the default level of compression, and 7 being the slowest but tightest level. Setting the level to 7 will increase the compression ratio to around 20 percent, but will take about twice as long to compress as Level 1. To disable compression, set the enable compression value to No. The compression subkey gets created after the first package is sent, so on a new install of SMS you can either send a test package to create the keys, or you can create the keys manually. Figure 4.16 shows the compression keys in case you want to create them manually. The only ones that need to be created manually are the Compression Level and Compression Enabled keys.

Tip

If most of the packages that you send are already compressed, it makes sense to disable compression before sending packages. The setting is a global one in that it affects all new packages sent. Changes to the compression values will not affect existing packages, but will affect all subsequent packages sent.

Figure 4.16.
SMS compression
keys and their
default values.

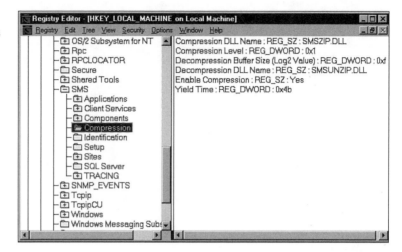

Summary

SMS is a complex application made of many services. By breaking down SMS into those services and comparing them to functions in a factory, you can begin to understand how SMS works. SMS is tightly integrated with both NT and SQL. By understanding the changes SMS makes when installed, you can better understand how SMS works and better troubleshoot problems when they occur.

- System Components:
  The Functions
  of SMS

- Understanding Sites
  and Site Hierarchies

- Communication
  Between Sites

CHAPTER 5

Understanding the SMS System

This chapter focuses on the components of SMS and how they work together to make an SMS site function. This chapter also covers having multiple SMS sites, and how to link those sites together.

Because SMS has so many pieces, each with its own responsibility and process, when you start to focus on the step-by-step processes of SMS, it is easy to miss the big picture of what SMS is trying to do. This chapter will focus on SMS but will also try to keep the big picture in mind. Figure 5.1 shows the major inputs and outputs of SMS, which will be covered in detail in this and later chapters.

Figure 5.1.
Major inputs and
outputs of SMS.

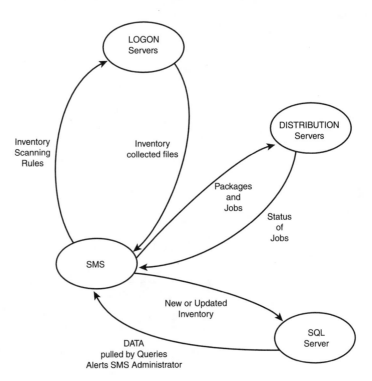

SYSTEM COMPONENTS: THE FUNCTIONS OF SMS

Taken as a whole, SMS seems all-encompassing in the tasks it can perform. In order to see exactly what SMS is doing, we need to break it down into its various services (which were introduced in Chapter 4, "SMS Server: Under the Hood") and watch the teamwork between these services. The SMS services rarely act alone—they usually act in concert as they pass configurations, files, and updates back and forth as they perform their tasks.

SMS has six basic functions. They are

- ◆ Administrative functions
- ◆ Inventory functions
- ◆ Software distribution functions
- ◆ Network-based application functions
- ◆ Troubleshooting functions
- ◆ SMS client functions

The remainder of this section will give you a better understanding of these functions.

ADMINISTRATIVE FUNCTIONS

Administrative functions include installing and maintaining SMS. Once SMS is installed, the SMS services help in maintaining the SMS installation and updating the configuration of SMS.

SMS creates a configuration file for the site, called Sitectrl.ct0. (See Figure 5.2 for an example.) This file contains settings for the site, as well as a list of what servers SMS has found and installed in the domain.

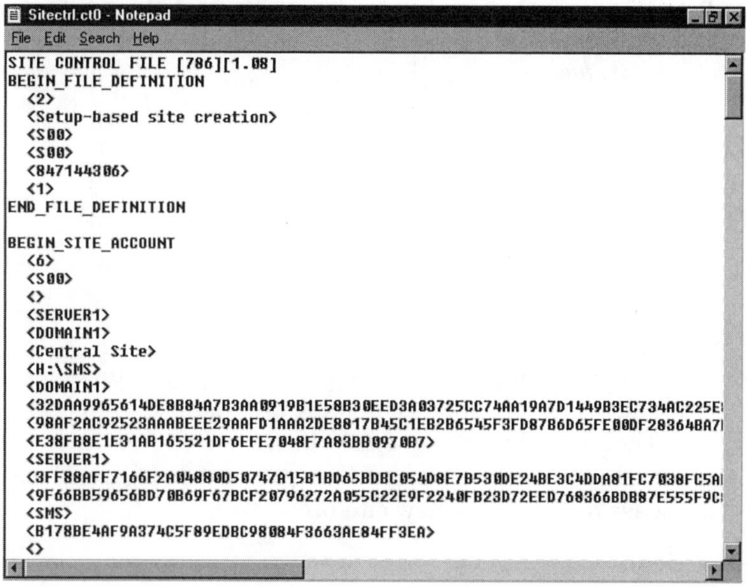

Figure 5.2.
Part of a
Sitectl.ct0
configuration file.

```
Sitectrl.ct0 - Notepad
File  Edit  Search  Help

SITE CONTROL FILE [786][1.08]
BEGIN_FILE_DEFINITION
    <2>
    <Setup-based site creation>
    <S00>
    <S00>
    <847144306>
    <1>
END_FILE_DEFINITION

BEGIN_SITE_ACCOUNT
    <6>
    <S00>
    <>
    <SERVER1>
    <DOMAIN1>
    <Central Site>
    <H:\SMS>
    <DOMAIN1>
    <32DAA9965614DE8B84A7B3AA0919B1E58B30EED3A03725CC74AA19A7D1449B3EC734AC225E
    <98AF2AC92523AAABEEE29AAFD1AAA2DE8817B45C1EB2B6545F3FD87B6D65FE00DF28364BA7
    <E38FB8E1E31AB165521DF6EFE7048F7A83BB0970B7>
    <SERVER1>
    <3FF88AFF7166F2A04880D50747A15B1BD65BDBC054D8E7B530DE24BE3C4DDA81FC7038FC5A
    <9F66BB59656BD70B69F67BCF20796272A055C22E9F2240FB23D72EED768366BDB87E555F9C
    <SMS>
    <B178BE4AF9A374C5F89EDBC98084F3663AE84FF3EA>
    <>
```

When a change is made to the site using SMS Administrator (see Figure 5.3), the SMS hierarchy manager creates a new file, called *.ct1, with the new configurations. (See Figure 5.4.)

Figure 5.3.
The SMS Administrator.

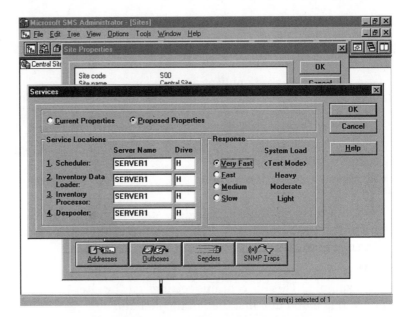

Figure 5.4.
The appearance
of the *.ct1 file.

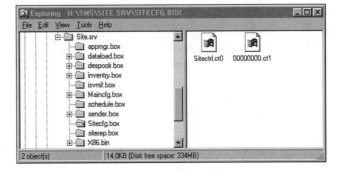

The SMS site configuration manager will then pick up that proposed change file and act on it. When it is finished making the changes, it creates a *.ct2 file. (See Figure 5.5.) The hierarchy manager picks up the .ct2 file and knows the changes have taken place. The hierarchy manager then connects to SQL and makes the changes to the database to reflect the new site properties.

The reason it is important to know how SMS makes changes to itself is so that when problems arrive, the configuration file process can be examined and either fixed or ruled out.

Figure 5.5.
The appearance
of the *.ct2 *file.*

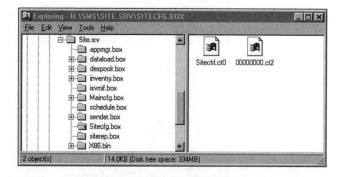

Tip

On a fast server, with the response time set to Very Fast (test mode), the files may appear for just a second or two, especially if the auto-refresh catches them just as they are being deleted. For troubleshooting, you will want to copy the *.ct1 or *.ct2 files somewhere else so you can look inside them at your leisure.

One of the key parameters is the response mode to which SMS is set. Changing the response mode was already covered in Chapter 4, but is repeated here because of its importance. To change the response mode, go to the Site Properties dialog and choose the Services button, which will take you to the Services window. (See Figure 5.6.) If SMS is set to Slow, the services only wake up every 30 minutes. In other words, if the services went back to sleep just before you made any change, it would take almost the full 30 minutes to take effect. Table 5.1 lists the settings and their effects.

TABLE 5.1. RESPONSE MODE SETTINGS: THEIR EFFECTS AND TIME INTERVALS.

Setting	Load on System	Time Interval
Very Fast	<Test Mode>	1 Minute
Fast	Heavy	5 Minutes
Medium	Moderate	15 Minutes
Slow	Light	30 Minutes

Figure 5.6.
Adjusting the
response time of
SMS.

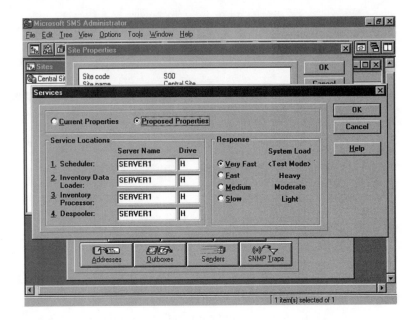

Truer Than Fiction

SMS installations that have dedicated servers for SMS can and do run at the Very Fast setting, although Microsoft says it is for test purposes only. It definitely makes SMS a lot more enjoyable to run when you only have to wait a minute or less for things to happen versus five minutes. Just be aware that anything else on that server will probably run noticeably slower.

Inventory Functions

The most important function of SMS is the inventory function, because it is the building block for the rest of the SMS site. Inventory has to be implemented before the other functions of SMS will work. Inventory is also one of the main reasons SMS gets approved and installed. After inventory is installed, the other SMS functions can be configured and used, as shown in Figure 5.7. Chapter 14, "Inventory: Knowledge Is Power," has more details on inventory.

Figure 5.7.
SMS inventory
as a building
block for other
functions.

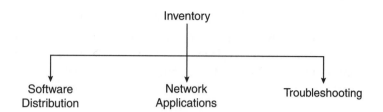

WHAT CLIENTS ARE SUPPORTED?

SMS 1.2 supports the following clients for inventory:

MS-DOS 5.0 or later

Windows 3.x

Windows 95

Windows NT

OS/2

Macintosh System 7

Various third-party software additions are available that will enable UNIX, VMS, or other types of operating systems to be part of the SMS site. See Chapter 13, "Installation of SMS Clients," and Appendix C, "Third-Party Integration—Making the Job Easier," for more details.

WHAT CAN BE INVENTORIED?

By default, SMS will inventory hardware. The specific hardware that SMS will inventory depends somewhat on the operating system and platform of the client, but the inventory will include things such as hard drive space, CPU, network card, and so on. Examples of platform-specific items that would be inventoried include such things as the model on a Macintosh platform, and the conventional, expanded, and extended memory on an Intel platform PC.

The inventory agents have the hardware scanning rules built into them. Although it is not possible to have the agents scan for additional hardware, programs can be written to inventory non-supported items. One example would be to write a Visual Basic application that would look in the .INI or Registry files and collect printer information (one item that is not collected by the agents). Appendix D, "Extending Inventory Collection," has more information on extending inventory collection.

How Often Are Things Inventoried?

Inventory can be set to occur automatically when a user logs into an NT domain, LAN Manager, or LAN Server, or even a NetWare server. Inventory can also be run manually at any time. By default, inventory will occur once every seven days. Hardware and software inventory frequencies can be scheduled independently of each other, and you can do this by using the Client Property button of the Site Properties dialog, which takes you to the Inventory window. (See Figure 5.8.)

Figure 5.8. Editing the inventory schedule.

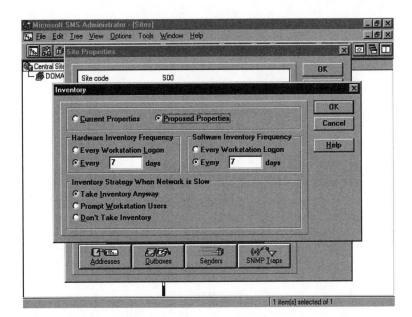

Stranger Than Fiction

At one site that had SMS installed, inventory was scheduled to occur every seven days. At the next scheduled inventory, some users would forget what the inventory agent looked like and would call the help line with reports of a virus! When the site switched to daily scans, the virus reports went away.

Note

For SMS 1.1, the default schedule for both software and hardware inventory is for every logon.

How the Services Help with Inventory

Services are involved with both the collecting of inventory, and the processing and uploading of inventory.

The Client Side of Inventory

The inventory process is initiated by the client either at logon, manually, or at preset intervals for servers. The inventory is moved to the SMS server, where it is processed and uploaded to SQL Server. The following paragraphs explain what happens, and Figure 5.9 diagrams the flow of data.

When a computer is inventoried, the agent will create a file called `*.raw` or `*.mif` (for OS/2 and Macintosh clients) in the `sms\logon.srv\inventry.box` directory on the server it authenticates to. This file will contain all of the hardware and software inventory for the client.

On MS-DOS, Windows 3.x, Windows 95, Macintosh, or OS/2 clients, the inventory agent can either be started automatically during logon script executions or it can be started manually by the user. Inventory will take a few seconds, after which the agent is unloaded from memory.

On NT workstations and servers, the inventory agent is a service that runs in the context of the system. Just like the MS-DOS or Windows 3.x clients, the agent on NT workstations will take inventory automatically at logon (if set) or manually.

On NT servers, the inventory agent wakes up every 24 hours and checks the number of days since the last inventory. If it has been longer than the interval set by the administrator, new inventory is taken.

Note

In SMS 1.1, the NT workstation inventory agent ran in the context of the user, so if the user didn't have sufficient privileges on his workstation, the agent could and did miss some items of inventory.

The Server Side of Inventory

The SMS maintenance manager monitors the `logon.srv\inventry.box` directory at the interval specified by the SMS response mode. When it finds one or more files, it moves them from the `logon.srv\inventry.box` directory to the `Site.srv\inventry.box` directory.

The inventory processor watches for new files in the `site.srv\inventry.box` directory, opens the file to get the client identification and inventory, compares the current inventory with the history for that client, and distills the differences into a `*.mif` file. The processor deletes the `*.raw` file and puts the `*.mif` file into the `site.srv\dataload.box\deltamif.col` directory.

The inventory data loader monitors the `site.srv\dataload.box\deltamif.col` directory for new files at the interval specified by the response mode. When it finds new files, it makes a connection to the SQL Server and either makes a new record or updates an existing one. See Figure 5.9 for a flowchart of how the inventory data is collected and updated.

Figure 5.9.
Flowchart of
inventory data.

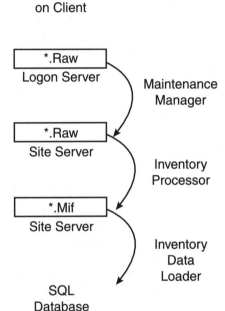

VIEWING THE INVENTORY

Inventory is viewed with SMS administrator by going to the site, then domain, and then choosing the properties of, or double-clicking on, a computer. (See Figure 5.10.) Different properties (hardware and software inventory) will be shown, depending on the type of client being viewed.

Figure 5.10.
Viewing proper-
ties of a client.

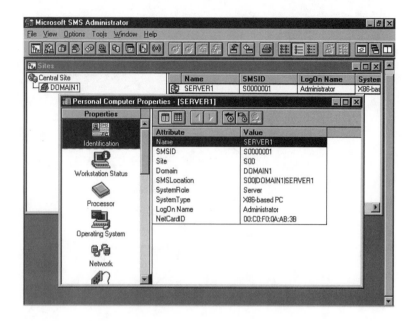

SOFTWARE DISTRIBUTION FUNCTIONS

SMS allows an administrator to remotely install, upgrade, or deinstall software on SMS clients. In order to distribute software, a package that defines the software to be distributed needs to be created. An SMS job is then defined that specifies which package goes to which client. The client then receives and runs the package. The following is a bulleted list for distributing software:

◆ Target computer is in SMS inventory database.

◆ Package is defined.

◆ Job is created.

◆ Client runs Package Command Manager.

SERVICES THAT CONTRIBUTE TO SOFTWARE DISTRIBUTION

Software packages take a somewhat convoluted route through the SMS system before clients can install them. Figure 5.11 shows the overall route of a package.

The first time a package is sent as part of a job, the SMS Scheduler reads the package and finds the source directory. The scheduler takes the entire directory structure (including all subdirectories) and compresses it into one file, named x.W00, where x is the ID number of the package. The compression levels and how to change them were discussed in Chapter 4. The scheduler stores the compressed copy in the site.srv\sender.box\tosend directory. This is the SMS site master copy that will be used to generate copies for other sites.

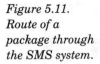

Figure 5.11.
Route of a
package through
the SMS system.

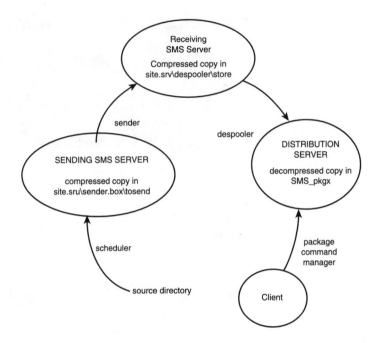

The scheduler then determines the best sender service to use in order to copy the file to the destination site. If there is only one SMS server in the entire enterprise, the file will still be copied to the target directory on the same hard drive using an SMS sender.

The scheduler will put a request in the appropriate directory for the sender it has chosen for that particular job. The default sender is the SMS_LAN_SENDER service, which can use TCP/IP, NWLink, or NetBEUI to connect to the various sites.

The sender will copy the file into the site.srv\despooler\receive directory.

The despooler will move the file into the site.srv\despooler\store directory and proceed to decompress the file. The despooler will make a directory called sms_pkgx, where x is the drive with the most room on it. Under the sms_pkgx directory, it will make a subdirectory for each package, named after the package ID number.

The Package Command Manager runs on the client and will list all the available packages for that particular client. When a package is run, it will make a connection to the package directory and install from there. The following are copies of the source code:

◆ Original source code (Uncompressed)

◆ Compressed copy in site.srv\sender.box\tosend

◆ Compressed copy in site.srv\despooler\store

◆ Decompressed copy of source code in sms_pkgx\s0000000x

NETWORK-BASED APPLICATION FUNCTIONS

SMS can install network versions of software so that the program resides on the server, with the groups and icons being built dynamically for any given user when he or she logs on.

Network applications work much like software distribution. A package is defined and a job is created to send the package out.

The additional part of creating a network application is defining the program group, which consists of choosing which package to include, giving the program group a name, and assigning NT groups to the program group. If LAN Manager, LAN Server, or NetWare servers are a part of the SMS site, their groups can also be assigned to the program group.

SERVICES THAT CONTRIBUTE TO NETWORK-BASED APPLICATIONS

When the job is created, the scheduler compresses the file and assigns an appropriate sender, just as in software distribution.

The application manager takes the program group that was created and makes instructions the SMS client can interpret.

The client runs program group control, which checks the membership of the user and finds any matching instructions. If there are matching instructions, the program group control then builds the new program group and icons. The following is a list of distributing software:

◆ Target computer is in SMS inventory database.

◆ Package is defined.

◆ Job is created.

◆ Program group is created and group(s) assigned.

◆ Client runs program group control to create the program group.

SMS NETWORK APPLICATIONS VERSUS SERVER-BASED PROFILES

Windows 95 and Windows NT allow a central profile to be kept on the server so that a person will get his or her environment no matter where he or she logs in from. Profiles are not available for Windows 3.x computers.

The question, then, is: What does the SMS Network Applications function give that profiles do not? Profiles are operating system-specific—that is, a Windows 95 profile cannot be used on a Windows NT computer, and vice versa. SMS Network applications are based on group membership, and as long as the program is compatible with the operating system, the program group will show up in Windows 3.x, Windows 95, and Windows NT.

TROUBLESHOOTING FUNCTIONS

SMS has real-time troubleshooting functions built into it, including remote control, remote reboot, chat, file transfer, and remote execute. Clients can set which functions will be allowed on their computer.

For MS-DOS, Windows 3.x, or Windows 95 clients, there are no services directly involved with the troubleshooting function of SMS. Of course, the client to be looked at must already be in the inventory database. For NT clients, the SMS Remote Control service must be started.

The troubleshooting functions of SMS are accessed by examining the properties of a computer and choosing Help Desk. (See Figure 5.12.)

Figure 5.12.
Establishing a
troubleshooting
connection to a
client.

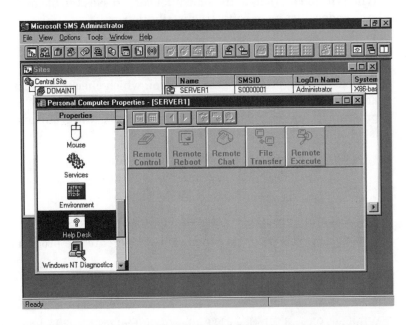

Note

In SMS 1.1, NT was not supported for real-time troubleshooting, thus the SMS Remote Control service for NT only shows up in SMS 1.2.

SMS CLIENT FUNCTIONS

There are several services that pertain to the NT computer as an SMS client, and are summarized in the next few paragraphs.

The Package Command Manager polls for new packages, runs mandatory packages, and allows the user to run optional packages. (See Figure 5.13.)

Figure 5.13.
The Package
Command
Manager.

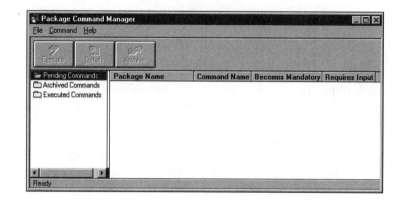

The inventory agent is a service on NT computers so that all possible hardware information can be collected.

The remote control service needs to be started on those NT clients that want to have the troubleshooting functions enabled. This service corresponds to the TSR that MS-DOS and Windows computers need to run.

UNDERSTANDING SITES AND SITE HIERARCHIES

The term SMS site corresponds to a complete installation of SMS. A site includes all of the types of servers that SMS needs in order to function correctly, such as NT servers, SMS servers, and SQL servers.

SMS can only be installed in an NT domain—in fact, the server that SMS is installed on must be either the NT Primary Domain Controller (PDC) or one of the NT Backup Domain Controllers (BDCs).

An SMS site can either keep its data in a unique, dedicated SQL database, or in a database from an existing SMS site. Sites that have their own databases are called primary sites, and those that store their data in an existing SMS database are called secondary sites.

Tip

> A primary site needs a dedicated SQL database, not a dedicated SQL server. An existing MS SQL server that has databases for other applications could easily be used for SMS, because SQL Server can hold as many as 32,000 databases! A single SQL server can hold the databases for many SMS sites—performance across the network would be the limiting factor.

THE REPORTING HIERARCHY

Relationships can be established between SMS sites so that a hierarchy for reporting and management exists. A hierarchy in SMS is always vertical—that is, sites at the top of the hierarchy have control over those at the bottom of the hierarchy. A site is called a parent site if it has a site below it. A site is called a child site if it has a site above it. (See Figure 5.14.) A primary site can be both a parent site (it has sites under it) and a child site (it reports to a higher site). Secondary sites are always children of the site whose database they exist in.

Figure 5.14.
An SMS site
hierarchy.

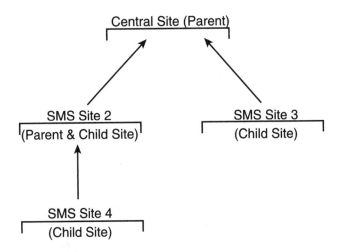

The site that is at the top of the hierarchy is considered the central site. A single central site for the entire company is not required—in fact, some companies have parallel central sites, as the entire company is not managed in a single SMS hierarchy. (See Figure 5.15.)

Figure 5.15.
Multiple central
sites.

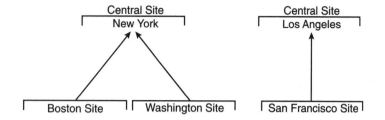

When SMS is installed into an NT domain, the SMS site encompasses the entire NT domain. Other NT domains can be added to the SMS site, but SMS will always consist of at least one NT domain. LAN Manager, LAN Server, and NetWare servers can also be added to an existing SMS site. (See Figure 5.16.)

Figure 5.16.
An SMS site
composed of
multiple servers.

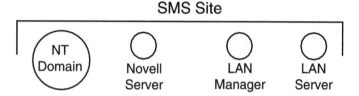

ONE LARGE SMS SITE COMPARED TO MANY SMALL SITES

An SMS site can contain one or more NT domains. If an SMS site contains multiple domains, the characteristics of the SMS site apply to all of the domains in the site.

Suppose you have one SMS site consisting of the Sales, Marketing, and Accounting domains. (See Figure 5.17.) If the Sales domain wanted inventory set to run every 7 days, but the accounting domain wanted inventory to run every 30 days, there would be a problem. In SMS, the properties that can be changed are site-specific, not domain-specific.

Figure 5.17.
The Sales,
Marketing, and
Accounting
domains in one
SMS site.

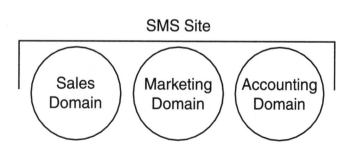

The question becomes one of licensing, performance, administration, and management. Chapter 7, "System Planning with SMS," has more details on design and performance issues.

The advantages of a single site are

◆ It is simple to manage and maintain.

◆ It is less expensive to license.

The disadvantages of a single site are

◆ All domains have to have the same properties under SMS.

◆ Administrators have control over all the domains in the site.

◆ Performance will probably be slower.

REPORTING TO A PARENT SITE

When there are multiple sites in the SMS hierarchy, addresses must be established, so SMS knows how to communicate between the sites. Addresses tell SMS which sender to use and what user to use to gain access to the other site. Adding an address is done by using the Address Properties dialog in SMS Administrator, accessed by selecting the Addresses button of the SMS Site Properties dialog. (See Figure 5.18.)

Figure 5.18.
Adding an
address to
another SMS site.

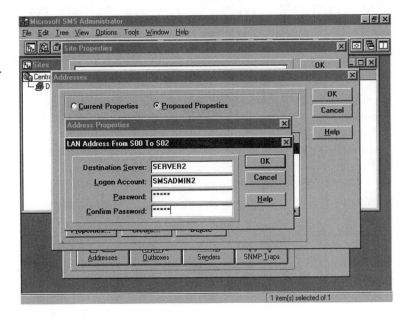

Because a parent site can administer its child and grandchild sites, it needs an address to all of the sites that are lower in the hierarchy. A child site needs an address to its immediate parent so it can send copies of its data up the hierarchy, and to any sites that are lower in the hierarchy. In Figure 5.19, site A needs addresses to sites B, C, D, E, and F. Because site C cannot manage or even see sites B or D, site C only needs addresses to site A and sites E and F.

Figure 5.19.
An SMS site
hierarchy.

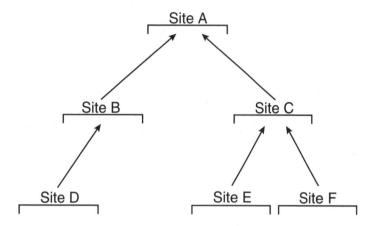

In order to create a reporting hierarchy, addresses must first be added that match the design. You can then attach the child sites to the parent sites by using the Parent Site button of the Site Properties dialog. (See Figure 5.20.)

Figure 5.20.
Attaching to a
parent site.

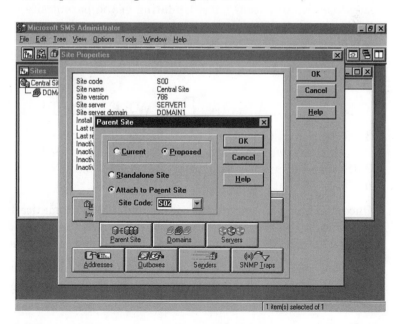

The following is a list for linking primary sites together:

1. Install each site as a stand-alone site (the default).
2. Make sure appropriate senders are installed and a common protocol is used.
3. Decide on a hierarchy.
4. Create addresses on the parent sites for all child and grandchild sites and so on.
5. Create addresses on the child sites for the parent site.
6. From the child site, attach to the parent site.

ADMINISTERING THE HIERARCHY

Once a site hierarchy has been established, child sites can be administered from the parent site. Any site you can see can be administered, so a site in the middle of the hierarchy would be able to administer its own site plus those below it (the child sites).

In the earlier example, site A could administer all SMS sites in the hierarchy, while site C could administer only sites C, E, and F. (Refer to Figure 5.19.)

Configurations, packages, jobs, and inventory scanning rules are examples of what a parent site can send to its child sites.

Inventory and the status of packages and jobs are the main types of data that child sites pass up to parent sites. Updating of the parent site is automatic once the hierarchy is established.

Administration is done through SMS Administrator, with the child sites being highlighted and then their properties examined.

COMMUNICATION BETWEEN SITES

SMS communicates across sites using the SMS senders. The default sender is the SMS_LAN_SENDER, which uses standard protocols across the local or wide area network. SMS can communicate with other sites using the LAN Sender, or one of the other five senders that can be installed.

Once something for the child site is created, SMS automatically sends it to the child site. The SMS senders each have outboxes that can be adjusted so that items can be held for later transmission, according to priorities or bandwidth restrictions.

The SMS site reporter service is in charge of the process that updates the parent site. It initiates system jobs to pass inventory up the hierarchy.

THE SENDERS

There are six possible senders that SMS can use to communicate between sites. The LAN Sender is the only one installed by default.

Three senders communicate through a Remote Access Server (RAS) including the MS_ASYNC_RAS_SENDER, which uses standard modems to communicate; the MS_ISDN_RAS_SENDER, which supports ISDN modems; and the MS_X25_RAS_SENDER, which supports communications using the X.25 specification. These senders require that a RAS server be installed somewhere in the domain.

Two senders communicate through the SNA protocol. Those senders are the MS_BATCH_SNA_SENDER, which supports communication via batch mode, and the MS_INTERACTIVE_SNA_SENDER, which supports immediate communication. These two senders require Microsoft SNA Server to be installed somewhere in the domain in order to work.

INSTALLING THE SENDERS

The senders are installed using SMS Administrator by selecting the Senders button of the Site Properties dialog, which calls up the Senders window. (See Figure 5.21.) Senders can be installed on any NT server in the SMS site.

Figure 5.21.
Installing a new
sender.

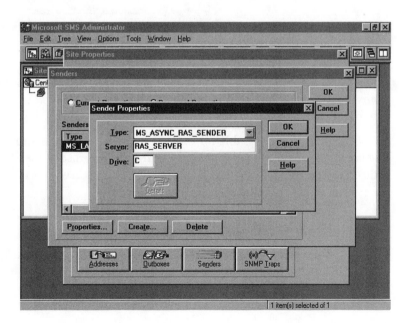

Before installing any RAS senders, you should first install a RAS server on the parent and child sites. Microsoft's SNA Server should also be installed in the parent and child sites prior to the SNA senders being installed.

MONITORING THE SENDERS

The two ways to monitor the senders are to watch for files actually being copied into their target directories, and to watch the log files of the services. Explorer or My Computer enables the directories to be monitored, whereas SMS Tracer enables real-time monitoring of the SMS log files. (See Figure 5.22.)

Figure 5.22.
SMS Tracer.

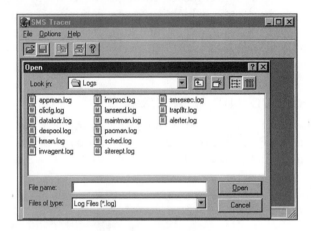

For SMS 1.1, the SMS Tracer executable was installed in the Site.srv*.bin directory but had no icon made for it. All that was needed to run SMS Tracer was to build the icon.

In SMS 1.2, the executable for SMS Tracer (SMSTRACE.EXE) and the supporting DLL (TRACER.DLL) need to be copied from the Support\Debug\X86 (for Intel platforms) directory on the CD-ROM to the Site.srv\X86.bin directory in order to run it.

> ### STRANGER THAN FICTION
>
> Upgrading to SMS 1.2 will actually delete the SMS 1.1 version of SMS Tracer off the local hard drive. SMS Tracer has to be reinstalled by copying it from the CD-ROM, as explained in the preceding paragraph.

Using Multiple Senders

Multiple addresses can be created to a single site. If multiple addresses exist, the scheduler will pick the most efficient address to use when communicating with that site. An example of multiple addresses would be sites that had modems with different phone numbers. Although a job will never be split among multiple addresses, concurrent jobs can occur.

Bandwidth Restrictions

The way the SMS senders use network bandwidth can be controlled with the SMS sender manager. Sender manager can be started from the Tools menu of SMS Administrator, or by using its own icon from the SMS program group. Sender manager lets you set bandwidth restrictions based on the sender (see Figure 5.23), or based on the site. (See Figure 5.24.) Restrictions can be set on an hour-by-hour basis.

Figure 5.23.
Setting restrictions based on the sender.

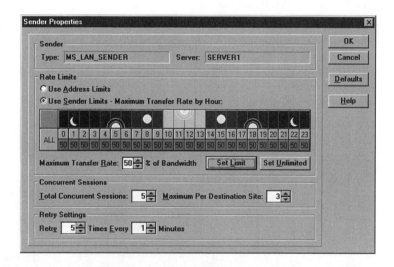

> ## Note
>
> In SMS 1.1, Sender manager does not get installed by default. It must be copied from the PSS tools directory on the CD-ROM to the Site.Srv\x86 directory (for Intel platforms) in order to use it.

Figure 5.24.
Setting restric-
tions based on
the address.

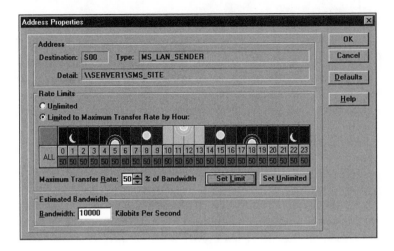

OUTBOX MANAGEMENT

You can change the scheduling and priorities of the jobs the senders will accept by using the Outboxes button of the Site Properties dialog, which will call up the Outbox window. (See Figure 5.25.) Priorities can be adjusted on an hourly basis such that only high-priority jobs are sent during working hours but all jobs are allowed after hours.

Figure 5.25.
Outbox properties
of a sender.

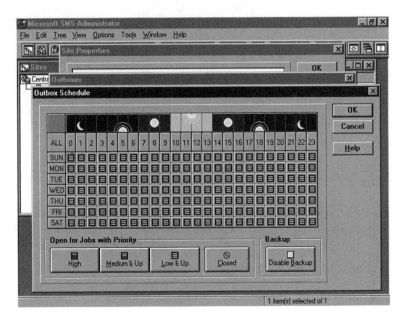

5

Tip

Outbox settings are especially important when using RAS senders. Expensive daytime rates can be kept to a minimum by blocking low- and medium-priority jobs during the day. That way, jobs can be assigned a high priority to make them happen immediately, or assigned low or medium priority to make them happen after hours. Low-priority jobs could even be blocked until after rates were at their lowest, thus maximizing savings.

The backup settings enable this outbox to be used for jobs from other outboxes that won't or can't be sent for three days. The scheduler will move the job between senders if multiple addresses are configured for any particular site.

SUMMARY

This chapter focused on the components of SMS and how they work together to make an SMS site function. This chapter also covered having multiple SMS sites, and how to link those sites together.

SMS functionality consists of individual services acting together to produce the desired output. Understanding the individual steps that SMS takes is required for troubleshooting, but should not be focused on exclusively.

SMS sites are built around NT domains, and can contain one or more domains. A site can also contain LAN Manager, LAN servers, and NetWare servers.

CHAPTER 6

SMS Site Components

This chapter focuses on the different types of SMS servers and how they interact to make an SMS site.

You use various tools that come with SMS to manage SMS. Some of the tools are installed by default, whereas others are not.

When SMS is installed into an NT domain, it adds functionality to the servers in the domain. This chapter looks at what SMS adds to the servers in a domain and their role in making the SMS site function.

THE TOOLS

You need various tools, utilities, and programs to administer and use SMS. The most common tools are installed by default, while other, more advanced tools have to be manually installed from the SMS CD-ROM. The following section describes both types of tools.

INSTALLED TOOLS

When SMS installs, it creates a program group called Systems Management Server. Within that program group are the following items (see Figure 6.1):

> SMS Administrator
> SMS Database Manager
> SMS Security Manager
> SMS Sender Manager
> SMS MIF Form Generator
> SMS Network Monitor
> SMS Service Manager
> SMS SQL View Generator
> SMS Setup
> SMS Books Online
> SMS Release Notes
> SMS What's New in 1.2

SMS ADMINISTRATOR

SMS Administrator is the primary program for configuring, maintaining, and using SMS. Because the SMS database is stored in SQL Server, a valid SQL logon is required to use SMS Administrator (see Figure 6.2). After the SQL logon, the first time you run SMS Administrator (and each time thereafter unless you remove the check from the Show this dialog at startup box), the Open SMS Window dialog appears and prompts you to open an SMS window or category. (See Figure 6.3.)

Figure 6.1.
The SMS Admin-
istrator group.

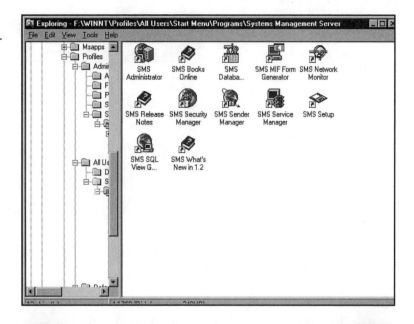

Figure 6.2.
Logging into SQL
Server.

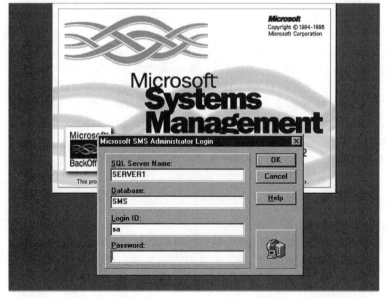

Figure 6.3.
Opening a
window inside
SMS Administra-
tor.

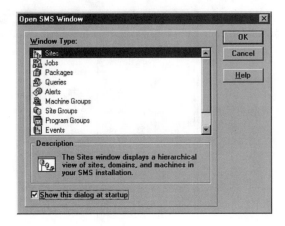

Many of the menu items have icon shortcuts, and ToolTips for the icons are available by passing the mouse over the icon.

CONNECTING TO SQL SERVER (LOGGING IN)

Because SMS stores its data in a SQL Server database, most of the utilities require you to log into SQL Server before the utility finishes loading (refer to Figure 6.2). SQL Server maintains its own database of user logons and passwords, but you can configure it to synchronize its database to that of the NT domain. See Chapter 9, "Installing and Upgrading SQL Server," for more details on SQL Server.

THE WINDOWS IN SMS ADMINISTRATOR

The Sites window contains a visual representation of the SMS site, with all computers in the site listed first by site and then by domain. You perform the inventory and troubleshooting tasks of SMS through the Sites window.

The Jobs window shows all current and past jobs and their status. You can observe the status of clients that are to receive the jobs by examining the properties of an individual job. Jobs are covered in detail in Chapter 19, "Jobs."

The Packages window shows all currently defined packages. Packages are defined with a source directory and instructions for their execution. Packages are covered in depth in Chapter 18, "Packages."

The Queries window displays the predefined queries that come with SMS, as well as queries that the administrator defines. Queries gather information from the database. You can define queries once and run or edit them at a later date. Queries are covered in Chapter 16, "Queries."

The Alerts window displays alerts that the administrator defines. An alert consists of a query and an action to perform if the query returns a certain result. Alerts are covered in Chapter 23, "Housecleaning in SMS."

The Machine Groups window is used to group computers. For example, you can make groups for servers, workstations by departments, and so on.

The Site Groups window is used to group SMS sites. For example, you can base groups of sites on geography or function. Machine and site groups are covered in Chapter 17, "Machine and Site Groups."

You use the Program Groups window to make program groups for network applications. The program groups contain a listing of packages and the user groups that get them. Program groups are covered in Chapter 20, "Making the Software Distribution."

The Events window opens all the SMS events that are logged. SMS events are also recorded as NT events in the application log, and you can view them with the NT Event Viewer.

The SNMP Traps window is used to view current traps in the database. SNMP traps are discussed in Chapter 23.

The SQL Messages window lets you see any new messages that SQL Server generates for SMS.

Figure 6.4 shows all the windows mentioned in this section.

Figure 6.4.
The windows in
SMS Administra-
tor.

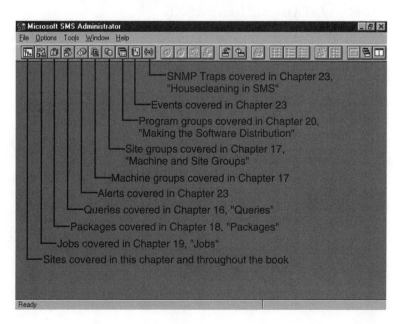

THE MENUBAR

The menubar changes, depending on which window (if any) is open.

The File menu enables you to open windows, make new items inside windows, execute queries, print, and exit Administrator.

The Edit menu enables you to copy data to the clipboard, and it sometimes offers a Delete Special item that lets you clean up old data from your database.

The View menu controls the appearance of the current window.

The Options menu controls how SMS Administrator operates.

The Tools menu enables you to start SMS Security Manager, SMS Service Manager, SMS Database Manager, or SMS Sender Manager from SMS Administrator.

The Window menu lets you cascade or tile multiple windows.

The Help menu gives you access to the online documentation and technical support resources.

Note

To see the credits for SMS (and a neat Easter egg), type `Hermes` when viewing the help screen.

SMS DATABASE MANAGER

The SMS Database Manager is useful for maintaining the SQL Server database. After the initial SQL Server logon, you can perform various maintenance tasks. (See Figure 6.5.)

Figure 6.5.
The SMS Data-
base Manager.

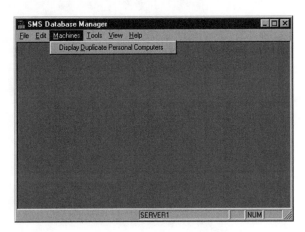

Using the Machines menu, you can search for duplicate computers, which you can then merge into a single record by highlighting the duplicates and using the Edit menu. Duplicates usually occur because the SMS.INI file was erased and reinstalled.

The Tools menu of the Database Manager can control what inventory data is saved and how the data is viewed. You can clean up old collected files from the Tools menu as well.

SMS SECURITY MANAGER

SMS security issues deal with a person's rights on an NT server so that he or she can install SMS, deinstall SMS, control SMS services, or perform other server-centric functions. SMS security also has to take into account a person's rights in the SMS database so he or she has enough rights to send packages, perform troubleshooting, change SMS configurations, and so on.

Rights that deal with NT issues are controlled by giving the NT user rights on the servers in the domain.

You control the rights that deal with the ongoing maintenance of SMS and using all the functions of SMS by giving appropriate rights within SQL Server to the SMS database.

You use SMS Security Manager to give rights inside the database (see Figure 6.6), but you need knowledge of SQL Server and SQL rights to successfully accomplish the task.

Figure 6.6.
The SMS Secu-
rity Manager.

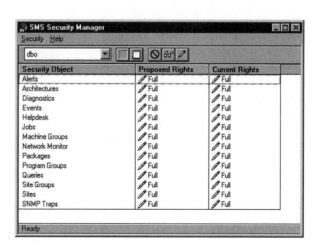

SMS Security Manager is a front-end application that distributes SQL Server rights easily, and it even comes with templates for common SMS administrative functions.

The first step to using SMS Security Manager is making a SQL Server user and assigning it to the SMS database. You must use SQL Enterprise Manager for this step. To add a user, simply open the SQL Server by clicking the plus sign in the box next to the server. Next, highlight the Logins folder, click the right mouse button, and select New Login. (See Figure 6.7.) Type the user's name and password, and put a check in the box next to the SMS database. (See Figure 6.8.) You can customize the user's rights with SMS Security Manager.

Figure 6.7.
Creating a new
SQL Server
login.

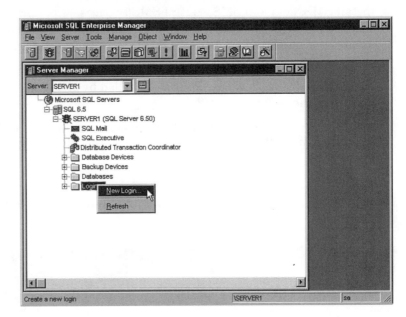

Several templates are included with SMS Security Manager that can either be used as is or modified to fit specific requirements. Figure 6.9 shows the Tech Support template loaded. The templates and their settings are described in the following list.

Figure 6.8.
Assigning a SQL
Server login to a
database.

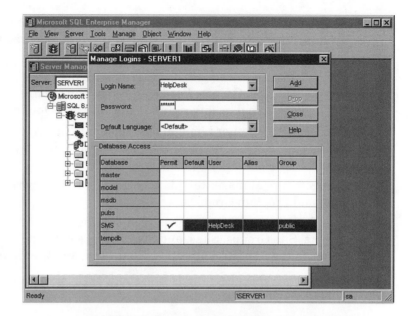

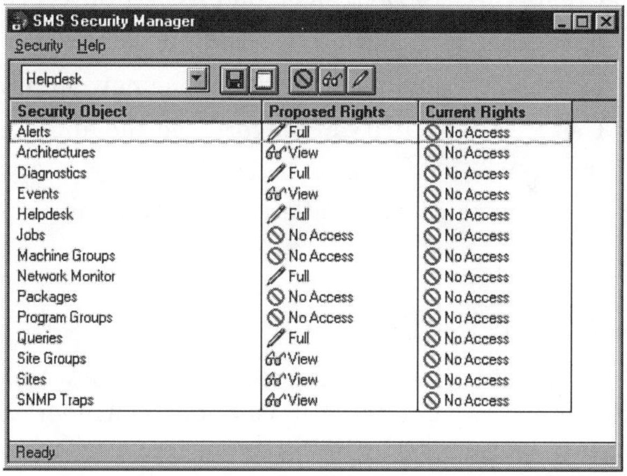

Figure 6.9.
The Tech Support
template in SMS
Security Man-
ager.

◆ The Asset Manager template has read-only rights to the Architectures, Events, Packages, Sites, and SNMP Traps data and read and modify rights to the Queries data of the SMS database.

◆ The Job Manager template has read-only rights to the Architectures, Events, Machine Groups, Packages, Sites, Site Groups, and SNMP Traps data and read and modify rights to the Jobs and Queries data.

◆ The Network Monitor template has read-only rights to the Architectures, Sites, and SNMP Traps data and read and modify rights to the Network Monitor data.

◆ The Software Manager template has read and modify rights to the Packages and Program Groups data.

◆ The Tech Support template has read-only rights to the Architectures, Events, Site Groups, Sites, and SNMP Traps data and read and modify rights to the Alerts, Diagnostics, Help Desk, and Queries data.

The following is a checklist for creating a new SQL logon for the SMS administration:

◆ Create the new SQL logon using SQL Enterprise Manager.

◆ Assign the new logon to the SMS database using SQL Enterprise Manager.

◆ Decide on the responsibilities of the new administrator.

◆ Using SMS Security Manager, load the appropriate template and modify as necessary.

◆ Save the new logon and give the logon and password to the new administrator.

SMS SENDER MANAGER

You use the SMS Sender Manager to control how SMS uses the bandwidth when it sends data between sites. See Chapter 5, "Understanding the SMS System," for more information on the SMS Sender Manager.

SMS MIF FORM GENERATOR

The SMS MIF Form Generator builds custom data entry forms. (See Figure 6.10.) After a user saves his form, the data is automatically uploaded to the SMS database during the inventory process. Creating new forms is covered in Appendix D, "Extending Inventory Collection."

Figure 6.10.
Creating a new
MIF form with
the MIF Form
Generator.

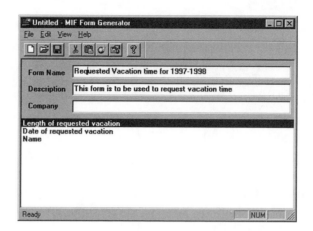

SMS Network Monitor

Network Monitor is a program that you can use to capture, filter, and analyze packets on the network. (See Figure 6.11.) Network Monitor is covered in Chapter 21, "Using the Network Monitor."

Figure 6.11.
Network Monitor.

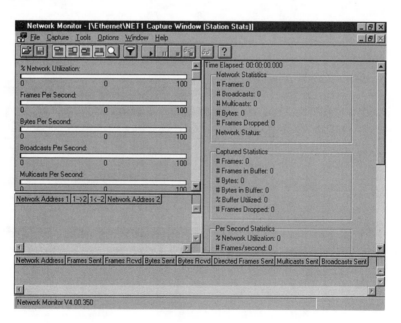

Note

Before NT 4.0, the only way to get Network Monitor was to buy SMS. It is estimated that acquiring Network Monitor was the primary incentive for more than 20 percent of the companies buying SMS.

SMS SERVICE MANAGER

The SMS Service Manager program enables you to see all the individual SMS services and change their trace file characteristics. (Figure 6.12 shows the file settings for the LAN Sender service.) The default setting for the trace files is to keep a 128KB file in the SMS\LOGS directory, with the next most recent log file renamed with a .LO_ extension. (See Figure 6.13.)

Figure 6.12.
Trace file settings
for the LAN
sender.

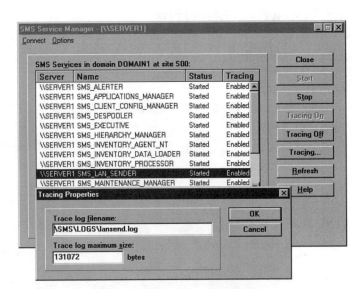

Figure 6.13.
Trace files in
Explorer.

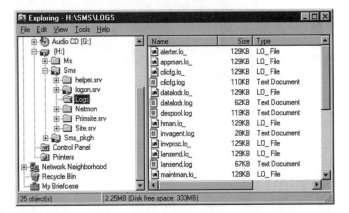

When you stop a service that is contained within SMS Executive, a warning states that stopping the service might make SMS Executive unstable. (See Figure 6.14.) You can still stop the service, but the results are unpredictable.

Figure 6.14.
Warnings before
stopping an SMS
service.

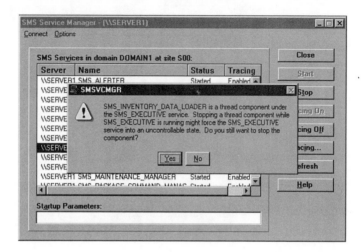

SMS SQL VIEW GENERATOR

The SMS database is relational in nature, with rows of data broken down into tables. Because the SMS database is stored on a SQL Server, you can easily use programs other than SMS to access the data. When you run a report or query, the data is recombined from the tables to make a complete record.

Data rows can be reconstructed from the tables every time a report or query is run, or you can define a view that reconstructs the data once and use it easily after that.

SMS SQL View Generator creates views that reconstruct the tables into some common categories such as hard drives, network cards, operating systems, memory, video, and network settings. (See Figure 6.15.) The views that SMS SQL View Generator creates always start with a lowercase v.

SMS SETUP

After you use SMS Setup for the initial installation, you can use it to install the administration tools on another Windows NT computer, install additional pieces of SMS from the CD-ROM (online documentation and so on), deinstall the site, or perform various other operations.

If you choose the Operations button, you can upgrade the current site (install service packs), reset the site, shut down the site, change the SMS service account, or change the SQL Server parameters. (See Figure 6.16.)

Figure 6.15.
Views created by
SQL View
Generator.

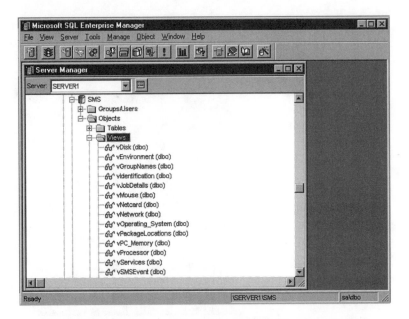

Figure 6.16.
Operations of
SMS Setup.

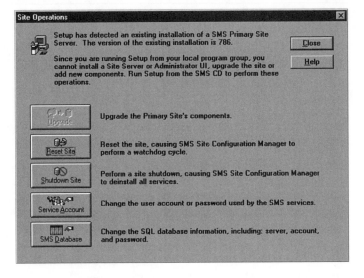

Resetting the site causes SMS to stop all the services, reinstall the SMS_SITE_CONFIG_MANAGER service, rewrite the site control files, and restart the SMS services.

Tip

> If SMS seems stuck or is acting strangely, choosing the Reset Site option often cures the problem.

Shutting down the site merely stops all the SMS services. You can restart them manually by rebooting the server or by performing a site reset.

If you change the SMS service account, you can change the user or password that the SMS services use. You should change the account and password by using SMS Setup and not Control Panel | Services because SMS Setup changes all the services at once.

You must change the SMS settings for SQL Server if the SQL Server or database changes name or the user or password for SQL Server access changes. Otherwise SMS will be unable to connect to SQL Server.

Other SMS Program Items

Other program items that are installed include the SMS Books Online, which contains the documentation for SMS; the SMS What's New in 1.2, which contains the new features of SMS 1.2; and the SMS Release Notes, which contains the latest release information about SMS 1.2.

The SMS Knowledge Base is on the CD-ROM in the Support directory.

Advanced Tools

Other diagnostic and maintenance tools come with SMS but are not installed by default. Some of these tools are command-line based and let you jump into the internal workings of SMS.

Most of these tools are in the Support\Debug\X86 directory for Intel-based servers (see Figure 6.17) of the CD-ROM and are not officially supported by Microsoft. You can find more information on these utilities in the Support\Debug directory. Not all of the utilities found in the Support\Debug\X86 directory are detailed in this chapter; you'll find only the utilities that are of interest to the majority of SMS administrators.

Figure 6.17.
Diagnostic tools
on the CD-ROM.

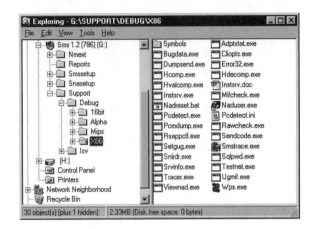

CRYSTAL REPORTS

One of the complaints about earlier versions of SMS was its lack of a sophisticated report generator. Microsoft's solution was to include Crystal Reports starting with SMS 1.1. Crystal Reports is superior to SMS's built-in report generator, and is capable of creating professional reports based on the SMS database with just a few minutes of effort.

Crystal Reports version 4.5 comes with SMS 1.2, and you can install it from the Reports directory on the CD-ROM or from the Autorun menu on NT 4.0. Crystal Reports has many prebuilt reports that you can easily run as is or alter for your specific requirements.

To use the prebuilt reports, you must first configure the Open Database Connectivity (ODBC) connection using the 32-bit ODBC Setup and Administration program. (See Figure 6.18.) ODBC is the standard that SQL Server uses for easy access by different front-end applications (such as Crystal Reports).

After you start Crystal Reports, you can open and refresh predefined reports using current data by choosing the Verify Database option. (See Figure 6.19.)

SMS TRACE

The SMS Trace program shows log files in real time as they are updated. This is one of the best programs to use in understanding and troubleshooting SMS. SMS Trace is covered in more detail in Chapter 5.

BUGDATA.EXE

The BUGDATA.EXE program compresses the SMS Registry keys, the log files, and the site control file for easy transmittal to Microsoft Technical Support. The file can be decompressed using the HDECOMP.EXE program.

Figure 6.18.
Configuring
ODBC support.

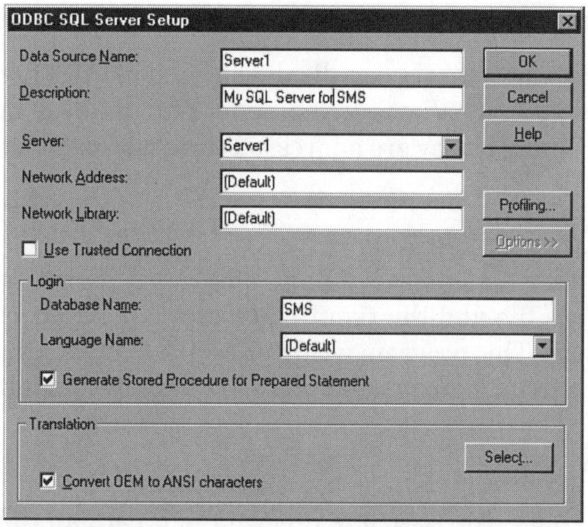

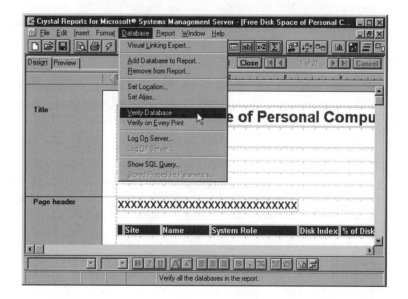

Figure 6.19.
Refreshing a
report in Crystal
Reports.

CLIOPTS.EXE

You can use the CLIOPTS.EXE program to change options for the client troubleshooting piece of SMS. A common use of this program is to change the default protocol that the remote control agent uses.

DUMPSEND.EXE

The DUMPSEND.EXE program displays a send request file in ASCII rather than its native binary format. Viewing the send request can help troubleshoot packages by determining if they are addressed correctly, or if the correct sender is being chosen.

FERRET.EXE

The FERRET.EXE program detects additional parameters on certain Compaq computers. This file and the required CPQBSSA.TXT file are found in the Support\Isv\Compaq directory. This program would allow the SMS administrator to get the special BIOS entries that Compaq computers are capable of storing into the SMS database.

HCOMP.EXE

You can use the HCOMP.EXE program to create an SMS package from the command prompt. The NT Scheduler service could then be used to create packages on a recurring basis, because the Scheduler service runs from a command prompt.

HDECOMP.EXE

You can use the HDECOMP.EXE program to decompress an SMS package from the command prompt. This would be used mostly for troubleshooting purposes or for when the despooler service has been corrupted or disabled.

HVALCOMP.EXE

You can use the HVALCOMP.EXE program to validate an SMS compressed package from the command prompt. This utility is good for troubleshooting, as a package can be validated before and after being sent, which would diagnose a corrupted sender service.

INSTSRV.EXE

The INSTSRV.EXE program can install and remove NT services. The instsrv.doc file documents how to use it. This is one of the more advanced tools here. Proper use would allow installation of services remotely, but improper usage could make a server unusable.

MIFCHECK.EXE

The MIFCHECK.EXE program checks a MIF file for errors. It should be used by programmers who are writing custom MIF files for extending the SMS database. See Appendix D for more details.

NADUSER.EXE

NADUSER.EXE is a 16-bit Windows application that shows you the NT global groups you belong to and which network application icons are available to your groups. One of the first steps in troubleshooting shared applications would be to run NADUSER to find out the groups that SMS thinks you belong to.

PCMDUMP.EXE

PCMDUMP.EXE is a 32-bit Windows application that displays the package command manager instructions in a readable format. This is invaluable for troubleshooting, as the Package Command Manager will not display packages that were not specifically sent to it. PCMDUMP will let you see the same instructions that the Package Command Manager sees, and you should be able to determine why the Package Command Manager isn't displaying the package.

RAWCHECK.EXE

The RAWCHECK.EXE program reads in a *.raw inventory file and checks it for corruption. To use the program, type **rawcheck filename.raw**, and the result is displayed. Used primarily for troubleshooting, this program may help you find the problem when a particular computer's inventory is always corrupt.

SENDCODE.EXE

The SENDCODE.EXE program lets you send commands directly to an SMS service. An example is **Sendcode SMS_Site_Config_Manager 192**, which initiates a watchdog cycle that verifies the installation, checks for new logon servers, reads any new configurations, and so on.

SETGUG.EXE

The SETGUG.EXE program lets you set the global group reporting interval for domains that are part of your SMS site. Usually, global groups are reported every day, but you can reduce this or even shut it off. The syntax is **Setgug [/E on¦Off] [/I days]** where *days* is 1 or more.

SNIRDR.EXE

The SNIRDR.EXE program displays the Despooler instruction file in a readable form. To use it, specify **Snirdr filename.ext**. Primarily used for troubleshooting, this program will help when the Despooler is not decompressing the package correctly.

SQLPWD.EXE

The SQLPWD.EXE program can change the SQL Server user and the password that SMS uses. This is the command prompt version that has the same functionality as going into SMS Setup and changing the SQL parameters from the options button.

TRACER.EXE

TRACER.EXE is the command-line equivalent to SMS Trace, but it can only show one log file at a time. To use it, type **Tracer filename.log**.

VIEWNAD.EXE

The VIEWNAD.EXE program lets you view network application groups that are available for the client to use. This utility is primarily used for troubleshooting shared network applications that are not showing up for a particular client.

WPS.EXE

WPS.EXE is a 16-bit Windows program that lets you view and terminate processes on Windows 3.*x* computers. This program is required if you want to stop the package command manager process on a 16-bit Windows platform.

THE SERVER TYPES AND THEIR ROLES IN THE SYSTEM

You must install SMS into an existing NT domain on either the Primary Domain Controller (PDC) or a Backup Domain Controller (BDC).

By default, SMS affects only the single server where it is installed, but you can configure it to automatically communicate with and incorporate the other domain controllers into the SMS site.

When you plan the SMS installation, the first decision to make is whether SMS will be installed as a primary or secondary site.

An SMS site is considered a primary site if it has its own SQL Server database. It is considered a secondary site if it uses the database of its parent site.

You must have at least one primary site in the hierarchy, but after that, any additional sites that are installed can be either primary or secondary. The considerations, advantages, and disadvantages of each type are covered in Chapter 7, "System Planning with SMS."

You use the SMS Setup program to install primary sites, but you install secondary sites using SMS Administrator.

PRIMARY SITE SERVERS

The computer where you install SMS is called the SMS Site Server, and the first site installed in a company must be a primary site.

THE PRIMARY SITE SERVER'S ROLE IN THE SMS SITE

The primary site server is the brains and the heart of the SMS site. It coordinates all the other pieces of the SMS site by copying configuration data internally among the other servers in the site, as well as communicating with other SMS sites.

The primary site server creates inventory rules based on changes made to SMS Administrator and sends those rules to the logon servers. In this way, SMS clients have the latest rules when inventory is run. The site server also collects inventory from the logon servers after the clients are inventoried.

The primary site also creates packages and jobs and sends those packages to the distribution servers (also known as application servers) in the site. SMS clients then install or run their applications from these distribution servers.

REQUIREMENTS FOR A PRIMARY SITE SERVER

A server must be installed as either the PDC or a BDC, and it must be running NT Server 3.51 with Service Pack 4 or NT Server 4.0.

The server must have an NTFS volume with at least 100MB of hard drive space. It should also have at least 32MB of RAM.

The server doesn't have to be dedicated to SMS, but performance of other applications suffers if the SMS site is very active or set to a faster response mode. Chapter 7 has more specifics on performance and planning issues.

INSTALLING THE PRIMARY SITE SERVER

Installation of SMS is covered in detail in Chapters 8 through 12, but the basic steps are to install NT, SQL Server, and then SMS.

Installing SMS creates the SMS directory on the NTFS volume with subdirectories for each of the types of servers that SMS installs.

CHANGES MADE TO THE PRIMARY SITE SERVER

SMS installs its services on the primary site server, creates directories, makes shares, and creates and edits Registry settings. Chapter 4, "SMS Server: Under the Hood," has more details on all the changes that SMS makes.

SECONDARY SITE SERVERS

When installing a secondary SMS site, you must specify the server. (See Figure 6.20.)

Figure 6.20. Installing a secondary SMS site.

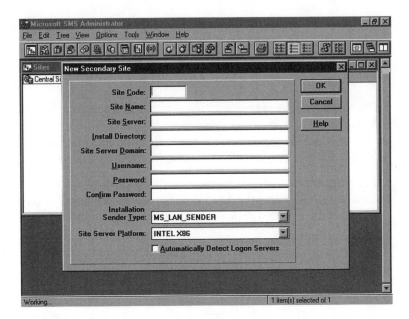

THE SECONDARY SITE SERVER'S ROLE IN THE SMS SITE

The secondary site server controls its site much like a primary site server. The main difference is that the secondary site is controlled from the parent site or from another site that is higher in the SMS hierarchy. In fact, the SMS tools are not even installed on a secondary site server.

The secondary site server creates new inventory rules, synchronizes them with its logon server, and collects inventory data.

The secondary site server can also create packages and send them to its distribution servers.

REQUIREMENTS FOR A SECONDARY SITE SERVER

A secondary site server must be running NT Server 3.51 with Service Pack 4 or NT Server 4.0. The server needs an NTFS volume with at least 100MB of free space and at least 32MB of RAM as well. The server needs to be a PDC or a BDC of an NT domain that is not already in the SMS site and does not already have SMS installed on it.

INSTALLING THE SECONDARY SITE SERVER

Installing and maintaining the secondary site is all accomplished from the SMS Administrator. By highlighting a primary site, you specify which one will be the parent of the secondary site. Choose New from the File menu, and you see the New Secondary Site window. (Refer to Figure 6.20.)

CHANGES MADE TO THE SECONDARY SITE SERVER

When SMS installs, it makes the same kinds of changes to the server that a primary site installation does, with one exception. The exception is that the SMS_INVENTORY_DATA_LOADER service is not installed because a secondary site doesn't have its own database. A secondary site sends its data directly to its parent site, and the parent site uploads the data to the parent site's SQL Server database.

HELPER SERVERS

SMS consists of many services, and you can move some of those services to other servers (called helper servers) to help balance the load. The services that you can move are the Scheduler, the Despooler, the Inventory Data Processor, and the Inventory Data Loader. You move the services by clicking the Services button of the Site Properties dialog. Figure 6.21 shows the Services dialog box that appears.

Figure 6.21.
Moving services
to a helper server.

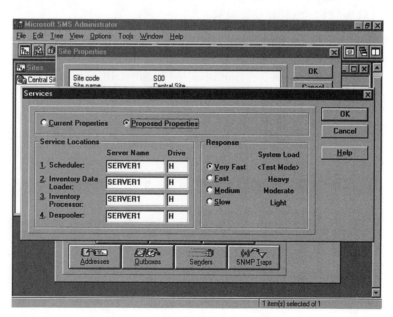

6

SMS SITE COMPONENTS

Note

SMS 1.1 required a separate SMS license for the helper server. SMS 1.2 licensing has changed, so helper servers no longer need a separate license.

SQL SERVERS

Because SMS stores its data in a SQL Server database, a SQL Server must be present where SMS can have access to it. SQL Server is an application that runs on NT Server and doesn't require a dedicated server in order to function, but it is often placed on a dedicated server for performance and reliability reasons.

One issue that may arise is security because SMS needs access to the SQL System Administrator (SA) account during installation. If the person or department that is in charge of the SQL Server is different from that of the SMS administrator, the SQL SA account and password might not be easily accessible.

Installing and configuring SQL Server is covered in Chapter 9.

DISTRIBUTION AND APPLICATION SHARE SERVERS

You can send SMS clients software or prepare network applications for them. The software to be distributed or run from a server must reside somewhere. The server that provides the location is called the distribution server. The server may also be called an application or package server.

THE DISTRIBUTION SERVER'S ROLE IN THE SMS SITE

The distribution server is merely a file warehouse that holds all the packages that have been created.

When a client runs Package Command Manager, a list of available packages (software distributions) is displayed. If the client selects one of the packages to install, it makes a connection to a distribution server and starts the installation (or deinstallation) program.

REQUIREMENTS FOR A DISTRIBUTION SERVER

Distribution servers need ample amounts of hard drive space because the software to be distributed or run exists in uncompressed form.

Any server in the SMS site can be a distribution server, including NT Server, NT Workstation, LAN Manager, and NetWare servers.

The SMS administrator account needs to have administrator or supervisor rights on the server before it is installed as a distribution server. For NT and LAN Manager computers, that means making the SMS user a member of the administrators local group. For NetWare servers, you need to make the SMS user account a supervisor equivalent.

INSTALLING A DISTRIBUTION SERVER

The SMS site server is installed as a distribution server by default. To add servers as distribution servers, first install them into the SMS site and assign them as distribution servers.

To install additional NT domain, LAN Manager, or NetWare servers into the SMS site, see the section "Adding Domains to the Site" later in this chapter.

To assign the servers as distribution servers, click the Servers button from SMS Administrator, which opens the Server Properties dialog box. (See Figure 6.22.)

Figure 6.22.
Assigning a new
distribution
server.

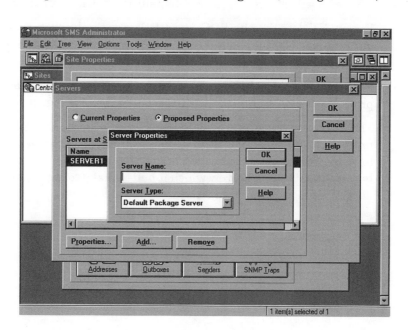

CHANGES MADE TO THE DISTRIBUTION SERVER

When decompressing a software distribution package to a distribution server, SMS creates an SMS_PKGx directory on the server, where x is the volume. Under the SMS_PKG directory, SMS creates a new subdirectory that corresponds to the ID number that SMS assigned to that package.

When a network application package is decompressed to the distribution server, the package definition specifies how the directory and its corresponding share name are made.

LOGON SERVERS

The initial installation of the SMS client and all subsequent inventories is driven by a batch file that the client runs. The batch file used to run the inventory process can be run manually or can be automated to run whenever the user logs into the domain or server. Because clients all log into either NT domains or NetWare servers, the servers providing authentication services are a natural place to look for automation of scripts.

THE LOGON SERVER'S ROLE IN THE SMS SITE

SMS uses logon scripts to automate running the client batch files. Logon scripts run whenever a user logs into the NT domain or when a user logs into a NetWare server.

For an NT domain, the PDC and BDCs are the logon servers because users are authenticated by these servers. The PDC and BDCs also contain the logon scripts, which are run by the users as they log onto the domain.

For NetWare clients, the NetWare server provides authentication services and also provides a logon script that the user runs when she logs in.

The logon servers also provide a place for the clients to store their inventory files until the SMS site server is ready to pick them up. That way, every client does not have to make a direct connection to the SMS site server—it just uses its connection to its authentication server (which it had to make to log on) and puts the inventory data in a file that the SMS site server retrieves later.

Requirements for a Logon Server

For NT domains, the PDC and BDCs can become logon servers. The services require approximately 3MB of RAM when they run and 10MB of hard drive space.

For NetWare servers, no additional RAM is needed, but they require 10MB or less of hard drive space.

Installing a Logon Server

Installing a logon server can happen automatically when SMS is installed or manually by specifying the server type and name.

During the initial installation, you see a checkbox marked Automatically Detect All Logon Servers. If the box is checked (the default is unchecked), then SMS detects all the logon servers (PDC and BDCs) in the domain and installs the logon services and directories to all of the logon servers in the domain. If the box is unchecked, you can select the radio button marked Use All Detected Servers (see Figure 6.23), or you must add each individual server to SMS so that the logon services and directories are copied to the logon servers.

Figure 6.23.
Changing an NT
domain to
automatically
detect all logon
servers.

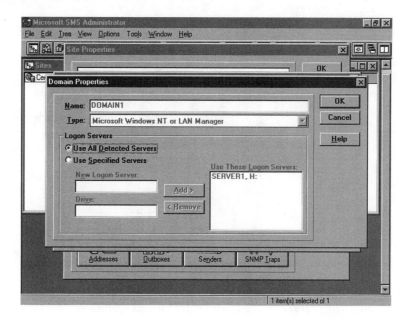

You add NetWare servers to the domain using the Domains button of SMS Administrator. Adding domains is covered in the "Adding Domains to the Site" section later in this chapter.

CHANGES MADE TO THE LOGON SERVER

SMS creates an SMS directory with a `Logon.Srv\Inventory.Box` directory structure on the logon servers. When clients log on and run the inventory agent, the agent saves its data in the `Inventory.Box` subdirectory.

Instructions for the Package Command Manager are also held on each logon server because a client may authenticate to any PDC or BDC in an NT domain. Instructions for each client are held in the `Pcmins.Box` directory.

If SMS is set to automatically install clients (see Figure 6.24), the logon scripts are then edited (or created) for all the users. SMS requires that you install directory replication on the NT domain controllers so that the edited logon scripts are propagated throughout the domain.

Figure 6.24.
Setting SMS to
automatically
install clients by
editing logon
scripts.

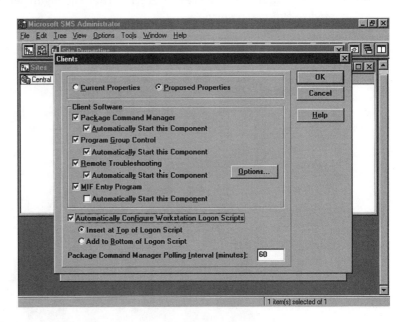

NetWare servers have their system logon scripts edited on a server-by-server basis for every server that is a part of the SMS site so that the client batch file runs at logon.

ADDING DOMAINS TO THE SITE

An SMS site has at least one NT domain. You can add other NT domains and LAN Manager and NetWare servers to an existing domain. (See Figure 6.25.)

Figure 6.25.
Adding domains
to the SMS site.

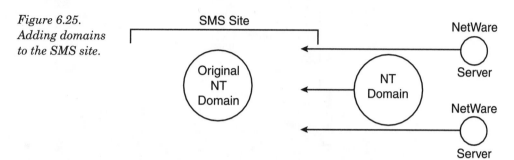

Adding additional domains to the SMS site lets the new domain participate fully in the site. Computers can be inventoried and software distributed to clients in the new domain as if they were part of the original domain.

To add an additional domain to the SMS site, the SMS administrator account must exist in the domain or server to be added and must have administrator rights (for NT and LAN Manager) or be a supervisor equivalent (for NetWare).

NetWare servers are supported for the native server versions 2.*x*, 3.*x*, and 4.*x* servers that have bindery emulation enabled.

NT DOMAINS

SMS uses just one account to communicate with all the NT servers and NetWare servers. That one account must exist on the NT domains and NetWare servers that are going to join the SMS site so SMS can properly install.

Before you can add NT domains to the SMS site, you have to establish appropriate trusts between the domains so the SMS administrator account from the original domain can have administrative rights on the domain to be added.

Add the new domain by clicking the Domains button of the SMS Administrator. (See Figure 6.26.) Make sure to specify that it is an NT or LAN Manager server (the other choice is NetWare).

6

SMS SITE COMPONENTS

Figure 6.26.
Adding a new
domain to the
SMS site.

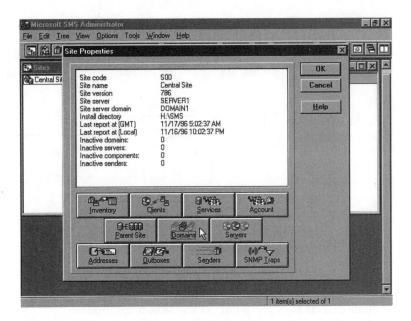

If you want SMS to automatically search for and install all the logon servers in the
domain, make sure that Use All Detected Servers is selected (the default). (See
Figure 6.27.)

Figure 6.27.
Adding an NT
domain to the
SMS site.

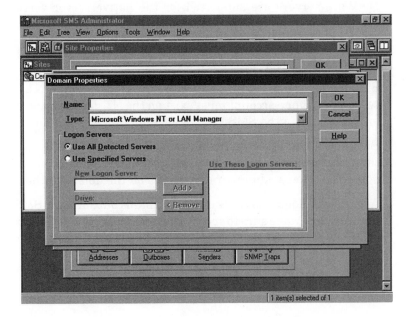

NetWare Servers

Before adding NetWare servers into the SMS site, the SMS administrator account must also exist on the NetWare server with the exact spelling and password as the NT user. The user must also be a supervisor equivalent (SE).

Add the new server by using the Domains button of SMS Administrator (refer to Figure 6.27), but be sure to change the default from the NT type of server to NetWare. (See Figure 6.28.)

Figure 6.28.
Adding a
NetWare server to
the SMS site.

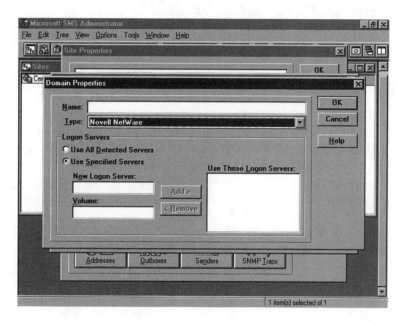

Because no services run on the NetWare server, data gets collected by the SMS site server on a much less frequent basis. The SMS site server connects every 24 hours to move all the inventory of the NetWare clients to the SMS server.

The Client/Server Relationship

Client/server is one of the buzzwords of the computer industry and has different meanings for different people. For our purposes, I define client/server as an application that resides on both the server and the client and needs both pieces to fully operate.

SMS is a client/server product, which means that it is composed of pieces that reside on the SMS servers and pieces that reside and run from the SMS clients.

SQL Server is also a client/server application, with the data residing on the server and the front-end applications that access the data residing on the clients.

THE SERVER SIDE OF SMS

The pieces of SMS that reside on the servers include the services that move, process, and store the data and services that control and update the configuration of SMS.

THE CLIENT SIDE OF SMS

The client side of SMS includes the administration and reporting applications and the actual clients and their programs and data that make up the SMS database.

Client administration programs include SMS Administrator and the other tools discussed earlier in this chapter.

SMS installs an SMS client group on every client in the site. The client for Windows-based computers has Package Command Manager, Program Group Control, Help Desk Options, MIF Entry, and SMS Client Help. (See Figure 6.29.)

Figure 6.29.
The SMS Client
group.

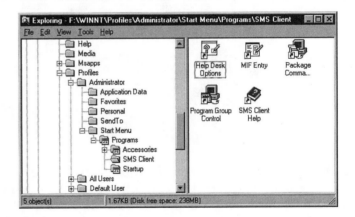

Package Command Manager (see Figure 6.30) displays the packages that the client can run.

Program Group Control looks for new network applications that are available to the user based on his group membership.

The Help Desk enables the user to control whether the troubleshooting options are active for her computer.

MIF Entry is used to fill out forms generated by the SMS administrator with the SMS MIF Form Generator.

Figure 6.30.
The Package
Command
Manager.

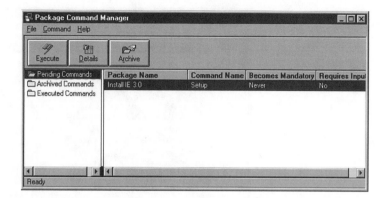

SMS Client Help is a help file for the client programs.

Note

Not all the client operating systems have support for all the possible client programs. Chapter 13, "Installation of SMS Clients," has more details on the various clients that SMS supports and their differences.

CLIENTS

An SMS client is a computer that gets inventoried in the database and can participate in the software distribution, network applications, or troubleshooting functions of SMS.

You can add clients to the SMS site either manually or automatically.

To add a client manually or to run the inventory agent manually, the client needs to connect to the sms_shr share on one of the logon servers and run the runsms batch file.

To add clients automatically, the NT domain must first have NT's directory replication running. When you click the Clients button of SMS Administrator, you can check the Automatically Configure Workstation Logon Scripts box in the Clients dialog box. (See Figure 6.31.) SMS then edits existing logon scripts to add the SMS client batch file or assign a new batch file for those clients who do not already have a logon script assigned.

6

SMS SITE COMPONENTS

Figure 6.31.
Setting the clients
to install auto-
matically.

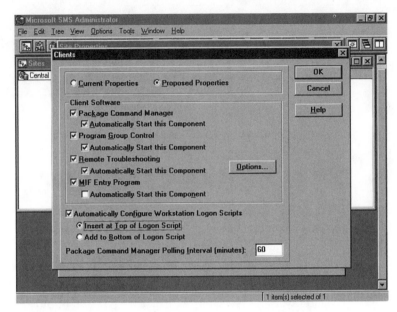

SUMMARY

An SMS site is composed of many different aspects—services running on servers, clients connecting to those servers to get instructions and software, and constant communication between the SMS Site Server and the other various pieces.

You can install SMS sites as primary sites, in which they maintain their own SQL Server database, or as secondary sites, where the database of a parent site is used to store its data.

SMS is a true client/server application because the data resides on a SQL Server and applications on the client perform all the configuration and management.

CHAPTER 7

System Planning with SMS

This chapter deals with planning the SMS site. Issues covered include site design variables, as well as server capacities and limitations.

PLANNING WITH SMS

Most people who are new to SMS imagine that it is like most other applications— easy to install and implement. Microsoft made complex server applications easy to install in the past, so what is different with SMS?

SMS is easily the most complex piece of BackOffice. Knowledge of NT Server, MS-DOS, Windows 3.*x*, Windows 95, SQL, and SMS is required just for basic sites. UNIX, NetWare, and other operating systems can just as easily be a part of SMS, so knowledge of those is needed as well.

Getting the full functionality out of SMS needn't be your whole life's work, however, because there are certain steps and procedures that can ensure both a smooth installation and a productive use of SMS.

Planning the SMS installation consists of more than scheduling a time to sit down at the server. Planning the site consists of steps that take the network, users, hardware, software, and the politics of administration into account.

Here's a list of questions to ask yourself when planning a site:

- ◆ What hardware will I use?
- ◆ What am I trying to accomplish?
- ◆ What will my site look like?
- ◆ Who will administer my site?
- ◆ How will I let my users know what is going on?
- ◆ How will I train my administrators?
- ◆ Does my network limit my decisions about my site?
- ◆ Am I planning for the future?
- ◆ What will SMS cost me and potentially save me?
- ◆ When am I going to install SMS?

ORGANIZING THE NETWORK INTO SITES

The SMS site is the building block of the entire SMS installation. Planning your site is one of the most important things you can do to ensure a smooth installation and ease of management. You should try to install SMS the way you want it, although you can change many aspects of your SMS site after installation.

Because SMS is based on NT domains, it makes sense to start planning for the SMS site by looking at (and in some cases planning) the NT domain. Usually, the reasons and arguments that guided the design of the NT domains are still present during the design of the SMS site.

NT Domain Planning

There are four generic models when it comes to planning an NT domain. These are meant to be models only and can be modified for your company as needed. The four models are

- The single domain model
- The master domain model
- The multiple master domain model
- The complete trust model

Trusts Between Domains

Domains are easily linked using trusts that are built between domains. A trust is like a bridge; just as a bridge doesn't actually move anything across (it just permits travel), the trust does not actually grant any rights to users between domains. However, it allows those users to be granted rights at a later date.

You can set trusts as a one-way link between domains, where you could give users from one domain rights to resources in another domain but not vice versa. In Figure 7.1, the arrow denotes the direction that users can travel; users from the sales domain can use resources in the marketing domain, but users in the marketing domain cannot use resources in the sales domain. You can also set trusts as two-way, giving users the capability to use resources of any domain to which they have rights. In Figure 7.2, users from the sales and marketing domains can use each other's resources.

Figure 7.1.
An example of a
one-way trust.

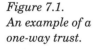

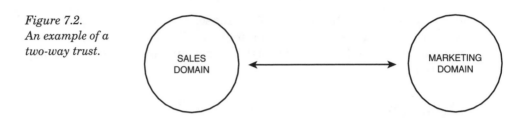

Figure 7.2.
An example of a
two-way trust.

Trusts are the key to account management in NT domains because they enable users to access resources on the entire network with a single logon into their domain.

THE SINGLE DOMAIN MODEL

The simplest model is a single domain. The first NT server is installed as the Primary Domain Controller (PDC), and other NT servers are installed as either Backup Domain Controllers (BDCs) or as application (member) servers. (See Figure 7.3.) The database of users, groups, and passwords is coordinated by the PDC and synchronized to the BDCs. Users can be validated by either the PDC or by a BDC.

Figure 7.3.
The single
domain model.

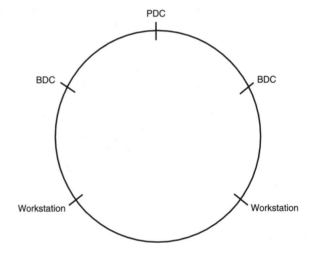

This model is easy to maintain and can have up to 20,000 users in it before it must be split into separate domains. For most companies, the domain is split for administrative, performance, geographic, or political reasons long before the 20,000-user limit is reached.

The single domain model is used extensively by small companies, especially those with a centralized information system.

In the single domain model, trusts are unnecessary because there is only one domain.

THE MASTER DOMAIN MODEL

The master domain model seeks to combine the advantages of central control that a single domain gives with the advantages of decentralized resource management that splitting into separate domains gives.

One domain is designated as the master, and it holds the database of users, groups, and passwords that the other domains use. The master domain is considered the account domain. The other domains are called resource domains because they contain printers, directories, and applications that the users access. The domains are linked with one-way trusts, which allows users a single logon into network resources. (See Figure 7.4.)

Figure 7.4.
The master
domain model.

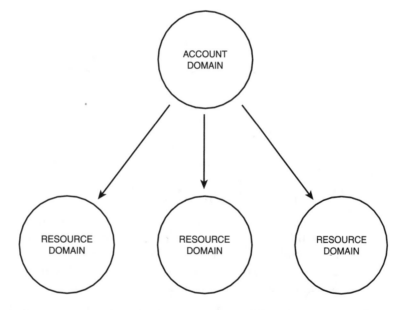

Because the domains are linked with trusts, the master domain can be in charge of all the users' accounts, whereas the resource domains can have their individual administrators who have rights over the resources in their domain.

THE MULTIPLE MASTER DOMAIN MODEL

When there are more than 20,000 users, or when there needs to be more than one controlling domain for geographic, functional, or political reasons, you can use a multiple master domain model. In a multiple master domain model, there are two or more domains at the controlling (or account) level and two or more at the resource level. You can place users in any of the master domains, and they can access the resources of any of the resource domains if they have enough rights.

This is probably the most complex of the models, but it may be necessary for very large companies. (See Figure 7.5.)

Figure 7.5.
The multiple
master domain
model.

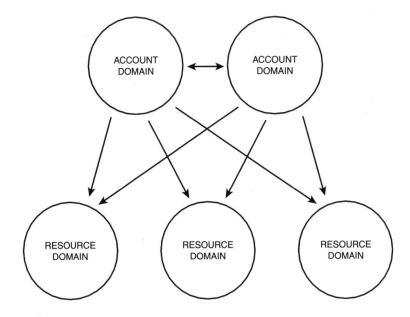

THE COMPLETE TRUST MODEL

For networks that are decentralized, or for domains with their own administrators who still want to access resources from other domains, you can use a complete trust model. A complete trust model has reciprocating trusts between all the domains. This allows users to access resources anywhere in the network while maintaining their logon in their particular domain. (See Figure 7.6.)

You can compute the number of trusts in a complete trust model by multiplying the number of domains times the number of domains minus one ($x \times (x-1)$). For example, four domains in a complete trust model have a total of 12 trusts ($4 \times (4-1)$).

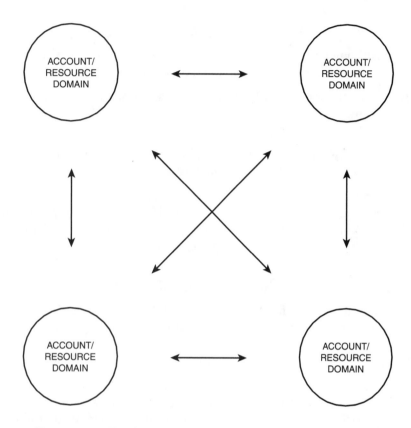

Figure 7.6.
The complete
trust model.

HOW BIG CAN A DOMAIN BE?

The theoretical limit on the size of a domain is based on the size of the database of users, groups, and passwords. The theoretical limit of the database is 40MB, after which the database becomes unresponsive.

Users and groups each take approximately 1KB, which means that 20,000 users and groups take about 20MB. The other 20MB of the database comes from entries for NT computers; each NT computer also takes approximately 1KB.

If your network is not using NT Workstation as the operating system for your users, then 40,000 users and groups is the maximum that you can have in a domain.

The database of users, groups, and passwords resides in memory on the PDC and BDCs. If the database is 10MB, an additional 10MB of RAM overhead is required on each of the PDC and BDCs.

SO WHAT MODEL IS BEST FOR YOU?

Although designing NT domains is a larger issue than this chapter can adequately cover, some generic recommendations can be made.

For networks with 10 or fewer servers, and with three or fewer WAN links, a single domain design is probably best. Remember that BDCs can help the authentication by being placed on the other side of WAN links.

For larger networks that have de-centralized information system support, a complete trust model could be the best fit.

Companies with many locations and servers will have to choose between the single master or the multiple master model. If the company naturally falls into regions, the multiple master may be better. If the company is centrally administrated and controlled, the single master might be a better fit.

INSTALLING NT AND CREATING DOMAINS

To create a new domain, simply install NT Server as a PDC in a new domain. Domain names must be unique on the network. Bizarre and unpredictable results appear (such as servers and workstations either disappearing or showing up in random domains during browsing) when a workgroup and domain are named the same.

After a PDC is installed and on the network, you can install the BDCs. To install a BDC, you must install the network card in the server before you set up NT. After choosing the BDC option, you need to enter the domain and administrator name and password. The setup program then connects to the PDC and copies the database of users, groups, and passwords to the BDC. After the initial installation, the PDC and BDC automatically synchronize their databases every five minutes by default.

You can also install NT Server as neither a PDC or BDC. The server has the advantages of NT Server but has none of the CPU or memory overhead of being a PDC or BDC. This type of server is often called an application or member server. SQL Server can reside on an application server, whereas SMS must reside on either the PDC or a BDC.

NT 3.51 OR NT 4.0

NT Server 3.51 and 4.0 can coexist on the same network and even the same domain. They can be PDC and BDCs for each other. The version of NT that you run is of no practical consideration to either SQL Server or SMS, although NT 4.0 should be faster than NT 3.51.

Security Planning

Security becomes a key issue when SMS is installed because the SMS administrator account and the SMS services have rights on server and client machines. Security issues involve all aspects of the network because SMS makes its presence felt almost everywhere (as it was designed to do).

NT Security

Because the SMS administrator account must have administrative rights on the servers in the domain, security issues involve that user account and its corresponding password. By assigning a user for SMS, you have to take off the default restrictions of forcing periodic password changes (because a service can't change a password). The administrator should change the password on a regular basis. It can be changed inside SMS using either SMS Setup or the Account button of the SMS site properties inside SMS Administrator.

Other NT security issues involve setting who has remote control rights (if any) to the NT servers.

NT security is discussed further in Chapter 8, "Installing and Upgrading Your NT Servers."

SQL Security

SQL rights and privileges play a major part in determining who can do what with SMS, as SMS administrative rights are dependent on access to the SMS database.

Rights to query the database, create packages and jobs, create software scanning rules, and create network applications can all be controlled by allocating rights within the SQL Server database.

You can easily control SQL Server rights using the SMS Security Manager, which was discussed in detail in Chapter 6, "SMS Site Components."

Backing up the SMS database should also be part of the security plan because failure of the SQL Server could occur.

SQL security is discussed further in Chapter 9, "Installing and Upgrading SQL Server."

SMS Security

SMS security refers to the overall plan of who will have what rights in SMS and which functions will be enabled.

Some sites that have high security requirements may choose not to install certain pieces of SMS, including remote control and troubleshooting.

SMS security is discussed further in Chapter 10, "Installing and Upgrading Primary Site Servers."

HIERARCHY SECURITY

By building an SMS hierarchy, you design which SMS sites can control other SMS sites.

Any site that is higher in the hierarchy is always able to control those sites that are below it.

Figure 7.7 shows that SMS site A is the central site and controls all the other sites. Site B controls site D, and site C controls those below it (sites E and F).

Figure 7.7.
An example of an
SMS hierarchy.

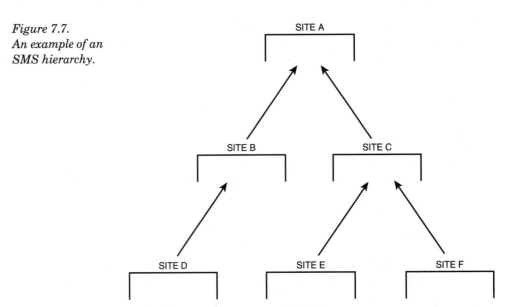

Hierarchies need not be built at all, or if they are built, they need not be built into a single central, all-controlling site.

WORKSTATION SECURITY

Deciding on what functions to enable at the client is a major part of SMS security. Client items need not be installed at all, or if they are installed, they need not be started automatically.

In SMS 1.1, the Inventory agent ran in the user's context, which means that if the user didn't have enough rights on his workstation, his inventory could be incomplete. SMS 1.2 runs the Inventory agent in the system context, which means that the agent always has enough rights to gather all the inventory data.

NETWORK MONITOR SECURITY

Network Monitor is a real-time utility that enables the administrator to capture and analyze packets from the network.

After you install and play with Network Monitor, it soon becomes apparent what a powerful tool it is. You can easily capture and view packets, and can even rebroadcast packets back onto the network.

Network Monitor requires the Network Monitor agent to be installed in order to capture packets. You can set a password on the Network Monitor agent so that packets from that workstation can be captured only by a user with the password. More details on the Network Monitor and agent can be found in Chapter 21, "Using the Network Monitor."

IS SMS TOO INVASIVE OR NOT INVASIVE ENOUGH?

One of the interesting things about SMS is how administrators perceive it. Administrators who come from the mainframe world see SMS as not doing enough. They are used to having absolute control over the workstations, and SMS usually isn't as invasive a product as they might have hoped.

SMS has come a long way in enabling the administrator to take more control of the workstations; remote control for NT was one of the major features of SMS 1.2, but some administrators will still be disappointed that SMS doesn't do more. For them, the system policies features of NT 4.0 and Windows 95 may fulfill their needs.

On the other hand, administrators who come from a personal computer environment see SMS as an amazing product that they wish they could have had years ago. Their main reservations are usually about how the end users will feel; administrators usually had to fight the appearance of a "big brother" image even before SMS came along. Once the features of SMS are enabled, they are afraid the users may rebel.

To help these administrators, you should remember that SMS need not be invasive at all. You can bring features online slowly to give users time to adjust to the idea that the SMS administrator has power over the users' desktops. Remote control functions probably scare users the worst—you can remind users that the remote control functions only work if they are permitted, and that the users will be able to see if and who is controlling them.

SMS Server Capacity Planning

How many servers do you need? This is one of the primary questions when dealing with SMS. Some salespeople contend that SMS can be installed on existing hardware; that is true as long as your existing hardware has excess capacity in CPU power, RAM, and hard drive space. Most companies end up buying additional hardware to run SMS and SQL Server. Details of RAM and hard drive requirements for the components are discussed in the following sections.

SQL Servers

Planning for the SQL Server is relatively straightforward. The most important decision concerns whether the SQL Server will be a separate computer from the SMS site server.

If the SQL Server and the SMS site server reside on the same box, network traffic is reduced, but the server has additional overhead. If both servers are on the same box, it is recommended that you either use a very fast CPU (Pentium 133 or higher) or install multiple CPUs in the server.

Hard Drive Space

SQL Server itself requires about 60MB of hard drive space, not including the online documentation, which is another 15MB. This includes the master database for SQL Server but not any user databases. The default SMS database is 55MB (45 for the data and 10 for the log). The total hard drive space for SQL Server and the database is then 130MB of hard drive space as a minimum.

If you make the backups of the master and SMS database to the hard drive first, each set will occupy 20MB to 65MB, depending on how full the databases are. SQL Server database backups are often done this way, with the backups initially saved to the hard drive and then copied to tape each night as part of the normal backup routine of the entire server.

When you use the default settings, the Backup Wizard of SQL Server 6.5 creates a task that backs up the master database weekly and keeps the four most recent copies of the backups. The backups range in size from 17MB to 22MB each, consuming no more than 88MB total for the master database backups.

The Backup Wizard of SQL Server 6.5 creates a task that backs up the SMS database weekly as well (if you use the defaults). Because the log file is truncated on a regular basis (and cannot be backed up separately), it is highly recommended that you back up the SMS database on a daily basis. If you do not change the default setting of keeping four weeks of backups, but you perform the backups on a daily basis, that means that SMS keeps the 28 most recent backups of the SMS database on the hard drive. Please refer to the SQL Administration manual for more details on backups and tasks.

For a worst-case scenario, a 45MB database with 28 copies amounts to 1260MB of hard drive space to keep the backups of the SMS database.

Although some databases are valuable enough to warrant four weeks of history, it is recommended that you either back up the SMS database on a less frequent basis (every third day or so) or change the number of weeks that SQL Server keeps old backups to one or two weeks.

MEMORY

SQL Server does its own caching of data and tends to become CPU- or memory-bound. Ample memory and a fast processor increase the speed of SQL Server dramatically. The minimum memory for SQL Server is 16MB total, with 4MB for SQL Server and the other 12MB for NT. Realistic memory is more like 64MB, with 48MB for SQL Server and 16MB for NT. Setting memory aside for SQL Server is one of the most important parameters to adjust. You can also track actual memory usage inside SQL Server with the DBCC MEMUSAGE command. (See Figure 7.8.)

If SQL Server is on its own box and is only supporting the SMS database, 32MB is a good minimum standard, with 64MB being quite adequate.

If SQL Server and SMS Server reside on the same box, that server should have at least 64MB of RAM, with at least 24MB dedicated to SQL Server to ensure adequate performance.

Figure 7.8.
Output from the
DBCC MEMUSAGE
SQL command.

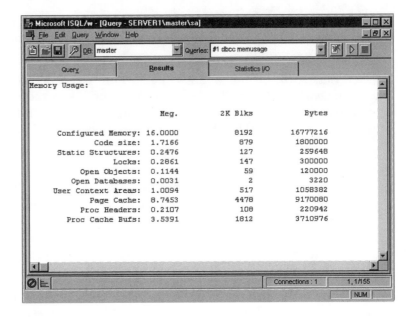

SMS SERVERS

The server that has SMS installed on it is the SMS site server. This server coordinates all the services and runs most of the services for the entire site. You can adjust the load that the services place on the server by changing the SMS response mode to a different setting.

HARD DRIVE SPACE

SMS site servers require approximately 40MB of hard drive space for the initial installation.

The files collected and the initial compressed copy of packages consume additional hard drive space. Designating the site server as a distribution server also consumes hard drive space.

There is not much you can do about collected files from active computers in your inventory, but you can easily delete orphan files, using the Database Manager.

The site server always has the master compressed copy of packages. The size of the compressed file is about 65 percent of the original (unless the original files were already compressed). The copy is stored in the Site.Srv\Sender.box\Tosend directory. After the package is sent, you can delete this copy safely. To automatically erase this copy, you have to delete the package, which might not always be what you want.

If the site server is also a distribution server (which is the default), there is another copy of the package. This copy is uncompressed so clients can attach and install the package. The uncompressed copy is in the SMS_PKG*id* directory, where the *id* is the ID of the package.

You cannot safely delete this copy by hand. To delete this copy, remove the site server from the list of distribution servers. (Just make sure there are enough distribution servers to satisfy the load from the clients.)

As a general rule, make sure the site server has 2GB to 4GB of hard drive space before installing SMS.

MEMORY

The SMS site server must already be installed as either the PDC or BDC, which requires at least 16MB of RAM. SMS takes approximately 8MB or more. (See Figure 7.9.)

Figure 7.9.
Memory usage of
SMS and SQL as
shown by Task
Manager.

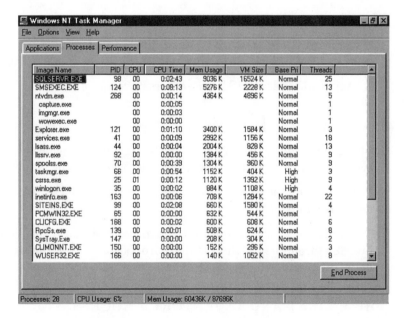

The SMS site server should have 32MB as a minimum and 64MB or more for optimal performance.

NT SERVERS

NT Servers in the domain might be logon servers or distribution servers, hold the original source code for packages, or just be SMS clients.

HARD DRIVE SPACE

The NT server that has source code installed on it needs hard drive space equal to that of the programs installed.

NT servers that are logon servers require approximately 10MB of hard drive space.

NT servers in domains that are a part of the SMS site can have the client software installed on them. Servers that are clients in the site require approximately 2MB for the client software, plus that space required for any software that is installed using SMS.

Distribution servers need hard drive space equal to the program being decompressed on them. Their hard drive space requirements are the same as that for a source code server.

If an NT server fills more than one role, its hard drive space requirements are the sum of all the roles it is fulfilling.

MEMORY

NT servers as either source code or distribution servers have no additional RAM overhead. Additional RAM may help with file caching, but it is not required.

NT servers that are SMS logon servers have approximately 3MB of RAM overhead.

BANDWIDTH ISSUES

Because SMS operates in a way that's like a batch mode, there is potential both to overwhelm the available bandwidth and to control the bandwidth that SMS uses.

To understand the bandwidth issues of SMS, you need to look at when and how SMS uses the bandwidth.

The major uses of bandwidth are the initial installation of clients, the collection of inventory from clients, the installation of Logon Server, the sending of packages, the updating of the SQL Server database, and the querying of the database.

THE CLIENT AND INVENTORY PROCESS

The initial installation of clients takes approximately 2MB. This only becomes a problem when large amounts of clients are installed at the same time. Imagine a company with 1,000 users all set to install at logon time on Monday morning. Approximately 2GB of extra traffic is going down to the client, in addition to the space used for the baseline inventory that takes place during the installation.

The collection of inventory from clients consists of creating a file on the logon server that holds the inventory data. The file is approximately 40KB or more in length, and it is created according to the inventory schedule (the default is every seven days).

The file is saved on the logon server that the client authenticated to, and, eventually, the Maintenance Manager copies the files to the site server. If any files are collected, they are also included inside the file.

If a huge file is mistakenly tagged to be collected, then every client is scanned for the file, and it is collected whenever it is found, possibly bogging down the network for hours.

The site server processes the files into delta or partial MIF files (about 6KB or so) and must then upload them to the SQL Server. If SQL Server is on the same box, no additional network traffic is generated; otherwise, a connection is made to SQL Server and the data is updated.

Things that you can do to lessen network traffic include taking inventory on a less frequent basis, being very careful only to collect small files, and keeping the SQL Server on the same box as the SMS site server.

Tip

If the SQL Server is on a different box from the SMS site server, you can move the Inventory Processor and Inventory Data Loader services to the SQL Server (thus making it into a helper server). This lessens network traffic but puts additional CPU and memory load on the SQL Server.

Sending Packages and Jobs

When a job is created, the package is compressed and sent to the receiving site. The default settings for SMS are for the sender to make connections on the network and get the job there as soon as possible. The job may consume huge portions of the bandwidth, unless you previously modified the bandwidth or sender properties.

If the priority of the sender was previously altered to hold low or medium priority jobs, then the administrator has some control over when the package is sent. The administrator can also set a time on the job during the initial creation of the job.

Once the job is sent to a receiving site, the site holds a copy of the compressed file so the sending site never has to send it again.

The despooler service on the receiving site then makes connections to each of the distribution servers and decompresses the file.

Ways to conserve network bandwidth include adjusting the sender outboxes to force low and medium priority jobs to run during off hours and adjusting bandwidth estimates so that the senders only consume a portion of the bandwidth.

Breaking SMS into sites based on geography may also help, because the site-to-site transmission of packages and inventory uses less bandwidth than one large site does.

SMS SITE PLANNING

You need to plan the structure of the SMS site before implementing it. You have two basic choices—a single SMS site or multiple SMS sites. Figure 7.10 shows a flow chart to help you decide which model to use.

Figure 7.10.
Flow chart for
planning SMS
sites.

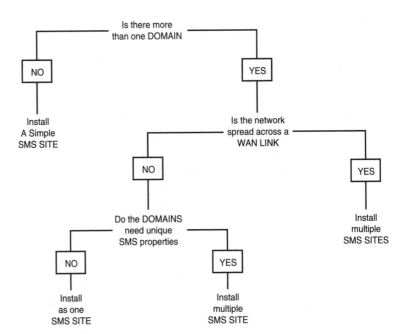

THE SINGLE SMS SITE

An SMS site must contain at least one NT domain, but it is easy to add additional NT domains to the SMS site. An SMS site can contain an unlimited number of NT domains. The limiting factor is performance or organization before technical reasons.

The advantages of a single site are

◆ It's easiest to install and maintain.

◆ Only one copy of SMS need be licensed.

The disadvantages of a single site are

◆ Performance may suffer on a large site.

◆ There is only one site server for the entire company (all settings must be set the same for the entire company).

Multiple SMS Sites

The advantages of multiple sites are

◆ The SMS hierarchy can match that of the company.

◆ Performance is better in large sites.

◆ Other parts still function when you take parts of SMS offline.

The disadvantages of multiple sites are

◆ They are more expensive.

◆ More administrators are needed.

Sample Companies and Their SMS Sites

Take a look at some sample companies and what their SMS site planning options look like.

Company A (Small Size)

Company A is a small company with one NT domain maintaining about 500 users. The entire company is located in one city, with two locations connected by a WAN. They have one PDC and two BDCs.

Company A has only one choice because they only have one NT domain. They can only install a single SMS site. (See Figure 7.11.)

Company A is unable to install multiple SMS sites until it has more than one NT domain.

Figure 7.11.
The single SMS
site with one
domain.

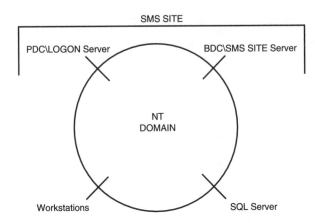

COMPANY B (MEDIUM SIZE—CENTRAL CONTROL)

Company B is a medium-size company with 2,000 users in four NT domains. This company has two locations per domain, all connected by a WAN. Their domains are based on geography, and they run in a master domain model, with trusts built between their account domain and the resource domains.

Company B could install just one SMS site that contained all four domains. A single site may be the best bet because the network is already under central control. (See Figure 7.12.)

Figure 7.12.
The single SMS
site with four
domains.

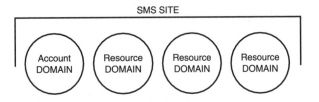

This company can install four SMS sites (one for each domain) and then link them in an SMS hierarchy that matches the NT domain design. (See Figure 7.13.) In a master domain model, the users all authenticate in one domain and then return to their domain to use resources. There isn't much, if any, performance gain because the SMS server of the account domain still has to do all the work (because the logons and inventory all occur in that domain).

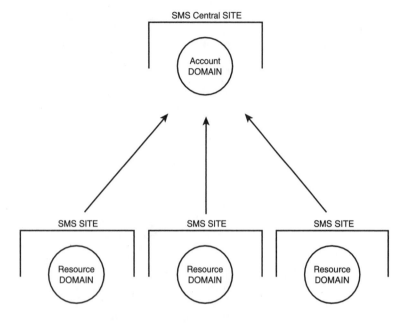

Figure 7.13.
Multiple SMS
sites.

Company C (Medium Size—Decentralized Control)

Company C is much like company B; they have 2,000 users in four NT domains, but their NT domain model is a complete trust model. There is no central domain that has control of the network, but all four domains contain their respective administrators and users.

The single SMS site that contains all four domains has the advantage of being easy to set up and administer, but you cannot adjust the properties of the domains on an individual basis. The peer-to-peer model of the NT domains is overridden by the centralized model of SMS.

If SMS is installed as one site, you should assign distribution servers in each domain, so users do not have to make connections across domains to install or run software. (See Figure 7.14.)

If you install SMS as four sites, the four separate domains can each control their copies of SMS. The question then concerns the necessity of linking the sites into a hierarchy and whose site is at the top (the central site). (See Figure 7.15.)

Figure 7.14.
The single SMS
site with multiple
domains.

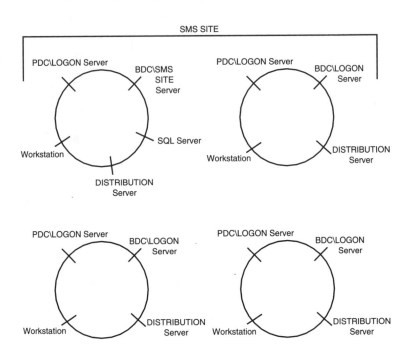

For performance reasons, the multiple site model is probably the best choice, because packages and inventory are passed around the SMS hierarchy in the most efficient manner, and you can install four separate SQL servers so SMS servers can connect to SQL servers in their domain.

This design also has the benefit that if one site were down, the other sites could still function normally.

COMPANY D (LARGE SIZE)

Company D is a large company with 20,000 users and 20 domains. Their domains are organized by department, and they use the multiple,Öaster NT domain model.

A single SMS site is not feasible for company D. It is simply too big and has too many transactions.

You need to install multiple SMS sites at company D. The question is one of design. The design of SMS should come naturally from the design of the network. Because there is a multiple master design in place, it seems logical to base SMS around that design.

Because the company is in a multiple master domain model, one of the first questions in designing the SMS site concerns a single SMS hierarchy with one central site (see Figure 7.16) or multiple SMS hierarchies with multiple central sites (see Figure 7.17).

Figure 7.15.
Multiple SMS
sites.

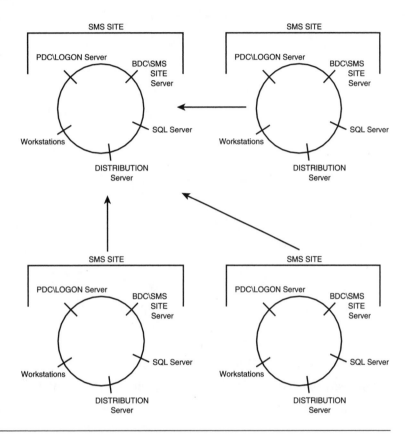

Figure 7.16.
One SMS
hierarchy.

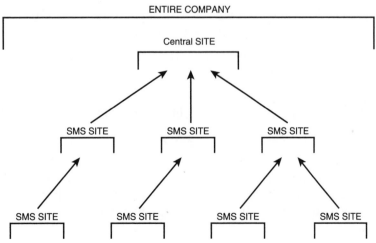

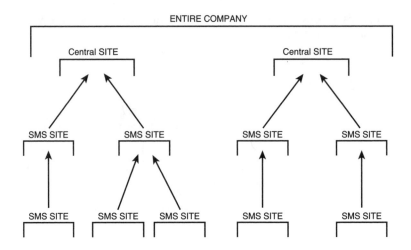

Figure 7.17.
Multiple SMS
hierarchies.

The creation of the smaller SMS sites depends on the geography and resources that each domain has.

PLANNING TO IMPLEMENT SMS

Many people assume that they can install SMS and use all the functions in less than a hour. The reality is that an SMS installation can go quite smoothly if planned and executed correctly, but it can turn into a nightmare if it is installed haphazardly with no previous planning.

One way to successfully plan and implement SMS is with a pilot study approach.

In the pilot study approach, you install SMS on a limited basis and work out all the bugs before implementing SMS on a large scale basis.

The pilot study will help you identify hardware, software, and security issues that you can resolve in a satisfactory manner.

The pilot study approach consists of the milestones or phases described in the following sections.

PLANNING THE PILOT STUDY AND THE FULL INSTALLATION

Planning the pilot study and the rest of the installation is key to keeping expectations in line with reality and being able to measure whether SMS is installed and used as was initially hoped. You should create timelines and identify key personnel for both the pilot study and the full installation.

Examples of a realistic plan and deadline are allowing the pilot study to last one month, at which point SMS should be ready to install to the entire company.

Key personnel should either be trained on SMS or be very familiar with the product. You should also train or identify personnel who are also experts in NT Server and SQL Server. Small installations might find it more cost-efficient to hire SQL Server consultants than to train their own people.

You should choose one department or division for the pilot study. A natural choice is the information systems (IS) department because the users are usually more computer literate than users in other departments, and they are more likely to be patient if they encounter server problems or intrusive visits to their workstations.

BEFORE THE PILOT STUDY

You should do several things before starting the pilot study. The following list summarizes the tasks, which mainly concern planning issues:

- Choose a pilot study group and servers.
- Recruit SMS administrators and decide whether further training is needed.
- Plan any additional inventory that will be collected.
- Limit the extent to which troubleshooting functions are implemented.
- Decide whether Network Monitor will be installed and supported.
- Choose which applications (if any) will be set up for software distribution.
- Choose which applications (if any) will be set up for network application support.
- Set the length of time for and the size of the pilot study.

THE PILOT CREW

In order for the pilot study (and later the full installation of SMS) to work, you need to have administrators who are familiar with SMS, NT Server, and SQL Server. Taking classes on NT, SQL Server, or SMS is always an option, but some experienced administrators might be able to pick up SMS by playing with it.

If you are planning a large site, a dedicated SMS administrator may be called for. Very large sites (5,000 or more clients, scattered geography, and so on) may call for more than one dedicated SMS person or a full-time person helped by several part-time people.

The users involved in the pilot study are almost as important as the administrators. Not only do they need to be patient if things go wrong, but they also need to supply constructive feedback to help the next generation of users.

You might need to spend extra time with the users of a pilot study in order to get their cooperation and their feedback.

THE PILOT STUDY

If the pilot study lasts for four weeks, it is easy to break the study into goals and milestones for each week.

WEEK 1

Primary Goals: Install SMS and ensure inventory is working.

Secondary Goals: Install Crystal Reports and query the database.

You should inform the users that there will be a pilot study of SMS and give them some details about the benefits of SMS and what to expect when their computers run the SMS inventory script.

You should identify which server will have SMS installed. You should also install the SQL Server (if necessary). If the division for the pilot study has its own NT domain, you should install clients manually at first and later set them to install automatically.

Gather inventory on all the servers and workstations in the pilot study and set SMS to gather inventory at each logon. Make changes to the workstations and servers (freeing hard drive space and so on) and rerun the inventory to verify that the new inventory is being recorded and the history of inventory is being kept.

Install Crystal Reports and refresh the default reports with the new data. Set the clients to install automatically (if this is a separate domain) and test the new client installation.

Create SMS administrators with rights to only the inventory aspects of SMS and then test them for security.

Document every problem encountered (and its solution).

The tasks for Week 1 of the pilot study are

- ◆ Inform the users of the pilot study.
- ◆ Install SMS.
- ◆ Add clients manually.
- ◆ Confirm inventory is being updated.

◆ Add clients automatically (if pilot is in separate domain).

◆ Install Crystal Reports.

◆ Create inventory administrators.

◆ Document potential problems and solutions.

WEEK 2

Primary Goals: Configure and test troubleshooting.

Secondary Goals: Install and test Network Monitor (if applicable).

This week consists of configuring and testing the troubleshooting aspects of SMS. You also install and test Network Monitor and capture packets from the network so you can begin to build a baseline of network traffic.

Remote control is usually the first item to configure and test. You install and test remote control first because it is fun to set up and see in action, and if remote control works, you are almost guaranteed that the other troubleshooting functions will work.

You should also test servers for remote control, if your company will allow it. Only administrators should be assigned the right to run remote control on the servers.

Install Network Monitor (if it wasn't installed during the initial installation) and run the Network Monitor agent on at least one computer in each subnet. You can create a baseline of network activity that gives you a good feel for when problems occur.

Assign passwords to the Network Monitor agent so unauthorized users can't monitor the network.

Create SMS administrators with troubleshooting and network monitoring rights and test them for potential security breaks.

The tasks for Week 2 of the pilot study are

◆ Configure SMS clients for troubleshooting.

◆ Configure SMS servers for troubleshooting.

◆ Test troubleshooting on clients and servers.

◆ Install and configure Network Monitor.

◆ Test Network Monitor.

◆ Document potential problems and solutions.

WEEK 3

Primary Goals: Create packages and jobs for software distribution.

Secondary Goals: Identify or create scripts for automated installations, and create inventory scanning rules.

The third week consists of getting software distribution working and customizing the inventory taken at the client level.

You should set up the software that was identified before the pilot study began in a package format. Create jobs to send the software out to the workstations and even to servers. Create and run mandatory jobs, especially if scripts will be used to install software.

Create packages to simply start the setup procedure or invoke scripts that do all the work for the user, letting the installation go unattended.

SMS comes with a variety of scripts for Microsoft products, but often you need a script that does not exist. You can use Microsoft MS-Test or Seagate's WinInstall to create scripts for SMS.

The Package Command Manager should be running on both the clients and servers so that you can send and run packages.

Create jobs that are both voluntary and mandatory and that are both manual and script-based.

If you restrict the bandwidth for SMS or restrict the outboxes for various senders to certain times of the day, you should test the changes by sending jobs with different priorities.

The tasks for Week 3 of the pilot study are

 ◆ Identify software to install on clients.
 ◆ Use manual installations or find or create scripts for automated installations.
 ◆ Install bandwidth and sender restrictions.
 ◆ Test the packages and bandwidth restrictions by creating jobs.
 ◆ Create new inventory scanning rules or packages.
 ◆ Test new inventory configurations.

WEEK 4

Primary Goals: Create packages, jobs, and program groups for network applications.

Secondary Goals: Identify new responsibilities that SMS can handle.

The goals for this week include setting up network applications, creating packages and jobs to send those network applications, and creating program groups that assign the network applications to groups.

On the initial evaluation of SMS, many sites think that they will not use the network application feature of SMS. Later, when they are more familiar with SMS and see the advantages that installing network applications gives them, they may decide to use that function.

If your site is not going to use network applications through SMS, this part of the pilot study may be considerably shorter.

The other goal of this week is to brainstorm other ways that SMS may work in your environment. Many administrators can see the potential in SMS after they are exposed to it for a little while.

The tasks for Week 4 are

- ◆ Create packages for shared applications.
- ◆ Create jobs for shared applications.
- ◆ Create program groups for network applications.
- ◆ Test network applications.
- ◆ Identify where SMS could also be used on the network.
- ◆ Document possible problems and their solutions.

The Follow-Up

The purpose of a pilot study is to work out the bugs of the system before implementing SMS on a large-scale basis. You should hold a debriefing meeting and possibly create a written report to share all the issues and their solutions.

Some problems may not have a technical solution but may be political in nature. Examples are SMS site design and hierarchy security issues.

Setting Up SMS on the Network

Once the pilot study is completed, you can begin the installation of the company-wide SMS site.

It will soon be time to install SMS in the rest of the company. If the rest of the company is on the same domain as the pilot study, you can include the rest of the company by simply making SMS install clients automatically.

INFORMING THE USERS

Among the critical components of the SMS installation are the users and their reaction to SMS. SMS changes the way their screens look when they log into the network, and it adds a new program group to their computers. Some will see it as a threat and as another example of the company trying to extend its control over them. Others may see the potential of SMS in helping them accomplish their work.

By taking time to let the user know what SMS looks like when it runs, how SMS will benefit the user, and what to expect, you can avoid many hours of trouble, as well as unnecessary calls to the help desk from confused users.

TRAINING THE ADMINISTRATORS

SMS is one of the most complex BackOffice products, and for administrators with little or no experience with network management products, it can be quite intimidating.

Administrators may want to take classes on SMS; the key is doing it before the major installation.

Some people like to install a product and play around with it before they consider a class. Those people might want to perform a small pilot study and then take a class to fill in the holes of their knowledge and experience.

IS ADMINISTERING SMS A FULL-TIME JOB?

Most administrators who install SMS soon realize that it can help automate many of the tedious tasks that they do on a regular basis. Keen administrators can see the potential of SMS and may want to spend the time it takes to configure SMS to do these tasks. However, most SMS administrators have other responsibilities in the company and soon realize that configuring SMS to work properly and take care of routine tasks can be a full-time job. They may not have the time it takes to get SMS running and configured to automate many of their tasks.

They are often stuck doing things the old way, frustrated that they have a tool that could make things easier if they only had the time to learn and configure SMS.

Time invested in setting up SMS to do tasks and installations is almost always a good investment; companies should be encouraged to free up time for the administrators to use SMS to its potential.

INSTALLING THE SOFTWARE

When it comes time to install SMS, you should follow a schedule similar to that of the pilot study.

Assigning priorities to the various functions allows you to see where the emphasis should be during the initial installation.

SUMMARY

Planning the SMS installation consists of taking stock of your current network and basing your SMS site around your NT domain.

Capacity planning for the servers that SMS will affect is necessary because SMS can have relatively large requirements.

Planning and executing a pilot study helps large sites by identifying problem areas and giving both users and administrators experience with SMS.

PART III

Implementing SMS— Setting Up Shop

CHAPTER 8

Installing and Upgrading NT Servers

This chapter focuses on the configuration of the NT operating system rather than the configuration of SMS. The chapter illustrates how to configure the operating system components to enable features within SMS.

I begin with a discussion of service accounts and permissions. Following that is a detailed discussion of the underlying pieces to the SMS senders, especially RAS and SNA servers. The next topic covers the requirements to support remote control and remote diagnostics. Then I discuss domain services such as time synchronization and directory replication. Finally, I give hints on configuring an NT server for peak performance as an SMS site server.

SECURITY ADMINISTRATION

SMS installations rely heavily on server-to-server communications for both intrasite and intersite interaction. No matter the mechanism, whether it is LAN, RAS, or SNA, the common thread upon which all communications depend is logon authentication. That is, no server-to-server or site-to-site communication occurs unless both parties agree upon a common security context or service account.

That point might seem like common sense, but often the implementation of common sense involves planning. With a single SMS site that spans a single NT domain, planning is simple: Simply create one service account and use it for any required senders. However, with an SMS installation that spans multiple NT domains that might or might not trust one another—and throw in 10 or 15 NetWare 3.x servers—things get complex fast.

The fewer service accounts, the better. A single service account from an NT domain trusted by all other NT domains provides the most reliable and flexible SMS installation. The same service account name and password should also exist on all NetWare servers involved in the SMS installation.

Sometimes security or political motivations require unique service accounts or passwords for each NT domain or NetWare server. In such cases, keep the following items in mind. A LAN sender must have at least read and write access to the SMS shares of the receiving server. If the logon server is a NetWare server, the service account must have supervisor authority and all permissions for all volumes on the NetWare server. A RAS sender also requires at least read and write access to the receiving server's SMS shares but must also have dial-in access to the RAS server accepting the incoming call. If the accepting RAS server is not the end point of the communication link, the accepting RAS server must allow access to the local network over the appropriate protocol. An SNA sender also requires at least read and write access to the receiving server's SMS shares. In addition, the SNA sender must have access to the Logical Unit (LU) connected to the remote SNA Server.

Tip

Although it is possible to change the password of the service account for SMS, changing both the user ID and the password is safer. If a problem occurs during the update process and the password is not saved properly for all services, some services might attempt to use the new password and the old password. The set of services using the old password will fail to start. However, if both the user ID and password are changed—even if a service or even an entire server does not properly update—they can continue to start using the old user ID and password.

CONFIGURING NETWORK COMPONENTS FOR INTER-SERVER COMMUNICATION

SMS inter-server communication can occur over three vehicles: RAS sender, SNA sender, and the LAN sender. Each sender offers specific advantages and disadvantages. In most implementations, the LAN sender is the sender of choice because it is the simplest and most flexible to configure. The RAS senders, ISDN and Async, are most useful when constant communication is not a requirement. The RAS senders are a less expensive alternative to full-time WAN links. The SNA sender takes advantage of existing IBM infrastructure and offers the capability to communicate across an existing SNA network, without introducing additional protocols.

Each of the senders requires the presence of their unique underlying protocol layers and networking hardware. Thus, the LAN sender requires a network interface card in each machine, a serviceable network, and a LAN protocol such as TCP/IP, IPX, or NetBEUI operating on both sides of a communication link. The RAS senders require properly configured RAS services when sending and receiving systems. The sending system must include phonebook entries to support dial-out, and the receiving system must support incoming calls. In addition, both the sending and receiving systems must have the appropriate telephone service and communications hardware, such as modems or ISDN adapters. The SNA sender requires an installation of Microsoft SNA Server in both of the sites. Each SNA server must have a LAN or WAN connection to its SMS site server as well as a connection to a common SNA network. In addition, the SNA servers must be previously configured with an APPC session between one another.

> **Note**
>
> The SNA sender does not support NetBIOS sessions or RPC. There-
> fore, it does not support Network Monitor or the Help Desk options
> such as remote control, remote diagnostics, and file transfer. It also
> does not support NT administration tools such as Server Manager or
> User Manager, or services such as file and print sharing that rely on
> the Server Message Block (SMB) protocol native to NT and LAN
> Manager.

PREPARING FOR RAS SENDERS

The RAS sender requires that the RAS service be installed on a server in both the
sending and receiving SMS sites. As illustrated in Figure 8.1, to install the RAS
service, click the Add button on the Services tab of the Network applet in the Control
Panel.

Figure 8.1.
Installing the
RAS service.

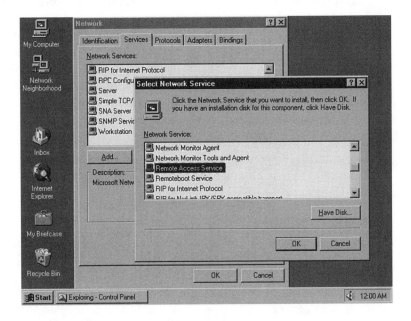

When installing RAS, the administrator selects which modem or modems to use and
from which communication ports they operate. As Figure 8.2 shows, the administrator must also choose the communication port, or ports, used by RAS. The sending
site's RAS server must be configured to dial out with the option "Dial out only" or
"Dial out and Receive calls." The receiving site's RAS server must be configured to
accept incoming calls with the option "Receive calls only" or "Dial out and Receive
calls."

Figure 8.2.
Configuring port
usage for RAS
service.

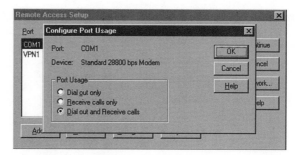

Tip

> Although RAS can use any serial port, it should not typically use the
> standard communication ports, which are usually COM1 or COM2.
> Multiport communication solutions such as DigiBoard and ECCI offer
> significantly lower CPU utilization and better total throughput.

Following the hardware definition phase of the installation process is the network configuration. Figure 8.3 depicts the Network Configuration dialog box that appears after selecting the appropriate communications port definition and clicking the Network button on the Remote Access Setup dialog box. This dialog box determines which protocols the RAS service supports, the limitations on the protocols, and security settings for dial-in sessions. In addition, in NT 4.0, the Network Configuration dialog box controls support for Multilink, which is the capability to bundle several separate physical RAS sessions into a single logical session.

The Dial out Protocols selections configure the RAS client and how it can attempt connections to other RAS servers. These selections determine which protocols the RAS client could possibly use during Point-to-Point Protocol (PPP) session setup. Selecting a particular protocol affects which protocols bind to the RAS client. It does not force the RAS client to use the protocol for every phonebook entry and does not guarantee that the receiving RAS server will support the protocol.

Note

> PPP is an Internet standard. It is tracked by the Internet Engineering
> Task Force (IETF) as STD-51 and, as of the writing of the book, is
> documented in RFC-1661 and RFC-1662. The protocol is responsible
> for establishing and maintaining a point-to-point link capable of
> encapsulating other protocols such as IP, IPX, NetBEUI, and others.
> PPP is typically used to create dial-up links between two networks or
> between a network and a remote system.

8

Figure 8.3.
Network configu-
ration of the RAS
service.

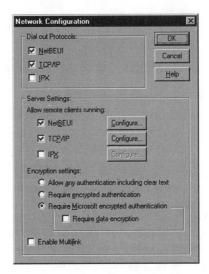

The Server Settings selections configure the RAS server and how it deals with incoming requests for connection. These selections determine the protocols for which the RAS server will honor requests and what limitations, if any, restrict the sessions using a given protocol.

The configuration options of each protocol enable the administrator to allow incoming sessions using the given protocol to access resources outside the RAS server or to limit the session's access to resources physically located on the RAS server. In addition, TCP/IP and IPX allow some choices for how the RAS client addresses are defined. For security purposes, it is usually considered a bad idea to allow the RAS client to request a specific address.

Caution

If you use TCP/IP as a RAS protocol and choose to meter out RAS client IP addresses using DHCP, be aware that the RAS server leases the IP addresses, not the RAS client. The RAS server does not give up those addresses until the RAS service is stopped. Therefore, after an administrator makes changes to the DHCP scope, the RAS service should be stopped and restarted.

Tip

> NetBEUI is the most efficient RAS protocol. If the RAS server's primary mission is to support the SMS RAS sender, use the NetBEUI protocol. If NetBEUI is *persona non grata* on your LAN, disable the NetBEUI binding to the LAN board in `Control Panel\Network\Bindings`. The RAS server will gateway the NetBEUI to either TCP/IP or IPX as the connection requirements of a particular LAN resource dictate.

The Encryption Settings selections primarily affect the logon process. The "Allow any authentication including clear text" and "Require encrypted authentication" selections provide support for non-Microsoft RAS clients. The "Require Microsoft encrypted authentication" selection is the default and should be used unless the server must also support non-Microsoft RAS clients.

There are many encryption algorithms. Often it is confusing to determine which algorithms are available and when to use them. Table 8.1 lists the algorithms supported by the Microsoft RAS server and RAS clients. The default settings support the logon process of the Windows 95 and NT RAS client in the most secure manner possible. To support Windows for Workgroups 3.11 or LAN Manager RAS clients, select "Require encrypted authentication" instead of "Require Microsoft encrypted authentication." The "Require encrypted authentication" option allows the RAS server to support the DES authentication used by older Microsoft RAS clients.

TABLE 8.1. SUPPORTED ENCRYPTION ALGORITHMS.

Node Type	PAP	SPAP	DES	MD4	MD5	RC4
NT RAS Server	X		X	X		X
NT RAS Client	X	X	X	X	X	
Windows 95 RAS Client	X	X	X	X	X	
Windows for Workgroups RAS Client			X			
LAN Manager RAS Client			X			

8

The Microsoft-encrypted authentication is very strong. It is the same Challenge-Handshake Authentication Protocol (CHAP) used for the LAN-based logon process. When the server receives a logon request, employing the user's password as the key, the server creates a 16-byte challenge using the Message-Digest 4 (MD4) algorithm documented in RFC-1320. The client receives the challenge, decrypts it using the password entered by the user, modifies the challenge in some agreed-upon manner, and then encrypts the response using MD4 again. The server receives the response and decrypts the message. If the client properly modified the challenge, the server knows the client used the proper password. Throughout the entire conversation, the actual password never crossed the wire, not even in encrypted form.

The MD4 algorithm is used only during the logon sequence. MD4 is a message-digest algorithm typically used to create a small message fingerprint that can be quickly processed by CPU-intensive digital-signature algorithms. It was not developed to encrypt streams of data like those that comprise network traffic. Selecting the option "Require data encryption" uses RSA Data Security's RC4 encryption algorithm to encrypt all traffic outbound from the RAS server. The RAS server expects the client to encrypt all inbound traffic.

Tip

The encryption utilized as a result of selecting the "Require data encryption" option uses the Remote Procedure Call (RPC) protocol. Older RAS clients, such as Windows for Workgroups or LAN Manager, do not support RPC. Those clients receive the message `NetBIOS Error 640: a NetBIOS error has occurred` when attempting connections to RAS server requiring encrypted data streams. Data encryption requires an NT or Windows 95 RAS client.

Note

MD4 and RC4 were developed by Ronald Rivest. MD4 was developed at the MIT Computer Laboratory and, along with MD2 and MD5, is an industry-standard algorithm released to the public domain. MD2 was developed for use on 8-bit systems and has little relevance on today's 32-bit platforms. MD4 was developed to operate quickly on 32-bit platforms. MD5 also was developed for 32-bit platforms and, although slower than MD4, is more secure.

RC4 is a proprietary algorithm developed and owned by RSA Data Security, Inc. Additional information about MD2, MD4, and MD5 is available from RSA Data Security, Inc., on their Web site at `http://www.rsa.com/rsalabs/faq/q99.html`. Their Web site also contains a wealth of information regarding encryption, located at `http://www.rsa.com/rsalabs/newfaq`.

After completely defining the RAS service, the location information and phonebook entry on the initiating RAS server must be created. The location information includes the country and area code of the initiating RAS server as well as dialing information, such as a number required to access an outside line and whether to use tone or pulse dialing. The phonebook entry holds the information required to set up the RAS session.

To create the phonebook entry, double-click the My Computer icon and then double-click Dial-Up Networking. The first time the Dial-Up Networking is accessed, the Location Information dialog box shown in Figure 8.4 appears. Completing the dialog box brings up the message in Figure 8.5. Clicking the OK button starts the New Phonebook Entry Wizard shown in Figure 8.6.

Figure 8.4.
Location
Information
dialog box.

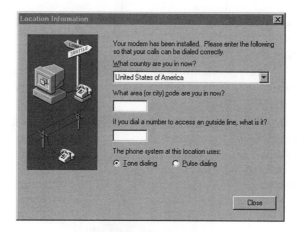

Figure 8.5.
Initial phonebook
message.

Figure 8.6.
New Phonebook
Entry Wizard.

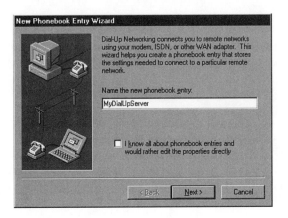

Checking the option that states you are familiar with the RAS options and you want to edit the properties directly displays the dialog box in Figure 8.7. The SMS Sender uses the Entry name to identify this phonebook entry. Enter the receiving server's area code and phone number in their respective fields. If multiple communication ports exist, ensure that the Dial using drop-down box specifies the appropriate port.

Figure 8.7.
Basic options in
the Edit
Phonebook Entry
dialog box.

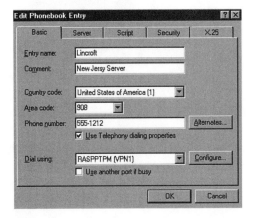

Select the Server tab to display the dialog box pictured in Figure 8.8. To support an SMS Sender, select PPP: Windows NT, Windows 95 Plus, Internet as the dial-up server type. Select the appropriate protocols from the Network protocols selections. The default TCP/IP settings allow the RAS server to assign IP information such as address, subnet mask, DNS, and WINS. It is best to leave the default.

Figure 8.8.
Server options of
the Edit
Phonebook Entry
dialog box.

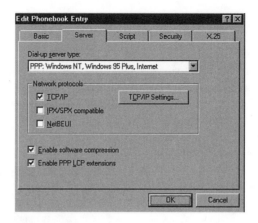

If the SMS Sender primarily supports the distribution of packages down to secondary sites, do not enable software compression. SMS compresses the package prior to distribution, and the package will not compress significantly more but will use additional CPU resources. If the SMS Sender will primarily support uploading of inventory data and collected files, enable software compression. The Script, Security, and X.25 tabs can be left at their defaults.

Double-clicking the Dial-Up Networking option after right-clicking the My Computer icon and selecting Properties displays the dialog box shown in Figure 8.9. Selecting the More button allows you to edit several properties of the phonebook entry.

Figure 8.9.
The Dial-Up
Networking
dialog box.

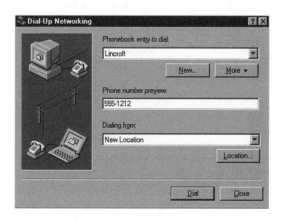

Selecting User preferences displays the dialog box in Figure 8.10. "Number of redial attempts" and "Seconds between redial attempts" define procedures to overcome poor quality lines and competition for RAS lines. Often, little can be done when the local phone system provides poor quality lines. However, a RAS line required by an SMS Sender should not be shared with other RAS clients. Leave "Idle seconds before hanging" at 0. SMS will terminate the connection when the connection is no longer required. Select "Redial on link failure" to allow RAS to re-establish the link if, for any reason, the link should fail.

Figure 8.10.
User Preferences
in the phonebook
entry.

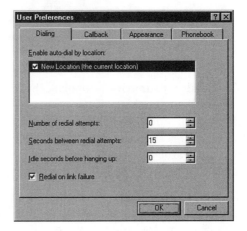

Clicking the Callback tab displays the screen in Figure 8.11. The callback level should usually be set to "No, skip call back." The link setup occurs faster, and callback security provides very little security against a skilled hacker.

In a callback security system, the client calls the server. The server then hangs up the line and calls the client at a preset number configured for that client's user account. The idea is that a hacker who discovers a user account, password, and modem number still cannot break into the network because he or she must dial from a specific telephone number. Callback security can stop the curious employee or novice hacker, but will not prevent more skilled intruders.

A benefit that callback security does provide is centralized billing for long distance telephone charges. Client calls typically last less than a minute. The longer, more costly calls are generated from the server at a central location. This allows organizations with multiple sites communicating to a central server to easily monitor the cost of RAS communications.

Figure 8.11.
Callback options
in the phonebook
entry.

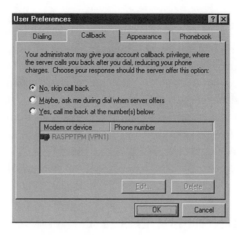

Clicking the Appearance tab displays the screen in Figure 8.12. Many of the Appearance options apply best to interactive RAS sessions, not the unattended sessions utilized by the SMS senders. The "Preview phone numbers before dialing," "Show location setting before dialing," "Show connection progress while dialing," and "Always prompt before auto-dialing" options should be turned off except during link testing or debugging. Their effects range from providing no benefit to inhibiting the automatic functioning of the RAS connection.

Figure 8.12.
Appearance
options in the
phonebook entry.

Note

> The SMS RAS sender requires additional information. The sending site must have a RAS-enabled account on the receiving RAS server and an account with read and write privileges on the receiving site server's SMS_SITE share. The accounts can be the same; however, typically the RAS-enabled account is an account local to the receiving RAS server or domain, and the SMS_SITE share-enabled account is either an account local to the site server's domain or an account from a domain trusted by the site server's domain.

PREPARING FOR SNA SENDERS

Similar to the RAS sender's dependence on the RAS service, the SNA sender depends on SNA server. An SNA server must be installed in each SMS site and LU pairs configured between the SNA servers before an SNA sender communicates between the SMS sites. Figure 8.13 depicts the initial screen of SNA Server 2.11.

Figure 8.13.
SNA Server 2.11
administration
application.

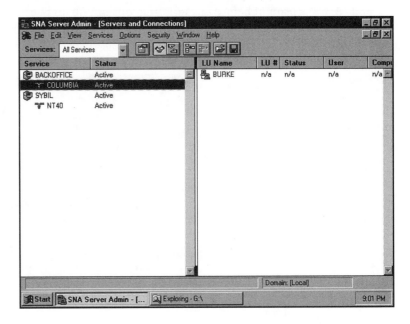

Tip

If you are installing a secondary site through an SNA sender, the receiving site server must be running SNA Server and must have the SNA receiver installed from the SMS CD-ROM.

Note

During the development of this book, Microsoft released SNA Server 3.0 Beta and Release Candidate 1. The administrative screens will no doubt look different but require the same configuration information.

Figure 8.14 illustrates the dialog box that appears after you select the Services menu option and choose the New Connections from the drop-down list. Select the appropriate protocol for the SNA network and click the OK button to display the dialog box shown in Figure 8.14.

Figure 8.14.
SNA Server 2.11
Insert Connection
dialog box.

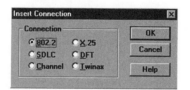

Figure 8.15 shows the dialog box that configures the connection properties. The Connection Name is the SNA server on which to create the connection. The Link Service drop-down list box shows all link services installed on the SNA server. Choose the appropriate link service for connecting to the target site. Select the Peer System option from the Remote End radio button list. Activation should be configured for On Server Startup because SMS makes frequent use of site-to-site links. Configure Allowed Directions for both Outgoing Calls and Incoming Calls to allow for package distribution as well as inventory reporting.

Clicking the Setup button on the Connection Properties dialog box displays the dialog box shown in Figure 8.16. This figure shows the properties required for an 802.2 DLC connection. Each link service has individual parameters that apply. These properties are the identifying characteristics of the SNA server on the other side of the SNA link.

Figure 8.15.
SNA Server 2.11
Connection
Properties
dialog box.

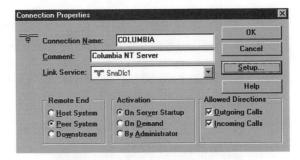

Figure 8.16.
SNA Server 2.11
802.2 Setup
submenu.

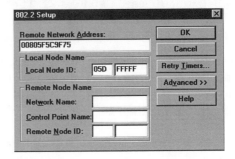

Figure 8.17 displays the dialog box that begins the last step in configuring a session between two SNA servers. This dialog box appears after you click the Assign LU list option from the Services menu option. Choosing the APPC [Remote] option displays the dialog box in Figure 8.18. Enter the characteristics of the LU defined in the SNA Server on the other side of the SNA link. Also select the Enable Automatic Partnering option.

Figure 8.17.
SNA Server 2.11
Insert LU
dialog box.

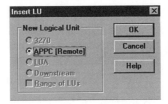

Figure 8.18.
SNA Server 2.11
APPC Remote LU
Properties
dialog box.

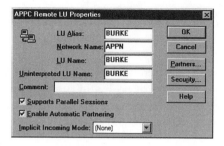

Perform the steps detailed previously at both ends of the SNA link. Create connections in both SNA servers and point them at one another. There are two more points worthy of note. The first is that after configuration, stopping and restarting the SNA service might be required. The second is that by default the SNA service installs as Manual start. Modifying the service in Services applet of Control Panel to Automatic start makes the link more reliable.

Caution

Lack of planning can cause SMS communications over an SNA link to disrupt the SNA network. A package sent over an interactive mode link uses all available bandwidth. Either schedule package transfers during off hours or use batch mode links, which do not disrupt the SNA network.

PREPARING FOR LAN SENDERS

The LAN sender is the simplest sender for which to prepare. If a full-time LAN or WAN link between the two sites has at least 56KB of unused bandwidth and supports TCP/IP, IPX, or NetBEUI, the LAN sender will function properly. When you use a LAN sender, SMS assumes that a full-time link is always up between the sites, spare capacity is always available, and no additional work is required for information to flow over the link. While those conditions exist, so will uneventful server-to-server and site-to-site communications.

8

BUILDING THE FOUNDATION FOR REMOTE CONTROL

The success of remote control depends heavily on the interaction among the client's protocol, the server's protocol, and the intervening network. The client and server must share a common protocol. In addition, that protocol and its associated name resolution procedures must traverse the network between the client and server.

Caution

Microsoft allows a computer name to have up to 15 characters. However, SMS can have problems connecting remote control to workstations with 15 characters. If you want to use SMS remote control, limit computer names to 14 characters.

Tip

By default, the RAS service does not support remote control of RAS clients. To enable remote control of RAS clients, make the following Registry update at the RAS server. Change the value of `HKEY_LOCAL_MACHINE\SYSTEM\CurrentControlSet\Services\RemoteAccess\Parameters\NetBIOSGateway` from 1 to 2. Stop and restart the RAS service for the change to take effect. As always, edit the Registry at your own risk.

USING TCP/IP

In versions 1.0 and 1.1 of SMS, remote control over TCP/IP required the SMS administrator to use either WINS or a properly configured LMHOSTS file. Version 1.2 remote control can operate without WINS or an LMHOSTS file if the inventory process captured the client's IP address and that address is still valid. In a DHCP environment, the SMS database might be out of date when the SMS administrator attempts the remote control session. The more child sites and tiers of sites in an architecture, the longer the update process takes.

If WINS is available, name resolution usually takes place quickly. However, if the SMS administrator and the remote client use different WINS servers, successful name resolution depends on proper WINS replication.

When the user double-clicks the Remote Control icon, the workstation posts one or more NetBIOS names to the WINS database. The first name, which is the workstation name with the letter C (43h) in the sixteenth position, allows the SMS administrator to connect a NetBIOS session for remote control of the client. The second name, which is the workstation name with an E (45h) in the sixteenth position, allows file transfer between the SMS administrator and the remote client. When the user closes the remote control agent, the workstation releases the previously created NetBIOS names relating to remote control.

Although this process occurs transparently in a WINS environment, an administrator must manually configure the NetBIOS names in an LMHOSTS environment. The machine on which the SMS administrator runs the remote control application must have three LMHOSTS file entries for each workstation that require remote control. The format of the entries are very specific, and Listing 8.1 illustrates a sample entry for workstations named Bert and Ernie. The last line of the table is not a valid LMHOSTS entry; it exists in this example as a guide to indicate the sixteenth character location.

Note

Although LAN Manager clients running Microsoft TCP/IP do support remote control under SMS, the client must have the latest version of the TCP/IP protocol, which was provided with LAN Manager 2.2c.

LISTING 8.1. SAMPLE LMHOSTS FILE ENTRIES FOR REMOTE CONTROL.

```
Bert    172.168.18.57
"Bert C"    172.168.18.57
"Bert E"    172.168.18.57
Ernie   172.168.20.60
"Ernie C"    172.168.20.60
"Ernie E"    172.168.20.60
```

Looking at the first of the three entries for Bert, the entry without quotes allows normal connectivity such as file sharing and message pop-up. The second and third entries allow the SMS administrator to locate the workstation and the NetBIOS ports on which the remote control agent is listening.

Tip

If you make a change to the LMHOSTS file on the SMS administrator's machine, it does not take effect until you run the NBTSTAT utility with the /R option to force reading of the LMHOSTS file. The proper syntax is NBTSTAT /R. The R must be uppercase; lowercase is not recognized.

Tip

By default, the RAS service does not support remote control of RAS clients. To enable remote control of RAS clients, make the following Registry update at the RAS server. Change the value of `HKEY_LOCAL_MACHINE\SYSTEM\CurrentControlSet\Services\RemoteAccess\Parameters \NetBIOSGateway` from 1 to 2. Stop and restart the RAS service for the change to take effect. As always, edit the Registry at your own risk.

USING IPX

IPX is a proprietary network protocol developed by Novell and based on the Xerox XNS protocol. For years, Novell NetWare was the only network operating system that used IPX. However, Microsoft's version of IPX, NWLINK, became available with Windows for Workgroups 3.11 and NT 3.1.

NWLINK allowed Windows for Workgroups and later NT to communicate with other Microsoft networking clients, but not necessarily with Novell NetWare. Novell used another protocol, NetWare Core Protocol (NCP), that ran on top of IPX to provide file and print services to NetWare clients. Until the release of NT Gateway Services for NT and the Windows 95 Client for NetWare Networks, Microsoft did not have a version of the NCP protocol that operated over NWLINK.

The previous information is not only an interesting bit of networking history, but it also helps in understanding some of the issues associated with IPX and remote control. Here are some of the known issues with remote control in a NetWare environment. Microsoft recognizes these issues and might correct the problems in a service pack or later release of SMS:

- When using Windows 95 with the Microsoft NetWare drivers instead of Novell's NetWare drivers, running the remote control agent causes the error `Unable to initialize IPX protocol`.
- When using both the NetWare IPX protocol and the Microsoft NWLINK on Windows for Workgroups, an attempt to remote control the client fails but does not generate an error.
- SMS NetWare login server clients support remote control using the IPX protocol but not TCP/IP.

The problem associated with the first bullet is an assumption made by the WUSER Remote Control TSR. Because NWLINK did not support the NCP protocol in Windows for Workgroups, when the WUSER TSR initially loads it assumes that because NetWare is the primary network provider, Novell's IPX is the network protocol in use. It ignores NWLINK and attempts to attach to the nonexistent Novell

IPX protocol. Installing the Novell Open Datalink Interface (ODI) drivers and the Novell IPX protocol gives WUSER the environment it expects and resolves the problem.

The problem associated with the second bullet is the inability of the Novell IPX and the Microsoft NWLINK protocols to play well together. The Windows for Workgroups NWLINK protocol ignores all traffic carrying NCP over IPX. However, the incoming IPX frame carrying the remote control request is not NCP; it is NetBIOS. NWLINK takes the NetBIOS remote control frame, but, as mentioned in the discussion of the previous bullet item, it does not have the capability to pass the request along to the WUSER TSR. Removing the NWLINK protocol allows the Novell IPX protocol to process the remote control request and pass it to the WUSER TSR.

The problem associated with the third bullet is the USERIPX TSR. The SMS software loaded onto a NetWare login client uses the USERIPX TSR to enable remote control. The USERIPX TSR, as the name implies, only supports the IPX protocol. Therefore, the NetWare login client can only support remote control over a version of the IPX protocol.

Tip

Remote control of NetWare login clients over a WAN requires IPX routing. The remote control agent registers a Service Advertising Protocol (SAP) with its login server and expects the server to broadcast the SAP to all other NetWare servers via the NetWare Routing Information Protocol (RIP). Without IPX routing, the SMS administrator cannot find the remote control agent.

USING NETBEUI

NetBEUI is the easiest protocol over which to operate SMS remote control. The SMS administrator and the remote control client are assumed to be on the same broadcast zone since the NetBEUI protocol cannot operate across multiple broadcast zones. The common broadcast zone permits the SMS administrator to easily locate the client, without any name service or network configuration.

Note

NetBEUI is sometimes improperly referred to as NetBIOS. NetBIOS is an API for inter-application communication. It is not, strictly speaking, a network protocol because it does not define a frame format on the wire. In the Microsoft networking environment, NetBIOS can operate over NetBEUI, IPX, or IP. NetBEUI is a network protocol that uses NetBIOS as its interface specification.

The common broadcast zone requirement of NetBEUI means that any router between the SMS Administrator and the remote control client must bridge the NetBEUI protocol. This requirement usually places a very heavy load on scarce and expensive WAN capacity. For this reason, most organizations do not normally bridge NetBEUI, making it impossible to use except within a single LAN segment.

NT DOMAIN SERVICES

SMS is a large and complex application; however, because it is an application, it depends on the operating system to provide a consistent set of services throughout the various sites in an organization. This section covers some options for time synchronization as well as the requirement for the directory replication service.

TIME SYNCHRONIZATION SERVICE

Properly synchronizing and sequencing events requires that NT keep the clocks in all systems consistent. Making all system clocks consistent enables the SMS administrators to ensure proper package delivery times. It also permits the NT administrators to view event logs from different servers, compare the entries, and know in what order the events occurred. Inconsistent system clocks prevent coordinated use of event logs, cause packages to cross the network at inappropriate times, and can prevent other services such as directory replication from operating properly.

An administrator could choose to adjust the clocks on each system manually. However, that would be inconvenient and unnecessary because several options exist for automatically synchronizing systems clocks. The NT Resource Kit includes a time service that is effective and easy to use. Microsoft's NT Server Web page maintains a list of NT utilities at http://www.microsoft.com/ntserver/tools. Included in the list are some commercial time servers. Other time servers are available and can be found by searching the Internet.

The time service available with the NT Resource Kit operates as a service on NT systems. It supports modem connections to organizations such as the US Naval Observatory, the BBC Radio Time Standard Dial-in Time Service, and other national time services throughout the world. Once configured, the service requires no manual intervention to maintain consistent time throughout an entire domain. The commercial time services offer similar configuration options but include installation programs and usually user support.

Note

Most of the time, services currently available for NT that support time synchronization over the Internet use SNTP (RFC 1769) or TIME (RFC 868). These protocols, although accurate in human terms, trade accuracy for simplicity. Applications that demand accuracy greater than plus or minus 50 milliseconds require radio synchronizing hardware or support for the full NTP protocol (RFC 1305).

DIRECTORY REPLICATION SERVICE

The primary responsibility of the directory replication service is to ensure that all servers capable of validating a domain logon request have the proper logon script and profile for every user. Each domain controller, whether it is a PDC or a BDC, should be running directory replication. The network and CPU overhead are minimal, and the increase in logon reliability is significant.

Servers participating in directory replication can be importers or exporters. Exporters hold the original copies of the files and are responsible for distributing the files to the importers.

When you install an SMS site, if directory replication is enabled on the site server and the SMS installation option Automatically Configure Workstation Logon Scripts is selected, the Site Configuration Manager copies the files required to use SMSLS.BAT as a logon script into the REPL$ share. From there, the files replicate to the NETLOGON share of all the domain controllers.

Caution

It is possible to create other subdirectories under the REPL$ share. However, remember the primary mission of directory replication is to support logon scripts, which are typically small and do not change often. On networks with limited available network capacity between nodes, using directory replication to disseminate large or frequently changing files can negatively impact the network.

The following steps explain the procedure for enabling directory replication within a domain:

1. Create a domain account in User Manager for Domains.
2. Add the account to the Replicator local group.

8

3. Give the account the Log on as a service right.

4. In Server Manager, double-click the server that will be the Export server and click the Replication button. The Directory Replication dialog box displayed in Figure 8.19 appears.

Figure 8.19.
The Directory
Replication
dialog box.

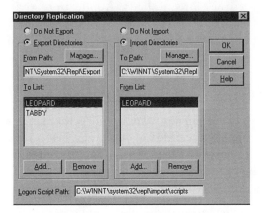

5. Click the Export Directories radio button. The From Path will automatically receive a default path.

6. Add the Primary Domain Controller (PDC) and all the Backup Domain Controllers (BDCs) in the domain.

7. Click the Import Directories radio button. The To Path will automatically receive a default path to the logon scripts.

8. Use the Add button underneath the From List to include the Export server in the From list.

9. Using Server Manager and the Computer/Properties/Replication menu option, repeat the two preceding steps for the PDC and each of the BDCs in the domain.

10. Using Server Manager and the Computer/Services menu option, configure the directory replication service on the PDC and each of the BDCs in the domain to use the account created in step 1, and set the Startup Type to Automatic.

11. Start the directory replication service on the PDC and all the BDCs.

Configuring NT for Optimum Performance

Any operating system, from DOS to NT to MVS, can run faster or slower depending on the configuration of the software and underlying hardware. Hardware tuning usually consists of spending more money, either for more or better parts. Software tuning is an art form with the curious goal of making the operating system or the application hardware-bound.

High Performance Hardware

The best and—if you place any value on your time—fastest way to speed up a system is using high-performance hardware. With memory, that means large quantities of fast RAM. An SMS server with less than 64MB of RAM will almost definitely improve performance with additional memory.

With disk I/O, high-performance hardware means multiple drives, multiple SCSI controllers, and hardware RAID. Hardware RAID has both speed and reliability advantages over NT Software RAID. Hardware RAID supports *hot swappable* drives, allowing online drive replacement and rebuilding. Software RAID requires a system shutdown to replace drives. Hardware RAID is significantly faster than NT software RAID. NT Software RAID places an additional load on the CPU, which increases as overall system load increases.

The SCSI versus IDE discussion often degenerates into a religious war. Proponents of SCSI push performance and expandability. Proponents of IDE push performance and price. In many workstations, the arguments of the IDE side are correct. On the other hand, in server environments, SCSI is the clear choice. In some situations, SCSI and IDE do have similar I/O throughput. However, the IDE controller uses Programmed I/O (PIO), which pays a heavy price in CPU utilization to achieve high throughput. The more expensive SCSI hardware has enough native intelligence to complete many operations without any additional CPU instructions after the initial request. In addition, virtually all the hardware RAID solutions require SCSI.

To improve throughput, install multiple SCSI channels. The system then can operate on both SCSI buses at the same time, effectively doubling I/O performance. Even a system with just two disk drives can show noticeable improvement from an additional SCSI channel. However, systems with four or more drives show the most dramatic improvement.

Tip

> Placing CD-ROM and tape drives on a separate SCSI channel from the disk drives will decrease file transfer and system backup duration.

Unless budgets are infinite, some investigation should precede hardware upgrades. Adding memory to a system constrained by disk I/O might not improve performance. Use Performance Monitor to examine existing systems to determine whether the system is hardware-bound before buying new hardware. Is the percentage of disk time consistently above 60 or 70 percent? You might need more disks or more controllers. Is the available memory below 5MB or 6MB and the percentage of pagefile utilization high? You might need more memory. Is your processor queue length consistently two or above? You might need a faster CPU.

Installing and Configuring NT for SMS

SMS is primarily I/O-intensive, although at times it can consume CPU cycles as well. Therefore, the system component that deserves the most consideration is the I/O subsystem, the disk drives. For the average SMS site server, there are two goals regarding I/O optimization. First, allow fast processing of inventory and collected files. This includes the Maintenance Manager's process of writing the incoming files to the SMS\SITE.SRV\INVENTORY.BOX directory as well the Inventory Processor's task of reading the files and writing applicable delta-MIFs. The second goal is to ensure that the SMS process does not compete with normal operating system I/O pagefile access as well as access to system executables and Dynamic Link Libraries (DLLs).

Ideally, an SMS site server should have hardware RAID providing RAID1 (disk mirroring) for the system partition, RAID0+1 (stripe-set mirroring) for an SMS partition, and an SQL partition. Each partition should have a separate SCSI channel. This configuration offers the highest I/O throughput as well as very good system and data availability. An I/O subsystem such as this could easily cost $30,000 or more, and that is before you buy the server to attach to it.

For those unwilling or unable to invest that much in disk subsystems, the ideal model can be to scale back. The first step back is to combine the RAID0+1 partitions for SMS and SQL into one RAID0+1 partition. In typical environments, except during the initial addition of clients to the site, there is usually little SQL I/O generated during inventory processing, because most of the inventory attributes remain static.

The next step back is to use RAID5 (stripe set with parity) for the combined SMS and SQL partition instead of RAID0+1. RAID5 performs poorly during write operations, which will slow down the arrival of incoming RAW files; however, it has good read performance and reliability. Performance will be slower, but in small to medium sites (less than 500 clients) the performance difference may be unobservable to the human eye.

An alternative to using a RAID5 partition is using a RAID1 partition with 4GB or 9GB drives. If a site can operate within a 4GB or 9GB file system, this alternative provides faster performance with fewer drives than a RAID5 solution. Of course, two 4GB drives can cost as much as three 2GB drives.

All of these solutions have two things in common. First, they assume the NT operating system is on a separate partition from the SMS and SQL applications. Second, they assume the use of multiple SCSI channels. These two common threads are the key to minimizing any competition for I/O resources between the NT operating system and the SMS and SQL applications.

SUMMARY

This chapter examined service accounts and permissions and looked at how NT and other applications provide the base functionality for SMS communication. The operation of the SMS senders depends on the proper configuration of the underlying NT and SNA server components. In addition, you have seen how remote control depends heavily on the proper choice and configuration of LAN protocols, and have examined the procedures for replicating logon scripts and maintaining consistent time throughout an organization. Finally, this chapter showed how to design and configure the NT operating system and file system to enable peak performance from the SMS site server.

CHAPTER 9

Installing and Upgrading SQL Server

SMS uses a SQL Server database to store configuration and inventory information. SQL Server is the only database that supports storing information for SMS. Although installing or upgrading SQL Server is a pretty straightforward process, there are several things to consider when configuring SQL Server for SMS. In this chapter, you walk through the process of installing and upgrading SQL Server. We also discuss planning and configuring SQL Server for SMS.

SMS 1.0 and 1.1 are supported by SQL 4.21a and SQL Server 6.0 and 6.5. SMS 1.2 is only supported by SQL 6.x. SQL Server 6.5 is the focus of this chapter, but we also point out some of the differences between the versions. This chapter also discusses a couple of bugs that were found when upgrading a client's SQL Servers from 6.0 to 6.5. (Refer to "Upgrading SQL Server" later in this chapter.) The topics covered in this chapter include

◆ Planning the install
◆ Planning the upgrade
◆ Installing SQL Server
◆ Upgrading SQL Server
◆ Manually creating the database and devices

PLANNING THE INSTALL

When planning the installation of SQL Server, you need to consider the following items:

◆ Platform
◆ Memory
◆ Storage

PLATFORM

SQL Server is only supported on the Windows NT operating system (OS), which eliminates the need to select an OS platform. The same restrictions on hardware for Windows NT are also applicable to SQL Server. Windows NT is a portable operating system that is supported by the following hardware platforms:

Digital Alpha AXP
Intel 32-bit $x86$ (486, Pentium, and so on)
MIPS
PowerPC

When choosing a hardware platform, do not pass Go; do not collect $200; go directly to the Windows NT Hardware Compatibility list to make sure the brand and model of machine you plan to use is on the list. If the machine is not on the list, download the latest list and check it (this list is constantly updated), or check with Microsoft or the hardware vendor.

REAL LIFE EXPERIENCE

Checking the Windows NT Hardware Compatibility list is a simple step that can prevent potential problems. Use only Microsoft-approved hardware. You might be able to get a no-name machine to work and save a few hundred dollars. I recall one instance where a client had several generic servers and added some 32MB SIMMs and upgraded the service packs. The upgrade went well (or so they thought). Over the course of the next week, some of the servers would suddenly lock up or crash when others were okay. By the time the client would get one server up, another one would crash! Thinking the service pack was the problem, all the servers were restored from tape after business hours. All looked well for the next day, but then the problems began again. After several hours of reading crash dumps and going all over the system, we found that the real problem was that some of the servers had a mixture of 16MB and 32MB SIMMS after the upgrade, which was a problem for this particular brand of machine. The moral of this story is that the few dollars saved in the beginning on the hardware is a lot less than the consulting hours the client paid for, not to mention the credibility of the IS staff from the user community. The second lesson to be learned is never change more than one thing at a time. Microsoft even recommends that you wait a few days after upgrading SQL Server 6.0 to 6.5 before you upgrade SMS 1.1 to 1.2.

You should also consider cost and the number of servers. There is no sense evaluating servers you cannot afford. Also consider maintenance when planning how many primary site servers to install. If you define multiple primary sites with their own SQL databases, you have multiple databases to administer. This decision becomes important when deciding to configure primary site servers to either configure several Primary Site Servers to a single SQL Server to store the SMS databases, or to configure each SMS Primary Site server with SQL configured on each server that is performing the function of Primary Site server. Although multiple primary site servers with their own SQL Servers provide some level of redundancy for the SQL Server databases, multiple servers require extra administration when administering security, configuring backups, maintaining the database, and upgrading the databases. Secondary sites do not have a separate database, which alleviates SQL maintenance. You cannot upgrade a Primary Site server with its own SQL Server remotely, which means upgrading SQL Server in the field requires a visit to all Primary Site servers configured with their own SQL servers.

Stranger than Fiction

When upgrading a Primary Site to SMS 1.2, it will automatically upgrade secondary site servers. A client with an upgrade problem experienced problems getting the secondary site servers to fully upgrade. The upgrade will show a construction icon and if you click on Site | Properties from the SMS Administrator, you will see that it reaches phase 4 of 5, but never seems to make it to the fifth final phase; it will not complete the upgrade. The `BOOTSTRAP.EXE` copies to the secondary site server but never seems to fully execute. The `BOOTSTRAP.LOG` file on the secondary site server did not give us much clue as to what was happening either. After a call to Microsoft, we found that using the `PREINST.EXE` command with the proper site code entry could reset the installation. The secondary site upgrade completed successfully! For detailed instructions on the use of the `PREINST` utility, type `preinst.exe /?` at the command prompt from the `<Drive>SMS \SITE.SRV\<architecture>.bin` directory for the switches to use to reset the site.

Another consideration is whether to use SMP (Symmetric Multiprocessing Processors). It is commonly known that SQL Server is very resource-intensive. Windows NT Server can natively support up to four processors. Some Original Equipment Manufacturers' implementations of Windows NT Server support up to 32 multiprocessors. (See the Hardware Compatibility List for supporting OEMs.) One thing to keep in mind is the store-and-forward nature of SMS. SQL Server is most resource-intensive when using a large number of transactions. SMS is not very transaction intense. One scenario where SMP improves performance with SQL 4.21a and 6.0 is the asynchronous process used for processing MIF entries. SQL 6.5 does not have this constraint. The primary performance increase is most noticeable when you perform queries from the SMS Administrator, which is transaction based.

From the SQL Server Enterprise Manager, you can select Server Configuration | Options to fine-tune SQL Server.

Note

SQL bottlenecks generally tend to be disk I/O intensive instead of processor intensive. The first knee-jerk reaction I have seen people do when performance slows down is add more processors. Usually, the real problem is that SQL Server has used all available RAM and begins caching to disk. You should monitor the disk activity with Performance Monitor to verify this. Remember to use the DISKPERF utility that comes with NT Server to enable monitoring of disk activity. Other items of particular interest are shown in the following table:

PERFORMANCE MONITOR OBJECT	COUNTER
Memory	Page Faults/sec
SQL Server	Cache Hit Ratio
SQL Server	I/O Page Reads/sec

The main objective when tuning SQL Server for memory is to maintain a high cache-hit ratio (this is the data being retrieved from cache), low physical I/O (disk I/O is low because data pages are in memory), and no page faults (page faults are an indication that not enough memory has been allocated to Windows NT, which causes the server to rely heavily on virtual memory). These values will not be available until after SQL Server is installed. SQL Server 6.5 also installs its own Performance Monitor for more detailed information on the SQL Server's statistics.

In short, I suggest that you monitor the system with Performance Monitor after installation to substantiate additional hardware.

MEMORY

The minimal memory requirement for a Primary Site server running Windows NT is 20MB. If the same server is running SQL Server, the minimal memory requirements are 28MB. I recommend 64 to 128MB of RAM for a server servicing about 500 clients, with at least 16MB dedicated to SQL. SQL Server manipulates memory very intelligently and can take advantage of as much memory as you allow it to. SQL

Server allocates memory as memory units. Each memory unit is 2KB of RAM. The default settings are 3,074 memory units or about 6MB RAM.

Table 9.1 represents my recommended memory allocation in MB for SQL Server for a Primary Site server servicing 500 clients. Keep in mind that you want to allocate storage for packages that can be up to four times their original size.

TABLE 9.1. RECOMMENDED MEMORY ALLOCATION.

Total Windows NT Memory	Recommended SQL Server Memory Allocation
28MB	10MB
32MB	16MB
64MB	40MB
128MB	80MB
256MB	160MB

When SQL Server is up and running, monitor it to pinpoint the amount of memory used by SQL Server and fine-tune from there.

Caution

Avoid setting the memory configuration option higher than the amount of physical memory installed. Using virtual memory can slow system performance.

You can configure the memory dedicated to SQL Server from the SQL Server Enterprise Manager utility. Select the server to be configured. To configure memory for SQL Server, perform the following steps:

1. From the Microsoft SQL Server 6.5 menu, select the SQL Enterprise Manager.
2. From the Server menu, select the SQL Server option and then the Configure option. The Server Configuration/Options window appears as shown in Figure 9.1.
3. Select the Configure tab to display the configuration options as shown in Figure 9.2.

9

Figure 9.1.
Server Configura-
tion / Options
dialog box.

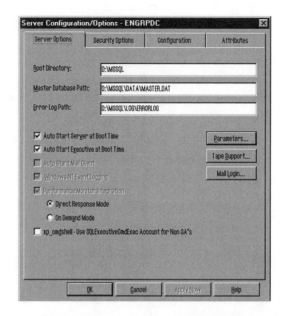

Note

Take advantage of the description box when you select a configuration parameter, as shown in Figure 9.2. The description text gives a summary of the selected parameter as well as when the change will take effect. Hats off to Microsoft developers for this feature. This makes tuning SQL Server so much easier. If you've used the sp_configure utility from SQL 4.21a to look up minimum and maximum values, you will appreciate the description box!

This illustration shows a SQL Server configured for 16MB RAM. Select the current options and click the OK button to save settings, and then exit.

Tip

SQL Server 6.0 has a bug that slowly utilizes all available memory. Service Pack 1 fixes the memory leak problem. Always research the most recent Service Pack for the product being installed.

In general, give SQL Server as much memory as you can afford.

Figure 9.2.
Configuring
memory units.

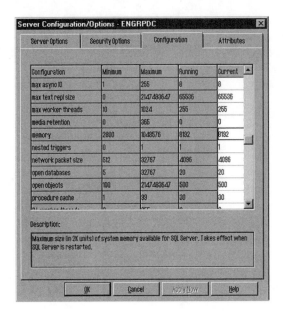

STORAGE

Even though SMS requires an NTFS file system, this is not necessarily true of SQL Server. The performance increase between NTFS (New Technology File System) and FAT (File Allocation Tables) file systems is negligible. Generally, NTFS performs faster during read operations, whereas FAT performs better during write operations. About the only significant advantage FAT poses is if you were required to have a dual-boot system with a non-FAT partition.

> NTFS is recommended over FAT because you can take advantage of Windows NT security and auditing features.

Prior to installing SMS, there are a few things you need to know; however, you do have to be a programmer to set up SQL for SMS. SMS uses SQL Server databases and devices to store information. A device is merely a predefined area that SQL Server uses to store information. This chapter only introduces the elements of SQL Server that you really need to know in order to administer an SMS system. For detailed information on SQL Server, refer to the SQL Administrator Guide for more in-depth information about SQL Server. The database and devices that must be configured for SMS include the following:

◆ SMS Database
◆ Log device
◆ Tempdb data device
◆ Tempdb log device

SMS stores inventory and configuration in a SQL database.

A SQL device is preallocated hard disk space. SMS requires two devices: one for the Site database and one for the transaction log.

The transaction log device stores before and after images of data that have been changed in the database. The transaction log is used to recover SMS in case of a system failure.

SMS DATABASE

You should calculate the site's database size based on the number of participating clients. The recommended figure is 35KB per machine.

Tip

> You might want to increase this number depending on the history to be kept, the number of administrators accessing the system, the number of queries to be run, the size of the tables being queried, and so on.

About 70KB is a good figure to use when calculating these requirements. The minimal requirement is 10KB. This size is the most important calculation because the other devices used by SMS use these values to determine their storage requirements.

TRANSACTION LOG DEVICE

The log device should be about 10 percent of the site database.

Tempdb DATA DEVICE

The Tempdb data device should be at least 20 percent of the site database device. A larger Tempdb increases performance for queries that contain sorts.

Tempdb LOG DEVICE

The `Tempdb` log device should be at least 20 percent of the `Tempdb` data device.

Note

> To prevent the `Tempdb` log device from filling up, enable the SQL Server's Truncate Log on Check Point option for `Tempdb` or back up the SMS database, which truncates the `Tempdb` log.

The `Tempdb` devices are created automatically upon install, but you might have to increase the size for SMS through the SQL Enterprise Manager utility.

Another thing to consider is the physical media (hard disks and controllers) to be used for the SQL Server. You might want to consider using a combination of RAID 5 for the Windows NT operating system and SMS. Place SQL Server on a non-striped drive and the databases on the striped partition, as displayed in Figure 9.3.

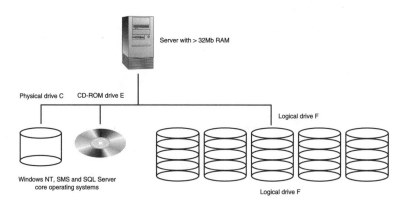

Figure 9.3.
Windows NT,
SMS, and SQL
Server hardware
configurations.

Server with > 32Mb RAM

Physical drive C   CD-ROM drive E

Logical drive F

Windows NT, SMS and SQL Server
core operating systems

Logical drive F

Keep in mind that stripe sets with parity require additional memory. Refer to the Windows NT Server documentation for more details on RAID 5 and optimizing Windows NT performance.

When installing SQL Server, see Table 9.2 for approximate storage requirements.

Caution

> Installing SMS into an existing database removes all existing data from the database.

TABLE 9.2. STORAGE REQUIREMENTS FOR SQL SERVER.

Upgrading from	Disk Space for Windows NT 4.0 and SQL Server	Storage Required for the Master Database	Storage Required for SMS Database (Default) and SMS Files	Space Required for SQL Books Online
New installation	106MB	25MB	157MB NTFS	1MB if run from CD-ROM; 15MB if installed to run from hard drive.
SQL Server 6.0	70MB	2MB	157MB NTFS	1MB if run from CD-ROM; 15MB if installed to run from hard drive.
SQL Server 4.21a	125MB	9MB	157MB NTFS	1MB if run from CD-ROM; 15MB if installed to run from hard drive.

Obviously, the storage requirements vary depending on the size of the database configured for SMS.

Tip

If space is available, install the Books Online to run from the hard drive. The SQL Server online documentation contains a wealth of information for tuning, configuring, and troubleshooting SQL Server.

The memory requirements for your site servers vary based upon the performance required, clients participating, files collected, and so on. Configure your site servers to produce the desired results for your requirements.

PLANNING THE UPGRADE

Planning an upgrade is somewhat different from planning an installation. Upgrading SQL Server differs from making a new installation because your existing database contains data used by the SMS infrastructure. Never underestimate an upgrade, and expect that anything that can go wrong, will go wrong. Extra time spent up front might save you a lot of time and headaches in the long run.

A SIMPLE UPGRADE?

I recall upgrading a customer's Windows NT server from 3.5 to 3.51 and from SMS 1.0 to SMS 1.2. A simple enough procedure—after all, these were not major revisions, right? Wrong! After the upgrade, I logged on to make sure all was well and sent out a test package through SMS. Oddly, the package never got to me. After checking a few things and realizing something was not right, I decided to return the server to its original state. Fortunately, I had backed up the registry and the server, and the next day, I replicated the problem in the lab. It took me the better part of two days to figure out that if you don't configure License Manager (which was new in NT Server 3.51) correctly, SMS will be refused IPC connections, which are required to connect and copy files. Fortunately, I was able to return it to its original state. I don't think the client would have been very happy if the system was inoperable for two days. It's odd, but being a consultant and going into several large companies experiencing connectivity issues, I have seen exactly the same problem with some systems being inoperable for weeks. The point here is to do your homework and always have a backup plan.

Before you upgrade the SQL Server, you should consider the following steps:

1. Set up the upgrade scenario in a lab. If you have technical support, contact them for any last-minute advice. Check Technet and any release notes that might have come with the product. Far too often, I have seen last-minute release notes that are not included in the documentation.

2. Determine required disk space. Table 9.2 lists the required disk space for the different versions.

3. Estimate the amount of down time you expect the upgrade to take. Include approximate time to back up, test, and restore the server if necessary. Remember, the larger the database, the longer the backup will take.

4. Perform maintenance with the DBCLEAN utility, which eliminates any out-dated records in the SQL Server database.

5. Verify that the number of SQL Server open databases configuration param-eter is greater than the total number of databases on the server. Use the SQL Server Enterprise Manager utility to check and configure this option. From the Enterprise Manager utility, select Server | Server Configuration | Option. Click the Configuration tab.

6. Shut down SQL Server with the Service Manager and use Windows NT backup facilities to back up all databases and all SQL Server and SMS directories.

Tip

> Use SQL Server's Service Manager utility to start and stop SQL services as shown in Figure 9.4.
>
> Most backup mechanisms require that SQL services be shut down to back up the SQL Server databases.

Figure 9.4.
SQL Service
Manager.

7. Back up the Registry. Some Windows NT backup facilities have this capa-bility in case you need to restore the system.

INSTALLING SQL SERVER

Now that you have gone through the planning process, it is time to install SQL Server 6.5:

1. Log on to the Windows NT server with an administrative account. The SQL setup procedure requires advanced rights to perform its installation, such as installing services, making Registry entries, creating directories, and so on. One of the most common problems that occurs is a message that reads Cannot Create Directories. This error is indicative of insufficient Windows NT privileges.

2. Installing SQL Server 6.5 requires running SETUP.EXE from the SQL Server 6.5 CD-ROM. There is a SETUP.EXE for different processor platforms:

\Alpha   Digital Alpha AXP

\I386   Intel 32-bit *x*86 (486, Pentium, and so on)

\MIPS   MIPS processors

\PPC   PowerPC

Select the appropriate directory for the machine type you are using and start the Setup program. Figure 9.5 displays the initial welcome window. Click the Continue button to proceed.

Figure 9.5.
SQL Server 6.5
Welcome screen.

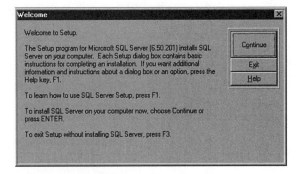

3. The Name and Organization dialog box appears. Fill in the Name, Organization, and Product ID fields and click Continue.

The Verify Name and Organization dialog box appears. (See Figure 9.6.) Verify that the information you provided is correct and click the Continue button.

Figure 9.6.
Verify Name and
Organization
dialog box.

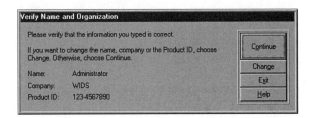

4. The SQL Server Options dialog box appears. (See Figure 9.7.) Make sure the Install SQL Server and Utilities radio button is selected and click the Continue button.

Figure 9.7.
Options window.

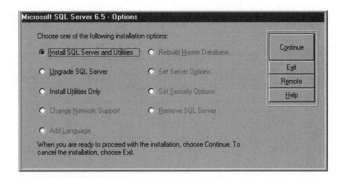

5. The Choose Licensing Mode window appears. (See Figure 9.8.) Select the correct licensing mode for your organization and select the Continue button. The licensing dialog appears. Read the agreement, verify that the license information is correct, click the verification box, and click the OK button.

Caution

If you select the Per Server option, do not leave this option set to 0. This setting can cause all kinds of strange connectivity problems, such as preventing you from logging into the database when all seems okay. If you select the Per Seat option, ensure that the domain is properly configured through License Manager and that you have sufficient licenses. Also, ensure that License Manager replication is properly configured. Figure 9.9 displays an improperly configured License Manager. Remember that License Manager should be configured higher than the number of users. Many of the BackOffice products initialize several Netlogon connections to perform tasks such as copy files and so on. These connections register as licensed or nonlicensed connections to License Manager. License Manager also must be configured for licenses for SMS 1.2. Licenses must be added for all versions of the product to be used, as well as other BackOffice products installed on Windows NT versions later than 3.5. The License Manager can be set up different ways and may require much care when configuring. In particular, look for the Domain Controller option and the replication option. Refer to the Windows NT 3.51 documentation or Technet for more details on License Manager.

Figure 9.8.
Choose Licensing
Mode dialog box.

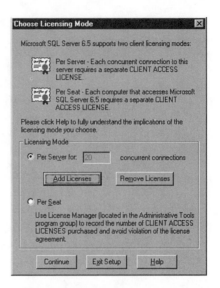

Figure 9.9.
An improperly
configured
License Manager.

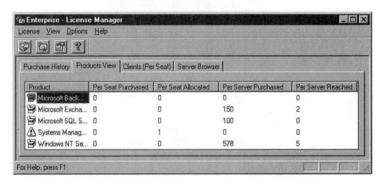

6. The SQL Server Installation Path window appears. (See Figure 9.10.) Verify the drive and directory. Also review the required and available space. The setup routines are not always the smartest at calculating disk space. Give yourself a little extra room if possible. Click the Continue button.

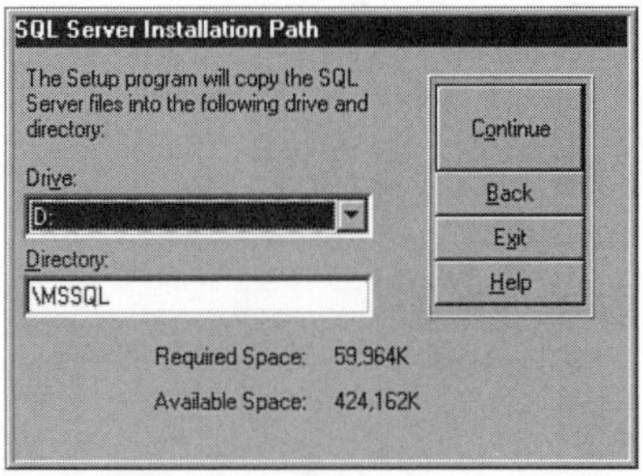

Figure 9.10.
SQL Server
Installation Path
window.

Tip

Avoid using version numbers in the installation directory; you'll experience much less confusion after an upgrade. Along the same lines, if you are using multiple SQL and SMS servers, try to keep the file, directory, database, and device names consistent. Also try keeping the Windows SQL Server's name the same as the Windows NT server name if it is installed on the same machine. Keeping up with domain and server naming conventions can be difficult enough, but it gets worse when you start customizing everything.

I have one client that made up codes for the devices to match the site codes in a 17-site infrastructure. When new sites were brought up, the naming was so complicated that remembering it in the field was difficult. The SMS/SQL Server logon process to get into a site could be a 2 to 10 minute process! Keeping things consistent is also helpful when speaking to technical support.

7. The Master Device Creation dialog box appears. (See Figure 9.11.) Verify the drive, directory, and size for the master device. Click the Continue button.

Figure 9.11.
Master Device
Creation dialog
box.

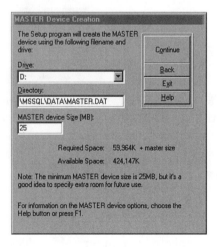

Tip

The minimal master device size is 25MB. I suggest that you make it about 40MB if you have the space. This provides for future expansion and a larger temporary database for performance. As SQL Server versions have changed, the requirement for free space on the master device has increased and decreased between 2 and 10MB free. Creating a larger master device may alleviate one more detail to handle during the next upgrade.

8. The SQL Server Books Online window appears. (See Figure 9.12.) Select the radio button for your choice and click Continue.

Figure 9.12.
SQL Server
Books Online
window.

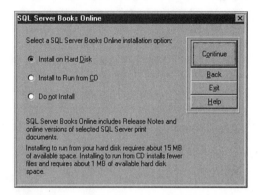

Tip

If you can spare the 15MB space on the hard drive, install the books on the hard disk. You know that the CD-ROM is never going to be around later when you really need it. Microsoft's Books Online is easy to use and provides a search capability that enables you to search on a specific error code in no time. Far gone are the days of fumbling through several manuals (if you can find them!) to hunt down a code.

9. The Installation Options window appears. (See Figure 9.13.) If the SQL Server is only to be used for SMS, select the default Character Set; ISO Character Set; and the default Sort Order, Dictionary Case Sensitive.

Click the Networks button to display the Select Network Protocols window. (See Figure 9.14.) Add additional protocols such as TCP/IP, NWLink, Banyan, and so on. Keep in mind that you will need to configure a common protocol for the SMS site servers to communicate. Also remember the NetBEUI is a non-routable protocol.

Figure 9.13.
Installation
Options window.

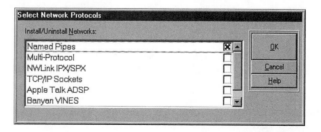

9

> When selecting the TCP/IP protocol, accept the default prompt for port 1433.

You are also given the option to auto start SQL Server and SQL Executive at boot time (refer to Figure 9.13). Select the Auto Start at boot time for both options. If this is a dedicated SMS server, you always want to run these services even if the server is rebooted.

Click the Continue button.

10. The SQL Executive Logon Account dialog box appears. If you have already set up a Windows NT account for this purpose, enter the Domain/Username and Password or select the Local/System Account option. Click the Continue button.

Figure 9.14.
Select Network
Protocols win-
dow.

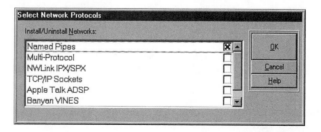

> Use the Local System account. This saves a lot of grief later if the Windows NT account password changes or expires.

The File copy in progress window appears. (See Figure 9.15.) You are advised that now is a good time to fill out your registration card. I recommend that you fill out your registration card, update your free weekly computer rag subscriptions, clean your desk, and so on. In short, this is a time-consuming process. It can take as little as five minutes or as much as a couple of hours, depending on the platform where you are installing SQL Server.

After the file copy is complete, the second installation process makes Registry modifications and installs services. (See Figure 9.16.)

Figure 9.15.
File copy in
progress window.

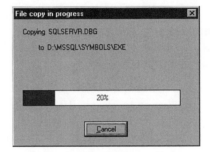

Figure 9.16.
SQL Server setup
creating the
master device.

11. Last but not least, the SQL Server 6.5 - Completed window appears. (See Figure 9.17.) Click the Exit to Windows NT button and the installation is complete!

The installation also installs the SQL client to manage the servers, as shown in Figure 9.18.

Figure 9.17.
SQL Server 6.5 -
Completed dialog
box.

Figure 9.18.
MS SQL Server
6.5 tools.

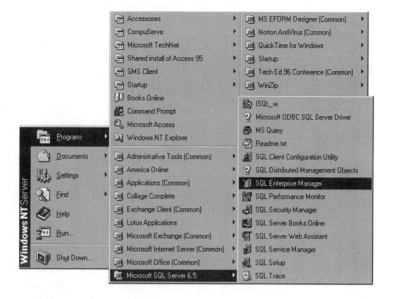

UPGRADING SQL SERVER

As discussed earlier, the upgrade process is a little different from a new installation. Most of the calculations have been performed, and SQL Server merely updates the Registry and files used.

STRANGER THAN FICTION

I have run into a couple of strange problems in the field during the SQL 6.0 to 6.5 upgrade process, though. One problem in particular left us scratching our heads, and hanging on the phone for a long support call to Microsoft. When attempting to upgrade the SQL Server 6.0 to 6.5 on the Primary Site servers, an error message appeared stating that You cannot upgrade a Beta version of SQL. After verifying that this was not a Beta version of SQL 6.0, and even trying to load the Service packs, we continued to receive this message. After a call to good old Microsoft (they did an excellent job of directing the call to the right people), we found that we had to rebuild the ODBC registration in the Registry to correct the problem. Refer to the Rebuild ODBC Registration section at the end of this chapter to correct this problem.

Don't forget to make backups of the Registry, devices, database, and all SMS/SQL Server directories in case you need them.

Note

You can install SQL Server 4.21a and SQL Server SQL 6.*x* on the same machine. You cannot, however, install SQL Server 6.0 and 6.5 on the same machine, because they have a common directory structure and Registry entries. Installing SQL Server 6.5 on the same machine where SQL Server 6.0 is installed results in an upgrade. Another thing to keep in mind is that after an upgrade, there is no going back unless you delete the install and restore from tape and Registry backup. Also, keep in mind that installing Service Packs of any BackOffice product cannot be uninstalled.

For existing SMS installations, it only makes sense to upgrade SQL Server 6.0 to 6.5 in the process, right? Be careful, though. Get your backups in place, because this may be a rocky road. I found only a couple of major gotchas in the upgrade process for existing site servers that did not appear on fresh installations in the lab. To begin the upgrade process, follow these steps:

1. Log on to the Windows NT server with an administrative account. The SQL setup procedure requires advanced rights to perform its installation, such as installing services, making Registry entries, creating directories, and so on. One of the most common problems that occurs is a message that reads `Cannot Create Directories`. This error is indicative of insufficient Windows NT privileges.

2. Installing SQL Server 6.5 requires running `SETUP.EXE` from the SQL Server 6.5 CD-ROM. There is a `SETUP.EXE` for different processor platforms:

   `\Alpha`   Digital Alpha AXP

   `\I386`   Intel 32-bit *x*86 (486, Pentium, and so on)

   `\MIPS`   MIPS processors

   `\PPC`   PowerPC

   Select the appropriate directory for the machine type you are using and start the Setup program. Figure 9.19 displays the initial Welcome window. Click the Continue button.

Figure 9.19.
SQL Server 6.5
Welcome screen.

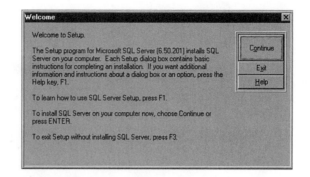

3. The SQL Server Already Installed window appears. (See Figure 9.20.)
   Verify the information and click the Continue button.

Figure 9.20.
SQL Server
Already Installed
window.

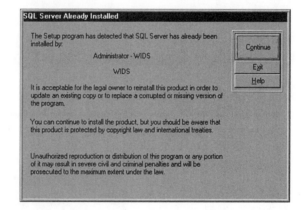

4. The SQL Options window appears. (See Figure 9.21.) Ensure the Upgrade
   radio button is selected and click the Continue button.

Figure 9.21.
Options window.

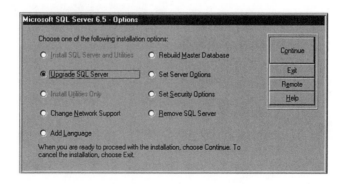

5. The Upgrade SQL Server dialog box appears. (See Figure 9.22.) Again, you are reminded of backup procedures. Click the Resume button to continue.

Figure 9.22.
Upgrade SQL
Server dialog box.

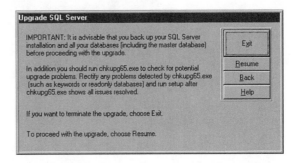

> ## Note
>
> As the dialog indicates, run the CHKUPG.EXE utility to verify database structure. This utility is included with the SQL 6.5 CD-ROM. When the server is used only by SMS, problems are seldom reported.

6. Another window appears, prompting you to confirm the path. Click Continue and the SQL Server Upgrade Path window appears. (See Figure 9.23.) Confirm that the information is correct for the master device and click the Continue button.

Figure 9.23.
SQL Server
Upgrade Path
window.

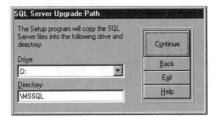

7. The Books Online menu appears. (Refer to Figure 9.12.) Select one of the options and click the Continue button.

8. The SA Password dialog box appears, prompting for the SA (SQL Server System Administrator) password. (See Figure 9.24.) Click the Continue button. The SQL Executive logon account dialog box appears. If you set up a Windows NT account for SQL, enter this information or select the local system account.

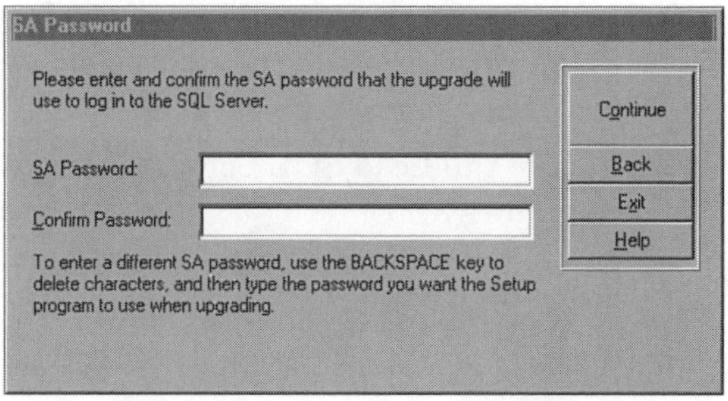

Figure 9.24.
SA Password
dialog box.

The Upgrade SQL Server window appears. (See Figure 9.25.) Click Continue. This process takes a while to complete because the setup routine completes the installation.

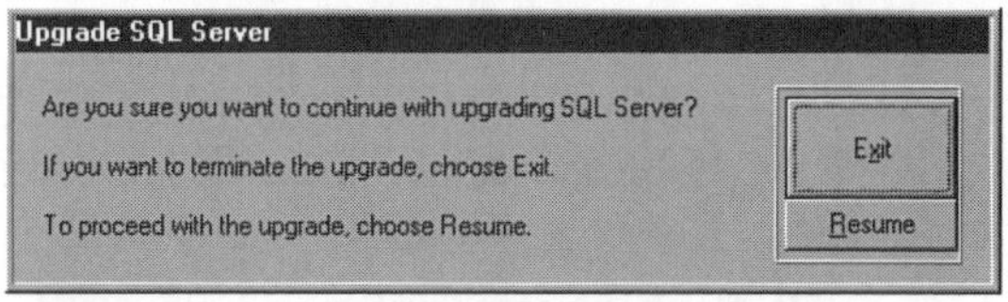

Figure 9.25.
Upgrade SQL
Server window.

STRANGER THAN FICTION

After successful upgrades in the lab, one of my customers started the upgrade process for SQL Server 6.0 to 6.5. Right at this point in the upgrade process you may receive a Dr. Watson error stating there is a sharing violation and the installation will abort! After several hours on the phone with Microsoft, we found that we had to rebuild the SQL Server 6.0 registry before we could continue the upgrade process. If you receive this Dr. Watson error, you can refer to the following lists to recover the upgrade:

Rebuild ODBC registration

1. Open File Manager.
2. Double-click the `<Drive>\<SQLSERVER>\Install\SQLOLE.REG` file.
3. From Program Manager open the SQL 6.0 program group.
4. Double-click the ISQL_w icon.
5. In the Connect To box, enter the Server name, Login ID, and password.
6. Click on the Connect button; this will connect you to the SQL Server and invoke the query prompt.

7. Ensure that the Query tab is selected and that the selection for dB: option is master.

8. Choose the Load SQL Script button, which is represented by the open file symbol.

9. Highlight the `<Drive>\<SQLSERVER>\Install\SQLOLE60.SQL` file and select the OK button to proceed.

10. Perform the query by selecting the green arrow on the toolbar.

11. When the query is complete, exit the ISQL_w tool.

12. Reboot the system and follow the procedures in the SQL Server Registry rebuild process.

SQL Server Registry rebuild process

1. Open a command prompt.

2. Change directory to the `<drive>\SQL\BINN` directory.

3. Type `SETUP /T RegistryRebuild = ON` at the command prompt and press Enter.

4. SQL Server setup will begin.

5. Enter name and company.

6. Enter license information to continue.

7. You will be prompted for the SQL Server path. Enter the path and click the Continue button to proceed.

8. You will be prompted for the size and location of the SQL Server Master Database file. Use File Manager to verify the size and location of the `MASTER.DB` file and enter the size and location. Click the Continue button to proceed.

9. Select the SQL Server Books option to be installed and select the Continue button to proceed.

10. Choose the Automatically start at boot for both options and select the Continue button to proceed.

11. Choose the Local/System option to run the SQL services and select the Continue button to proceed.

12. The Registry Rebuild process will re-create the program group and icons for SQL Server 6.5.

13. Reboot the system after the Registry has been rebuilt. You are now ready to proceed to the "Manually Reconfigure SQL Server from Single User Mode" section.

> **Manually Reconfigure SQL Server from Single User Mode**
>
> 1. Always take great caution when using the Registry editor! Start `Regedit32.EXE` from the `<Drive>\<%System root>\SYSTEM32` directory.
> 2. Locate the `HKEY_LOCAL_MACHINE\Software\Microsoft\MSSQLServer\Parameters` registry key. In this location are several registry keys with the `SQLArg<number>:Reg_SZ:<registry value>`.
> 3. Locate the registry value that is set to `=-m`. This is the single-user mode option.
> 4. Select the Edit | Delete option to remove the registry key.
> 5. Reboot the system to proceed.

When installation is complete, the setup routine prompts you to exit to Windows NT. Exit to Windows NT and reboot the server, and the upgrade is complete.

MANUALLY CREATING DEVICES

You can install SQL on the local Primary Site server or another server running SQL.

If SQL Server is on a machine other than the site server, you have to manually create the devices through SQL Server Enterprise Manager. If SQL is installed on the same computer as the site server, SMS can automatically create the devices upon installation. (See Chapter 10, "Installing and Upgrading Primary Site Servers.")

SUMMARY

This chapter walked you through the SQL Server install and upgrade process. Although you may run into a couple of strange things, overall it is not a very complicated process. Always do your homework and have a backup strategy! The next chapter guides you through the installation of SMS.

CHAPTER 10

Installing and Upgrading Primary Site Servers

After planning how your sites will be implemented, it's time to proceed with the installation. If you are involved with the installation of a central primary site server, one task at hand is to determine the initial size requirements for the SMS database (SQL Server) based on your environment. This chapter discusses the installation of the single central primary site, keeping in mind site expansion and the possibility of other sites in the hierarchy.

By this time, you have done your lab testing, documentation, and created a model of how you will implement your site. It is suggested you use the BackOffice deployment templates in getting ready to install and implement SMS.

Some organizations may only need to upgrade their primary site servers because they are already using a previous version of SMS. This chapter will outline some issues you should be aware of when upgrading a site. Because SMS is dependent on SQL Server, the person who is implementing the installation of the SMS site should have some experience with SQL Server.

Finally, this chapter will discuss the requirements and implications of running SQL Server and SMS on the same server. The SMS Security Manager, SMS Administrator, and the role of the distribution and logon servers in the environment, including a brief discussion on setting up clients for inventory collection, will also be discussed.

HARDWARE REQUIREMENTS

As SMS is a robust application, there are some general hardware requirements for your SMS Server. Additionally, there are guidelines for the SMS environment as a whole, and these are covered in Chapter 24, "Optimizing SMS Performance." The hardware requirements for an SMS Site Server are the following:

- ◆ 486 DX2 66 or higher (higher is recommended)
- ◆ 32MB of RAM
- ◆ 100MB of free hard disk space
- ◆ NTFS partition
- ◆ Windows NT Server 3.51 with Service Pack 3 or later (SP4 is recommended or Windows NT Server 4.0)
- ◆ Server is a PDC or BDC (Primary/Backup Domain Controller)
- ◆ SQL Server 6.x for Windows NT

Note

It is not required, but suggested, to have hardware that is on the Hardware Compatibility List, because it has been tested by Microsoft.

Note

Additional space will be needed for software packages, if you decide to use the software distribution feature in SMS.

Note

Different requirements exist if SQL Server will exist on the same server with SMS. See the section on "Dual-Role Server (SQL and SMS)."

SQL Server with SMS

SMS version 1.2 requires SQL Server version 6.0 or SQL version 6.5; SQL Server version 4.*xx* is no longer supported. SMS uses SQL Server as its data repository, and the overall requirements for SMS will vary based on the location of SQL Server. Obviously, if SQL Server and SMS reside on the same server, resource requirements for that server will be much greater than the individual server requirements necessary when SMS and SQL Server coexist separately.

Requirements for SQL Server

SQL Server requirements will vary based on whether it will be used only to support the SMS application, or as a generic database application server where SMS is one of several applications utilizing SQL Server. The requirements can be broken down into several categories, as follows:

- ◆ Processor requirements
- ◆ Memory requirements
- ◆ Storage space requirements

The effects of these requirements are discussed in Chapter 24.

A Pentium-based processor is suggested as a minimum requirement for SQL Server. If you will be running SMS and SQL Server on the same machine, it should be Pentium-based.

The memory requirements for SQL Server will be based on the number of users (connections) to be supported and the amount of data being served. In addition to each connection using memory resources, the data caching techniques employed by SQL Server are directly dependent on memory being available. Lastly, don't forget to account for the base memory that the NT operating system will need to operate by default.

When calculating storage requirements, assume that between 25 and 35KB of space will be required, per client, in the database. As database storage calculations are never totally accurate, be sure to increase your final calculation by 30 percent. Keep in mind that SQL Server will create and use the *master* and *tempdb* databases in addition to logging transactions (the transaction log) for recovery purposes. This needs to be factored into the overall disk usage totals. As the saying goes, disk space is cheap, so buy more than required.

DUAL-ROLE SERVER (SQL AND SMS)

SMS Server requires a fair amount of memory and when SQL Server is added to that same server, even more RAM is required. It is not suggested to run a dual-role server, where SMS and SQL Server reside on the same machine. The processing overhead required by each product does not make this scenario the best performer. If, for some reason (such as cost), you must implement your site this way, contemplate installing SMS, SQL Server data, and the NT operating system on separate disk drives and assure a minimum of 64MB of RAM.

Caution

If you put SMS and SQL Server on one computer, you reduce the level of fault tolerance. If that computer incurs problems, you lose both processes, which could make recovery more difficult.

TWO INDEPENDENT SERVERS (SQL AND SMS)

Having two independent servers is a more reasonable way to set up your SMS environment, one to run SQL Server, and the other for SMS. Although this increases network I/O between the servers, you could put them on a separate segment, or put a high-speed link between them. If the SQL Server and the SMS Server reside in two completely different domains, you need to verify that the account that you are using to install SMS is valid on the remote SQL Server. This can cause an authentication problem, which will keep you from accessing the SQL Server during SMS installation. If you are going to run two independent servers, it is recommended for both servers to employ a RAID level 5 hardware subsystem.

PREPARING THE SQL SERVER

You should log on to SQL Server with a privileged account that exists on the SQL Server. Generally, this is the sa account, which is short for system administrator. An account, which will be used for SMS, needs to be created with (at least) the following permissions:

◆ Create a database

◆ Dump a database

◆ Dump a transaction

Once these permission requirements are in place, it is time to create the actual devices.

CREATING A DATABASE DEVICE

Creating a database device can be done using the SQL Enterprise Manager. Using this tool, you can create a database device by assigning it a name and initial size. SMS will create its database itself, using the device you specify. In Figure 10.1, the SQL Enterprise Manager is shown with the right mouse button being used to create a new device. In Figure 10.2, you see the New Database Device window. The following steps allow you to create a database device:

1. Start SQL Enterprise Manager.
2. Click the Manage menu and select Database Devices.
3. Click the Create New Device button.
4. Enter the name location and size of device.
5. Click Create Now.

You have now created a database *data* device, which will contain the data of a database. Finally, you need to create a *log* device, which will be used to log or journal all transactions that occur in the database (updates, deletes, and inserts).

CREATING A LOG DEVICE

It is important to create a log device for a database as it will be used in the event of a failure. The log device will contain a history of transactions against the database. In the event of a failure, this "transaction log"—in addition to the last full backup of the database—will allow you to restore an otherwise corrupted database to its most current state. In Figure 10.3, the log devices are listed in the SQL Enterprise Manager. Creating a log device is identical in procedure to creating a database data device. You specify it as a log device within the SMS installation. Generally, it is good to name it with a .LOG extension so that any other database administrator will know that it is a log file.

Figure 10.1.
The SQL Enter-
prise Manager
with the right
mouse function.

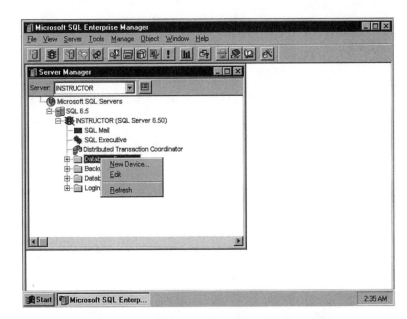

Figure 10.2.
The database
device setup
window.

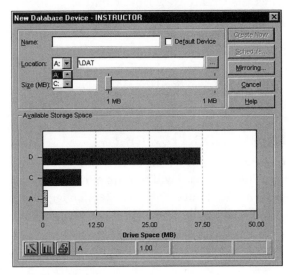

Figure 10.3.
The log device
listed in the SQL
Enterprise
Manager.

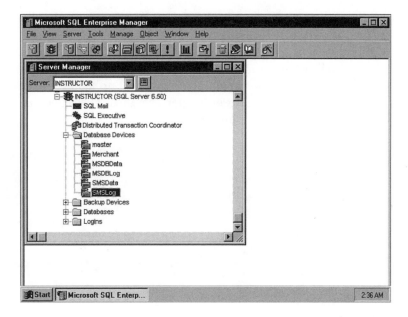

10

SPECIAL CONSIDERATIONS

If SQL Server exists on the same computer as SMS, SMS can actually create the database data device and log device. If both are running on separate computers as independent servers, SMS cannot create the devices and they will have to be manually created via the SQL Enterprise Manager. To create a device on a dual-role during SMS installation, click the device creation button and enter the device parameters.

SQL SERVER CONFIGURATION PARAMETERS

Although Chapter 24 covers many of the SQL Server configuration parameters, the following list shows some that will be discussed as they are directly relevant to the installation of a SMS Site Server:

- ◆ User Connections. SMS installation requires a minimum of 20 connections. For each SMS Administrator (program) instance, you will need at least five user connections.

- ◆ Open Objects. This is 500 by default and should be incremented to between 5,000 and 10,000 for very large sites.

- ◆ Memory. The default allotment of memory to SQL Server is 8MB. You will want to increase this to improve the performance of SQL Server as it will use this memory for caching and its own internal processing. If you are running other applications on the server, it is important not to increase memory usage to the point where the NT operating system and those applications are lacking memory. You should always leave 16MB of memory just for the NT operating system alone. You can always change the amount based on observed performance. These settings are talked about in more detail in Chapter 24.

Note

Make sure that the SQL Server and SMS Server are time-synchronized. Otherwise, this could cause problems when executing jobs.

INSTALLING THE CENTRAL PRIMARY SITE SERVERS

It is now time to start setting up the actual SMS site via the SMS installation program. I have discussed SQL Server and its requirements prior to installation. The type of server discussed in this section is the Central Primary Site Server, which exists at the top of the hierarchy in an SMS environment. Creating additional primary sites and secondary sites is covered in Chapter 11, "Installation of Additional Site Servers."

To install SMS, run setup from the SMS CD. There are several stages in the SMS setup. The first stage analyzes your system to determine if your machine meets the requirements necessary to install SMS and checks whether you have a previous version of SMS, in which case you will need to upgrade. There are two modes for installing SMS: default and custom. In Figure 10.4, the Setup Install Options dialog is shown, where you can select to run the custom installation.

DEFAULT

The default installation of SMS allows you to install the following:

- ◆ Intel Client
- ◆ Intel Network Monitor
- ◆ Intel Server
- ◆ Intel SMS Administrator
- ◆ Scripts

These are installed when you choose Continue and forgo a custom installation.

Figure 10.4.
Setup Install
Options dialog.

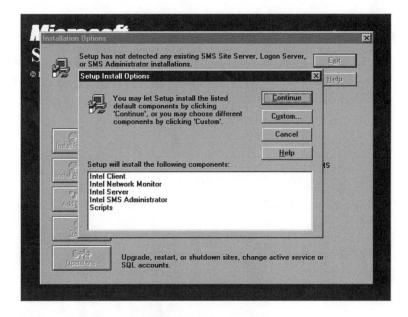

CUSTOM

When choosing to initiate Custom install, you can exclude the installation of software based on your environment. One such option would be the exclusion of the Macintosh clients. No need to install it if Macs do not exist in your environment. In Figure 10.5, the Custom installation options are shown where you can add or remove different items to or from your installation.

Figure 10.5.
The Custom
installation
options in the
SMS Setup.

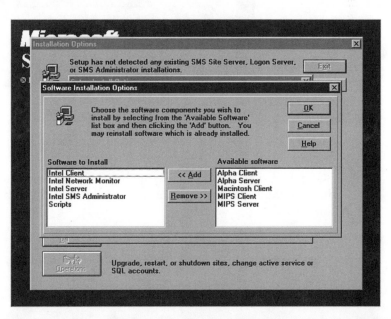

INSTALLING SMS

Several configuration parameters are requested when installing SMS for the first time. These configuration parameters pertain to the Central Primary SMS Site and the SQL Server that SMS is going to use. The dialogs that you will see in the middle of installation are the following:

◆ SQL Database Configuration

◆ Primary Site Configuration Information

SQL DATABASE CONFIGURATION

Using the dialog shown in Figure 10.6, the SQL Server database can be created.

Figure 10.6.
SQL Database
Configuration
dialog.

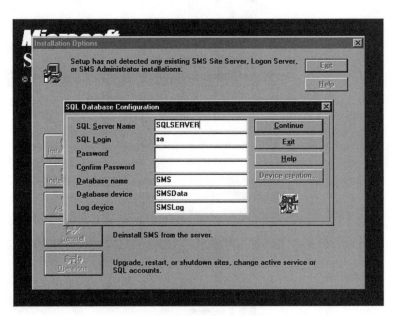

In this dialog, the following information is requested:

SQL Server Name. The name of the server that is running the SQL Server Services and will contain the database data and log devices.

SQL Login. The login account, having the permission to create a database, dump a database, and dump a transaction, which will be used on the SQL Server.

Password. The password for this account.

Confirm Password. The confirmation of the password entered.

Database name. The name of the database to be created on the SQL Server using the database data device below.

Database device. The database data device that you created on the SQL Server to hold the database.

Log device. The database log device that you created for logging database transactions.

Caution

At this point, you may get the error "Not enough SQL connections." If you receive this error, increase the number of SQL Server user connections so SMS can properly connect to SQL Server. Even so, SMS installation can continue and the user connections parameter can be configured afterwards, prior to SMS startup.

PRIMARY SITE CONFIGURATION INFORMATION

Figure 10.7 shows the Primary Site Configuration Information dialog. For the site information, the following is requested, with their definitions:

Site Code. A unique number that identifies the SMS site. This identification is also used in the ID of other processes and operations in the SMS site.

Site Name. A unique name given to the site.

Site Server. The server on which SMS is being installed.

Site Server Domain. The domain in which this site server exists.

Automatically detect all logon servers. SMS will attempt to detect and automatically perform the setup for any logon servers in the environment.

COMPLETING THE INSTALLATION

At this point, there are three steps remaining in order to complete the SMS installation:

◆ File installation

◆ SQL database creation

◆ System initialization

Figure 10.7.
The Primary Site
Configuration
Information
dialog.

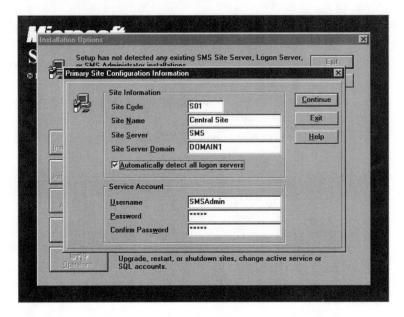

During the installation, both file installation and SQL database creation will occur at the same time. Once these steps have completed, the system initialization step begins, which installs and starts the SMS services. In Figure 10.8, the program group for SMS is shown. Note that several different program items have been installed in your SMS group. These program items are the following:

SMS Administrator. Main administrative program for setup, viewing, and maintenance of the SMS site.

SMS Network Monitor. Network trace (sniffer) program for analyzation of the network.

SMS Security Manager. Security management of the SMS database.

SMS Service Manager. This allows the administrator to view and manage (stop, start, and debug) the services that are used by SMS.

SMS MIF Form Generator. A tool to set up custom data forms.

SMS Setup. Used to re-initiate SMS setup and modify setup parameters or remove the site server.

SMS Books Online. All of the SMS online documentation is available here.

SMS Release Notes. Gives some last-minute information about the SMS product (from Microsoft) for the administrator.

SMS Database Manager. Also referred to as DBCLEAN, this program will help the SMS administrator clean up old, unused, or duplicate data in the database.

SMS Sender Manager. Program for managing or controlling the way the senders operate.

SMS SQL View Generator. Used to create specific SQL views on the SMS database, which can be used by ODBC applications.

SMS What's New in 1.2. Covers current changes and updates.

Figure 10.8.
The SMS pro-
gram group in the
Start menu.

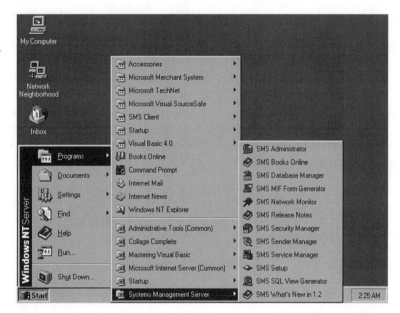

SMS is comprised of several NT services that were installed during setup. You can view these services via the Services icon in the Control Panel. The SMS services are

- ◆ SMS_Hierarchy_Manager
- ◆ SMS_Site_Config_Manager
- ◆ SMS_EXECUTIVE
- ◆ SMS_INVENTORY_AGENT_NT
- ◆ SMS_PACKAGE_COMMAND_MANAGER NT
- ◆ SMS_CLIENT_CONFIG_MANAGER
- ◆ SMS_REMOTE_CONTROL_AGENT

Additionally, the following *shares* were created:

- ◆ SMS_SHR—This share represents SMS/Logon.SRV on the site server.
- ◆ SMS_SHRd—This share designates the root of the SMS installation where d represents the drive.

◆ SMS_Site—This share points to the SMS/SITE.SRV/DESPOOLR.BOX/RECEIVE directory, which contains instruction files and packages destined for site delivery.

UPGRADING SITE SERVERS

This section covers the SMS upgrade process and outlines steps for success.

UPGRADE PROCESS

When upgrading to SMS 1.2, the process will differ, depending on whether your current version is 1.0 or 1.1. If you have SMS version 1.0, you need to make sure that you manually shut down the site from the Operations menu and then upgrade your SQL Server from 4.21 to 6.x. Once that has been done, you can reset the site and upgrade as normal. SMS version 1.2 does not support SQL version 4.21a, thus you need to upgrade SQL Server to 6.x prior to upgrading to SMS 1.2.

Note

If you are not using SQL Server 6.x, the suggested upgrade path entails upgrading SQL Server first, then continuing with the SMS upgrade.

The general phases of an SMS upgrade are the following:

◆ Shut down of all the SMS Services
◆ File installation and reconfiguration
◆ System restart

UPGRADE STEPS

When upgrading, you use the standard SMS setup procedure that you used when first installing a site. Prior to actually upgrading the site, make sure that all SMS databases have been properly backed up and that there are no active connections. Active connections could result in an incomplete upgrade, which is what having clean backup will cure.

Additionally, prior to upgrading, verify that all of your secondary sites are up. If your secondary sites are not up, they will not be included in the upgrade process. You can verify they are being upgraded by selecting the site (via the site icon) and noting that its status shows that an upgrade is in process.

In Figure 10.9, the SMS upgrade cycle is shown; this dialog will be shown while the SMS upgrade is in process. The following steps will initiate the upgrade process on your SMS site:

1. Start the SMS setup from the SMS CD.
2. Click Continue.
3. The system will analyze and find that there is a current installation; click Continue.
4. Click Operations in the Installation Options menu.
5. Click Upgrade.
6. You will be asked to confirm the upgrade; click Yes.

*Figure 10.9.
The SMS up-
grade cycle is
shown.*

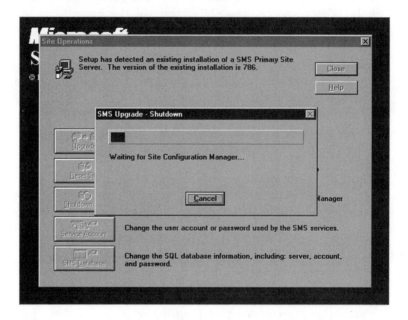

At this point, the three-phase upgrade process will take place starting with the shutdown, followed by file installation, and then the restart of all of the SMS Services. Once this is done, the SMS upgrade will be complete.

UPGRADING THE CLIENTS

If, for some reason, you update your clients with a different operating system, you will also need to upgrade the SMS client software. To do this, you need to connect to the SMS_SHR and run the appropriate upgrade command file for the client operating system. This will then update your SMS client with the proper files for the new OS. This is necessary because the previous SMS client components are not going to operate properly under the new operating system.

SMS SECURITY IN THE SMS SECURITY MANAGER PROGRAM

SMS security encompasses Windows NT , SQL Server, and the SMS Site Server. NT security is relevant as it is the underlying operating system for SQL Server and SMS. SQL Server, in turn, facilitates a secure SMS database.

In general, an administrator should take advantage of all security avenues available. With respect to the SMS database, the inventory and software information should be secured so not just anyone can access this organizational data. You should set up SMS user security based on the *role* of each person involved in the maintenance of the SMS environment. There are several roles in the SMS environment, which are discussed in this section. One standard feature of SMS Security is that the use of the SMS Administrator program requires an SQL Server account. This automatically provides an internal level of security.

SETTING UP ACCOUNTS IN SMS

The SMS Security Manager is used to set up accounts in SMS. This is independent of the related SQL Server database security that may also need to be provided. Much of that is done in the SQL Security Manager, which is discussed later in this section. Figure 10.10 shows the SMS Security Manager. SMS Security is comprised of the following:

◆ Security objects
◆ User rights

These classify the level of security of a person who has a role in the SMS environment. The security objects in the SMS Security Manager include

◆ Alerts
◆ Architecture
◆ Diagnostics
◆ Events
◆ Help Desk
◆ Jobs
◆ Machine groups

- ◆ Network monitor
- ◆ Packages
- ◆ Program groups
- ◆ Queries
- ◆ Site groups
- ◆ Sites

Figure 10.10.
The SMS Secu-
rity Manager.

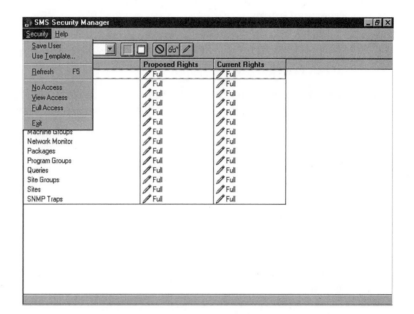

10

PRIMARY SITE SERVERS

This should look familiar to you as these objects are on the toolbar in the SMS Administrator. You can restrict access to these objects by defining what are called user rights. There are three levels of rights that can be applied to the security objects for a user:

- ◆ No access. The user has no access to the specific object.
- ◆ View access. User can view the specific object information but cannot modify it.
- ◆ Full access. The user has complete control of the specific object.

Default combinations of security objects and user rights have already been created with the templates SMS provides. These templates simplify security for the SMS administrator by categorizing specific roles, and assigning default rights based on these roles. The following templates are provided in the SMS Security Manager:

- ◆ Asset Manager. Allows view rights for Architecture, Events, Packages, Sites, and SNMP traps, with full rights to Queries
- ◆ Job Manager. Allows view rights to Architecture, Events, Machine Groups, Site Groups, SNMP traps, and full rights to Jobs and Queries
- ◆ Network Monitor. Allows view rights to Architecture, Sites, and SNMP traps, with full rights to the Network Monitor
- ◆ Software Manager. Allows no view rights but full rights to Packages in Program Groups
- ◆ Text Support. Allows view rights to Architecture, Events, Site Groups, Sites, and SNMP traps, with full rights to Alerts, Diagnostics, Help Desk, and Queries

With these roles, you can automatically assign rights to users on the SMS Security Manager to allow them to use the SMS Administrator to view or modify an object at their discretion.

ASSIGNING RIGHTS

To assign rights, you use the SMS Security Manager as follows:

1. Start the SMS Security Manager.
2. When the SMS Security Manager login appears, log in with the appropriate information and click OK.
3. Choose the user you would like to modify in the top left corner of the screen.
4. Set the rights for the user either individually or as a template. To do it individually, use the Security menu and choose the rights you want to grant. Using the template, make sure you choose Use Template on the Security menu. Figure 10.10 shows the Security menu in the SMS Security Manager.
5. Choose Save User on the Security menu.

Once this is done, you have set the rights for that user. Note that you must save (Save User) your changes for them to take effect.

SETTING UP A LOGIN FOR A SITE

A login for a site is set up in the SQL Security Manager, which is used for defining database (SQL Server) security. In the SQL Security Manager, you will basically assign access rights for the SMS database and its tables. If no access is given, one will not be able to run the SMS Administrator or the SMS Database Manager. Over time, this procedure should be tasked out so that SMS database security is done by the same person or group—all the time. This may end up being the general SQL Server administration group in your organization.

Many organizations do not set a password on the sa account for the SQL Server. It is important that for any of the SQL Server accounts that you are going to use, you do set a password. You also have the option of running what is called integrated or mixed security, which allows you to use the Windows NT Security Account Manager to provide security for the SQL Server. When you install SQL Server, the administrator's groups automatically give the administrator rights to the SQL Server. If your organization is small, it is generally OK to leave it this way; however larger organizations normally have a separate group that will actually be doing the SQL management, and they are not generally a part of the NT Server Administrators group. Also, be aware that if the SQL Server and SMS server exist in separate domains, the same accounts should reside in both domains, thus allowing logon validation onto SQL Server.

LOGGING INTO THE SITE

To log into the site, you will be required to supply a user ID and password that have been set up in the SQL Security Manager. After validation, the SMS Administration program will start and you will be able to administer SMS as defined by your user rights specified in the SMS Security Manager. (See Figure 10.11.)

Figure 10.11.
The login for the
SMS Administra-
tor.

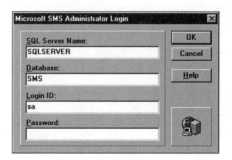

SMS ADMINISTRATOR PROGRAM

In Figure 10.12, the SMS Administrator program is shown. There are several objects in the SMS Administrator that can be opened and viewed. Any of the information that you create or modify within the SMS Administrator is updated in the SMS Database. This, in essence, makes the SMS Administrator program a front-end for the SMS Database on the SQL Server.

Figure 10.12.
The SMS Admin-
istrator with
descriptions.

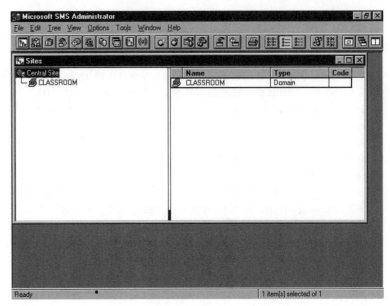

SMS OBJECTS

SMS objects are the components or building blocks that comprise SMS. Again, they are the following:

- ◆ Alerts
- ◆ Events
- ◆ Jobs
- ◆ Machine groups
- ◆ Sites
- ◆ Site groups
- ◆ SNMP traps
- ◆ Queries
- ◆ Program groups
- ◆ Packages

Packages and Jobs are used for software distribution. Alerts, Events, and SNMP traps can provide information on network devices (including PCs) and overall environment stability. Via Machine and Site groups, you can group machines and sites into logical entities for special SMS-related operations. Utilizing Program Groups enables you to do manage-shared applications.

SMS Administrator provides an interface to these operations and to the SMS database itself. When you first open the SMS Administrator, you see a list of the different objects as shown in Figure 10.13, which contains all of the different objects that are accessible in the SMS Administrator.

10

PRIMARY SITE SERVERS

Note

Note that the SMS Administrator only works on Windows NT computers. However, using a third-party application made by Computing Edge, you can run the SMS Administrator on a Windows 95 client. For more information, go to www.ComputingEdge.com or look at Appendix D, "Extending Inventory Collection."

Figure 10.13.
The objects to
choose when the
SMS Administra-
tor is first open.

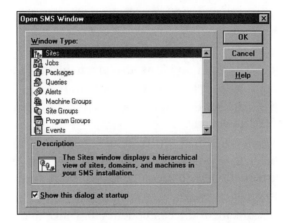

Note

It is suggested that SMS administrators run the SMS Administrator from a client computer instead of running it from the SMS Site Server, which can easily be done by installing the SMS Administrator tools on a non-site server. This is discussed in Chapter 13, "Installation of SMS Clients."

VIEWING AND MODIFYING SITE PROPERTIES

Once a site has been installed, it is time to configure the site. You can view the current configuration of a site and modify whatever configurations need to be made to change how the site operates. There are services that are directly related to viewing and modifying the site. These services facilitate changing the configuration of the site. The services are

◆ SMS_Hierarchy Manager
◆ SMS_Site Configuration Manager

These two services carry out any site modifications made.

SITE PROPERTIES

The SMS site has now been installed, and you want to view information about the site. The Site Properties dialog provides a view of the properties that exist for your site. Figure 10.14 shows the Site Properties dialog. The properties list the basic configuration of the site. Once SMS has been installed, these base configuration details cannot be changed. It is static to the site itself. The following properties are listed in the Site Properties dialog:

Site code. An SMS site has to be identified by a unique ID. This ID is called the site code.

Site name. This is the name of the SMS site that is listed in a site's window. The site name was also given during installation.

Site version. The SMS version (build) number of all the SMS components that are installed on that site. The latest revision is 786 for the final release of SMS version 1.2.

Parent site. If the site has a site above it in the hierarchy, this will be listed under parent site. All of the site's inventory will then be reported to the parent site and jobs can be moved down to this site from the parent site.

Site server. The computer that actually is the primary site server that contains all of the components for SMS, manages the entire site, and is the final collection point for inventory and instructions.

Site server domain. Domain of the site server. A suggestion is to put this into a separate domain outside of the domain that your user exists in, as described in Chapter 24.

Install directory. The path where the SMS installation files have been installed. It is the root directory of SMS on the site server.

Last report at (GMT). The actual time that the Site Configuration Manager has sent the configuration and structure to the site control file to be updated.

Last report at (LOCAL). The local time that this update has been made to the site control file by the Site Configuration Manager.

Inactive domains. The recorded number of SMS domains that could not be verified the last time the monitoring occurred.

Inactive servers. The number of logon servers that could not be verified at the last monitoring interval that occurred.

Inactive components. At the last monitoring interval, the SMS services and components that were not running or could not be started.

Inactive senders. The number of senders that were not running or could not be started when the last monitoring interval was run.

With this information under the site properties, you can get a basic idea of how your SMS site is configured and operating.

Figure 10.14.
The Site Proper-
ties dialog.

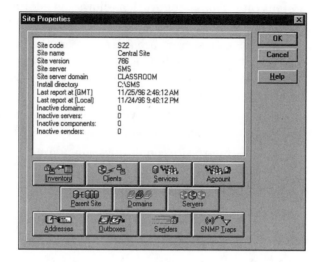

PROPERTY BUTTONS

In the Site Properties dialog, there are also property buttons that you can choose to do different tasks. Via property buttons, an SMS administrator can configure logon server senders, outboxes, clients, and other properties that can change the site's operations. Many of these site properties are discussed throughout the book, but a brief description of each of these property buttons follows.

Inventory. This allows the administrator to select the frequency of inventory and to set the configuration for a slow link when inventory is to be taken.

Clients. The client tools can be chosen here for installation on the clients. If, for some reason, an administrator wants to keep a particular utility from going to the desktop on the clients, he would choose this property button. Also, the option to automatically configure workstation logon scripts is configured here with the option of adding to the bottom or top of the logon script that is to be configured. Other specific options for Windows NT clients can also be chosen here.

Services. Helper Servers can be configured here via the services button. This allows the administrator to offload particular services such as the Inventory Data Loader, Inventory Processor, Scheduler, and Despooler to another Windows NT Server. It also allows the response time for the SMS Site Server to be configured.

Account. This allows the SMS administrator to change the SMS Services account for the SMS site.

Parent Site. This configuration allows the administrator to specify whether a parent site exists for this site or if it is a standalone site.

Domains. Logon servers are selected from the Domains property button. You have two options: to use all detected logon servers or to choose Specify Servers and manually enter them. One can select the type of server: NetWare, LAN Manager, or Windows NT.

Servers. This button allows you to set up a distribution server. This will require you to specify a default package server for this site.

Addresses. Site-to-site communication addresses (for senders) are set up via this button.

Outboxes. Outbox configuration details.

Senders. The configuration for the type of senders used in site-to-site communication. These include RAS, SNA, or LAN senders. By default, a LAN sender is installed.

SNMP Traps. SNMP trap management.

MAKING A PROPOSED PROPERTY CHANGE

Upon the selection of one of these property buttons, you see two radio buttons to choose from in the resulting dialog. One is the Current Properties, which shows the current properties that have already been designated, so the administrator's only choice is Proposed Properties. Once Proposed Properties is selected, you will be able to make changes. Once this is done, the two services discussed earlier, the Site Configuration Manager and Hierarchy Manager, will configure the site and apply your changes. These changes are not considered complete until the services finish the task. Their timeframe is based on the response time that is designated in the Services property button under the site configuration. If this property button is set on very fast, it only takes one minute; fast, 5 minutes; medium, 15 minutes; and slow, 30 minutes.

The Hierarchy Manager constantly polls the SMS database to see if any changes have been made. Once it sees that a change has been made, it creates what is called a .CT1 file containing the proposed site changes. The .CT1 file is then handed off to the Site Configuration Manager which performs the update on the master site control file, which is a .CT0 file, and generates a .CT2 file. Thus, while the .CT1 contains the proposed site changes, the .CT2 file is simply the .CT0 master site control file after the changes have been made. This master site control file is, namely, the `SITECTRL.CTO` file that exists in the `SITE.SRV/SITECTRL.BOX` directory. Once the master site control file is updated, the proposed changes become current properties for the site. If you find that the properties have not been changed, you should look in the log file for both of these services to see if any errors occurred.

> ## *Note*
>
> Once you have made a proposed change, you can use Explorer to view the change being made to the master site control file. Another way to see that it has been changed is to look at the time and date on the master site control file. The master site control file size should be somewhere between 6 and 8MB.

10

PRIMARY SITE SERVERS

ADDING DOMAIN DISTRIBUTION AND LOGON SERVERS

These servers work in conjunction with the site server in the management of the SMS site. They retrieve and deliver data to and from the client.

ADDING A LOGON SERVER

The logon server gives the SMS Site Server a means of obtaining a client's inventory and delivering instructions to the client for specific packages that have to be delivered. It works closely with the SMS site using the Maintenance Manager. The vehicle that the logon server uses to interact with the client is the login script, generally the `SMSLS.BAT` or `RUNSMS.BAT`, depending on whether the login script is run automatically or manually. Upon execution, the logon server receives a client's inventory, which is then delivered up to the SMS Site Server and up the hierarchy. You can configure the logon server via the Domains property button under the Site Properties. When configuring a logon server, you are actually setting up an SMS domain reference on the SMS Site Server. A logon server can be Novell NetWare, LAN Manager, or Windows NT. All files for the logon server are stored in the `\LOGON.SRV`; this is initiated by the SMS Site Server. Logon servers are set up via the Domains property button. In Figure 10.15, the Domain Properties dialog is shown; this dialog is displayed using the following steps:

1. Start SMS Administrator.
2. Highlight sites, go to the File menu, and select Properties.
3. Click the Domains property button.

4. Click on Proposed Properties.

5. Select either Use All Detected Servers or Use Specified Servers.

6. Select Use Specified Servers and select the server type.

7. Click OK.

8. Click Yes to update the site.

The SMS Site Server will now install the necessary files onto the logon server specified.

Figure 10.15.
The Domain
Properties dialog.

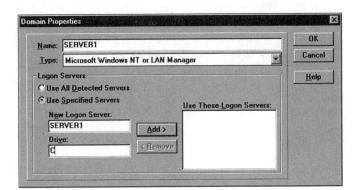

ADDING A DISTRIBUTION SERVER

Another key component is the distribution server. This is used to deliver packages to the client. Generally, you want to select a server that offers enough storage space to store the packages to be delivered. The distribution server creates a share called SMS_PKGE to actually store the packages. Once a package is stored here, a job can be used to deliver the package to a specific client. Because it is going to be delivering packages, the distribution server is the default package server. There can be more than one default package server, but try to span distribution servers wisely across your network. Generally, the number of clients and the location of the clients will define the location and need for a distribution server. Once a package has been delivered, you can choose to delete it or keep it there for future installations.

Installation of a distribution server is very similar to that of a logon server. In Figure 10.16, the Servers property button has been selected to display the Server Properties dialog for the default package server. Here, you can specify what server you want to operate as the default package server. To display this dialog, do the following:

1. Start SMS Administrator.

2. Highlight the site, go to the File menu, and select Properties.

3. Click the Servers property button.

4. Click Proposed Properties.

5. Enter the distribution server and click Add.

6. Click OK.

7. Click OK.

8. Click Yes to update the site.

You have now updated the SMS Site Server and installed and configured a distribution server. When creating a job, you can specify the specific distribution server you want to send the job to or send it to all distribution servers. If sending to all distribution servers, all the distribution servers listed in the Servers dialog under the Site Properties will receive the package.

Figure 10.16.
Configuring the
distribution
server.

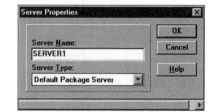

SETTING UP CLIENT INVENTORY COLLECTION

The SMS site is now installed, but the clients haven't been set up to deliver inventory to the SMS site via the logon server. The client can be configured to run the inventory procedures automatically, or the user can execute them manually on the client.

NETWARE SERVERS

If you have Novell NetWare servers, the system login script is updated with what is called the SMSLS.SCR. Then, when a NetWare user logs in, the client information and inventory will be collected and saved on the logon server, which is the Novell NetWare Server. This data will then be sent up to the SMS Site Server.

Note

In the Clients Property dialog, you should select Automatically Configure Workstation Logon Scripts. This will automatically find all of the Novell NetWare servers and configure their logon scripts to make them all logon servers.

WINDOWS NT OR LAN MANAGER

Unfortunately, you have to click Automatically Configure Workstation Logon Scripts and Use All Detected Logon Servers to automatically set these up. If this was not done, there are work-arounds.

The first option is that you can execute RUNSMS.BAT, which exists in the \LOGON.SRV directory. This will initiate a manual client inventory collection, and install when executed for the first time. If you are selecting Automatically Configure Workstation Logon Scripts and Use All Detected Logon Servers, the directory replication service needs to be enabled on these servers to actually propagate the logon scripts. These logon scripts will, of course, include the SMSLS.BAT, which will automatically be configured in the user's profile under his or her logon script. This is because you have chosen to automatically configure the logon script so that all users will automatically install the SMS client and send inventory upon login. Beware of automatically configuring your logon servers as all servers found will be configured. It may make more sense for you to manually choose your logon servers.

Another option for manual collection is to include the RUNSMS.BAT in the AUTOEXEC.BAT or the Startup group of your Windows-based client. In doing this, you can somewhat automate the execution of the SMS client software.

AUTOMATICALLY CONFIGURE WORKSTATION LOGON SCRIPTS

This option allows the administrator to automatically configure all of the user's logon scripts. You can choose where the collection executables install—either at the top or bottom of the logon script.

USING ALL DETECTED LOGON SERVERS

This specifies that all servers in the environment that accept logins will automatically become logon servers. All files are copied from the SMS Site Server to the logon server for setup.

Note

Details on setting up the client and client inventory collection are discussed in Chapter 13, "Installation of SMS Clients," and Chapter 14, "Inventory: Knowledge Is Power." Chapter 13 covers using clients and Chapter 14 covers inventory.

TROUBLESHOOTING THE SMS INSTALLATION AND CONFIGURATION

When you encounter troubles during SMS installation or configuration, it is important to verify the operation of all components: Windows NT Server, SQL Server, and the SMS software. Additionally, verify that SMS setup ran correctly; view the SMSSetup.Log file located in the root directory of the SMS root drive. This log may help you diagnose any problems the SMS setup process may have encountered. The notable areas of failure include the following:

◆ Services

◆ SQL Server communication and configuration

◆ Authentication

◆ Drive considerations

◆ Server configurations

The following section covers problems that may occur relative to the areas in the preceding list.

SERVICES

The Hierarchy Manager may not have properly initialized (will not start). If this happens, verify the following:

◆ The SMS Service account has the proper permissions and can access the SQL Server.

◆ Trust relationships exist if there are multiple domains.

SQL COMMUNICATION AND CONFIGURATION

◆ Device for SMS Database is Not Available.

Verify that the database devices have been created properly using the SQL Enterprise Manager.

◆ Not Enough User Connections for SQL Server.

Increase the user connection limit on SQL Server. For SMS, increase it to around 35. If you have other applications accessing SQL Server, consult with Database Administrator.

10

PRIMARY SITE SERVERS

AUTHENTICATION

Verify that the SMS site service account (userid) created for the SMS services has the Logon As Service right and administrator privileges.

SERVER CONSIDERATIONS

Make sure that the server is a PDC or BDC.

These are general notes that may help an administrator resolve the more common problems or errors encountered during SMS installation.

TROUBLESHOOTING THE SMS CLIENT INSTALLATION

Tip

To view the client installation process, you can set the environment variable, SMS.LS, to equal one. This will enable you to see exactly what is going on during the SMS client installation, step by step.

The most common problems encountered on an SMS client, and their possible solutions, are in the following bulleted list:

◆ SMSLS does not appear to run automatically.

Verify that Automatically Configure Workstation Logon Scripts has been selected. If so, check to see if the scripts were modified.

Make sure you have selected Autodetect Logon Servers.

Make sure you have selected and set up directory replicator service.

Look to make sure that there is a REPL$ share that exists on the primary domain controller.

Check the REPL$/scripts directory to see if the SMS files have been put there; if not, check the event log and the SCMAN.LOG.

◆ Unable to install files on clients.

Make sure that the SMS.INI can be created on the C:\.

Make sure there is enough free space for the client software on the workstation.

SUMMARY

This chapter discussed SMS installation and configuration. It also covered the upgrading of a SMS site, noting the differences between upgrading SMS 1.0 and 1.1. To successfully manage an SMS environment, it is important to understand that SMS is an integration of several software components and many, often disparate, client and server environments. SMS has clear mechanisms for viewing and modifying the information and properties of a site; this functionality emphasizes the SMS Administrator and the security aspects of the SMS Security Manager.

10

PRIMARY SITE SERVERS

CHAPTER 11

Installation of Additional Site Servers

Now that you have created your central primary site, you are ready to add additional sites to the hierarchy as needed. Generally, a company will add sites to the hierarchy due to company growth or the addition of other (physical) geographical locations. Your initial goal is determining what *type* of site server you need to add. You have two options:

◆ Primary site

◆ Secondary site

By definition, when you add sites, you create a site hierarchy. Figure 11.1 shows a typical site hierarchy with both parent and child sites. A site is either a parent or child site; parent sites have sites below them (at least one child site, and possibly more parent sites) in the hierarchy.

Figure 11.1.
Typical site
hierarchy with
both parent and
child.

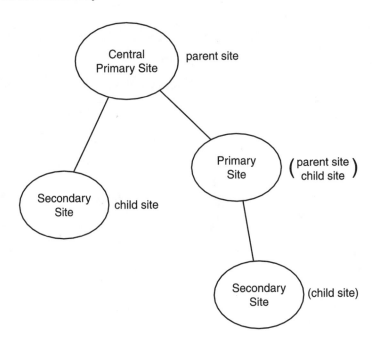

PARENT SITE

A parent site controls its own site and the child sites beneath it, although a parent can also be a child site. The only type of site server that can be a parent site is a primary site. Secondary sites cannot contain child sites. Because a parent site can only be a primary site, a SQL server will always exist at the parent site. Information is forwarded from the child sites to the parent sites by a process called the Site Reporter, which reports information about the sites beneath it in the site hierarchy. A parent site is generally placed where some level of server management can be implemented by a local administrator.

CHILD SITE

A child site exists beneath the parent in the site hierarchy and reports its information up to the parent site. A child site can be a primary or secondary site. If it is a primary site, that site will contain a SQL server. If it is a secondary site, it does not contain a SQL server and generally needs no IS people local to that site. The secondary site simply acts as a primary site "representative," pooling and forwarding its information to the primary site. Figure 11.1 shows the child site in the site hierarchy. If the child site loses its parent, the child site ends up becoming an orphan.

PARENT AND CHILD RELATIONSHIP

Just as a parent and a child have a certain type of relationship in real life, within SMS there is a relationship between child and parent. This relationship is fundamental to the site hierarchy and actually enables SMS to operate the way it does. The relationship requires the child site to send the parent its site information, including its inventory and site configuration file. This site configuration file, which was covered in Chapter 10, "Installing and Upgrading Primary Site Servers," enables the parent site to understand the configuration of its child and correctly deposit the inventory it has for the child into the SMS database. The administrator of the parent site can look at the site configuration for its children and the inventory information of the clients that exist on those child sites. The administrator at the parent site has complete control of the hierarchy at this level.

Lastly, all this information eventually propagates all the way up to the central primary site at the top of the site hierarchy. At each level, on the path to the central primary site, all parent sites will store the information of the sites below it (its child sites).

Caution

It is important to make sure that the parent site's Tempdb database is sized in accordance with the size of the child sites. This should be monitored and adjusted when adding new site installations.

ADDING PRIMARY SITE SERVERS

This section covers how to create an additional primary site. Because it is *additional*, it is automatically going to be a child. It is going to exist under your central primary site server or under another primary site to make it a child site. It may also serve as a parent site. There are several steps in creating an additional primary site.

You do much of this, of course, using the Site Properties dialog, as shown in Figure 11.2. The first step involves the set up and installation of the primary site, stand-alone, via SMS setup. Once this is done, you can then attach it to a parent site, which will be yet another primary site above it. This attachment is implemented via Addresses; you actually address the site above it. This site will then be attached to the parent site (above it), which is the central primary site or another primary site.

Figure 11.2.
Site Properties
dialog.

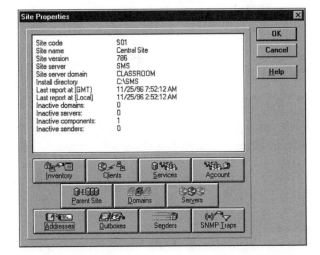

> ## Note
>
> Make sure that you use the same naming convention you use on the parent site. Create a naming convention for your whole SMS environment and stay consistent when installing your additional primary sites.

CONFIGURING ADDRESSES

Configuring addresses is the first step in attaching a primary site to a parent primary site. When doing this, it is important to understand that the primary site that you have just installed to be the child is where you start when configuring the addresses. The address configuration is done in the Site Properties dialog. When you set this address, you have virtually set up a path of communication between the child and parent sites. In order to specify the address, there are three fields required:

◆ Destination site code. The destination site code is the site code of the destination (the other site). You need to set this on both sides so that the site code you input on the parent site is the child site code, and vice versa.

◆ Sender type. The sender type denotes the form of communication (which sender) you will use in communicating between the sites. Both of these designations will be the same on the parent and child sites. You have three options:

> LAN sender
>
> RAS sender
>
> SNA sender

Make sure that you know all three items, or you will not be able to set up the site communication.

◆ SMS service account. The SMS service account exists in the destination site. This is used to authenticate and enable communication between the sites.

Note

If you change the password that you have designated in the address properties, site communication will fail.

RAS SENDER ADDRESS

If you select an RAS sender, a properties dialog prompts you to enter information for RAS communication. (See Figure 11.3.) In this dialog, there are several items required to configure the RAS sender address for proper communication with the other site using RAS site-to-site communication.

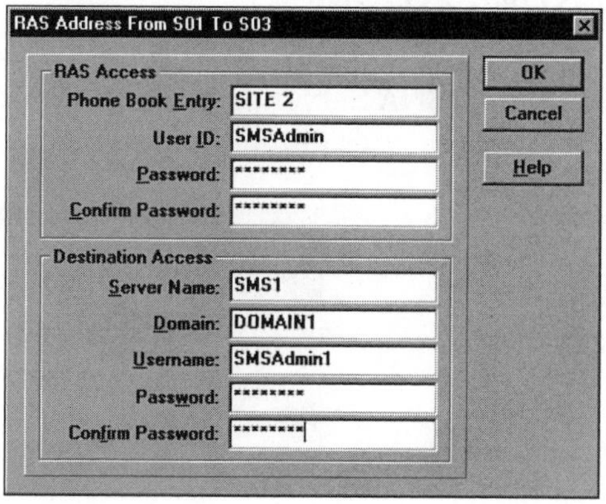

Figure 11.3.
RAS configuration.

The following points describe the settings related to configuring the RAS sender address:

◆ Phone Book Entry. The phone book entry is the description of this connection, which is already provided.

◆ User ID. The user ID is an RAS account that will be authenticated by the RAS server. It is important to make sure that the access permissions exist on the RAS server for this account.

◆ Password (RAS Access). The password for this account.

◆ Confirm Password (RAS Access). Password confirmation.

◆ Server Name. The server name is the destination site server name.

◆ Domain. The domain item is the destination site server's domain name.

◆ User Name. The user name is the name of the account that will be used to access the destination site server. It is important to make sure that this account has full control permissions to the sms_SITE share on the destination site server.

◆ Password (Destination Access). The password for the user name account.

◆ Confirm Password (Destination Access). Password confirmation of the password above.

Note

The Remote Access Service must be set up on both servers.

SNA SENDER ADDRESS

When selecting the SNA sender type in the Address Properties dialog, it is necessary to have set up your SNA Server properly. However, you do have to configure some settings to allow both sites to communicate using·SNA. (See Figure 11.4).

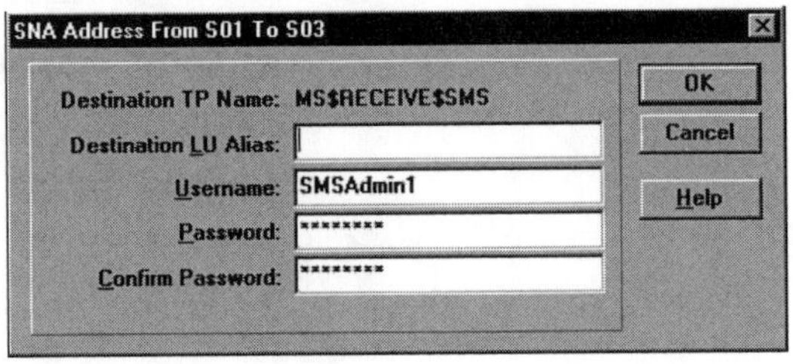

Figure 11.4.
Settings that
must be config-
ured for SNA
senders.

The settings are described in the following list:

◆ Destination LU Alias. The destination LU alias is the LU alias that is defined on the destination site. The LU alias will match a *remote* LU alias defined on the SNA Server in the other site. LU stands for Logical Unit and is relevant in SNA inter-networking. Contact your SNA administrator for help with the setup of this sender.

◆ Username. The username for accessing the destination site. This user must have full control permissions to the sms_SITE share on the destination site server.

◆ Password. The password for this username.

◆ Confirm Password. Password confirmation.

Note

SNA Server should be set up on both servers.

Steps for Configuring an Address

There are steps for configuring an address on both sites. It is important to make sure that, prior to configuring the address, you have both the site code and the SMS service account for both sites with the password. Figure 11.5 shows the Address Properties dialog. This is where you actually configure the address and enable both sites to communicate. Figure 11.6 shows the LAN Address dialog asking for the SMS site services account and destination server. To configure the address, you must do the following:

1. Start SMS Administrator.
2. Highlight the site, go to the File menu, and choose Properties.
3. Click the Address Properties button.
4. Click Proposed Properties.
5. Click Create.
6. Enter the destination site code and sender type, and click Details.
7. Make sure you enter the destination server in the SMS service account with a password and click OK.
8. Click OK.
9. Click OK.
10. Click Yes to update the site.

Figure 11.5.
Address Proper-
ties dialog.

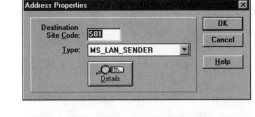

Figure 11.6.
LAN address
service account
and destination
server.

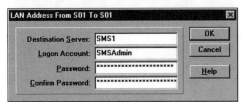

ATTACHING TO THE PARENT SITE

Once you set up the address, you need to attach the child site to the parent site. This is done on the primary site via Site Properties. Figure 11.7 shows the Parent Site dialog, which enables you to attach a child site to a parent site by specifying the site code. After successful attachment to the parent site, the inventory for the child site is forwarded to the parent site and stored in the database. Thus, the parent site administrator can manage the parent site data, in addition to the child site data, because the child site inventory has been uploaded. Once you make the change to attach to the parent site, SMS notifies the hierarchy manager, which subsequently updates the site configuration (file) and begins propagating the child inventory to the parent site.

Figure 11.7.
Parent Site
dialog.

STEPS FOR ATTACHING TO THE PARENT SITE

Here's how you set up the child site to attach to a parent site:

1. Start SMS Administrator.
2. Highlight the site, go to the File menu, and select Properties.
3. Click the Parent Site properties button.

4. Click Proposed.

5. Select Attach to Parent Site.

6. Choose Site Code.

7. Click OK.

8. Click OK.

9. Click Yes to update the site.

You have now set up the child site to report its information to a parent site.

ADDING A SECONDARY SITE

The characteristics of a secondary site are that it can only exist as a child site and it does not contain a SQL Server at its site. It moves all its information about the site hierarchy to the other parent sites. It uses what is called an *agent*. An agent operates at a site, but does not require all the resources of a primary site. This is generally feasible for an environment that has no IS department or does not have the resources for a SQL Server. Another good reason you might want to implement a secondary site is if you have a small site outside of the IS "umbrella" that has a minimum number of clients. Installing a secondary site makes it a lot easier for a small site to gather information and not incur the cost of implementing a full primary site. The secondary site is initiated by the primary site.

For primary-site to primary-site communication, I discussed installing the primary site standalone and then setting up communication. This is not the case with the secondary site. The secondary site is *spawned* off the primary site. When using a primary site, you can spawn a secondary site off to exist between the primary site and a set of clients so that their inventory information can be brought up to the primary site. In this scenario, the primary site is the parent of the secondary site, which is just a child. When installing a secondary site server, you must set up several different configuration settings for that secondary site. These settings give the secondary site some unique properties that do not exist on any other site. It also allows the primary site, which is the parent site, to identify the secondary site and identify the information that is forwarded from the secondary site. Figure 11.8 shows the New Secondary Site dialog, where you can enter the configuration information needed to create a secondary site.

The settings are described in the following list:

◆ Site Code. The site code is the unique three-character code for the new secondary site.

◆ Site Name. The site name is the unique name that you give the new site. This name identifies the secondary site. It is important to make sure that you give it a name that indicates it is a secondary site for clarity.

11

INSTALLATION OF ADDITIONAL SITE SERVERS

◆ Site Server. The site server is the name of the Windows NT Server that you want to be the secondary site server.

◆ Install Directory. The install directory is the directory path to use for installation of the secondary site.

◆ Site Server Domain. The site server domain is the Windows NT domain that is going to contain the secondary site.

◆ Username. The username that will be your SMS site services account, which must have the logon as a service right.

◆ Password. The password for the SMS site services account.

◆ Confirm Password. Password confirmation.

◆ Installation Sender Type. The installation sender type that you will use to install the secondary site server—LAN, RAS, or SNA.

◆ Site Server Platform. The site server platform is the type of processor used on the secondary site. This will assure the correct executables are installed.

Figure 11.8.
New Secondary
Site dialog.

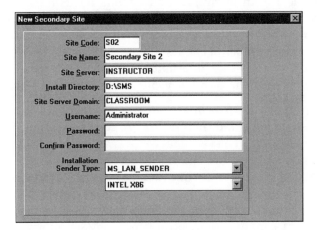

AUTOMATICALLY DETECT LOGON SERVERS

The Automatically Detect Logon Servers option, when selected, will detect and add all logon servers located in the new site. (An internal formula is used to determine if a server is logon server capable.)

Tip

When entering this information, be sure to follow the naming convention you have used elsewhere in your environment. This makes overall site administration easier.

Tip

> Make sure the directory path that you specified for the install directory exists on an NTFS partition. Otherwise, the secondary site server will not install correctly.

Note

> It is important to make sure that you check the secondary site to verify the files have been copied. Also, check the other sites and verify they have not transgressed to retry or fail status.

SECONDARY SITE INSTALLATION PROCESS

The two key services used during secondary site installation are the SMS Hierarchy Manager and the SMS Site Configuration Manager. The following steps detail what automatically occurs to facilitate the setup of the secondary site:

1. First, the Hierarchy Manager checks the database to see whether anything was changed in the site control file. If the Hierarchy Manager notices a change, it then submits a send request to the Scheduler. These sender instructions are then initiated via the Scheduler to start and set up the installation directory on the new secondary site.

2. The Hierarchy Manager also installs a Bootstrap service. This Bootstrap service will actually start the secondary site.

3. The sender then connects to the server that is going to be the secondary site and starts executing the instructions that were requested by the Scheduler.

4. Once the Bootstrap service starts, the Hierarchy Manager at the parent site creates two packages. One is for the SMS site software, and the other is for the site control file. Once there has been a check for enough free disk space and for an NTFS partition, the Bootstrap service starts decompressing these packages onto the SMS secondary site server. It expands and creates the SMS directory structure while copying the files into the structure.

5. The Bootstrap service starts the Site Configuration Manager on the secondary site. Once this happens, the Bootstrap service stops, as its purpose has been fulfilled. The Site Configuration Manager controls events from this point on.

6. The Site Configuration Manager starts installing the secondary site using the site control file that was sent by the Hierarchy Manager. This site control file was generated from the configuration information entered by

the administrator for the secondary site installation. Then, the Site Configuration Manager reports any errors or messages to the Site Reporter, which will forward them to the primary site.

7. The Site Configuration Manager starts all the SMS services on the secondary site. Once these have been started, it creates a .CT2 file, which then updates the database on the primary site to be put into the SQL Server.

The four services that are involved in this process must complete their respective tasks successfully; therefore, it is important to check their log files if you encounter a problem during this installation. The four services follow:

◆ Hierarchy Manager

◆ Site Configuration Manager

◆ Bootstrap service

◆ Scheduler

Using these four services, the secondary site server is installed and can forward its information to the primary site.

SECONDARY SITE INSTALLATION STEPS

Installing the secondary site requires only a few steps. However, there does need to be a constant monitoring, and you must meet some prerequisites to make sure that the secondary site can be installed. You need to check the following things before installing the secondary site:

◆ Windows NT Server 3.51 or later

◆ NTFS partition

◆ At least 50MB of free hard disk space

With these prerequisites met, you are ready to install the secondary site. The following steps allow you to set up a secondary site:

1. Start SMS Administrator.

2. Highlight the site, go to the File menu, and select New.

3. Enter the information needed to set up the secondary site in the options boxes.

4. Click OK.

5. Start looking at the properties of the secondary site to see if the site creation has been initiated.

Now your secondary site is beginning to be installed. You can check the status of the installation of the site by looking at the properties of the secondary site. A status window, as shown in Figure 11.9, will be displayed. As this installation is initiated by system jobs, you can see these jobs in the Jobs window. It is important to watch these jobs and make sure that they have not failed or are not retrying but are continually active and eventually complete. If they have retried or failed, you may have a secondary site installation problem and should verify you have met all of the secondary site prerequisites. The three systems jobs that execute are

◆ Site preinstall
◆ Site install
◆ Site control jobs

Figure 11.9.
Site Properties
dialog showing
secondary site
installation
status.

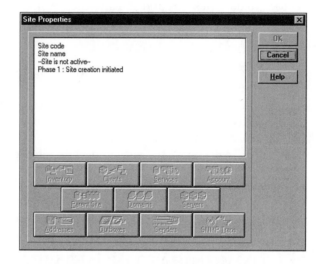

REMOVING A PRIMARY OR SECONDARY SITE

You can thoroughly remove a primary or secondary site. As this process is irreversible, be absolutely sure that you want to remove the site.

REMOVING A PRIMARY SITE

Removing a primary site requires three steps. First, you must remove any of the site hierarchy that exists below the primary site. It is important to also detach any primary sites that are children. You can do this in the Site Properties dialog by modifying them to be standalone sites via the Parent Sites button.

Second, begin removing your site clients. To do this, you want the SMS clients to attach to the SMS_SHR that exists on the logon server and run the Deinstall program. If you do not do this, the SMS client remains on the workstations and you will have no primary site to then deinstall the SMS client. This will necessitate manual intervention and become very messy.

Finally, after you remove the site clients, you can remove the site itself via SMS setup. When you run SMS setup, you are given an option to deinstall the site. The deinstall removes the services and directories from your server. To deinstall, you must perform the following steps:

1. Start SMS setup from the SMS CD-ROM.
2. Click Continue.
3. Click Deinstall on the Installation Options menu.
4. You are then asked to drop the database and log devices, which you can choose to do. Click OK and the site then deinstalls.

Removing a Secondary Site

Removing a secondary site is easier. As when you installed the secondary site, a Bootstrap service is started, which then initiates the deletion of that site. It also removes all the server files on all the logon and distribution servers of the site, although it won't remove the client files or any packages installed on the client. To do this, you will need to execute the deinstall on the client, prior to deinstalling the secondary site. To deinstall the secondary site, do the following:

1. Start SMS Administrator.
2. Go to the Sites window and highlight the secondary site.
3. Go to the Edit menu and select Delete. This then deletes the secondary site.

SMS Communication Between Sites

The key components that enable two SMS sites to communicate are

◆ Addresses
◆ Sender
◆ Outbox

Configuring addresses was discussed earlier in this chapter. This section covers senders, outboxes, and the different operations in which they are involved. The majority of activity involving senders and outboxes is based on jobs initiated by the Scheduler.

Sender

The sender is used to transfer information from a site outbox to the site that is addressed. The sender operates just like a copy program in that it just copies information from one site to another. There are three types of senders:

- ◆ LAN sender
- ◆ RAS sender
- ◆ SNA sender

The RAS sender and SNA sender require additional software to run.

LAN SENDER

The LAN sender is generally used on a local area network or wide area network. The LAN sender is automatically installed by default when you install the site. When using the LAN sender, you have a choice of three protocols:

- ◆ NetBEUI
- ◆ TCP/IP
- ◆ IPX/SPX

These three protocols can be used to transfer data via the LAN sender. The LAN sender can be used for LAN or WAN traffic.

RAS SENDER

Windows NT includes the Remote Access Service right out of the box. Used for dial-up connections, RAS supports three methods of transportation:

- ◆ ASYNC
- ◆ ISDN
- ◆ X.25

Use of RAS requires the Remote Access Service to be running in the environment. If your network or site server is overloaded, you may want to consider offloading the Remote Access Service to a server that is independent of the SMS site server.

SNA SENDER

Most organizations that already have SNA Server in use take advantage of the SNA sender. It uses the Microsoft SNA Server Advanced Program-to-Program Communication (APPC, another SNA term) to facilitate communication between the two sites. There are two flavors of SNA senders:

- ◆ Batch
- ◆ Interactive

As with the RAS Server, you might want to assign SNA Server to a server other than your SMS site server. In larger SNA sites, this is probably already the case to begin with.

SENDER'S TASKS

Sender communication is covered in Chapter 24, "Optimizing SMS Performance." This section discusses the three functions of the sender:

◆ Monitoring the outbox

◆ Moving data to the destination site

◆ Notifying the Scheduler of its status

These three functions comprise the sender's responsibilities. When monitoring an outbox, the sender looks for .SRQ (Send ReQuest) files that are placed in the outbox by the Scheduler. The presence of .SRQ files signifies to the sender that there is information to be sent. The .SRQ files contain instructions for sending the package and despooler information to the destination site.

Note

Monitoring the outbox allows the sender to automatically start a job that has been scheduled via the Scheduler. Conversely, a sender can also be manually scheduled and configured for a particular package. Sender configuration is discussed in more depth in Chapter 24.

If part of this process fails, the sender will retry the request. Once the sender starts to process the request, it renames the .SRQ file to .SRS, which indicates that the send is progressing. If any errors happen in the middle of transmittal, the .SRS file posts the error, which the scheduler notes and thus realizes that there has been an error in sending the package.

Once the entire file is sent, the sender has then completed the operation, and a complete status is given to the .SRS file. Once the scheduler sees this complete status, it then deletes the .SRS file.

SENDER STATUS FILE

Once the .SRQ file is renamed to an .SRS file, you are able to view it. To view it, you will need DUMPSEND.EXE, which is on the SMS CD-ROM in the /Support/DeBug/Platform directory. This file contains a lot of information on how the job was sent to the other site. It is important to view this file if you feel that the job was not sent correctly to the other site. If the .SRS file was deleted, then the request obviously completed successfully.

MULTIPLE SENDERS

A good way to augment fault tolerance and performance is to utilize multiple senders. Adding multiple senders provides fault tolerance, in that if one sender is not working correctly, the other sender can be used. It also increases performance by load balancing between senders. If you use a sender that is LAN-based over a wide area network, it is suggested that you create an RAS sender using ASYNC to back up the LAN sender in the event of a problem.

ADD THE SENDER

When adding a sender, you should verify that communication to the target site is already in place. In Figure 11.10, the Senders dialog shows you a list of the senders that have been installed. In Figure 11.11, the Sender Properties dialog depicts what sender type you are installing on what server and what drive. It is important to understand that you can install a sender on a separate server. If you choose to run RAS or SNA on a separate server, you will want to install the sender on that same server. Sometimes it is advantageous to offload the sender tasks to another machine so your SMS site server does not handle the additional overhead of those operations. To add a sender, do the following:

1. Start SMS Administrator.
2. Highlight the site, go to the File menu, and click Properties.
3. Click the Sender Properties button.
4. Select Proposed Properties.
5. Click Create.
6. Enter the server and the location where you want the sender installed.
7. If this is an SNA sender, select Batch or Interactive, click Details, and enter the sender LU alias.
8. Click OK.
9. Click OK.
10. Click OK.
11. Click Yes to update the site.

You can now communicate with the other site. To configure how the sender will operate, you can use the Sender Manager tool. This is discussed in Chapter 24.

11

INSTALLATION OF ADDITIONAL SITE SERVERS

Figure 11.10.
The Senders
dialog showing
what senders
have been
installed.

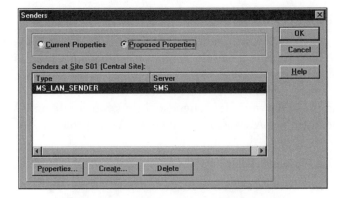

Figure 11.11.
The Sender
Properties dialog.

OUTBOX

The outbox is where information is put by the Scheduler to be picked up by the sender, which will then send it to the site and deliver it to the inbox. The two outbox configurations are

◆ Priority

◆ Backup

You can set priorities for the jobs being sent by configuring multiple outboxes with different priorities. Based on the outbox priority and which outbox receives the job, one can dictate the overall priority of many jobs. The Scheduler recognizes outbox priorities and takes this into consideration.

The backup outbox is simply a second outbox in case the default outbox fails. For example, an outbox has no jobs sent or serviced for three days. The Scheduler can load those jobs into another outbox that is set up for backup jobs. If an outbox has not been set up for backup, the Scheduler leaves the job in the Site.SRV/Schedule.BOX until an outbox is available.

The outbox is just a directory that holds the package instructions and sends request files for the senders. It is a "buffer" used by the Scheduler and sender.

CONFIGURING THE OUTBOX

To configure the outbox, you perform the same steps as when you configured the sender and the addresses using the Site Properties:

1. Start SMS Administrator.
2. Highlight the site, go to the File menu, and select Properties.
3. Click the Outbox properties button.
4. Click Proposed Properties.
5. Select the outbox you want to configure and click Properties.
6. Click Schedule.
7. Select the outbox configuration and click OK.
8. Click OK.
9. Click OK.
10. Click Yes to update the site.

SHUTTING DOWN AND RESETTING SITES

Shutting down and resetting a site is generally done when an administrator wants to perform a backup of the SMS database. Before you perform the backup, make sure that you shut down the site. When the backup is complete, you will need to reset the site. These procedures are initiated via the Operations menu that is available in the Installation Options menu.

Shutdown, and a subsequent reset, are also necessary if you plan on upgrading SMS or SQL Server. In Figure 11.12, the Site Operations dialog shows the shutdown of the site.

SHUTTING DOWN THE SITE

When you shut down the site, it stops all services on the SMS site. It also updates the site control file with the current date and time information. Figure 11.12 shows the Site Operations dialog. The second and third buttons perform an SMS site reset and shutdown, respectively. Once these services are shut down, you can backup the SMS database via the SQL Enterprise Manager. To shut down the site, you must do the following:

1. Start the SMS setup program from the SMS CD-ROM.
2. Click Continue.
3. Click Continue.

4. On the Installation Options menu, click Operations.

5. The Operations menu appears (see Figure 11.12); click Shutdown Site.

6. Click OK when the site has been shut down. (See Figure 11.13.)

Figure 11.12.
Site Operations
dialog showing
shutdown of a
site.

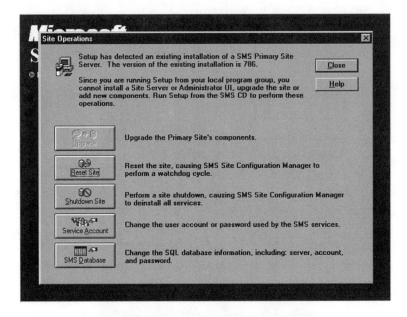

Figure 11.13.
Site shutdown.

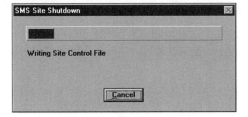

RESETTING A SITE

Once you have shut down a site and completed your operations, you can reset the site. Resetting a site actually restarts the SMS services, which forces the Site Configuration Manager to perform what is called the *watchdog cycle*. This cycle shuts down the Site Configuration Manager and then reinstalls the site services. Once it has done this, it writes any changes it made to the site control file. Figure 11.14 shows the SMS System Reset resetting a site.

Also verified at this time are any outstanding requests that may have been waiting to be serviced while the SMS site was shut down. Resetting the site generally takes a little bit longer than shutting down, due to process/service startup and the outstanding requests search. To reset a site, do the following:

1. Start the SMS Setup from the SMS CD-ROM.
2. Click Continue.
3. Click Continue.
4. From the Installation Options menu, click Operations.
5. From the Operations menu, click Reset Site.
6. Click OK after the site has been reset.

Figure 11.14.
SMS System
Reset.

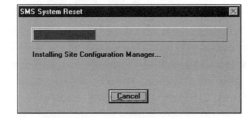

MOVING SITES

Moving a site is extremely easy. For a primary site, you simply detach and then reattach it to another primary site. For a secondary site, you just have to remove the components from the current site and reinstall them in another primary site.

SYNCHRONIZING TIME AND TIME ZONE CONSIDERATIONS

It is very important to make sure that your SQL server time and your SMS site server time are synchronized. When the times are not synchronized, jobs that are created do not finish because the SQL server time and the SMS server time do not match. Most of the problems that you will encounter with jobs are generally time synchronization issues. One also needs to consider time zones, although this is dependent on your Windows NT network more than SMS itself. You want to make sure that your Windows NT network servers have correct time and time zone settings. To synchronize the time on an SMS site server with the SQL server, type the following in a Command window:

```
net time \\computername \set /y
```

Using this command, you can synchronize one server's time with another. It is also important to assure that the site's client PCs are synchronized with the SMS site server.

SITE HIERARCHY

When managing the site hierarchy, it is important to follow several rules. The key is to understand how the site hierarchy works.

SMS can use two types of site servers: a primary site server and a secondary site server. These two site servers help manage and facilitate all the clients in the site by pooling inventory and allowing software distribution to be pushed to these computers. The design of SMS is based on a hierarchy.

If a site exists above another site and it supports that site, it is called the parent site. The site below it is the child. The child site is responsible for moving information about its clients to the parent site. The first question to ask about your site is does it have an administrator and does it have the resources to have a SQL Server? If so, you can generally put a primary site at this site. Thus, you install the primary site and then attach it to another primary site, which ends up becoming its parent. Once this parent is established, the child site, which is also a primary site, moves information up the hierarchy, using the Site Reporter, to the parent primary site. The parent primary site stores this information in the SMS database, so any site that is a parent site contains its own database and that of the sites below it.

A child site can be either a primary or secondary site. If it is a secondary site, it is generally because you do not have an administrator in that site or do not have the resources for a SQL Server. If this is the case, you spawn off a secondary site from a primary site by installing it from the primary site. Once this secondary site becomes a child site, it then moves the inventory information to the primary site. The secondary site does not have a local SQL Server for an administrator to be able to look at its information locally. All the information about its site must be viewed from the parent site.

One key thing to think about when setting up your site hierarchy is determining the resources in each of your geographical locations. When speaking of resources, I mean hardware and software. The other concern, of course, is human resources; how many administrators are in that site and how many of them are going to be active in the SMS environment?

NETWORK LINK CONNECTION CONSIDERATIONS

When connecting sites, it is important to understand that a certain amount of network bandwidth is required for letting these sites communicate. This is part of managing the site hierarchy. Sometimes, an administrator must get a status report of what percentage of the bandwidth is left for SMS to operate. One suggestion for an administrator who worries about network bandwidth within his or her site hierarchy is to make sure that most of the processes, such as job delivery and inventory collection, run at night. This frees up the network during the day when other operations take place.

If you set up two sites, try to get a 56KB per second line or faster. It is possible to use RAS connections with regular modems to connect two sites as a redundant line. However, such a connection should not be the primary connection between two sites because a 28KB per second connection is not fast enough to send jobs and bring inventory on a constant basis. If you have a large amount of inventory and jobs to be sent at night, it might take a lot longer than the time allotted. It is important to understand the current status of your network bandwidth and its overall potential. This can give you some insight into how you need to set up your site.

STORAGE SPACE CONSIDERATIONS

When managing the site hierarchy, a key point that people generally do not understand or consider is that the parent site needs to have more storage space than generally required because the child sites will bring their information to the parent site. Make sure you take into consideration not only the clients that exist at your own site, but also the clients that exist beneath you, because they are going to take the same amount of space as if they were in your own site. This is discussed more thoroughly in Chapter 24.

SERVER PROCESSES

If you find that more than one of the server processes have a problem running on the same server, it may be time to offload some of these processes. Fortunately, SMS gives you the ability to do this. SMS lets you create what is called a helper server, which allows you to move some of the services from other servers. This becomes very important for parent sites because they not only have to process their own information, but also the information of their child sites. Moving server processes to other servers can only help your SMS environment and never hurt it.

SUMMARY

When considering additional site servers, primary or secondary, you need to view your SMS environment as a whole. Pay particular attention to the site hierarchy and what it actually provides. Once you create these additional sites, you are basically creating agents and other locations for your SMS central primary site server to represent itself so that information can be brought for your central IS department to manage. It also gives you the flexibility to have local IS departments operate and manage their own environments with no interference from the central IS department at the top of the hierarchy. SMS also includes a mechanism for creating an agent called the secondary site, that actually represents the primary site without any human interaction at all. The secondary site is good for small sites or sites with little or no resources. It is important to take advantage of the flexibility SMS offers, by personalizing it to match your own site hierarchy.

CHAPTER 12

Installing Server Tools

The tools for SMS are installed by default on the site server that you set up for your SMS site. Systems administrators do not generally run and administer their SMS sites from their SMS site servers. It is more common to administer the SMS sites from Windows NT workstations. This machine is generally the SMS administrator's computer that is located at his or her desk. As an SMS administrator, your machine must be capable of installing the server tools needed for SMS. If you have a Windows NT machine, it is relatively easy to install the server tools. If you have a Windows 95 machine, you must use a third-party tool. The two server tools I discuss that are Microsoft-specific are the SMS Administrator and the Network Monitor. This chapter describes how you can install the SMS Administrator on a Windows NT machine.

The other product that I discuss is the Network Monitor. The Network Monitor gives you the ability to monitor statistics about the network on which your SMS site runs, as well as any other Microsoft environment, for that matter. The Network Monitor, which is supplied with SMS, can run on both Windows NT Server and Windows NT Workstation machines.

INSTALLING THE SMS ADMINISTRATOR ON WINDOWS NT

As mentioned previously, you should generally install the SMS Administrator on a Windows NT workstation. By default, the SMS Administrator is installed automatically with the administrative utilities. The SMS Administrator in SMS version 1.1 has limited capabilities, compared to SMS version 1.2. Many of the administrative utilities that you had to run separately in SMS version 1.1 are integrated in SMS version 1.2's SMS Administrator. These tools include

◆ SMS Database Manager

◆ SMS Sender Manager

◆ SMS Security Manager

◆ SMS Service Manager

Figure 12.1 shows that the Tools menu in the Microsoft SMS Administrator on SMS version 1.2 lists these managers. Also included under the Tools menu are the following Windows NT administrative tools:

◆ Windows NT Event Viewer

◆ Windows NT Server Manager

◆ Windows NT User Manager

◆ Windows NT Performance Monitor

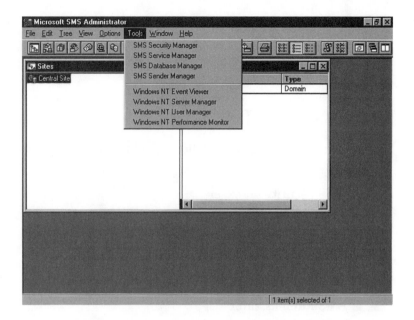

Figure 12.1.
The SMS
Administrator's
Tools menu
showing the
integrated tools.

SMS version 1.1 does not install these Windows NT administrative options with the SMS Administrator. You must run these administrative tools from the administrative tools program group, and you must run the SMS database and sender managers from their executables. With SMS version 1.1, the SMS security and service managers are also icons in the SMS program group.

What Is the SMS Administrator?

The SMS Administrator is an application that acts as a front end to the SQL Server database. It provides the SMS administrator with a more user-friendly interface for viewing and administering the SMS database on the SQL Server.

Requirements

For Windows NT machines, the following list outlines the requirements for running SMS version 1.2 on a non-site server or for installing the SMS Administrator:

◆ Machine running Windows NT 3.51 operating system or later

◆ Service Pack 3 or later (Service Pack 4 recommended)

◆ 50MB of free disk space (70MB recommended)

> *Note*
>
> You do not have to install the SMS Administrator tools on an NT
> server. They can also be installed on an NT workstation.

WHAT GETS INSTALLED

SMS version 1.1 installs the following administrative tools:

- ◆ SMS Administrator
- ◆ SMS Security Manager
- ◆ SMS Network Monitor (optional)
- ◆ SMS MIF Form Generator
- ◆ SMS Help

SMS version 1.2 installs the following administrative tools:

- ◆ SMS Administrator
- ◆ SMS Security Manager
- ◆ SMS Service Manager
- ◆ SMS Database Manager
- ◆ SMS Sender Manager
- ◆ SMS MIF Form Generator
- ◆ SMS SQL View Generator
- ◆ SMS Setup
- ◆ SMS Books Online
- ◆ SMS Release Notes

SMS ADMINISTRATION PROGRAM GROUP

Now you know the different programs that both versions of SMS install. Figure 12.2
shows the Program menu for SMS version 1.2.

Figure 12.2.
The Program
menu for SMS
version 1.2 after
installing the
administrative
tools.

INSTALLATION OF SMS ADMINISTRATIVE TOOLS

You install the administrative tools for the SMS with the same steps you use when installing a primary site server, but you do choose different options. When installing the SMS installation tools, use an account with administrator privileges on the computer; you must have administrator privileges on the site server's domain. Install the administrative tools on a non-site server for an SMS version 1.1 or 1.2 site by following these instructions:

1. Make sure the machine that you are using has Windows NT 3.51 or later.
2. Insert the SMS CD-ROM and switch to the CD-ROM drive.
3. Go to the \SMSSETUP directory.
4. Select the directory for the processor type of the machine you are using.
5. Run SETUP.EXE.
6. Click Continue in the dialog box.
7. Fill in the information in the registration dialog box, including your name, your organization's name, and your product identification number. Then, click Continue.
8. Select Install Admin Tools.
9. Enter the path where you want the SMS Administrator to be installed on your Windows NT computer. If the directory exists, Setup installs the SMS Administrator files into the directory. If it does not exist, SMS creates the directory for you.

12

10. Click Continue.

11. The default components for the admin tools are listed in the dialog box. To select components other than the defaults, you can click the Custom button. Otherwise, click Continue to install the default components.

12. If you click Custom, select the components you want and then click OK.

13. You see a list of all the items that will be installed. Click Continue.

14. A message states that the SMS installation is complete. Click OK.

In Windows NT 3.51, the program items for the SMS Administrator and administrative utilities appear in your SMS program group. In Windows NT version 4.0, you see the program items under the SMS Program menu.

Caution

If you install the SMS Administrator on a machine that is also part of a secondary site server, helper server, logon server, or distribution server, you should set up the administrative tools in a different directory. Otherwise, you could experience problems with your existing SMS site.

When installing the SMS installation tools, make sure that you use an account with administrator privileges on the computer and that you also have administrator privileges on the site server's domain.

Installing the SMS administrative tools on a Windows 95 machine requires a program called Administrator +Plus from ComputingEdge, which is discussed in Appendix C, "Third-Party Integration—Making the Job Easier."

THE NETWORK MONITOR

The Network Monitor gives you the ability to monitor information and detect problems on networks that are either LAN-based or WAN-based. It allows you to capture and display information about the components on your network.

There are actually two sources for Network Monitor: the Network Monitor tools provided with Windows NT version 4.0, and the Network Monitor tool provided with SMS. The network monitor tool that comes with SMS has more protocol parsers and is a more robust product. The Network Monitor with Windows NT only allows you to look at network traffic coming in and going out on a local computer. It does not allow you to analyze traffic between other computers on the network. I discuss the Network Monitor from the SMS CD-ROM, which offers the capability to monitor specific clients listed in the SMS Administrator while you view the properties of the computer. You can monitor specific traffic on a selected computer, but you must first make sure the NT machine is running the Network Monitor agent. Figure 12.3 shows how you install the Network Monitor from the Services tab of the Network applet in the Control Panel:

1. Click the Start Menu.
2. Select the Settings menu.
3. Click the Control Panel.
4. Double-click Network.
5. Click the Services tab.
6. Click Add.
7. Select Network Monitor Agent.
8. Click OK.
9. Enter the path of the Windows NT files.
10. Click Continue.
11. Click OK.

Figure 12.3.
The Select
Network Service
dialog box for
installing the
Network Monitor.

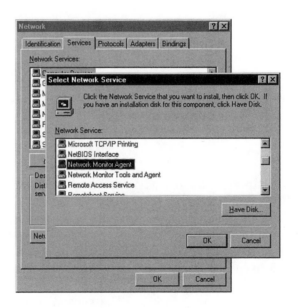

INSTALLING NETWORK MONITOR

To install the Network Monitor, you can perform the same operation that you used to install the administrative tools. You must choose the Network Monitor when you select the administrative tools. Setup then installs the Network Monitor on the machine. It is important that you choose the SMS Network Monitor if you have a choice between the Windows NT Network Monitor and the SMS Network Monitor. If you are going to use both, it is important to install the Windows NT Network Monitor before installing the SMS Network Monitor.

SPECIAL CONSIDERATION

When working on a computer with a monolithic NDIS 4.0 driver, you might discover that you capture only one-way network traffic instead of two-way network traffic. There is a workaround for this situation. The fix requires that you change the system Registry:

1. Start the Registry Editor (REGEDT32.EXE).
2. Go to HKEY_Local_Machine/SYSTEM/CurrentControlSet/ Services/bh/Linkage.
3. Note the value for bind and write down the string after device.
4. Go to HKEY_Local_Machine/SYSTEMS/CurrentControlSet/Services/ bh/Parameters.
5. Go to the Edit menu and click Add Key. Select the key name field and type **ForcePmode.**
6. Go to the Edit menu and click Add Value. Select the value name field and type **the value written down earlier.**
7. Select the data type field REG_DWORD and then select the data field and type the numeral 1.
8. Select OK.
9. Exit the Registry Editor.

SUMMARY

In this chapter, you learned how to install the administrative tools, which include the SMS Administrator and additional administration utilities for both SMS version 1.1 and SMS version 1.2. I also discussed installing the Network Monitor. It is important to understand that you do not use these tools from your SMS site server. The administration tools belong on the SMS administrator's computer, which is usually a Windows 95 or Windows NT machine. The tools' features allow an SMS administrator to physically lock up his servers and perform full administration from his own desktop. The convenience and security of administering servers from a non-site computer will make any SMS administrator's life easier. For further information about Network Monitor, see Chapter 22, "SMS on the Internet."

- Client Features

- Installing the SMS Client

- SMS Client Setup Program

- Client Components

- Troubleshooting and Maintaining the Client Installation

CHAPTER 13

Installation of SMS Clients

After the SMS site servers are installed, it is time to prepare the clients. This chapter discusses the different features of the SMS client on all client platforms. I also include information on installing the clients and special considerations for the different clients on the different platforms. Installing the clients is the foundation of the SMS operation. None of the SMS operations is possible unless you install the client so that you can start to inventory the clients. I provide a breakdown of all the features the client offers in relationship to the actual programs that are integrated with the SMS client. This chapter also introduces the different directories and files on the clients, in order to make troubleshooting the client installation a much easier process.

Client Features

The SMS client offers the administrator many features that are integrated with the SMS servers. The client gives the administrator the flexibility to make changes to the client environment as required. This flexibility allows the administrator to install software on the client and make clients consistent with the standards of the organization. The features of the SMS client are as follows:

◆ Inventory Agent

◆ Package Command Manager

◆ Program Group Control

◆ Remote troubleshooting

◆ MIF entry

These features help SMS cover the gamut of operations that it performs.

Inventory Agent

The Inventory Agent is one of the key components in the SMS client. It provides the capability to scan the client for all hardware and software that is requested by the SMS administrator. The Inventory Agent runs on all the SMS clients and generates the inventory that is put into the SMS database. Configured on the SMS Administrator, the timing mechanism for the Inventory Agent is set on an interval basis. When an inventory scan is done, the logon server provides the information to the site server using the Maintenance Manager. Chapter 14, "Inventory: Knowledge Is Power," covers inventories in more detail.

The Inventory Agent runs in two forms. On a Windows NT machine, it can run as a service, and on the other clients it runs as a regular program. One of the key reasons the Inventory Agent is the most important component for the SMS client is that the SMS Administrator must have an active inventory of the SMS client to perform any operations with that client. All SMS operations require that the machine have an inventory. When the client installs the first time, it provides an inventory of the machine to the logon server.

PACKAGE COMMAND MANAGER

The Package Command Manager's (PCM) main responsibility is to run operations that are sent by the SMS administrator with Run Command on Workstation jobs. Packages created on the SMS site server are sent with a job, which specifies what is to be done with the package. A package used in a Run Command on Workstation job is processed by the Package Command Manager on the specified client. The Package Command Manager scans and monitors the SMS logon server for any package instructions that are designated for that client. The PCM has three different types of commands:

- Pending
- Archived
- Executed

A pending command is waiting to be run. An archived command is archived by the user to be run at a later date. An executed command has already run successfully or has failed. The SMS Administrator sets client packages as either mandatory or optional. Mandatory packages must be executed by the end-user before a time specified by the administrator. If this is not done, the package will be automatically executed when that time comes. Optional packages need not be executed, if the user so desires. Figure 13.1 shows the Package Command Manager.

PROGRAM GROUP CONTROL

The Program Group Control allows the SMS Administrator to distribute program groups containing program items so the SMS clients can run shared applications. These shared applications run off specified servers. The package is created, paired with a job, and designated as a Share Package on Server job. Share Package on Server jobs ensure that the package makes its way to the appropriate distribution server and is ready to run. Program Groups, set up with the SMS Administrator, provide instructions on the logon server about which groups of users the package should be available to. This allows the SMS Administrator to create a standard desktop for all the SMS clients. The Program Group Control allows software to run off servers, whereas the Package Command Manager allows software to be installed on the client computer.

Figure 13.1.
The Package
Command
Manager main
window.

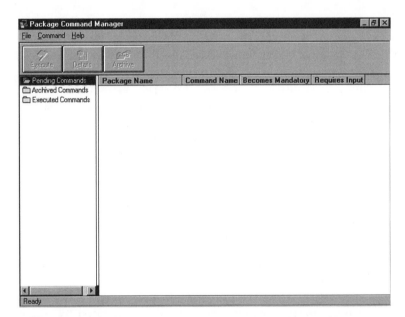

Note

People who are new to the SMS environment often confuse the Program Group Control with the Package Command Manager. Any command to be run on the workstation uses the Package Command Manager; any shared applications to be delivered to the SMS client use the Program Group Control.

REMOTE TROUBLESHOOTING

Remote troubleshooting seems to be the most attractive feature for many SMS administrators. It is the "ooh" and "wow" of SMS because it gives you the capability to remotely control the workstations. Remote troubleshooting also offers the capability to perform diagnostic analysis. You can run different diagnostics tools on MS-DOS and Windows-based clients, which allows you to troubleshoot errors and problems with the clients in the SMS environment.

The remote operations offered to the SMS administrator include the following:

◆ Remote control

◆ Remote execute

◆ Remote reboot

◆ Remote chat

◆ Remote file transfer

These remote features are discussed in Chapter 15, "Using Help Desk Utilities and Diagnostic Tools."

MIF ENTRY

Many SMS administrators overlook the power of the MIF entry facility, producing Management Information Format files. The MIF entry allows the user of the SMS client to enter specific information that is tagged with inventory. Many pieces of information can be collected with the MIF entry. The MIF entry provides a form-based tool for the user to add information that is specific to that machine. Users can provide the following information with an MIF entry:

◆ User profile

◆ Location

◆ Serial number

If you use your imagination, you can tag many other things with the computer. The MIF entry is collected with the inventory for the SMS database.

INSTALLING THE SMS CLIENT

To take advantage of the client features that make SMS what it is, you must install SMS. Installing SMS is not a difficult process, although it involves some knowledge of SMS administration. The two main installation programs for the SMS client on Windows-based machines are

◆ SMSLS.BAT

◆ RUNSMS.BAT

These two files, which allow the SMS Administrator to inventory the client, run in two different ways. I discuss how to run both of these files for Windows-based machines, as well as how to install MS-DOS, OS/2, and Macintosh clients.

> *Note*
>
> Not all client features are offered on all clients. The MS-DOS, OS/2, and Macintosh clients do not offer all the client features. This will be discussed later in the chapter in "Supportive Client Platforms."

SMSLS.BAT

One method of running the SMS client setup allows SMS to automatically configure logon scripts for the users to log in and run what is called the registration process. During the registration process, the inventory program scans the computer and provides an inventory to SMS. The first time this happens is when the SMS client is installed on the workstation. The client is registered with SMS so that its inventory record is kept at the site server's database and moved up the site hierarchy if the site is a child site. The SMSLS.BAT allows you to configure logon scripts to automatically let clients log in and register with the SMS site server. This automation is convenient if you have a large number of clients and you want to take inventory on an interval basis.

To take advantage of logon scripts, you must install the SMS clients in a certain way. You install the SMSLS.BAT differently according to whether the environment is a Windows NT domain or a NetWare environment. There are actually two main files for these environments. For the NetWare environment, you add the SMSLS.SCR to the system logon script of the NetWare server. You use the SMSLS.BAT in the Windows NT domain environment by adding it to the user's logon script field. You can configure SMSLS.BAT for the NT environment with the following steps:

1. Start the SMS Administrator.
2. Highlight the site and choose Properties from the File menu.
3. Select the clients.
4. Select the proposed properties.
5. Check the option titled Automatically Configure Workstation Logon Scripts. If a logon script is already present, you can add the SMS logon script to the top or the bottom of the existing logon script by clicking the appropriately marked button.
6. Click OK.
7. Update all the sites by clicking Yes.

Figure 13.2 shows the Automatically Configure Workstation Logon Scripts selection in the client's properties under the site configuration.

Figure 13.2.
The client's
properties
window under the
site configuration.

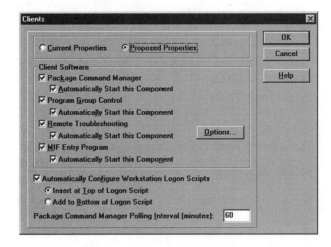

If you now look in the user's information under the Profile tab, you see a logon script that SMS configures for all the users. In network domains, it adds the SMSLS.SCR to either the bottom or top of the system logon script depending on what you chose in the client configuration box. When you log into that network server, you are part of the SMS domain. Inventory is delivered to the designated logon server.

When running Windows NT domains, LAN Manager, or LAN Server, the logon script is automatically set up as long as you choose to automatically configure the workstation logon script and use all the detected logon servers. If you choose specified servers options, SMS does not automatically set up the logon scripts for you.

With NetWare servers, you can either select a server, use all the detected servers, or use specified servers in order to be able to automatically configure the workstation logon scripts.

Tip

You can configure the SMSLS.BAT by adjusting the SMSLS.INI. This gives you the flexibility to map the workstations of the SMS domain. If you do not map the workstations, they automatically default to the Windows NT logon server domain.

Note

Existing NT server logon scripts that are in the NETLOGON share are adjusted if you choose to have SMS automatically provide users with SMSLS.BAT. The adjustment adds a call to SMSLS.BAT and puts it either at the top or bottom of the logon script, depending on what you selected for the client configuration.

DIRECTORY REPLICATOR SERVICE

To copy the automatically configured logon scripts to all the Windows NT logon servers, you must turn on the Directory Replicator Service. This is the easiest way to replicate the logon scripts to different logon servers. The Directory Replicator Service automatically copies all the files necessary to install the SMS client and log in the clients. It copies them from NETLOGON share on the designated server to the NETLOGON share on other servers. To start the Directory Replicator Service for an SMS record, you create a user that is in a replicator group and start the service using a user account. To do this, follow these steps:

1. Start User Manager for Domains.
2. Click User and click Add.
3. In the User Name field, type `replicate`.
4. Uncheck the option User Must Change Password at Next Logon.
5. Click Groups.
6. Select the replicator group and backup operator group and click Add.
7. Click OK.
8. Complete the Password and Confirm Password fields.
9. Click OK.
10. Click the Policies menu and select User Rights.
11. Click the box to show advanced user rights.
12. Select logon as a service.
13. Click Add and select the replicate account, which you just created.
14. Click OK.

You created a user that is a member of the replicator operators group with the right to log on as a service. This user can start the service as the system account so that

13

the Directory Replicator Service causes it to run. To configure the Directory Replicator Service, do the following steps:

1. Go to the Control Panel.
2. Double-click the Services icon.
3. Select the Directory Replicator Service and click Start Up.
4. Click Automatic.
5. Click System Account.
6. In the User Name field, type `replicate`.
7. In the Password and Confirm Password fields, enter the password for the replicate account, which you just created.
8. Click OK.
9. Make sure the service has started.

Configuring the replicator service means the logon scripts are automatically propagated to the NETLOGON shares used by the clients.

RUNSMS.BAT

The SMSLS.BAT procedure is called by logon scripts, or is used as one. It contains logic that handles special situations, such as slow network links (for example, when the user is dialed in to the server). When just performing a manual installation of the SMS client, you can use RUNSMS.BAT to activate the SMS client setup and go through the registration process. RUNSMS.BAT is on the SMS_SHR. SMS_SHR is the logon.SVR directory on an SMS logon server. To operate the SMS client manually, you perform the following steps:

1. Connect to the SMS_SHR share.
2. Execute the RUNSMS.BAT file.

Running the SMS client setup manually is not often necessary. The computer inventory is still added to the logon server, and the machine is still added to the SMS domain. The RUNSMS.BAT is much the same as the SMSLS.BAT.

Tip

You can set up the RUNSMS.BAT to run automatically by putting it in the AUTOEXEC.BAT or the startup group in the Windows environment. Figure 13.3 shows the SMS client installation.

Figure 13.3.
The SMS client
installation.

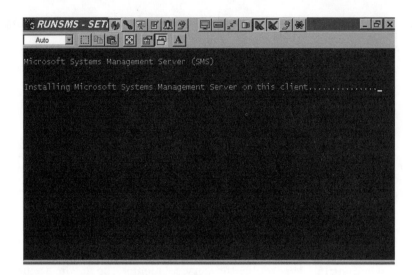

SMSLS.BAT VERSUS RUNSMS.BAT

The SMSLS.BAT is ideal for a NetWare or NT environment that requires all its users to log in and send inventory to the site. The RUNSMS.BAT gives the administrator more control over how to run the logon script. The SMSLS.BAT must run in the logon script and takes some of the flexibility away from the administrator. If the administrator wants to use the AUTOEXEC.BAT or the startup group in Windows or perform manual inventories, RUNSMS.BAT is the appropriate choice. Most environments use the SMSLS.BAT. Some clients can run either RUNSMS.BAT or SMSLS.BAT, depending on possible inventory intervals.

Much of the decision about which SMS client setup to use depends on the inventory intervals that you require. If you require inventory intervals on a constant basis, it is probably more beneficial to use SMSLS.BAT because it automatically starts at the user's logon. You can use RUNSMS.BAT if you are going to use the startup group or AUTOEXEC.BAT.

SMS CLIENT SETUP PROGRAM

The SMS client setup program performs many different operations to install and maintain the SMS client on a constant basis. This maintenance and installation runs on all the clients that the SMSLS.BAT runs on. Every time the SMS client runs, it verifies the client configuration. It helps by automatically maintaining a client if any files are needed. The SMS client setup prepares the workstation with the SMS client by doing the following:

◆ Assigning a unique SMS ID to identify the client

◆ Creating an sms.ini file, which holds system information for the client

◆ Determining which components to install and remove for the SMS client

◆ Determining the operating system and language used on the client

◆ Copying the SMS files to the client

◆ Configuring all the components according to the site configuration

SITE CONFIGURATION

The site configuration in the SMS Administrator has a Client's button that allows you to configure the clients. It offers several different settings for the different components you want to install when the SMS client setup runs. Depending on what options you pick, the client setup determines what client components are put onto the workstation. Refer to Figure 13.2 to see the client configuration with the different selections you can choose.

SUPPORTIVE CLIENT PLATFORMS

The beauty of SMS is that it provides support for the majority of client platforms that run in any network environment. The majority of supportive platforms run the SMSLS.BAT or RUNSMS.BAT. The special considerations for some of the other clients are discussed later in this section. The supportive client platforms are as follows:

◆ Windows NT 3.5 or later

◆ Windows 95

◆ Windows 3.1/Windows for Workgroups 3.11

◆ MS-DOS 5.0 or later

◆ OS/2 1.3, 2.11 or later

◆ Macintosh 7.0 or later

Note

A unique client support option is provided by a third-party tool made by ComputingEdge.

Windows NT

The Windows NT SMS client is similar to the Windows 95 and Windows 3.1 clients, although it is somewhat different in how the SMS client runs. The CCM (Client Configuration Manager) Service helps install, upgrade, and remove the different components for the SMS client. It runs three very important components:

◆ Inventory Agent Service

◆ Remote Control Service

◆ SNMP Event to Trap Translator

The CCM Service uses an SMS services account that must be created on the NT server. The CCM Service runs on any Windows NT server that is also an SMS logon server. The SMS client puts all its configuration information into the Registry. Much of the information for the Program Group Control is set in the Registry as reference information so that specific shared applications can pull information about the shared package. Windows NT 3.51 and Windows NT 4.0 are both supported as SMS clients. After you have installed the SMS client and an inventory is taken by the site server, you can then run the Windows NT administrative tools for the Windows NT server from the client's properties inside the SMS Administrator. Figure 13.4 shows the client properties for a Windows NT server, which allows the administrator to invoke the administrative tools for Windows NT.

Figure 13.4.
Client properties
for a Windows
NT server show
the administra-
tive tools.

Note

> To run remote control with Windows NT, you must have Version 3.51 or later.

SMS_CLIENT_CONFIG_MANAGER (CLIENT CONFIGURATION MANAGER) SERVICE

The Client Configuration Manager Service helps update the Windows NT machine and the components that are installed on the SMS client. Its responsibility is to install, upgrade, and remove the different client components on the Windows NT computer. When the SMS client needs to perform any tasks, it calls on the CCM Service; the CCM Service then carries out the task.

Figure 13.5 shows the CCM Service running on a Windows NT computer.

Figure 13.5.
Services dialog
box with the CCM
Service running.

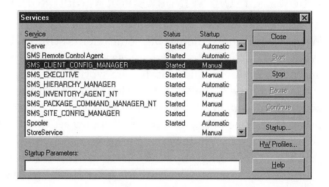

Note

> The CCM Service requires that you create an SMS service account that has administrative privileges. Without the account, CCM cannot install the SMS components.

WINDOWS 95

One of the most popular clients in SMS environments is Windows 95. These clients operate much like the other Windows-based clients but have special considerations. You must configure the client configuration box under the site configuration for the different components to be installed on the Windows 95 workstation. The majority of the support files for the Windows 95 SMS client are very similar to the files for

Windows 3.1 clients, with a few differences because of the Windows 95 operating system architecture. However, much of the process of how the client runs is the same. I discuss these files later in the section "Client Components." Figure 13.6 shows the Windows 95 workstation and Program menu for the SMS client.

Figure 13.6.
The Program
menu for the
SMS client on the
Windows 95
workstation.

WINDOWS 3.1 AND WINDOWS FOR WORKGROUPS 3.11

Even though many companies are migrating and upgrading their machines to Windows NT and Windows 95, some clients still run Windows 3.1 and Windows for Workgroups. SMS offers a seamless installation of the SMS client with these older operating systems. The installation works much like the Windows 95 SMS client setup using the same SMSLS.BAT. However, when the operating system is detected, some of the copied files are different—with the main difference between the files being that some of the files in the Windows 95 installation are 32-bit. The files for Windows 3.1 and Windows for Workgroups 3.11 must all be 16-bit. Windows 3.1 and Windows for Workgroups 3.11 have no limitation on the features of the client components, which is also true for all of the Windows-based SMS clients.

With the Windows for Workgroups SMS client, it's important to update your Windows for Workgroups workstation before installing the SMS client. Get the latest patch from the Windows NT server's CD-ROM. The NT server CD-ROM has a WFW/Update directory in the client's directory that contains the files you need to update the Windows for Workgroups client and install the SMS client correctly.

Note

> With Windows 3.1 and Network Client 3.0 for MS-DOS, you cannot run the SMS client and set up the inventory from the site server. One solution is to run the LAN Manager version 2.1 or later or Windows for Workgroups.

MS-DOS

The MS-DOS SMS client setup runs similarly to the Windows-based setup with some considerations and differences. You can run all the client components except the Program Group Control on the MS-DOS–based machine. Many of the client components that make up the MS-DOS SMS client are discussed later in this chapter, in the section "Client Components." The MS-DOS client runs the SMSLS.BAT or the RUNSMS.BAT to do the SMS client setup. The setup takes an inventory of the MS-DOS machine just as it does in the Windows-based environments. All client components are then installed and set up to be run.

There are several ways to set up the MS-DOS client, but you generally use the AUTOEXEC.BAT. That is the only way to initiate any operation to be executed automatically at startup. The other consideration is the logon script. MS-DOS–based clients can run the SMSLS logon script when logging into the Windows NT domain. This allows them to use the SMSLS also. One key issue for the MS-DOS SMS client is that it doesn't run the Program Group Control. It does run Package Command Manager as a separate program that must be run since it is not a TSR (Terminate and Stay Resident program). It is run whenever you want to initialize and search to see if there is a package waiting to be run. It takes about 420KB of conventional memory.

Note

It is important to understand that MS-DOS supports only MS-DOS version 5.0 and later. Some documentation from Microsoft incorrectly states MS-DOS version 3.3 or later.

OS/2

OS/2 clients are few and far between, although they still exist in some environments. The key file for allowing the OS/2 SMS clients to initiate is the SMSLS.CMD. This file is very similar to the SMSLS.BAT that you use with Windows-based clients. One difference between the OS/2 client and the Windows-based clients is that the OS/2 workstation doesn't support any remote troubleshooting utilities.

The SMS client setup can inventory the OS/2 workstation. The other key components that the OS/2 client cannot support are the diagnostic tools. The Package Command Manager used on the Windows 3.*x* clients is the same one that is installed when the OS/2 SMSLS.CMD runs. It is important to note that in order for OS/2 clients to install the SMS client programs, their user logon scripts must run the SMSLS.CMD. This allows the setup program to inventory the clients and set up the SMS client. Later in this chapter, I discuss the client components run on the OS/2 client that are different from the clients for Windows and Windows for Workgroups.

Note

To run the SMS client setup on an OS/2 computer, OS/2 needs to be installed on drive C.

MACINTOSH

The Macintosh still exists in client/server environments. SMS provides support for the Apple Macintosh, which allows you to install some of the features of the SMS components on a Macintosh client. The SMS environment can also inventory the Macintosh client. The SMS client setup on the Macintosh is not as automated as it is in the Windows, MS-DOS, and OS/2 environments. The administrator must manually run the client setup at the Macintosh. The basic requirements for running a Macintosh client in the SMS environment are as follows:

◆ Apple System 7.0 or later

◆ Apple Installer version 3.4 or later

◆ Services for Macintosh on the NT server

SMS SERVER MACINTOSH COMPONENTS

When you meet the Macintosh requirements, use the Apple Installer to install the Macintosh SMS client. Put the Apple Installer in the Site.SRV/MAINCFG.Box/CLIENT.SRC/MAC.BIN directory on the SMS site server. There is an Apple Installer compatible SMS script in the logon server parameter under MAC.BIN. Running this tool installs the client on the Macintosh. After it does this, the components that have been installed include the Inventory Agent and the Package Command Manager program. The Macintosh components are discussed later in this chapter, in the section "Client Components."

SMS ID

Installing the SMS client assigns a unique SMS ID to each client. This unique SMS ID allows the SMS server to identify which clients are in the environment. The ID is derived from the unique ID file on the system logon server. The logon server is what actually gives the SMS clients their unique ID. Each logon server is given a unique range by the SMS site server.

The SMS site constructs the client SMS ID by using 36 different characters, plus the site codes. The characters include the numeric value of zero to nine and the alphabetical characters of A to Z. The first three characters of the SMS client ID comprise the unique site code. This site code is designated for the site itself, and all clients within the cycle share the same site code. The last three characters of the

SMS ID sequentially increment as they are allocated through the client, so each client with the last three characters of the SMS ID increments the number by one. Once this number is incremented, the last client that was installed sticks the next increment to the SMS site in a file called SMS_SHR/SMSID/SMSIDx.ID. Once a logon server has issued 44,065 SMS IDs, a new site code should be allocated to that logon server. These features of the SMS were implemented to make sure that all SMS clients carry the unique ID.

Note

> If a workstation moves from one site to another site, the original SMS ID for the client is moved to the new site database once the workstation has run three successful logons on the new site. The only way that the SMS ID is altered is if the client experiences a deinstall and reinstall procedure.

CLIENT COMPONENTS

In the same way that it is important to understand all the parts of an automobile to be able to fix a problem, it is important to understand the components of the SMS client. This understanding allows an administrator to troubleshoot and make sure the client is working properly. The components for the SMS client allow the SMS client to interface with the main operations of the SMS site server. All the SMS client components are files that either run as a service or a program. The SMS client takes about one to three megabytes of disk space.

SMS CLIENT INSTALLATION

A group of files that actually initiate the SMS client installation differ according to the platforms where they are run. The installation sends one to three megabytes of files to the client and makes an inventory of the client. Figure 13.3 shows the SMS client installation being run. The four files that actually kick off the SMS client installation include the following:

◆ CLI_NT.EXE for Windows NT

◆ CLI_DOS for MS-DOS, Windows 3.1, and Windows for Workgroups

◆ CLI_W95 for Windows 95

◆ CLI_OS/2 for OS/2

These files start the SMS client setup and deliver the SMS client components to the workstation.

INVENTORY AGENT

The inventory agent is one of the key SMS client components. Depending on the platform that the client is running, one of several different files allow the setup to gather the inventory:

◆ INVWIN32 for Windows NT

◆ INVDOS for MS-DOS

◆ INVMAC for Macintosh

◆ INVOS/2 for OS/2

Note

Windows NT computers that do not operate as SMS servers run the INV32CLI.EXE to act as their inventory agents. INV32CLI.EXE uses a local system account to kick off the service.

Two components that work together to resolve where the computer exists are the SetLSx.com and the SMSLS.INI. The SMSLS.INI maps the client to its position in the SMS environment. With three types of mappings, you can map a client to a specific SMS domain underneath the workgroup heading in the SMSLS.INI. You can make a mapping to a specific logon server in the SMSLS.INI under the machine heading. You can also map to a specific site using the domain heading in the SMSLS.INI. These client mappings only apply to LAN Manager, LAN Server, and Windows NT domains. The SetLS program looks at this SMSLS.INI to see whether there are any entries about how to add the computer into the site hierarchy. If these mapping entries are here, SetLS then uses the SMSLS.INI entries to set the machine in the site. The SetLS program also runs certain SMS programs off the logon server wherever the SMSLS.BAT file was run. The SetLS program you use depends on the program environment that you run:

◆ SETLS32.EXE for Windows NT

◆ SETLS16.EXE for MS-DOS and Windows

◆ SETLSOS2.EXE for OS/2

Note

The first program that is run when you run the SMS client is called NETSPEED.COM. It is used to determine the speed of the network. When it detects a slow network setup, it asks the user if it should proceed with the inventory (if the site's configuration allow that option).

PROGRAM GROUP CONTROL

The Program Group Control pulls shared applications from the logon server. These shared applications are delivered from the site server. The Program Group Control requires two main files to perform this operation. The first file is APPSTART, which is in the c:\Windows directory. The second file can be one of the following three files:

◆ APPCTL16 for Windows 3.1 and Windows for Workgroups 3.11

◆ APPCTL32 for Windows NT

◆ APPCTL95 for Windows 95

The APPCTL file acts as the Program Group Control for the SMS client, which allows the desktops to show program groups that are shared from the site server. These program groups also include the program items with logical pointers to the shared applications that exist on the specific server.

Note

> The program that actually puts the program groups on the desktop and then sets up the desktop is SMSRUN16.EXE or SMSRUN32.EXE. The 16-bit application is for the Windows version 3.1 platform, and the 32-bit application is for the Windows NT platform.

PACKAGE COMMAND MANAGER

The Package Command Manager allows the SMS client to examine the SMS logon server and distribution server for a set of packaged instructions to run workstation jobs. The Package Command Manager runs as a file for all the client platforms except Windows NT. The Windows NT runs the Package Command Manager agent as a service. The Package Command Manager files used for the different client platforms are as follows:

◆ PCMWIN32.EXE for Windows NT

◆ PCMWIN16.EXE for Windows, Windows for Workgroups, Windows 95, and OS/2

◆ PCMDOS.EXE for MS-DOS

◆ PCMMAC.EXE for Macintosh

Note

> The Windows NT client platform also has a file named PCMSVC32.EXE on the logon server that does the PCM function as a service.

REMOTE TROUBLESHOOTING UTILITIES

You must meet a lot of criteria to use remote control. One issue that seems to be a problem for many people is maintaining a common protocol—making sure that the default host protocol on your client is the same as what is on your server.

Most importantly, however, you need to install several files on the client that act as components when the SMS client's setup is done. The box to be controlled remotely must have one of two files, depending on its platform. Windows-based clients use WUSER.EXE and WUSER32.EXE. WUSER.EXE is for Windows 3.1, Windows 95, and Windows for Workgroups clients. WUSER32.EXE is for Windows NT machines. SMS also supports a TSR to allow you to remotely control MS-DOS and Windows 3.1 clients. The two TSRs are USERTSR and USERIPX. USERIPX is for clients using an IPX/SPX transport protocol. USERTSR is for clients with any other type of transport protocol.

The other component that comes with the SMS client is the help desk options program, which allows the client to specify to what degree an administrator can remotely control the client. When an administrator attempts to remotely control a client, the client is asked if the administrator is allowed to come in and remotely control the desktop. Figure 13.7 shows the Help Desk Options dialog box.

Figure 13.7.
The Help Desk
Options dialog
box.

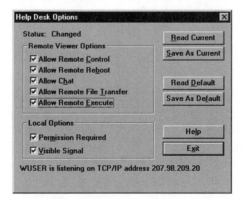

Note

The executable that actually runs the help desk options is EDITINI.EXE. This allows the client to configure the remote control options for the machine.

MIF Entry

All platforms allow users to add user information to the client inventory with an MIF entry form. The administrator can change the MIF entry form by using the MIF entry form generator. Some components that the SMS client setup installs deal with the MIF entry. The first component is the MIF entry program, which is MIFDOS.EXE or MIFWIN.EXE, depending on the client that is installed. UINFO.XNF is an MIF entry form file that allows the MIF entry program to collect information about the user. UINFO.XNF is installed by default during the SMS client installation. The administrator can change and configure the UINFO.XNF to create a different form.

Troubleshooting and Maintaining the Client Installation

After your client is set up, you need to consider many different factors for maintaining and troubleshooting the client. Several different maintenance mechanisms are built in for the client in case you want to either install the client or upgrade the client because the operating system has upgraded or changed. There are also key issues to watch while maintaining and troubleshooting the SMS client for the different operations that the SMS site will provide.

Upgrading the SMS Client

If you change the client platform on the SMS client to a different operating system, you must connect to the SMS_SHR on the logon server to upgrade your SMS client. Run UPGRADE.BAT to upgrade your client to the new operating system.

The Deinstallation of the SMS Client

To install the SMS client, you must connect to the logon server's SMS_SHR and run DEINSTAL.BAT. DEINSTAL.BAT removes all the components of the SMS client and pulls your client out of the SMS database.

Common Troubleshooting Problems

You should make sure that everything is in order so that the SMS client setup doesn't experience any problems when installing the SMS client. Two common problems with the SMS client concern disk space and the time setting.

Make sure that the SMS client has enough disk space to install the SMS component files. The installation procedure looks on the SMS client for a disk with the largest amount of disk space. The procedure needs between 1MB and 3MB of space to install the SMS client.

The time setting on the SMS client must be in sync with the setting on the SMS site server. Updating the inventory and the Package Command Manager is time-sensitive. In order to ensure the time is synchronized, you should adjust the users' logon scripts to include the command, `net time \\computer_name /set /y`.

NEEDED SETUP FOR REMOTE CONTROL

If you run network clients using IPX/SPX and run Windows 3.x, you must have the following files:

◆ NWNETAPI.DLL

◆ NWCALLS.DLL

◆ NWIPXSPX.DLL

These files generally come with the NetWare client. If they are not installed, you will not be able to run the remote control agent. Make sure that the LANA number for your protocol is set up correctly. Check the `protocol.INI`, and make sure that the default protocol is the same as the default protocol on the SMS site server. This lack of protocol commonality is sometimes one of the key problems in setting up remote control. For Windows NT machines, make sure that you set up an SMS services account to allow the SMS site server to run the Remote Control Agent Service on the Windows NT machine.

SUMMARY

When installing the SMS client, you have to take many factors into consideration. Many of these factors vary according to the different SMS operations that are active in your SMS environment. Depending on the platform that you run in the SMS environment, it is important that you follow the appropriate steps in installing your client and also examine the key factors for maintaining and troubleshooting your client. Follow the rules and steps detailed in this chapter in order to keep your SMS environment stable and consistent. This chapter provided an in-depth look at the SMS client and the different components that help it operate. With the information about maintaining and troubleshooting your environment, you should be able to keep your SMS environment as stable and consistent as possible.

P A R T   IV

Operating SMS— Running the Shop

CHAPTER 14

Inventory: Knowledge Is Power

What is the inventory process in the SMS world? The SMS inventory process is the core of the SMS system. The inventory process is that part of SMS that enables the other processes and components. The enabling is accomplished because the inventory process populates the SQL database. Many SMS activities hinge on the requirement that the machines participating in the SMS system are listed in the SQL database. This is the foundation of SMS activities.

The inventory process is the process that first recognizes and makes possible a machine's participation in the SMS hierarchy. Once a machine is recognized by the SMS system and inventoried, it can be used for all functions and procedures in the SMS system. The activities include Help Desk operations, software distribution, and overall administration of enterprise-level operations. Although some of the functions included with SMS may be considered optional, the inventory process is necessary and always performed.

One might also consider the question, "How can I use the inventory of my organization's machines?" This is the golden opportunity to organize and present information to further dazzle the managers in your life and impress on them the fact that you now have total control of strategic-level data because you are using SMS. When considering the investment that large companies make in their computer equipment, the control of the equipment is, in fact, a strategic-level requirement and critical to the success of the company. Better yet, you now have the ability to present the data in a variety of formats, from spreadsheets to charts.

There are many uses for inventories of machines. In the enterprise environment, the inventory database allows the network administrator to do extensive asset tracking as well as provides the capability to track the flow of equipment. You can perform asset tracking by making reports based on the information in the database. Additionally, the database information can be exported to any ODBC-compliant software package. Think of the impact of this: If a manager is hooked on Microsoft Access reporting methods, you can supply the manager with data that he or she can use with his or her favorite database package.

SMS also allows tracking of the flow of equipment, such as movement from department to department or from location to location. Because SMS maintains a history of the machine, it is also obvious when equipment, such as memory modules, disappears! This history-keeping capability is also helpful in the diagnostic and troubleshooting activities typically found at a help desk. It is now possible to look at the history of a machine and realize that something new was added. This takes the pressure off the end user in that he or she must no longer respond to the question, "Is there anything new on your machine?" Of course, it was always a rhetorical question; inevitably, the person did not realize the connection between work on his or her machine and problems.

Another powerful capability with the inventory data is the luxury of fully pre-planning a roll-out of any application. This includes the capability to know whether the hardware can run the application, the capability to know whether there are any problem drivers or DLLs, and the capability to see what is happening in the configuration files.

WHAT IS INVENTORY COLLECTION IN SMS?

Understanding the overview of the inventory process, the general flow is the first step in understanding the details of operations and developing troubleshooting techniques. The inventory process collects information about hardware and software for designated machines. Hardware inventory is enabled by default. The hardware and software information is processed and loaded into the site database.

Figure 14.1 shows the general process of inventory collection.

*Figure 14.1.
The inventory
flow from a
non-detailed
perspective.*

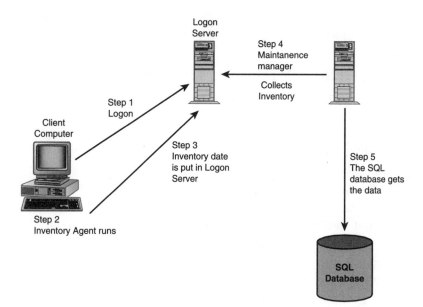

The inventory process follows these steps:

1. The client computer logs onto the logon server (discussed in "Logging onto the Logon Server").

2. The client computer performs the inventory process, either by a program or service (discussed in "Performing the Inventory Process").

3. The inventory information is sent back to the logon server (discussed in "Sending Information to the Logon Server").

4. The primary site server collects the inventory (discussed in "Collecting the Inventory").

5. The SQL database receives the inventory information (discussed in "Receiving the Inventory Information").

Understanding the inventory process at this level is most helpful for troubleshooting. For example, it is possible to correlate the steps to the questions that should be asked in the event of an inventory collection failure. The first question to be asked might concern finding out if the client was able to log into the logon server. This might be the easiest of all issues to correct. Next, one might consider looking at the client workstation to determine whether the inventory process ran at all. Was there output from the collection process, and did it get placed on the logon server? Lastly, you might consider checking the directories on the primary site server for the existence of the inventory files. At the end of this chapter, you will have the specific information you need to look for the answers.

Re-examine the steps in the flow of the inventory process for specific and detailed information.

Logging onto the Logon Server

Logging onto a logon server is the first step. As discussed in Chapter 5, "Understanding the SMS System," you must define a logon server in the SMS hierarchy. This definition of the server is in terms of a domain, which means a server was added to a domain defined in the SMS world. The logon server supports the SMS functions needed for inventory processing.

This support is evident in a number of ways. The logon server gets the inventory information from the client machine and stores it in designated directories. Also, the logon server stores the client components used for the inventory process.

The inventory information is placed on the logon server in the form of either a .RAW file or a .MIF file. The .RAW files are from the inventory agent program that runs on Windows NT, Windows 95, Windows 3.x, and MS-DOS machines. These .RAW files are encoded binary files. Other machines, such as OS/2 and Macintosh machines, using the other inventory agents, generate a .MIF file. The .MIF files are text files.

Both of these types of files are placed on the logon server by the inventory agent, which is discussed in the next step. Figure 14.2 shows the directories that receive these files.

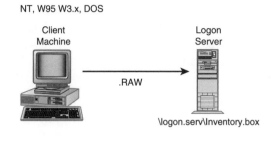

Figure 14.2.
The specific
directories that
receive inventory
files.

NT, W95 W3.x, DOS

Client
Machine

Logon
Server

.RAW

\logon.serv\Inventory.box

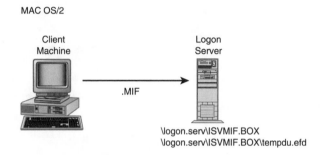

MAC OS/2

Client
Machine

Logon
Server

.MIF

\logon.serv\ISVMIF.BOX
\logon.serv\ISVMIF.BOX\tempdu.efd

The Windows NT, Windows 95, Windows 3.*x*, and MS-DOS machines put their .RAW files in the \logon.srv\inventory.box directory. Macintosh and OS/2 machines put their inventory in either the \logon.srv\isvmif.box directory or in the case of a customized inventory collection by an Independent Software Vendor (ISV), \logon.srv\isvmif.box\tempdir.cfd. NetWare servers also have inventory information placed in that directory.

The other supporting function performed by the logon server is storing and supplying the client components that are used in the inventory process. These components are located in the platform.bin directory on the logon server and some are installed on the client machine. The client component used in the inventory process is the inventory agent application, which brings us to step two of the inventory process.

PERFORMING THE INVENTORY PROCESS

The idea of the inventory step is that the inventory is run when the user logs onto the system. This is fine if the user logs in once. To prevent the inventory process from running more than once in the specified time interval, the inventory agent looks at the information kept in the SMS.INI file to determine if the inventory should be run. If the time interval has elapsed, the inventory is run; otherwise, it is not. There is a section of the SMS.INI file that keeps track of the scanning interval and the time interval for the inventory agent services. After the inventory is taken, the inventory agent updates the SMS.INI file to indicate when the last inventory was done. You can view SMS.INI using Notepad. SMS.INI is in the client's root directory as a hidden file. The inventory settings in the SMS.INI file correspond to the Inventory Frequency setting in the Inventory dialog box of the site properties.

You access the Inventory dialog box in Figure 14.3 from the Site Properties dialog by clicking the inventory button. This is where you control the inventory frequency.

Figure 14.3.
The SMS admin-
istrator can
control inventory
frequency.

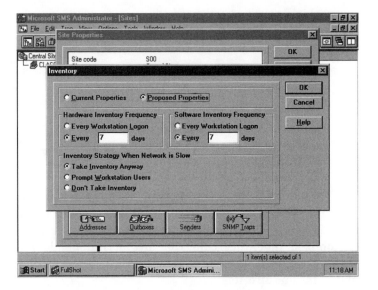

In addition to considering the time interval since the last scan, the inventory agent also considers the speed of the network. A utility called Netspeed.com determines whether the connection is a slow link. If the connection is a slow link, the inventory agent uses the designated strategy for that location. A slow link, by default, is defined in terms of the length of time it takes to read one kilobyte of data (in milliseconds) from the logon server. The default is 500 milliseconds. The SMS administrator has the opportunity to define what should be done in the event that a slow link is detected. The steps that should be taken if a slow link exists are called the strategy. The slow link strategy choices include take the inventory anyway, prompt the user about what to do, and don't take the inventory at all.

This presents two important issues for the SMS administrator. First is the issue of the definition of a slow link, and second is the actual designation of the strategy. The setting for the slow link threshold is in the Registry. The key to set the threshold transmission rate is

```
HKEY_LOCAL_MACHINE\SOFTWARE\Microsoft
➥\SMS\Components\SMS_MAINTENANCEMANAGER\Slow Net Threshold Speed
```

This value is copied to a file named NETSPEED.DAT for use by the Netspeed.com program.

The configuration of the strategy is done from the same screen that inventory frequency is specified. Look at the bottom of Figure 14.3 to see where the selections are offered.

There are three ways to take the inventory. One option is to run the SMSLS batch file from an automatically configured logon script. Another option is to run the SMSLS batch file from a manually configured logon script. The last option is to have the client machine connect to the SMS logon server and run the file.

Ideally, the logon script defined on the logon server runs the inventory agent application. The script language code that calls the inventory agent application should be in the logon script. How can you change all those logon scripts so they run the inventory agent application? You can make the script language changes either automatically or manually. Your first reaction might be, "Well, let's do it automatically and save all the work." However, there is a requirement. The requirement is that if you want to use the Automatically Configure Workstation Logon Scripts option, you must also select the Automatically Detect Logon Servers option during the installation of the primary site server. Figure 14.4 shows the screen that offers the option for Automatically Detect Logon Servers.

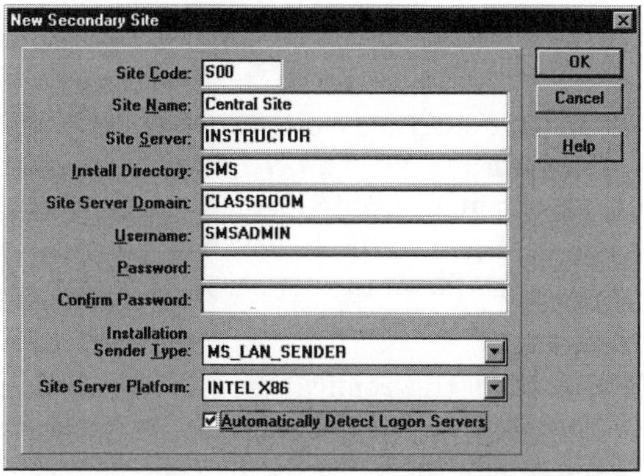

Figure 14.4.
The Automatically Detect
Logon Servers
box should be
checked.

If that option is checked during primary site installation, the administrator can check the Automatically Configure Workstation Logon Scripts option shown in Figure 14.5.

To have the luxury of automatically configuring the logon scripts, you must check both of these options. You can find the first option when specifying the properties of the particular site during the installation, and the second option appears in the properties of the site, under the client button.

Figure 14.5.
The Automati-
cally Configure
Workstation
Logon Scripts
option must also
be checked.

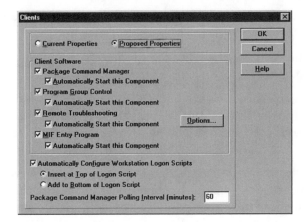

What actually happens when these options are selected? Of course, it depends on the operating platform of the logon server and the logon scripts. The intention of this option is to add lines of the script language to the logon scripts so that when the user logs in, the inventory agent application is invoked. When you realize that this option changes all the logon scripts, you can see the value of this time-saving option. If you don't change the logon scripts automatically, you must consider how they will be changed to run the inventory agent at sign-on time. This involves manually changing each logon script and adding the appropriate script statements to start the inventory agent.

If the Automatic Configure Workstation Logon Scripts option is enabled on domains that use logon scripts, such as Windows NT or LAN Manager, the SMSLS.BAT file is replicated to the appropriate logon servers. Although SMS adds the appropriate statements to a logon script, it does not recognize logon scripts that are lacking an extension. This is a factor to consider in the event you want a machine excluded from the group.

SMS fully utilizes the replication services of Windows NT and LAN Manager. Because SMS is a BackOffice product, it works with Windows NT and uses the features and capabilities. As a result, SMS uses the replication service to distribute the batch file.

Tip

It is wise to verify the operation of the replication service. It would be a shame to waste time trying to debug an SMS problem when, in fact, it could be an issue with the setup of the replication service!

On NetWare servers, which also use logon scripts, the logon script is changed to call SMSLS.SCR. Macintosh systems connect to the SMS_SHR on the server and run the installer program. This server must be running Services for Macintosh. The Macintosh systems use their startup folders for the inventory agent, which means that the inventory agent checks to see if it is time to run every time the system is started.

The manner in which the inventory agent starts is a factor in determining the client's SMS domain. The domain membership is significant when the inventory is displayed. This is a factor to consider for ease of administration. Consider how you will be accessing machines. Do you want the machines displayed in groups that are defined by which logon server is being used? Or would you like the organization of your inventory to be based on the logical organization of your company?

If you changed the logon scripts automatically or if you changed the logon scripts yourself, then the SMS domain membership information is determined by the settings in the SMSLS.INI file. This file enables you to map the domain membership as you choose. This is particularly useful if you are using a Windows NT domain model in which all users have their accounts on one machine. You can then create logically meaningful SMS domain membership for the viewing and management of inventory. For example, a logical organization of domain membership could be based on the organization of your business. If, on the other hand, you had the client connect to the logon server and run SMSLS, then the domain membership is on that particular logon domain.

Now that the logon scripts are configured to call the inventory agent application, the next piece of information that is useful for troubleshooting and debugging is which inventory application is used for which operating system platform. Table 14.1 provides that information.

TABLE 14.1. INVENTORY AGENTS.

SMS Role	Operating System	Specific Inventory Agent	Type
Client	Windows 95	INVDOS.EXE	Executable
Client	Windows 3.x	INVDOS.EXE	Executable
Client	MS-DOS	INVDOS.EXE	Executable
Client	OS/2	INVOS2.EXE	Executable
Client	Macintosh System 7	INVMAC	Executable
Client	Windows NT Workstation	INV32CLI.EXE	Service
SMS Server	Windows NT Server	SMS_Inventory Agent_NT	Service
SMS Server	LAN Manager	SMS_Inv_OS2LM	Service

Tip

> It is always possible to run an inventory from the command prompt. Use the /F parameter with the appropriate inventory agent. Also, using the /V parameter displays additional output for additional information.

Notice that for SMS servers, including logon servers and helper servers, the inventory agent is run as a service. This service does not run under the user's account but instead runs under the SMS service account. As with some of the other services in the Windows NT environment, it may run when the user is not logged on. Another difference between the service and the executable is the fact that the service has a default wake-up interval of 24 hours, at which time the service checks the hardware and software scanning intervals. The wake-up interval for the service is in the Registry at the HKEY_LOCAL_MACHINE_SOFTWARE\MICROSOFT\SMS\Components ➥\SMS_MAINTENANCE_MANAGER key. You can change the scanning interval on the Site Properties dialog button. (Refer to Figure 14.3.)

When the inventory agent is actually running, it has a time-saving, resource-saving feature. This feature handles situations in which the client's machine has not changed since the last inventory. Remember the other time-saving feature, in which the inventory only runs if the appropriate amount of time has elapsed? Well, the designers of SMS also considered the case of a machine not having anything to report, even if the time interval indicates that an inventory should be taken. SMS keeps track of each inventory collection file on the local machine and does a comparison. If there is no change, the inventory agent doesn't even bother to write another file; things are left alone. This collection history file is kept in the directory \MS\SMS\Colfile.His.

Note

> SMS version 1.2 now uses a service for NT Workstation instead of an executable. The advantage of this is that the inventory agent can run without complications arising from access rights of the user.

SENDING INFORMATION TO THE LOGON SERVER

Once the user logs on and the appropriate inventory agent performs the inventory process, the information is sent back to the logon server. If the particular agent has network access, then a .TMP file is created on the logon server and the files are copied at the same time the inventory takes place. When everything is finished, the .TMP is renamed to a .RAW filename. The exceptions to this are the Macintosh and OS/2 inventories, which are written directly to .MIF files. If the inventory agent does not have network access, it is kept on the local machine until it can be copied to the logon server.

Macintosh machines are handled differently. These machines require that the (Windows NT Server) SMS logon server run Services for Macintosh (SFM). These machines use the INVMAC inventory agent, which performs the copying of the files to the logon server.

The Windows NT machines and the LAN Manager Server machines that participate in the SMS world as SMS servers use the SMS_Inventory_Agent_NT or SMS_Inv_OS2LM services. Those services perform the copying.

For the machines that do not participate as SMS servers and are either a Windows NT Server or Workstation, CLIMONNT.EXE performs the copy. The service (which does not have network access) puts the .RAW inventory files into a local directory, and when the user logs on, the CLIMONNT.EXE program performs the copying to the logon server.

The next step showcases the sophistication of SMS when the primary site collects the inventory files from the logon servers.

COLLECTING THE INVENTORY

Did I say the primary site server does the collection? Of course, you know that there is another component of SMS designed for that purpose. The component that actually performs the collection is the Maintenance Manager. The Maintenance Manager collects the inventory files from all of the logon servers. This is not the only function of the Maintenance Manager, but this is the significant function in reference to the inventory process. The Maintenance Manager is installed on every site server in the SMS hierarchy. It scans the logon servers at a designated polling interval. You can control this configuration parameter, like the others already discussed, from the properties of the site server, with the Services button. (See Figure 14.6.)

Figure 14.6.
The Response
setting correlates
to the polling
interval used by
the Maintenance
Manager.

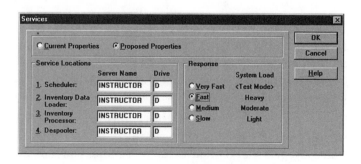

Table 14.2 indicates what the Maintenance Manager does with the different settings.

TABLE 14.2. MAINTENANCE MANAGER AND THE POLLING INTERVAL.

Response Time	Frequency of Maintenance Manager Scans
Very Fast	12 per minute
Fast	60 per minute
Medium	180 per minute
Slow	360 per minute

Tip

Although it is tempting to set the Response setting to Very Fast, the SMS administrator must consider the effects on performance before using that option.

After the Maintenance Manager gets the inventory files from the logon server, another component called the inventory processor takes over. The inventory processor runs on all site servers. The inventory processor takes a careful look at the .RAW and .MIF files. Remember, the .MIF files are generated from the Macintosh and OS/2 machines, whereas the rest of the machines produce .RAW inventory files. The inventory processor makes a comparison between these files and the history files. The history files are kept on the site server in the Site.Srv\Inventry.box\History directory.

Note

Processing the .RAW file involves parsing and verifying the syntax in reference to the Management Information Format (MIF). The parsing is done before the comparison to the history files.

The naming convention of the history file follows the SMS unique identifier, and each file has the .HMS extension. The .MIF generating clients have a history file with an .SMH extension. The .MIF generating clients use a file called HISTORY.MAP to track the computer and the associated history file. Additionally, the HISTORY.MAP file provides identifying information such as the SMSLocation, the SMSID, and the NetcardID.

The whole concept of comparing inventory to the history files is in line with the time-saving, resource-saving approach taken by the SMS designers. Right along with that concept is the creation of a delta .MIF file. You remember from your math classes that the delta is a Greek symbol that means change. A delta .MIF file contains only the inventory changes. Typically, a delta .MIF file is about 5KB in size.

When the inventory processor takes over in order to create the delta .MIF, it makes a comparison to the history file. The inventory processor follows the algorithm described here:

```
If this is a NEW inventory file
then
     write a history file
     write a delta mif file
     send to the inventory data loader
else (not a NEW file)
then
     If this is the SAME as the matching history file
     then
     no delta mif file is sent to the Inventory Loader, unless
     four days have passed
          send heartbeat delta mif file to the inventory loader (see note)
     else (not the same as the matching history file)
     then
          write a history file
          write a delta mif file
          send to the inventory data loader
          endif
endif
```

14

Note

The four-day time span that is mentioned in the preceding algorithm is called the heartbeat interval. If, in fact, the four days pass without a delta .MIF being sent to the inventory loader, then a heartbeat delta .MIF is sent. This small file (2KB) is just an indication that the machine is still connected and participating in the SMS system.

As you can see from the algorithm, the general idea is that the inventory processor sends the delta .MIFs to the inventory loader. The delta .MIF files are put in the SITE.SRV\DATALOAD.BOX\DELTAMIL.COL directory on the site server. The next step is that the inventory loader loads the inventory data into the SQL database.

Receiving the Inventory Information

When the inventory loader gets the delta .MIF files, they are marked to indicate the type of changes that are included. The structure of the inventory is divided into groups. The contents of the delta .MIF file are structured in reference to these groups. The delta .MIF file communicates what to do with a group; for instance, the group might be added, updated, or deleted. The statements that communicate the changes are called pragma statements. The default pragma statement is the add. The pragma statement shows inconsistencies for the data loader. If the pragma statement indicates an update and the record does not exist, then there is a problem.

The inventory loader must determine whether the delta .MIF is for a machine already in the database. In other words, is the delta .MIF an update, or is the delta .MIF for a new participant in the SMS system?

The inventory data loader has a number of different ways to uniquely identify the entry. First, it considers the computer name; the next item is the network card ID, and the last is the SMSID. The SMSID is stored in the SMS.INI file. The most fixed value of these three items is the SMSID. Consider how easy it is for a client to change the name of his machine or how often he or she might put a different network card in a machine. The SMSID has the final say in any questions about the identity of a machine. As with the issues surrounding the delta .MIF, you can also understand this issue in terms of an algorithm.

When all three identifiers match the delta .MIF, the database is updated without any problem. When none of the three identifiers match any entries in the database, it is obviously a new client machine.

If only the SMSID has changed and the other identifiers are still the same, there could be a problem. SMS is smart enough to enter the record as a new record, but it also generates a warning to the SMS Administrator. The warning indicates that there might be a duplicate record. In this situation, it is wise to investigate. You can see the warning in the event log.

If the SMSID did not change but some of the other identifiers did, then there could be a problem. SMS issues a warning in this case also, but the warning indicates that there have been some attribute changes. In this case, SMS does not create another record in the database. SMS assumes that either the computer name or network card number was changed for a good reason. This is probably the most common situation you will encounter.

There is also the possibility that the database has inconsistencies. This could be a situation where the delta .MIF exists and the pragma statements are not adds, which happens with a new entry into the database. This type of situation could occur if the computer was deleted from the database but the associated SMS client software was not deleted from the machine. This situation generates a message to the event log. This situation also generates a RESYNC command. When the RESYNC command is issued, the history file for the offending computer is deleted. The RESYNC command causes SMS to take a complete inventory again to verify the status of the machine. When the inventory data loader issues the RESYNC command, a file called RESYNC.CFG is placed in the \Site.Srv\Maincfg.box\Invdom.box\domain_name directory. The contents of the RESYNC.CFG file are the name of the offending computer and the time the RESYNC command was issued. This file is read when the inventory agent starts, and the inventory is taken regardless of the last scanned value. When the information returns to the inventory loader (through all the same steps again), previous files are deleted to avoid complications.

COMPUTER INVENTORY

The general flow described in the preceding section covered the inventory process and did not make a distinction between hardware and software. You probably noticed in Figure 14.3 that you could set up the hardware and software inventories for different time intervals. Software inventory can be taken in with the hardware inventory, or a software audit can be taken. I will outline the steps necessary to enable software inventory first, and then I will discuss auditing software.

Note

Hardware inventory is enabled by default; software inventory requires special configuration.

SOFTWARE INVENTORY

The software inventory process supports the SMS Administrator for the task of controlling desktop software. This is one of the most critical administrative tasks in the enterprise networking environment. For example, consider the information that is needed before you can perform a simple software upgrade. The questions include whether a client machine already has the package, as well as details about configuration files and drivers. Through careful analysis of configuration files, an administrator can identify and tag potentially problematic installation situations. The capability to take a software inventory before performing software administration activities puts the administrator in a favorable position.

You enable a software inventory by creating an inventory package and designating the software to be inventoried and the files to be collected. The following steps demonstrate the procedure:

1. From the SMS System Administrator application, select the Packages window (see Figure 14.7) when first starting the SMS System Administrator or choose the File | New option from the menu bar.

2. From the Packages window, select File | New to create a new inventory package. (See Figure 14.8.) Take the time to enter meaningful comments and any other extra information for later use.

Figure 14.7.
The Packages
window when
first opened.

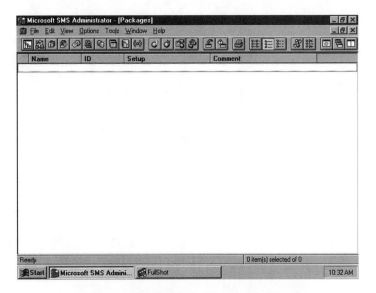

Figure 14.8.
Defining package
properties.

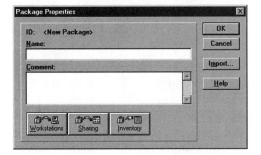

3. Click the Inventory button to enter the information about the software you want to inventory. (See Figure 14.9.)

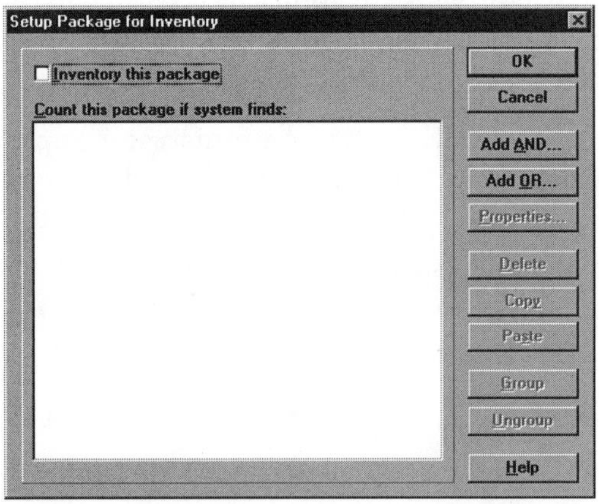

Figure 14.9.
Selecting specific
packages to be
inventoried or
collected.

4. Select the Add button to access the File Properties dialog, shown in Figure 14.10. This screen allows you to select the files by attributes or by browsing.

Figure 14.10. Selecting the files to be inventoried or collected.

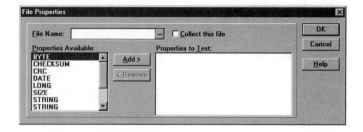

14

5. The process of designating a file to be collected requires entering the file name and checking the Collect this file box. (See Figure 14.11.)

Figure 14.11. You can collect configuration files.

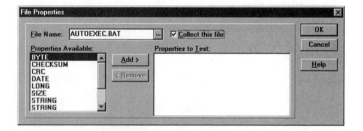

6. The final Setup Package for Inventory window might look like Figure 14.12.

Figure 14.12. A completed package might look like this.

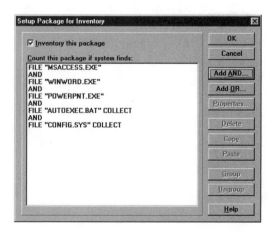

7. The SMS administrator gets the two confirmation messages shown in Figure 14.13 and 14.14.

Figure 14.13.
The update
confirmation
message for the
inventory rules.

Figure 14.14.
The update
confirmation
message for the
packages.

8. The package is ready to send; notice the package identifier that is used throughout the process for identification. (See Figure 14.15.) Also notice the comment that the SMS administrator entered when the package was first created.

Figure 14.15.
Inventory
package in
the Packages
window.

The procedure for adding software inventory is direct. Typically, you might perform software inventory once a week and hardware inventory once a day.

AUDITING SOFTWARE

Auditing software is not the same thing as taking a software inventory. We will outline the differences before we describe the steps to implement software auditing. The differences are related to how they are set up and what their purposes are. Software inventory is performed in a similar manner to hardware inventory.

The setup of the software inventory is similar to the setup of the hardware inventory, and they are both done at the same time, although not necessarily at the same frequency. Remember also that the inventory process is run by the inventory agent. The setup of the auditing is completely separate from the setup of the hardware inventory. Auditing is executed from the client's workstation with the AUDIT16.EXE or the AUDIT32.EXE. The AUDIT16.EXE or AUDIT32.EXE uses the customized rule file as the input for the designation of the files that the SMS administrator wants to audit. Most often, the audit process is run to check for versions of a specific file or the existence of problematic drivers and DLLs. Software inventory is used for the most frequent, continuous inventory purposes, whereas software auditing is used for specific situations and occasional use.

The auditing process follows these steps:

1. Find the AUDIT.RUL file. This file has the rules, unique descriptive characteristics, for over 5,000 commercial software packages. Using the Find command, as shown in Figure 14.16, double-click the file and Wordpad starts.

Figure 14.16.
The AUDIT.RUL
file is in the
\SMS\PRIMSITE.
SRV\AUDIT
directory.

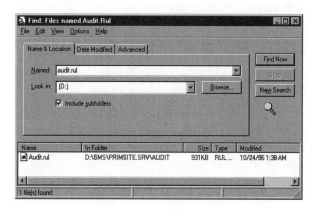

2. Using the Find command in Wordpad, locate the sections that are related to your auditing requirements and select those lines. Use the selection to start another Wordpad file, saving it as text. Don't call the file AUDIT.RUL, because then you lose the thousands of other descriptions. For this example, the new .RUL file is called MYAUDIT.RUL.

3. From the command prompt, compile the file called MYAUDIT.RUL. The compilation process generates an output file called AUDIT.CFG. This output file is always called AUDIT.CFG, regardless of what the .RUL file is called. Figure 14.17 shows the syntax and the desired outcome of the compilation process.

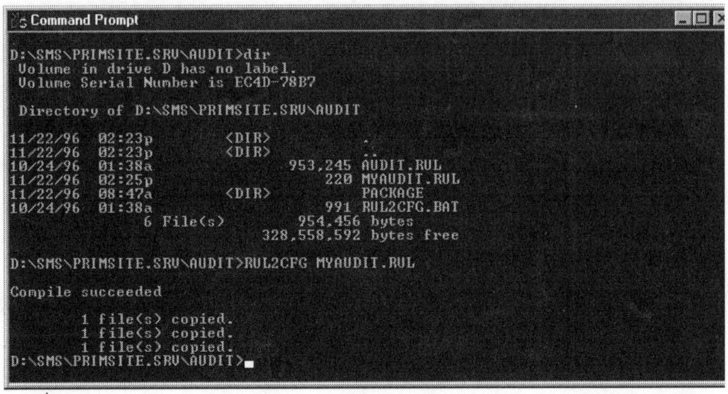

Figure 14.17. Use the RUL2CFG.BAT *file to compile the audit* .RUL *file that you made.*

The client then must run the audit executable file from the workstation. The SMS Administrator has options in this area. Typically, an audit is sent using a Run Command On Workstation job. This gives the administrator the flexibility to be very specific about which machines are going to be audited. Chapters 18, "Packages," and 19, "Jobs," answer the question of how the rule file is distributed so that it can execute at the client's workstation.

INVENTORY FAILURE

Although we all hate to admit it, sometimes things don't go exactly as they should! For example, what if the inventory process fails? Let's consider just such a calamity.

When the inventory agent runs, it considers the possibility of a hardware failure to position the SMS administrator so that he can recover. This preparation done by SMS creates a file named SMSSAFE.TMP. As the extension indicates, SMSSAFE.TMP is a temporary file used to leave traces in the event of a hardware failure. While the inventory agent is working, any failed hardware tests are written to this file, which is kept in the \Ms\SMS\Data directory. If, in fact, there were some hardware failures, the inventory agent copies that information into the SMS.INI file for future reference. At this point, the temporary file is erased. The section in the SMS.INI file referred to as the [WorkstationStatus] section has an entry named FailedHardwareChecks. SMS is smart enough to have the inventory agent read this section so that the same failing hardware test is not performed again.

MS-DOS machines face an interesting situation. These old-fashioned machines are not particular about direct hardware calls. (That's why all those game software programmers love DOS; they can take over everything for speed!) Because of this, the machine might be stopped from the inventory process before the inventory agent can even write the problem to the temporary file. At least the inventory agent is able to create the temporary file, even though the system goes down before it can write the information about the problem.

The next time that inventory runs, the inventory agent sees the SMSSAFE temporary file and concludes that there was a crash before the inventory agent could write the information about the crash. How can the inventory agent determine which hardware test caused the problem?

SMS has a very elegant solution for this situation. The inventory agent writes a line in the file about each test that reads component=Crashed. When the test is successful, the inventory agent returns to the file and writes component=Completed. When the inventory agent starts again and finds the SMSSAFE temporary file still there, it can determine the problem.

Although the inventory agent deletes the temporary file after everything is running properly, the SMS administrator needs to change the information in the SMS.INI file on the client's workstation. The SMS administrator must remove the FailedHardwareChecks section from the [WorkstationStatus] section in the SMS.INI file. The SMS administrator has that remote control capability available from the Help Desk utilities.

INVENTORY STRUCTURE

You can understand the structure of the inventory from a hierarchical perspective. Inventory consists of objects that are viewed and manipulated. The objects are things such as computers and software, which reflect the categorization of the inventory process, hardware and software. The inventory of these objects follows a hierarchical structure. The architecture establishes the structure for a number of objects. Each object has groups, and the groups have attributes. The attributes have the actual values.

The highest level of the structure is the architecture. The architecture has a unique name and various identification groups. An example of this is the Personal Computer architecture, which has identification groups for inventory related to PCs, such as processor, network, operating system, and others, as indicated in Figure 14.18. The other architectures are JobDetails, Package Location, UserGroups, SNMP Traps, and SMSEvents. The SMS administrator will be concerned mainly with the Personal Computer architecture.

Figure 14.18.
The idea of the
architecture, the
group, the
attributes, and
the values for the
attributes.

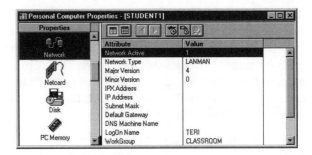

It is possible to extend the inventory capabilities. SMS is an open system, and this flexibility allows SMS administrators to collect inventory that is meaningful to their own operating environments. That means that an administrator could add a new architecture. For example, one might consider adding an architecture related to peripheral devices and call the architecture Peripherals. The groups would be printers, scanners, and so on. The attributes on the scanner would be color, full page, and so on. The values for the attributes would be yes for the color attribute and no for the full page attribute.

Figure 14.18 shows the Personal Computer architecture. The group illustrated is the Network group. The list of attribute starts is headed by the Network Active attribute, and the value for the Network Active attribute is 1.

The structure is the way that the data is organized, but it still doesn't illustrate what is actually kept in the inventory. The contents of the inventory vary according to the machine. For example, if no files have been collected, that group is not going to appear in the Properties section of the Personal Computer architecture. The Personal Computer architecture contains the following groups, in order of appearance, as found on a typical machine:

- ◆ Identification
- ◆ Workstation Status
- ◆ Processor
- ◆ Operating System
- ◆ Network
- ◆ Netcard
- ◆ Disk
- ◆ PC Memory
- ◆ Serial Port
- ◆ Parallel Port
- ◆ Video
- ◆ Mouse

- ◆ PC BIOS
- ◆ IRQ Table
- ◆ Packages (if packages have been used)
- ◆ Collected Files (if any have been collected)

Note

The Properties list includes other entries for convenient access. Examples include the icon to access the Help Desk functions, the icon for the Network Monitor, and, on server machines, the icon for Windows NT Administration. These icons are not actually inventory but are shown in the Properties list for convenient access.

VIEWING THE INVENTORY

Viewing the inventory is when the data actually turns into information after the SMS administrator puts it all together.

You first select the site of interest as indicated in Figure 14.19.

*Figure 14.19.
The screen where
you select the site,
the domain, and
the particular
machine of
interest.*

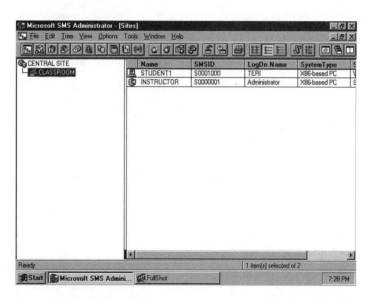

In this example, the site is called the Central Site, the domain name is classroom, and the machine of interest is Student1. When you double-click the computer name, the Properties screen shows the list of properties. Refer to Figure 14.18 to see the properties, attributes, and values.

SMS also gives the SMS administrator the capability to see the history of the inventory. Every time the inventory is updated for a machine, a time and date stamp is put on the record. That time and date stamp is used by the system to keep track of the inventory history. The Personal Computer architecture uses colors to distinguish between historical data and current data. An attribute listed in red indicates the data is different from the last inventory. If the attribute is black, there has been no change. This fast way to tell whether there have been any changes on a system is especially helpful for the Help Desk. The technical support person can check the inventory history for a clear indication of work that has been done on a machine. History is not maintained for any other architecture.

The procedure to view the history begins the same way as the procedure to view inventory data:

1. After you select the site, the domain, and the computer, double-click the computer to access the properties.

2. From the View menu, select Previous History Record. Figure 14.20 shows the differences in viewing a history record.

Figure 14.20.
The bar at the top
of the screen has
the machine
name with the
time and date
stamp.

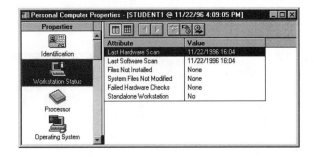

This is the previous inventory! The View menu has three selections related to the history records. The first option is to view the previous record, as shown in Figure 14.20. The next choice gives the option to view the next history record, which either opens the next record or opens the current inventory record if there is no next record. The last choice on the View menu is to display the History dialog, shown in Figure 14.21.

Figure 14.21.
This screen gives
you the opportu-
nity to specify
more detailed
information to
select the history
record.

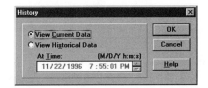

Managing the Inventory

In the broadest sense, you have only very basic functions for working with an inventory. Think of it: All that you might ever do is put things in the inventory (that's the inventory process), take things out of the inventory, move things around, and clean up to make sure there is one of everything. There can be no duplicates. Table 14.3 shows a list of typical management tasks.

Table 14.3. Common inventory management tasks.

Any Inventory	SMS Inventory
Put things in the inventory.	As described in the inventory process.
Take things out of the inventory.	Remove computers from the inventory.
Move things around.	Move computers to various sites and domains.
Clean up things.	Remove files from the various sites.
Ensure that there is one of each.	Remove duplicates.

Taking Things Out of the Inventory

You might think that the simplest of all the management tasks is taking something out of the inventory. However, if you really think about the complexity of the inventory process, you realize that there are pieces of that machine all over—pieces of data related to the existence of that machine. The actual process of deleting a machine from the inventory is a multi-step function.

Taking things out of the inventory involves removing the machine from the inventory, removing the history, and removing any SMS files on the computer. There are three different approaches for this task. You can use the Delete key, the Delete Special key, or the Database Manager Utility (DBCLEAN.EXE).

Using the Delete key is the most direct way to remove a machine. The resulting deletion is not a complete deletion, because the history of that machine is left intact.

To remove the associated history of the machine, you use the Delete Special key. The Delete Special feature deletes the machine and its history. The Delete Special key is on the Edit menu. Figure 14.22 shows the screen that the Delete Special key displays in the Sites window.

Figure 14.22.
The Delete
Special key
removes the
machine and its
history.

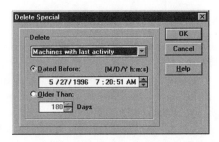

> ## *Note*
>
> The Delete Special key is context sensitive. If you use the Delete Special key for sites, as shown in this example, it deletes machines. If you use the Delete Special key for jobs, it deletes any finished job. If you use the Delete Special key for events or SNMP traps, it acts on those components.

Another way to perform a deletion is by using the SMS Database Manager. The SMS Database Manager is one of the administrative tools in the SMS menu group, as shown in Figure 14.23.

Figure 14.23.
The SMS Data-
base Manager is
accessible from
the Systems
Management
Server group.

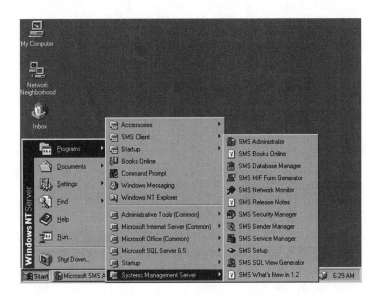

The SMS Database Manager program, DBCLEAN.EXE, is the tool to use for deletions from the database. This utility finds duplicates and unused machines using any of the identifying characteristics you indicate. As discussed earlier in the chapter, the three most significant characteristics are the computer name, the SMSID, and the netcard ID.

Tip

> You can remove the SMS client software from a machine by connecting to the SMS_SHR on the logon server and running DEINSTAL.BAT. If the logon script was changed to run the inventory, it will also need modification. Check the logon script for the SMSLS.BAT file.

MOVING THINGS AROUND IN THE SMS INVENTORY

In the real world of network administration, moving machines is one of the greatest preoccupations. Considering all the structuring and restructuring and the sizing and downsizing of corporations, most machines are moved at least once or twice in their lives! Some machines move even more often. SMS records this movement automatically.

When the client logs onto the new domain, SMS recognizes from the information in the SMS.INI file that the domain code and the site code are different. The SMS word for this is the FalseLogon setting. By default, the FalseLogon setting is 3. The SMS system considers the possibility that this might be just a temporary change and only makes a record of the difference.

This tracking of a different domain logon is also kept in the SMS.INI file. The inventory agent creates a new section in the SMS.INI for tracking this kind of activity. The inventory agent adds a section called the [LogonHistory]. The LogonHistory section has two entries that track what is going on. The first entry is the name of the new domain and site. The second entry is the counter. The counter entry counts the number of times that this location is used for the logon.

At this point, because the inventory agent is not totally sure of where the inventory data should go, the inventory agent does not perform the inventory. The inventory agent allows two logons with the new location data. On the third logon at the new location, the inventory agent understands it is a real move and takes the inventory with the new information. The client machine keeps the original SMSID, and the other information is scanned and updated in the SMS database.

Tip

> You can change the default number of FalseLogon from the Registry under the HKEY_LOCAL_MACHINE\SOFTWARE\Microsoft\SMS\Components\ SMS_MAINTENANCE_MANAGER FalseLogon Limit entry. The value of this key is kept in the DOMAIN.INI file under the InvAgentFalseLogonCount entry of the [SMS] section. This updates the InvAgeFalseLogonCount entry in the SMS.INI file.

Cleaning Up Files Left at the Various Sites

If the inventory process was used to collect files as well as collect the inventory, you might need to delete some of the files. This collection of files is typically a collection of configuration files, such as the AUTOEXEC.BAT, CONFIG.SYS, and INI files. In this case, you can perform the deletion with the Database Administrator program (DBCLEAN.EXE). DBCLEAN.EXE removes the collected files in the site database as well as on the site server.

Ensure One of Each

Duplicates in any database system are a problem. One of the fundamental concepts of database theory is that each record has a unique identifier. The SMS database, of course, requires a unique identifier to keep track of the records.

When the inventory records are being loaded in the inventory process, SMS examines the record being added to the database. The inventory loader is faced with the problem of inserting a record in the database that may already exist with a different identifier. The various reasons that this might happen relate mostly to movement of machines and equipment. An example is the deletion of the SMS.INI file, which contains the SMSID. The inventory process sees the machine as new and gives it a new ID. The computer is in the inventory list twice.

You should not delete a machine unless you determine that the machine is truly a duplicate. Assuming this is the case, you perform the deletion from the SMS Database Manager, as described earlier.

Sometimes, investigating duplicates reveals that, in fact, there is only one machine. In this situation, the records must be merged. Merging is a special function of the SMS Database Manager that allows the preservation of the history of the machine.

The SMS Database Manager displays duplicate machines. You choose the Machines menu and Display Duplicate Personal Computers. Once you display them, you can merge the duplicates by selecting Merge History for Selected PCs from the Edit menu.

Customizing the Inventory

SMS was designed for total management of the systems within your organization. The structure and contents of the inventory are a comprehensive representative of what is typically found in the vast majority of corporate environments. To accommodate the need for different kinds of inventory requirements, SMS includes methods to extend the database. This high degree of flexibility is another feature of SMS that makes it so great to use.

THE PROCESS OF CUSTOMIZING THE INVENTORY

The first step in customizing the inventory is creating a form for the collection of the desired data. You create the form in the Form Generator utility. After the form is created, it is distributed to the client machines, usually with a Run Command On Workstation job. The client enters the desired data, and the data is collected by the inventory process. You can view the new data with the other inventory information from the Sites window. This relatively simple process takes advantage of the already existing structures and processes within SMS.

FORM GENERATION

The inventory data must be in the .MIF format. The SMS database uses a format called the Management Information Format (MIF). MIF is a standard format created by the Desktop Management Task Force (DMTF), whose function is to develop standards for the desktop environment.

The SMS Form Generator utility creates the forms used to collect the data from the client. The .MIF form creates an output file in the appropriate format for assimilation into the SMS database. The SMS administrator has the option of editing the default form, UINFO.XNF, or creating a completely new form. The default form is in the SMS\SITE.SRV\MAINCFG.BOX\CLIENT.SRC\platform.BIN directory. The SMS administrator must run this Form Generator utility from a Windows NT machine.

This demonstration modifies the default form, UINFO.XNF:

1. From the Programs menu, open the Systems Management Server group, select the Forms Generator, and open the default form, UINFO.XNF. It is located in the SMS\SITE.SRV\MAINCFG.BOX\CLIENT.SRC\platform.BIN directory. (See Figure 14.24.)

Figure 14.24.
The existing
structure of the
default form.

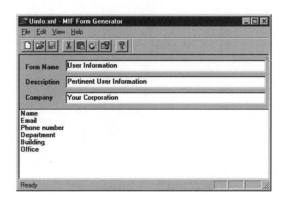

14

INVENTORY: KNOWLEDGE IS POWER

2. You can add three kinds of fields to any form: the Text field, the Number field, and the List field. From the Edit menu, select New Field | Add and choose the Text Field type. The screen looks like Figure 14.25.

Figure 14.25.
Entering a Text
Item field.

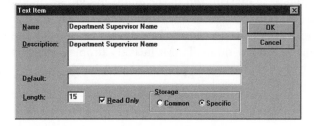

You can also use Number fields, as shown in Figure 14.26.

Figure 14.26.
Entering a
Number field.

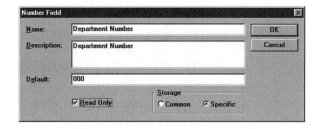

You can also use lists, as shown in Figure 14.27.

Figure 14.27.
Entering a List
field.

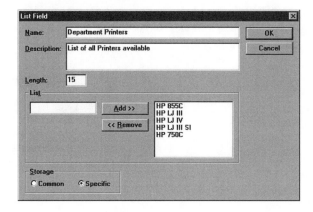

3. Save the form.

The screens for the various field types have extra options. The Read Only option relates to how the information is displayed; the viewer cannot change the data. It has no significance to the client that is entering the data. The Length option concerns the maximum length of the field. The Storage option that offers either Common or Specific relates to how the data is kept within the database. If there are going to be many common answers—for example, yes or no—the SMS database stores it in a different manner to avoid redundancy. The Specific choice indicates that there are so many different answers, it is not worth trying to find a pattern of repeating answers to economize on storage requirements. After adding to the existing user information form, you save the modified UINFO.XNF form.

FORM DISTRIBUTION AND COLLECTION

Distribution of the .XNF files is handled in one of two ways. A new form is distributed as a Run Command On Workstation job, using the inventory agent as the file to run. If the default user UINFO.XNF form was modified, it is handled in the normal fashion by the inventory agent.

After the client completes and saves the form, the data is written by the form generator process. The SMS.INI tells the form generator where to write the .MIF file by naming the directory in the MachineISVMIFPath entry. Although you can change this directory, the default directory listed after this entry is MS\SMS\NOIDMIFS. When the inventory agent runs the next time, it finds the .MIF file and adds it to the .RAW file, and the processing continues.

VIEWING THE CUSTOMIZED INVENTORY

You can view the customized data in the Properties window of the selected computer. The customization shows in the screen under the category of user information.

ACCOMPLISHING YOUR REPORTING GOALS WITH SMS

The goals of the SMS administrator are diversified. Of course, one of the primary goals is to keep management satisfied. In the corporate environment, that means extensive reporting capabilities for management. You can use inventory to accomplish this goal by considering and using the features of SMS. For example, with the capability to add to the inventory, the SMS administrator has total control over managing and tracking corporate resources. Integral to this goal is the capability to perform the type of reporting that managers expect, such as strategic-level reporting. You can achieve this type of reporting by using Crystal Reports, which comes with SMS. Additionally, if an SMS administrator is already entrenched in another reporting tool, such as Microsoft Access, then he or she can use that, too. The SMS database, which is kept in Microsoft SQL, is ODBC-compliant. This means that it follows the most common standard of compatibility in the database world and can communicate with any ODBC-compliant reporting tool.

Before you can use Crystal Reports, you must create SMS views and then complete the ODBC configuration. To summarize the complete process, first run SMSVIEW and then install Crystal Reports and configure the ODBC setup.

SMS views are created by running a program called SMSVIEW. This program works on the SQL database. It creates a representation (such as another copy) in which the internal SQL storage format is made usable for ODBC-compliant software. What actually happens is transparent to the SMS administrator. No messages are displayed; the representations are just created for later use.

You can run SMSVIEW from the SMS program group or from the command line. If you run it from the program group, select SMS SQL View Generator. See the dialog box in Figure 14.28.

Figure 14.28.
The logon screen
that gives access
to the SQL
database.

From the sign-on point, nothing else shows on the screen; however, if your machine's hard drive cranks, you hear it cranking. After it is finished, you see the screen shown in Figure 14.29.

Figure 14.29.
The SMSVIEW
program is
finished.

You run the command-line version of SMSVIEW from the SMS\SITE.SRV*platform*.bin directory. The syntax is as follows:

```
SMSVIEW options
```

options is the logon identification information for the SQL database:

/S	Server name
/L	Logon name
/P	Password
/D	Name of the database

An example is SMSVIEW /S:INSTRUCTOR /L:SA /P:PASSWORD /D:SMS.

If you run SMSVIEW from the command line instead of the SMS program group, the success or failure of the process is recorded in the Windows NT event log under the applications section.

The next step is to install Crystal Reports on the installation CD-ROM. This straightforward installation takes a short amount of time. Installation choices relate to where Crystal Reports is installed and whether other machines will use it. Installing Crystal Reports also installs the ODBC software.

After installing Crystal Reports, you need to configure the ODBC. You can do this from the last step of the Crystal Reports installation or from the ODBC icon in the Control Panel of the Windows NT machine. The ODBC configuration wants information about what database you will be using. In the situation of installing this with SMS, the SQL server drivers are used. Again, this is a direct installation.

SUMMARY

This chapter's discussion covered the inventory process, followed by a discussion of the common administrative tasks associated with the inventory. Truly, inventory is the focal point of the SMS system.

CHAPTER 15

Using Help Desk Utilities and Diagnostic Tools

The "ooh" and "wow" of SMS have always been the Help Desk utilities and diagnostic tools. They provide a means for the administrator to remotely execute specific operations on the SMS client. They also provide a mechanism for doing different diagnostics on the client. Many other operations of SMS enable you to pull information, although the information is not in real time. With the Help Desk utilities and diagnostic tools, the administrator can obtain real-time information. This increases the power that the administrator has at his or her desktop. The people who benefit from this feature the most are the people that it is named after— the help desk. Over the years, help desks have tended to cause much confusion for an information services (IS) department. Help desk people cannot always help all the people who need help at a given time. The Help Desk utilities enable the help desk to become more productive in the amount of time given. This, of course, is going to save money for the company because less labor is required.

The tools given for troubleshooting the desktops fall into two categories. The Help Desk utilities provide remote operation of the user's workstation. The diagnostic tools enable a help desk person or administrator to pull diagnostics information about the workstation. These two functions make this feature complete for a help desk person to provide support for the users in their environment, which in effect saves time, money, and increases efficiency in the IS department.

Using the Help Desk Utilities

The Help Desk utilities provide several different remote options that enable the help desk person to act as if he were at the user's machine. The five Help Desk utilities that come with SMS version 1.2 can offer a lot of power in controlling the desktop:

◆ Remote Control

◆ Remote Reboot

◆ Remote Execute

◆ Remote File Transfer

◆ Remote Chat

Figure 15.1 shows the Help Desk utilities in the computer's inventory under the SMS Administrator. Not all client platforms support the Help Desk utilities function. The Help Desk utilities function runs only on the following selected platforms:

◆ MS-DOS

◆ Windows 3.1 and Windows for Workgroups 3.11

◆ Windows 95

◆ Windows NT version 3.51 or later

Figure 15.1.
The Help Desk
utilities shown in
the SMS Admin-
istrator.

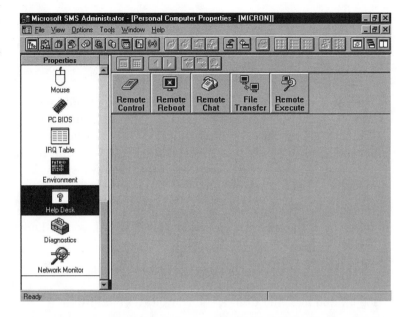

> ## Note
>
> Macintosh and OS/2 clients are not supported under the Help Desk utilities.

REQUIREMENTS FOR USING THE HELP DESK UTILITIES

Before running the Help Desk utilities, you need to fulfill a few requirements. The first requirement is that the SMS client needs to be part of the SMS database. You have to inventory the client to allow it to be remotely controlled. Another key factor in running the Help Desk utilities is to make sure that the machine running the SMS Administrator has the same common network transport protocol as the machine being supported. It is important to make sure when setting up the common protocol that the LANA number is the same as the Remote Control TSR running on the host. If the remote host is running MS-DOS, Windows 3.1, or Windows for Workgroups, it is important that it has at least a 386 or higher processor. The last requirement is to make sure that the remote client allows you to access his or her machine. You can set this up in the Help Desk options. By default, an administrator is disallowed from running any of the Help Desk utilities for security reasons. These requirements are specific to the MS-DOS, Windows 3.1, and Windows for Workgroups machines.

15

HELP DESK UTILITIES AND DIAGNOSTIC TOOLS

Note

You cannot use the Help Desk utilities over a connection that uses IBM's SNA network protocol.

The requirements for Windows NT differ to some degree. It is important to make sure that the administrator running SMS Administrator who tries to access the Windows NT machine by using the Help Desk utilities is part of the local machine's administrators group. It is important to make sure that the LANA 0 protocol is set up the same way as the same protocol that is set up on the SMS Administrator's machine. This can be configured in the Registry.

It is important to follow these requirements for controlling the Windows NT–based desktops. If these requirements are not fulfilled, you will have trouble configuring the desktops themselves.

With Windows NT, a user does not have to be logged on for the administrator to be able to remotely control them. This gives you the option of being able to log on and log off and lock and unlock the workstation at any time.

Allowing the administrator to access the workstation is up to the user. This is set up in the Help Desk options. By default, the administrator is not allowed to run the Help Desk utilities. Figure 15.2 shows the Help Desk options on the client, which doesn't disallows the administrator from coming in.

Note

All operations done with any of the Help Desk utilities are logged under the security log in the Windows NT Event Viewer.

REMOTE CONTROL

The capability to remotely control the workstation has been very fascinating for people over the years. There have been several packages such as PC-Anywhere and Remoteware that allow people to do this over modems. One of the great powers of Remote Control is that it does work over RAS. This gives it the capability to use a modem to remotely control an SMS client. When SMS version 1.0 first came out, there were many problems with the Help Desk utilities, especially Remote Control. Now, it is a much more powerful and stable tool in the later versions. SMS version 1.2 provides a very sound way of remotely controlling workstations.

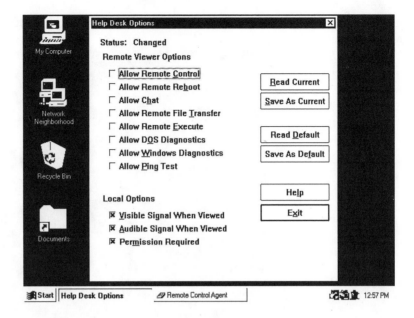

Figure 15.2. The Help Desk Options menu disallowing administrators from running Help Desk utilities.

One of the benefits of SMS version 1.2 is that it allows Windows NT machines to be remotely controlled, although they must have at least version 3.51 or later. Now that SMS has support for Windows NT, it is much more enticing to use the Help Desk utilities. Although many people use the Help Desk utilities with Windows 3.1 and Windows for Workgroups workstations, many companies are now moving to Windows NT, which makes Remote Control much more needed for these environments.

To allow Remote Control to work, it is important to have the Remote Control agent running on the client. After the client has been inventoried, the SMS client programs are installed onto the client. One of these programs is the Remote Control agent. Windows NT machines have an actual service that is part of the Client Configuration Manager Service, which allows the Remote Control agent to run. Once the requirements are filled, these files and tasks can be run to allow the administrator to access the desktop. It is important also to understand that the Help Desk options of the SMS client tools allow the administrator to remotely perform operations.

Once the agent is running, the administrator can remotely control the desktop by performing the following steps:

1. Start SMS Administrator.
2. Expand the client's inventory.
3. Move the scrollbar down and choose Help Desk.
4. Choose the Remote Control button.

In Figure 15.3, the administrator is remotely controlling a Windows 95 workstation.

Figure 15.3.
A Windows 95
client being
controlled
remotely.

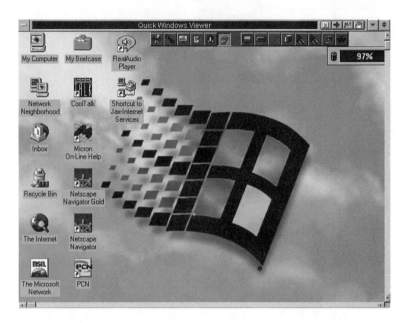

REMOTE EXECUTE

Remote Execute is a tool that many people would never expect a help desk person to run. However, it offers much power to the help desk person for providing support to the desktop, especially for things such as virus scans. Once a remote execute has been initiated, it runs only on the SMS client. The SMS administrator does not see any of the actions of the remote execute. When the actual command is completed, no other function operates after that command. Remote Execute can be very important in updating operating system software. Many patches and different updates that are sent out in executables can actually be run on your workstations with a remote execute.

Figure 15.4 shows the Run Program at User's Workstation dialog in SMS Administrator. To allow a remote execute to happen, you need to do the following:

1. Start the SMS Administrator.
2. Expand the client's inventory.
3. Move the scrollbar down and choose Help Desk.
4. Choose the Remote Execute button.

Figure 15.4.
The Run Program
at User's Work-
station dialog.

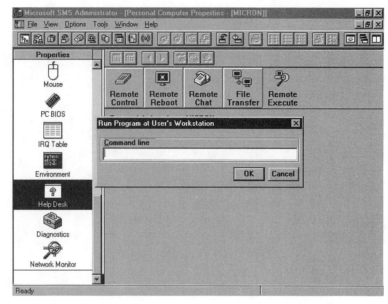

REMOTE FILE TRANSFER

Remote File Transfer is one of the most unbelievable tools that Microsoft has developed. You can use Remote File Transfer to send updated configuration files to the workstation. For example, it is much easier to update a workstation's CONFIG.SYS by using the Remote File Transfer. The Remote File Transfer provides you a view that shows you both the remote and local workstation drives and directories so that movement of files is very simple. You can then place that configuration file in a specific directory.

Figure 15.5 shows the Remote File Transfer utility. To enable an SMS administrator to use the Remote File Transfer utility, you must do the following:

1. Start the SMS Administrator.
2. Expand the client's inventory.
3. Move the scrollbar down and choose Help Desk.
4. Choose the Remote File Transfer button.

The Remote File Transfer utility allows an administrator to update not only configuration files but also executable files (or any other kind of file). This function allows a possibly corrupt DLL file to be updated instantaneously. The Remote File Transfer utility is another tool that is increasingly popular due to its real-time functionality.

Figure 15.5.
The Remote
Transfer File
utility.

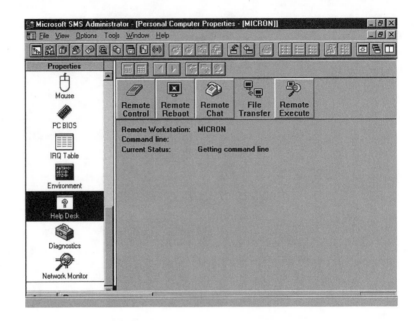

REMOTE CHAT

The Remote Chat function allows the help desk person to chat with the client at the desktop. This function becomes extremely beneficial for communication between the help desk person and the client at the desktop. When using this tool it is important to understand that it is generally used as a supplement for quick and spontaneous messages across the network. Because of the availability of telephones, Remote Chat isn't a popular tool in most organizations. It is very popular when you deal with a client at a remote distance. This decreases the amount of long distance charges for a corporation.

To allow Remote Chat to work, the administrator needs to do the following:

1. Start the SMS Administrator.
2. Expand the client's inventory.
3. Move the scrollbar down and choose Help Desk.
4. Choose the Remote Chat button.

Note

The Remote Chat feature was put into SMS version 1.1. This feature was not included in version 1.0, although it is documented as a utility in the product.

Figure 15.6 shows the Remote Chat window in the SMS Administrator.

Figure 15.6.
The Remote Chat
utility.

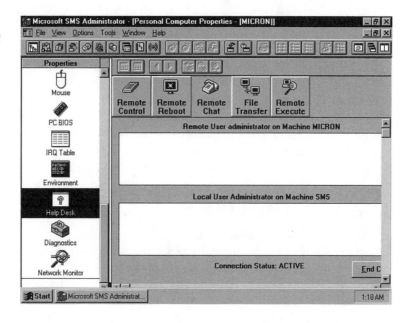

REMOTE REBOOT

The Remote Reboot utility allows an administrator to remotely reboot a workstation from the SMS Administrator. This function is important when some type of configuration requires a reboot. The only requirement is that the user must log back on to the workstation for the SMS Administrator help desk person to remotely control it again.

One of the most important situations for this utility occurs when a workstation is locked up, there is nothing that the SMS Administrator help desk person can do, and the user isn't sure exactly what to do. In this situation, the help desk person can reboot the workstation to allow it to come back up. Remote Reboot is even more beneficial on Windows NT machines because you can remotely control them again; the Remote Agent can still run, even though a user is not logged in.

To kick off the Remote Reboot, the administrator needs to perform the following tasks:

1. Start SMS Administrator.
2. Expand the computer's inventory.
3. Move the scrollbar down and pick Help Desk.
4. Select the Remote Reboot button.

TRAINING TIPS

When you control a workstation remotely, the user is aware of exactly what you are doing. It is the only operation that is a real-time operation performed by the SMS Administrator. When initially developing a training plan for your users in your environment, it is important to spend a lot of time explaining the Help Desk options. The reason for this is that when an administrator attempts to access the Help Desk options, the user is prompted for permission. If the user does not answer yes, it prevents the administrator from accessing the workstation. Another possible problem is that the user can deselect the Allow Remote buttons in the Help Desk options program. This keeps an administrator from performing any remote operations on the client, which is extremely detrimental if the client is in a remote site.

DIAGNOSTIC TOOLS

SMS also provides another troubleshooting feature, the diagnostic tools. This feature allows an administrator or help desk person to look at the current machine's parameters. The parameters can include a great deal of information. There is a difference in diagnostic tools for each client platform. Depending on the client used, the set of diagnostic tools changes. The MS-DOS diagnostic tools offer one set of options, but the Windows-based clients are different. It is important to understand the differences. Figure 15.7 shows the diagnostic tools for a client workstation. The diagnostic tools you see are Windows-based tools, which provide options to diagnose a Windows-based client.

Figure 15.7.
The diagnostic tools.

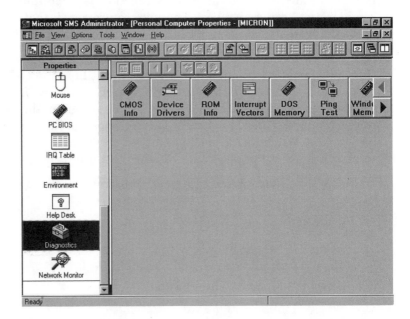

The diagnostic options for the MS-DOS platform include the following:

- ◆ CMOS Info
- ◆ Device Drivers
- ◆ ROM Info
- ◆ Interrupt Vectors
- ◆ DOS Memory
- ◆ PING Test

Windows-based clients offer some additional options:

- ◆ Windows Memory
- ◆ Windows Modules
- ◆ Windows Tasks
- ◆ Windows Classes
- ◆ Global Heaps
- ◆ GDI Heaps

The type of options you can select depends on the platform you are running.

CMOS Info

The CMOS (complementary metal-oxide semiconductor) Info selection offers you information about the CMOS static configuration memory in each computer. This information tells you about the major subcomponents of your machine. The CMOS contains all the low-level settings for hardware subcomponents of each computer, and also keeps track of the time. You can view this information using the CMOS Info button.

Device Drivers

The Device Drivers selection tells you what device drivers are loaded into memory. This is important for a help desk person or administrator who needs to view the different drivers that a workstation is running. The information helps the administrator figure out if there might be an invalid device driver loading on a workstation.

ROM Info

The ROM Info option tells the administrator what ROM chips are installed in the machine. For example, a SCSI controller includes a ROM chip, which contains a program that tells the controller how to do its job. You can view information about that ROM chip by using the ROM Info option.

INTERRUPT VECTORS

One of the biggest things that happens to workstations is a conflict between different hardware devices. For a help desk person, this can be frustrating because the user does not have enough information to figure out what might be wrong with the machine. The Interrupt Vectors option gives the help desk person the capability to see if different devices are conflicting with each other.

DOS MEMORY

The DOS Memory selection tells you how much memory is being used by DOS programs (the amount of memory taken by programs that are loaded between 0 and 640KB). This can sometimes give an administrator information about conventional memory. Workstations may have problems running specific MS-DOS programs because they do not have enough conventional memory. The DOS Memory feature enables you to troubleshoot that problem.

PING TEST

Many times, it is hard for an administrator to make sure that a workstation is up and running on the network. If you are running TCP/IP, you can use the PING utility. If TCP/IP is used, SMS allows an administrator or help desk person to make sure that the network is able to find the workstation.

Note

All the functions described for MS-DOS are also provided on the Windows-based clients. The Windows-based clients also have an extra set of tools, which are described in the following section.

WINDOWS DIAGNOSTIC TOOLS

The features described in this section are only for Windows-based clients who are not using Windows NT. Windows NT clients are not included in the options provided for Windows-based clients. See the section "Windows NT" later in this chapter for information about the diagnostic tools for that platform. You run the Windows NT diagnostics to diagnose a Windows NT machine.

WINDOWS MEMORY

Windows Memory allows the administrator to see what amount of memory Windows has used and what amount is available. This gives the administrator a grip on what actual memory is left on a Windows workstation. This becomes a great benefit when troubleshooting many issues relating to running programs. Even though Windows handles memory a lot better than MS-DOS, memory sometimes becomes a problem on a Windows workstation.

WINDOWS MODULES

Sometimes, it is important for a help desk person or administrator to understand the different modules that are running on a Windows machine. Some modules can conflict with others, especially when memory is involved. The Windows Modules option details the specific modules that are currently running on the Windows machine.

WINDOWS TASKS

The Windows Tasks option enables you to look at the different tasks that are running in Windows. It gives you information much like what a Task Manager or Task List does in a specific Windows-based client. The administrator can see what tasks are currently running on the workstation in case there is conflict between the different applications.

WINDOW CLASSES

The Window Classes option provides information on the different classes used to construct the Windows programs. Classes of windows are used for different purposes within Microsoft Windows. Some provide messages, others provide specific types of dialog boxes (such as About boxes), and others are the primary window of an application. These are not to be confused with the newer use of the term classes, which refers to definitions of objects, in object-oriented programming. These classes can be spelled out by the Windows Classes option.

GLOBAL HEAP

The Global Heap option provides information for the administrator that gauges the amount of free memory available for all applications to run on the workstation. This is not to be confused with Local Heap, which provides information to the administrator about free memory for a specific application. With the Global Heap option, administrators can get detailed information on what amount of memory is left on the workstation. This becomes increasingly important for many Windows-based clients because many of the Windows-based applications take a great deal of memory and that amount of memory must be tracked. This gauge can also give you specific information on what objects actually take that memory, which is important to find out if there is a runaway object that keeps taking up memory that it shouldn't.

GDI HEAP

The Graphic Device Interface (GDI) offers support for various graphical devices, such as computer display and printing functionality, and it takes a great deal of memory. Using the GDI Heap option, an administrator can easily track the amount of memory being used by the GDI for these functions. Tracking the memory becomes increasingly important when working with a workstation because the GDI is one of the most important resources for the workstation to operate.

TROUBLESHOOTING CONSIDERATIONS

It is important when working with the remote troubleshooting packages to take into consideration the different mechanisms for troubleshooting the communication of the workstation using the Help Desk utilities or the diagnostic tools. Many factors come into play when making sure that these processes are intact. The following list describes a few things that the administrator needs to consider when troubleshooting with the Help Desk utilities and diagnostic tools:

◆ Make sure the client is accessible from the network.

◆ Make sure the proper TSR is loaded (USERTSR, USERIPX).

◆ Make sure the protocol running on the SMS Administrator program machine is the same as the common default protocol on the host. Possibly, the wrong LANA number was allocated on the client.

◆ Ensure that the SMS client hasn't changed its NetBIOS (computer) name since the client was last inventoried.

◆ Ensure the client is running the Remote Control agent.

◆ Make sure a compatible video display driver is being used.

◆ If running NetWare, make sure the appropriate TSR (USERIPX) is being used.

WINDOWS NT

The Help Desk utilities discussed so far apply to all Windows-based clients, although the diagnostic tools dealt only with Windows 3.1, Windows for Workgroups, and Windows 95–based clients. With Windows NT, the rules are a little different. When viewing a Windows NT workstation's inventory in the SMS Administrator, you see the administrative tools for the Windows NT machine. With this, you can execute various administrative tools. Figure 15.8 shows the administrative tools for Windows NT, which can run the following applications:

◆ User Manager for Domains

◆ Performance Monitor

- ◆ Server Manager
- ◆ Event to Trap Translator
- ◆ Event Viewer

Figure 15.8.
The administra-
tive tools for
Windows NT.

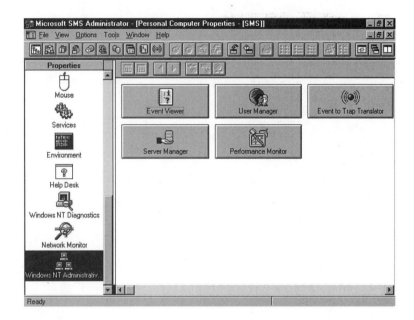

Windows NT Diagnostic Tools

With the Windows NT diagnostic tools, you can pull the same diagnostic information that you can with the MS-DOS–based and Windows-based clients and also find additional information that helps you access several different performance gauging events and specific permission problems. This gives the administrator the upper hand in being able to control Windows NT clients.

Summary

The Help Desk utilities and diagnostic tools are the most popular tools in SMS. There are many things that can benefit an administrator or a help desk person who is supporting desktop computers. The Help Desk utilities and diagnostic tools facilitate the work of the administrator by putting control of the workstation into his or her hands. The power of this control provides efficiency, time, and (ultimately) more money for the company that uses SMS.

CHAPTER 16

Queries

The query is arguably the most powerful aspect of SMS. Gathering client hardware statistics, software versions, and the myriad of other details serves little purpose without the capability to access, group, and massage data to aid in making sound business decisions. Your ability to do this by making intelligent requests based on business need will undoubtedly enhance the value of SMS in your organization.

Inventory information is the most obvious information to retrieve from your SMS database. There is, however, much more to SMS queries. SMS itself is a concatenation of many pieces that give you a finished product. The piece you are concerned with in this chapter is the front end to the SQL Server database. Keeping the idea of the front end in mind, you can see the underlying power in SMS. It is this power that allows you to use queries to trigger alerts or view the details of a job, such as type and status, and to group client PCs in any manner that suits you.

Note

> For the purposes of this chapter, all sample queries were conducted on SMS 1.2. I used SQL Server 6.5 on the same test server, although this does not matter technically. It only allows for faster queries as long as the platform is adequately powered. Finally, the primary site server was a primary domain controller running Windows NT 4.0.
>
> I used a combination of SMS, SQL Server, and Windows NT for no other reason than that was the non-production server assigned for this task. I conducted the same or similar tests with combinations of SMS 1.1 and 1.2 Beta, SQL 6.0 and 6.5, and Windows NT 3.51.

WHAT IS A QUERY?

Queries are, in their simplest form, an attempt at retrieving information. SMS, with a Microsoft SQL Server back end, contains a wealth of information waiting for retrieval. In this context, a query is a structured request based on a user-constructed set of criteria. Query execution results in an output derived from information within the SMS database.

The query itself contains one or more expressions separated by logical operators. Each expression derives structure from an architecture. Each architecture contains attributes for comparison by a relational operator to a value that either you or SMS supplies. The expression uses relational operators to compare an attribute's value stored in the SMS database to a value that is either entered by you or is a stored value supplied by SMS.

TYPES OF QUERIES

There are essentially two types of queries, the saved query and the ad hoc query. (Detailed information on ad hoc queries follows in the section "Ad Hoc Queries.") A saved query can be either a canned Microsoft query, denoted by SMS in the first three characters of the ID, or one you create, denoted by the site code in the first three characters of the ID. (See Figure 16.1.) These predefined queries provide some useful queries and the capability to add or delete any criteria contained therein. Additionally, you may delete predefined queries if so desired. However, they are a good reference for an administrator new to queries, and you should not delete them before you explore their usefulness.

Figure 16.1.
The query
window.

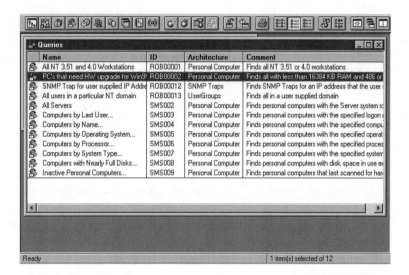

The queries mentioned so far lend themselves to being either attended or unattended. I am referring to automating your query. Unattended queries require no input upon execution. Unattended queries include premeditated input to satisfy the need for comparison value. Attended (non-automated) queries require administrator intervention upon execution. For example, you can define a query that checks for machines with RAM less than or equal to an unknown quantity. SMS then prompts you to enter the amount before executing the query.

THE QUERY WINDOW

Before you delve into creating the query, it is important to understand the query window and some of its components. Figure 16.1 shows an example of a query window. From left to right, the query window displays the saved query name, its ID, the architecture queried, and an administrator-supplied comment.

16

A new query requires a query name, ideally a useful one, to describe its function. The field supplied is 50 characters long and must be unique. No two query names can be the same. This caveat makes perfect sense in that you would never know which one to pick without examining the properties. Further, it helps to be as self-explanatory as possible in your naming convention because others (and you) may become confused by nondescriptive names.

The ID field is also unique, but it is generated by SMS. Three-character prefixes matching the site code precede the queries you create. For example, if your site code is ROB, your query identifier also uses this code. The number following the site code is a hexadecimal number that is simply the next number in sequence.

Tip

To list your saved queries together, click the ID column on the description bar. The query window lists by the column you select in alphabetical order.

You choose the architecture, and SMS supplies the attributes. Each architecture supplies a different set of criteria from which the administrator derives query details. Architectures are discussed later in this chapter in the section "Architectures."

The far right column, Comment, describes what the creator of the query envisioned as the query's purpose. You have 256 characters to describe what you intend the query to do. This field should always contain as detailed a description as possible. Properly documented queries, when compared to the actual logic in the query, reveal the original intention. The comment then becomes a textual representation of the logic.

CREATING QUERIES

Before you can create a query, you should be well versed in the various components. The following discussion examines the components of a query and what you will see in the Query and Query Properties dialogs. It also provides an explanation of architectures, clauses and subclauses, precedence, logical operators, relational operators, and expressions. If you are familiar with all these components of a query, you can skip ahead to the section "Steps to Creating a Query."

Queries are actually several components working with each other to give you the information you need. Each query must have criteria that may be a particular architecture with or without additional expressions connected by logical operators. Additionally, grouping tells SMS to consider the expressions connected by logical operators as a like entity.

The Query Properties dialog shown in Figure 16.2 shows the query name at the top. Below are the comment and architecture fields. The large text box in the lower left, Find all [architecture] items where:, is for the expression list. Later sections of this chapter will explore the buttons to the right that show expressions and logical operators.

Figure 16.2.
The Query
Properties dialog.

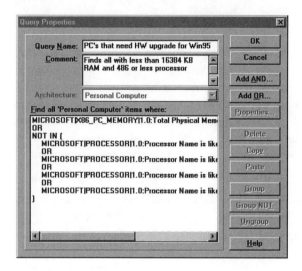

ARCHITECTURES

SMS defines architectures containing attributes you use to create a query. Each architecture contains various differing criteria from which to choose.

Each architecture has attributes, and each attribute is a member of a group. In SMS terms, an attribute is a property of a group. SMS structures like attributes into groups as a way of inventorying. A particular item such as the network card falls into an inventory group—in this case, the Network group.

SMS stores information from inventories such as the network card (or any other item) as values for each attribute (that is, IRQ, Port Address, Manufacturer, and so on). For example, if the attribute is IRQ, a typical value is 5.

SMS also uses class names for group identification. Each class name may not be unique within a group. For example, in the architecture Personal Computer, the class MICROSOFT|OPERATING_SYSTEM|1.0 is unique within the group Operating System. However, the group Operating System may have more than one class. SMS uses class to distinguish between groups that may have the same name. Class entails organization, the group name, and the version number. Organization refers to the organization that defined the group, so the name MICROSOFT appears in every class but American Power Conversion or internally generated MIFs.

16

Note

When you choose your architecture, keep in mind that once an expression is created from that architecture, the option to change architectures is grayed out. You can only query from a single architecture at a time with SMS. It is possible to use a third-party product to create hybrid queries.

Table 16.1 lists some of the most commonly used architectures, groups, attributes, and a description. This table is not all-inclusive; it is merely an overview of the features in the various architectures. You only need to choose between them. Personal Computer is the default and appears in the Query Properties dialog, and if you do not change it, the query is based on this architecture. This architecture is the default because it is the most commonly used; it has the most extensive list of attributes, and arguably, it is the most important.

TABLE 16.1. ARCHITECTURES.

Architecture	Description
Personal Computer	Contains American Power Conversion (Firmware Revision, Low Battery, and so on), Disk (Percent Free, Size, File System, and so on), Environment (variables), Identification (SMS Identifiers), IRQ Table (Values, Handlers, Addresses, and so on), Mouse (Manufacturer, Hardware, and so on), Netcard (IRQ, Port Address, and so on), Network (LogOn Name, Subnet Mask, Workgroup, and so on), Operating System (Name, Version, Build Number, and so on), Parallel Port (Parallel Port Index, Port Address), PC BIOS (BIOS Manufacturer, Release Date, and so on), PC Memory (Base Memory, Total Physical Memory, and so on), Processor (Name, Type, Quantity), Serial Port (Carrier Detect, Current Baud Rate, and so on), Services (Name, Start Time, and so on), User Information (user added Name, Department, and so on), Video (Adapter Type, Display Type, and so on), Workstation Status (Failed Hardware Check, Last Hardware Scan, and so on). The information here is the most extensive of all the architectures and thus is used most often.

Architecture	Description
PackageLocation	Contains package location identifiers such as MasterCopy, PackageID, Package Type, ServerName, and so on. Used to determine location of packages within your SMS installation.
UserGroups	Contains group identifiers: Domain, SiteCode, and UserGroup.
JobDetails	Contains job detail identifiers such as DetailData, JobID, RequestID, and Status. SMS tracks and logs information associated with jobs so the administrator can determine results.
SMSEvent	Contains SMS event identifiers such as EventType, MachineName, and SMSID. These apply to events generated by SMS and logged in the SMS event log.
SNMP Traps	New to SMS 1.2: SMS now stores SNMP traps such as NT Event Source, Time Ticks, and IP Address. These traps can be used to trigger alerts and send to other network management packages.

THE EXPRESSION

The following discussion serves, among other things, as a query expression reference. You can read the entire section or reference only those topics relating to a portion of an expression.

The expression, as you will see in the examples that follow, performs one comparison. Technically, a query without expressions works, but your search returns all the records in the database. Expressions serve to narrow your search by directing SMS to search a given record or object for a relationship you have defined.

In simple terms, you are asking for information from a database that matches your criteria. In SMS terms, you search a given architecture for a specific attribute and match a value to that attribute. An expression is a single request for this attribute-to-value matching. Figure 16.3 shows a single expression to search the SMS database for all machines with a VGA adapter.

Figure 16.3.
A single expres-
sion.

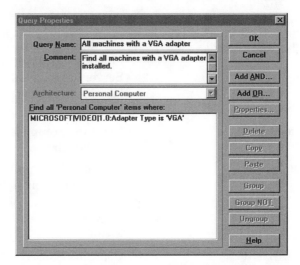

> ## Note
>
> Class name appears first in the expression. This can be confusing for administrators accustomed to looking for the group name. The second part from the left is the group to which the attribute belongs.

Clauses and Subclauses

A subclause is two expressions with a logical operator between them that is part of a greater whole, such as a clause. SMS views the subclause as a single logical expression. Clauses are multiple expressions having a logical operator between them. Clauses can also be the combination of subclauses. In either case, the clause includes the adjacent operator. In Figure 16.4, you can see a clause and a subclause within the same query.

Another powerful tool in queries is the group. It allows you to combine several expressions together so SMS views them as a single entity. Parentheses show both you and SMS that there is a relationship between the expressions listed. In Figure 16.5, you can see that grouping two clauses puts parentheses before and after the clause. In this case, I opted to use an OR. You may use any combination or nest groups. In the examples that follow, you will see practical application.

The group NOT, which is new with SMS 1.2, differs in appearance from a group in that preceding the first parenthesis are the words NOT IN. Its function is much different. Later in this chapter, you will see a group NOT in several examples.

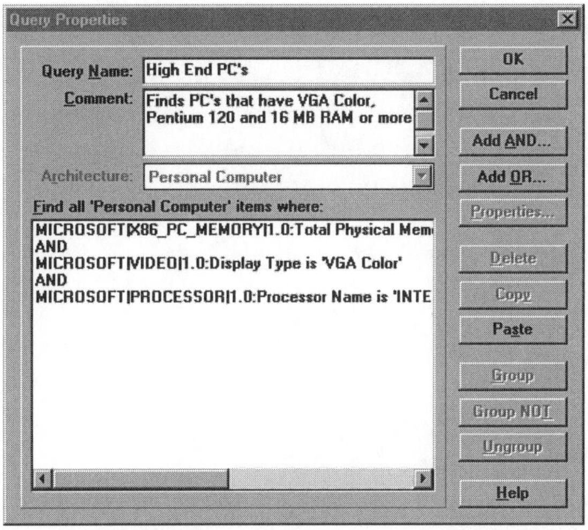

Figure 16.4.
Clauses and
subclauses.

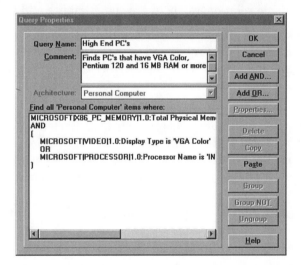

Figure 16.5.
Grouping.

PRECEDENCE

Before delving into examples of logical operators, groups, and complex queries, you must first understand the precedence of operator execution. This knowledge is of the utmost importance. A slight misunderstanding may cause some queries to return erroneous information. Basing business decisions on erroneous data constitutes a recipe for disaster.

The first item to be evaluated is anything in parentheses. Next is the AND, and finally the OR. This seems very straightforward, but it sometimes causes problems if you have not seen what slight changes to a query will do. Examples are given later in the section "Troubleshooting."

Caution

> Due to the way SMS performs a search, you have to be familiar with all the rules of the game before starting. For example, suppose you want to search for all blue or red balls that are also plastic. Using three expressions separated by an OR and an AND without a group does not give you the results that you desire. SMS evaluates the AND first so SMS looks for red and plastic to meet one condition and blue to meet another. All balls that were both blue and plastic will be missing from your results.

Relational Operators

The relational operator works with an expression's attribute in making a comparison. You enter a value for an attribute that you want to find and use an operator to establish a relationship between the attribute and the value.

The key is to choose the operator that best suits your query. You have a limited amount and type of relational operator to choose from depending on the attribute. For example, for an attribute that stores a numerical value, you do not see operators for date and time.

At the risk of stating the obvious, numeric operators are for querying numeric data and string operators are for string data. Each attribute's associated data is either a string or a numeral. SMS restricts operator options to only those that coincide with the attribute's data type. For example, the attribute WorkGroup is a string; therefore, you only enter a string as your comparison value.

Caution

> The relational operator you use requires a specific data type. Putting a non-numeric value with a numeric data type causes your query to fail. Using single or double quotations included as your value on either a string or numeric data type also causes the query to fail. SMS does not mask input.

Numeric Operators

When you use numeric operators, you are limited to the data you can input for comparison. A successful query includes only decimal or hexadecimal values. Hexadecimal values must start with 0x. Table 16.2 lists numerical operators and their use.

TABLE 16.2. NUMERICAL OPERATORS.

Operator	Use
is equal to	Numerically equal (for example, attribute=1, your value=1).
is not equal to	Numerically not equal (for example, attribute=1, your value=2).
is greater than	Is your value numerically greater than attribute?
is less than	Is your value numerically less than attribute?
is greater than or equal to	Is your value numerically greater than or equal to attribute?
is less than or equal to	Is your value numerically less than or equal to attribute?

STRING OPERATORS

Strings use operators that seem less precise than numerical operators. They are not imprecise—they just follow a different set of evaluation rules. SMS evaluates a string according to the code page installed with the SQL Server installation that powers the SMS database. A code page determines the character set to be used (for example, U.S. English, Spanish, and so on). SMS then follows its internal rules for evaluating a string.

Note

The operators vary depending on the code page that you use. Check your SQL Server documentation for a description of code pages.

16

Table 16.3 lists and describes relational operators used with strings (U.S. English code page). Each of the following has a case-sensitive counterpart. This rendition uses the SQL UPPER function to convert the object's value in the database and your string to uppercase. A normal comparison occurs after the conversion.

TABLE 16.3. STRINGS.

Operator	Use
is	Finds exact literal matches. Attribute matches your string value.
is not	Finds any attribute's value that does not match your string value.
is like	Finds any attribute's value that matches the pattern in your value string.
is not like	Finds any attribute's value that does not match the pattern in your value string.
comes after	Finds any attribute's value that has a greater value than your string value.
is same as or comes after	Finds any attribute's value that equals or has a greater value than your string value.
comes before	Finds any attribute's value that has a lesser value than your string value.
is same as or comes before	Finds any attribute's value that equals or has a lesser value than your string value.

> ## Note
>
> SMS does not treat all seemingly numeric attribute values as numeric. The IP address in the Personal Computer architecture, for example, seems to be a numeric value. Its treatment, however, is that of a string. Hence, to find all IP addresses greater than 200.0.1.1, you use the relational operator for strings, comes after.

is, is not, is like, is not like

A common use of relational operators is comparing logon names. Suppose you have four users named Gary, GaryH, GaryG, and GaryL, and you want to search for Gary. For your query results to contain only the objects associated to Gary, you must use the relational operator is as demonstrated in the following expression:

```
MICROSOFT¦NETWORK¦1.0:LogOn is 'Gary'
```

Because is is an exact literal operator, only those records with a network logon name of Gary satisfy the search. Conversely, if you use the operator is like, your results contain all four records.

Negating the preceding example with `is not` has the effect of asking the database for all network logon names except Gary. This returns all records because SMS still looks for an exact literal match for Gary and then excludes it.

If your intention is to exclude all variations of the logon Gary, you simply change the relational operator to `is not like`.

Comes after AND is same as or comes after

The operators `comes after` and `is same as or comes after` are functionally the same except that the latter includes your string in the comparison. Using the same example of four users with variations on Gary, you get wildly different results with either of these operators.

If your query searches for GaryL using `comes after`, the query results exclude Gary, GaryG, GaryH, and GaryL because the first three come alphanumerically before. GaryL, the comparison value, is implicitly excluded in this type of search. Further, all other logon names alphanumerically after GaryL are included in your results. The results far exceed a narrow search for GaryX.

Using `is same as or comes after` includes GaryL in the query results. No other changes occur.

comes before AND is same as or comes after

The operators `comes before` and `is same as or comes before` are functionally the same except for the latter's inclusion of the comparison string in the results. A search for Gary using `comes before` returns only those records that are alphanumerically less than Gary, but not including Gary. Using `is same as or comes after` includes the record that matched the comparison string in the query results.

PRACTICAL APPLICATION OF After AND Before OPERATORS

The examples you have seen so far are only a demonstration of how each operator works in a given situation and the limitations of using any given one. A more practical use is for software version control. In large networks, manually checking each workstation is cost-prohibitive. For example, assume you were charged with upgrading everyone to version 3 of MySoftware that is on the network in versions 1 and 2. The catch is that version 3 requires version 2 for an upgrade. Sound familiar?

You could use `is same as or comes after` to list all software alphanumerically of greater value, or you could combine it with `is like`. The ensuing expression looks like this:

```
MICROSOFT¦SOFTWARE¦1.0:MySoftware Name is same as or comes after MySoftware 1.0
AND
MICROSOFT¦SOFTWARE¦1.0:MySoftware Name is like MySoftware%
```

The preceding example is a mid-level query using the logical operator AND. This query also uses %, a wild card, which is explained later in this chapter.

DATE AND TIME OPERATORS

Time and date operators are slightly different from numeric or string operators. To begin with, there are more of them. Each portion of time (that is, hours, minutes, and seconds) and each portion of the date (that is, year, month, and day) has a distinct part of an operator. Additionally, there is an operator for date and time as a whole. Table 16.4 shows the basic operators used with date and time queries.

TABLE 16.4. DATE AND TIME OPERATORS.

Operator	Use
is	An exact match (for example, attribute value = 3/2/66 and the comparison value = 3/2/66).
is not	Returns all except the exact match (for example, comparison value = 10/8/70, so the return value is all dates other than 10/8/70).
is after	After a date or time (for example, comparison value = 2:18 PM, so acceptable attribute values are later in time than 2:18). Query results do not include any objects matching 2:18.
is on or after	This is the same as is after but includes objects matching the comparison value.
is before	Before a date or time (for example, comparison value = 6/28/96, so all acceptable attribute values have a later date than 6/28/96). Query results do not include any objects matching 6/28/96.
is on or before	This is the same as is before but includes objects matching the comparison value.

For more granular searches, you may use a specific time or date prefix. For example, to query for only the day from an object that has the date, you use the operator with the word day preceding it (that is, day is before or day is and so on).

LOGICAL OPERATORS AND GROUPS

There are two logical operators, AND and OR. AND and OR work by combining two single expressions, an expression and a group, or multiple groups. Logical operators and groups can be used in any combination to form complex queries.

Tip

First, articulate your search and apply the rules of precedence. For complex queries (that is, combining multiple logical operators), write pseudo queries once you can articulate what it is that you want. Use parentheses to show which expressions should be addressed as a logical unit. From there, you can choose an architecture, add expressions, and group them more easily.

A firm understanding of AND and OR is the foundation from which you build simple queries. Groups and groups NOT are the foundations of complex queries. As you move along, you will explore increasingly more complex logic to include nesting groups. Figure 16.6 shows the Query Properties dialog and the buttons used for adding and grouping expressions.

Figure 16.6.
Query Properties
dialog buttons.

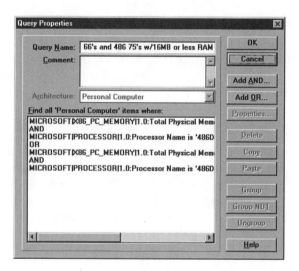

AND

The button Add AND located on the right of the Query Properties dialog gives you the opportunity to add an AND expression. If this is your second expression, the AND appears between the two. Your query has two criteria to match.

To further develop this point, consider a query using an AND between expressions comparing the values of X and Y. Such a query returns all records whose objects match X and Y. For example, suppose that you want to find all PCs with at least 16MB of RAM and a Pentium 120 for a Windows 95 pilot you are conducting. Your expression list looks like this:

16

```
MICROSOFT¦PROCESSOR¦1.0:Processor Name is 'INTEL PENTIUM-120'
AND
MICROSOFT¦X86_PC_MEMORY¦1.0:Total Physical Memory (Kbyte)
➥ is greater than or equal to '16384'
```

The query results list all PCs in the SMS database that have 16MB of RAM or more and a Pentium 120 (that is, a PC with 24MB of RAM and a 486 processor are not listed because of the 486 processor). In the case of the AND, both criteria must be met for an SMS record to be displayed.

You can add multiple AND operators to your expression list to further narrow the search. Take the last example and add another AND operator with an expression that requires 100MB of free hard drive space. The modified expression list looks like this:

```
MICROSOFT¦PROCESSOR¦1.0:Processor Name is 'INTEL PENTIUM-120'
AND
MICROSOFT¦X86_PC_MEMORY¦1.0:Total Physical Memory (Kbyte)
➥ is greater than or equal to '16384'
AND
MICROSOFT¦DISK¦1.0:Free Storage (Mbyte) is greater than or equal to '100'
```

Now your query requires all PCs to have at least 100MB of free hard drive space in addition to the previous criteria to be listed. If a current and accurate inventory exists, your query results provide you with a list of machines that could potentially be in the Windows 95 pilot.

Note

You need not be concerned which button you choose, Add AND or Add OR, for your first expression. No logical operator appears until you add a second expression. The logical operator used is determined by the button you choose for the second expression, not the first.

OR

The button Add OR located on the right of the Query Properties dialog gives you the opportunity to add an OR expression. If this is your second expression, the OR appears between the two. Your query has either criteria to match.

Queries using the OR operator return all machines meeting X or Y. That is to say, either X or Y satisfies the query. For example, if you want to know which machines have less than 16MB RAM or a 486DX-75 processor, you make an expression list that looks like this:

```
MICROSOFT¦PROCESSOR¦1.0:Processor Name is '486DX-75'
OR
MICROSOFT¦X86_PC_MEMORY¦1.0:Total Physical Memory (Kbyte) is less than 16384'
```

Your query results list all machines that met either condition or both conditions. Unlike an AND, the OR's condition could be met by either expression but does not exclude X if Y's condition is not met.

As with the AND, you can have multiple ORs (that is, X or Y or Z). Building upon this, suppose you want to broaden your search to include all machines with a 486DX-66 processor. You simply add another OR condition to your expression list:

```
MICROSOFT¦PROCESSOR¦1.0:Processor Name is '486DX-75'
OR
MICROSOFT¦PROCESSOR¦1.0:Processor Name is '486DX-66'
OR
MICROSOFT¦X86_PC_MEMORY¦1.0:Total Physical Memory (Kbyte) is less than '16384'
```

Adding ORs has the opposite effect of adding ANDs. In other words, you widen the search with an OR. The query results include machines that meet at least one of the criteria you specified.

AND/OR COMBINATIONS

Now that you have seen AND and OR work independently, take a look at using them together. Sometimes requiring records to match all criteria (AND) narrows the search too much, whereas allowing records to match any one of the criteria (OR) broadens the search so much as to return excessive records that may not be useful.

The alternative is to use AND and OR together. In keeping with the same theme of a Windows 95 upgrade, suppose you have decided that any machine that has either a 486DX-75 or a 486DX-66 and 16MB of RAM or less is a candidate for an upgrade. Your expression list looks like this:

```
MICROSOFT¦PROCESSOR¦1.0:Processor Name is '486DX-75'
OR
MICROSOFT¦PROCESSOR¦1.0:Processor Name is '486DX-66'
AND
MICROSOFT¦X86_PC_MEMORY¦1.0:Total Physical Memory (Kbyte)
➥ is less than or equal to '16384'
```

According to precedence of execution, SMS evaluates each record that matches the AND operator and then evaluates the record's compliance with the OR operator. The query results give you all 486DX-66 machines with less than or equal to 16MB of RAM and then evaluate the OR, giving you all 486DX-75s with no regard to the amount of RAM.

A more probable query searches for 16MB of RAM or less and either a 486DX-75 or 486DX-66. To accomplish this, you can do the following:

```
MICROSOFT¦PROCESSOR¦1.0:Processor Name is '486DX-75'
AND
MICROSOFT¦X86_PC_MEMORY¦1.0:Total Physical Memory (Kbyte)
➥ is less than or equal to '16384'
OR
```

16

```
MICROSOFT¦PROCESSOR¦1.0:Processor Name is '486DX-66'
AND
MICROSOFT¦X86_PC_MEMORY¦1.0:Total Physical Memory (Kbyte)
➡is less than or equal to '16384'
```

Here you see the precedence of logical operator execution evaluate the AND statements and then the OR. 486DX-75 machines with 16MB of RAM or less or 486DX-66 machines with 16MB of RAM or less meet the criteria.

GROUP

An alternative approach to the example in the preceding section is to group two expressions together. SMS then views the two-expression group as a single entity.

From the example in the preceding section, you can see that an AND OR combination falls short rather quickly in that there are three logical operators and four expressions. To check for another processor type requires two additional expressions and two logical operators. As you can see, you will soon be inundated with expressions and operators. Rather than try to guess if your logic will work or create a confusing ungrouped search, you should take the earlier example and use a group:

```
(
MICROSOFT¦PROCESSOR¦1.0:Processor Name is '486DX-75'
OR
MICROSOFT¦PROCESSOR¦1.0:Processor Name is '486DX-66'
)
AND
MICROSOFT¦X86_PC_MEMORY¦1.0:Total Physical Memory (Kbyte)
➡is less than or equal to '16384'
```

This example reduces both expressions and operators and is far easier to read. In order of precedence, the group (everything in the parentheses) is evaluated first. All 486DX-75 or 486DX-66 machines meet the first evaluation criteria. Next, all those machines must also have 16MB of RAM or less.

GROUP NOT

A group NOT effectively negates a group. As you have seen before, a group is evaluated first and at face value. Using a group NOT precedes the group parenthesis with NOT IN, saying all those not in this group meet the criteria.

```
NOT IN (
MICROSOFT¦PROCESSOR¦1.0:Processor Name is '486DX-75'
OR
MICROSOFT¦PROCESSOR¦1.0:Processor Name is '486DX-66'
)
AND
MICROSOFT¦X86_PC_MEMORY¦1.0:Total Physical Memory (Kbyte)
➡ is less than or equal to '16384'
```

Unlike a group, this query returns everything but the processors listed. It still proceeds to evaluate the AND as before, but your results are vastly different.

Tip

From an existing query that returns a given set of records, you can change to a group NOT to list the other group. This may be especially useful, for example, if you list a query that shows all machines with VGA color and you want to list all machines that do not. This way, you do not have to recreate the logic of your original.

NESTED GROUP

Nesting refers to the technique of embedding a group within a group. Nested groups add a degree of difficulty to the query. By nature, nesting is intricate in that you not only group, but it is implied that you are using AND OR combinations. The following example demonstrates the increased complexity:

```
(
    MICROSOFT¦NETWORK¦1.0:LogOn Name is like 'Rob'
    AND
    (
        MICROSOFT¦NETWORK¦1.0:IP Address comes after '200.0.1.1'
        AND
        MICROSOFT¦NETWORK¦1.0:IP Address comes before '200.0.1.75'
    )
)
AND
MICROSOFT¦WORKSTATION_STATUS¦1.0:Last Hardware Scan date/time is before 12/31/96
```

Now follow the nested logic. Precedence is also nested here in that SMS evaluates the inner set of parentheses looking for IP addresses that come after 200.0.1.1 and before 200.0.1.75. Next, SMS evaluates the AND within the next set of parentheses that looks for the logon name 'Rob'. Finally, the AND outside the nesting seeks those hardware scans before 12/31/96. Another way to articulate this is that all records with IP addresses that fall between 1 and 75 and are associated with the logon name Rob and then have a hardware scan before 12/31/96 will be listed.

Queries this intricate might be necessary if you track hardware and software on thousands of clients.

GROUPING EXPRESSIONS

You now know how you can effectively use a group and a group NOT to aid in logically organizing a query. To use either the group or group NOT, you simply do the following:

1. Add the two or more expressions to be grouped as described earlier.
2. Select the first expression to include. The entire expression excluding any adjacent logical operators is highlighted.

3. Holding the Shift key, find and click the bottom-most expression to be grouped. All expressions between the top and the bottom including the logical operators are highlighted.

4. On the right side, click the Group button or Group NOT button. If you choose Group, parentheses appear before and after the expressions you highlighted. For Group NOT, you see the words NOT IN appear before the opening parenthesis.

STEPS TO CREATING A QUERY

The actual creation of the query can be tricky. You should be familiar with each of its components discussed in the section "The Expression"—therein lies the tricky part. Without the understanding of the previous discussion, creating the query becomes difficult.

The following instructions provide more detail on the steps shown in Figure 16.7:

1. Articulate and write down your query in pseudo code. This is important for complex queries. Also, you should choose the architecture.

2. From the menu, choose File | Open and choose Queries, or click the Queries button on the toolbar. The Query window opens.

3. From the menu, choose File | New, or click the New button on the toolbar. The Query Properties window appears.

4. Enter a name and comment in the Name and Comment fields, respectively.

5. Choose an architecture from the drop-down list. Personal Computer is the default.

6. Based on your pseudo code, enter expressions using the Add AND and Add OR buttons. For more details on what constitutes an expression, refer to the section "The Expression."

7. Group as necessary. For more details, refer to the sections on expressions, groups, and operators.

8. When finished entering expressions and grouping, click the OK button.

9. Immediately execute the query to check the results. For more details, refer to the section "Executing a Query."

10. If the results are not what you expected, edit and execute. For more details on editing a query, refer to the section "Modifying a Query."

11. If you are satisfied with the output, you are done.

Figure 16.7.
Flow Chart for
creating a query.

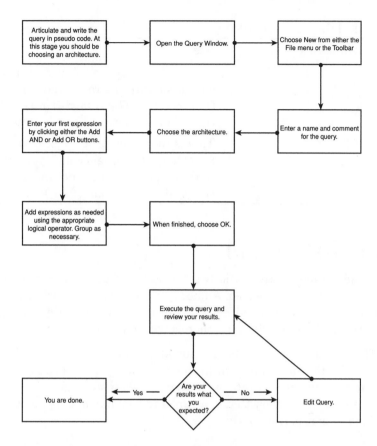

ADVANCED QUERIES USING WILDCARDS

When working with strings, you might not always know the correct spelling, or you may opt to enter part of a string to retrieve all records that are close. Behind the scenes, an ANSI-compliant SQL LIKE comparison takes place. Table 16.4 covers wildcards that can be used for the is like and is not like operators.

TABLE 16.4. WILDCARDS.

Wildcard	Use
%	Can be used to represent any number of characters including 0. (For example, Gar% can represent Gary, GaryH, GaryG, and so on.)
_	The underscore can be used to represent any single character. (For example, Gary_ can represent to represent GaryH, GaryG, and so on.)

continues

TABLE 16.4. CONTINUED

Wildcard	Use
[]	Square brackets can be used to represent a single character with the range indicated by the brackets. (For example, Gary[defghi] or Gary[d-i] will loop through each of the letters between the brackets.)
[^]	This is the opposite of the preceding wildcard. It also represents any single character within a range, but in this case to exclude, not include (for example, Gary[^defhgi] or Gary[^d-i]).

AD HOC QUERIES

An ad hoc query is essentially a "throwaway" query. It is a single-use query that is not, and cannot be, saved. Ad hoc queries are particularly useful when you have a simple query that need not be run again. Additionally, due to their temporary nature, ad hoc queries lend themselves to immediate execution.

These special queries, as mentioned, are not saved in the SMS database. Consequently, they do not appear in the query window as the saved queries do. This has some significant advantages in that you do not inundate your query window with every one-time query that you run, and you may modify an existing query without damaging it permanently.

Tip

An ad hoc query is a quick way to get SMS information easily. You should use it only for simple queries. Advanced, complex queries are best saved so that you do not have to rethink the logic later.

CREATING AN ORIGINAL AD HOC QUERY

There are two kinds of ad hoc queries, each having a special purpose. The first is a simple ad hoc query not based on a saved query, and the second is a little more sophisticated, based on an existing query. This section starts by exploring the former.

To create and execute a simple ad hoc query, you perform the following steps:

1. Choose File | Execute Query, or click the Execute Query button on the toolbar. The query window need not be opened. The Execute Query dialog

appears as shown in Figure 16.8. At this point, the windows that you previously opened determine what you see in the Query drop-down box. If you had the Queries window open, you do not see <Ad Hoc Query> in the Query drop-down box. Instead, the query selected in the Queries window appears. SMS anticipates that you want to run that query. For example, if you previously created and saved a query called "Every PC in the Home Office" and that query happened to be selected, SMS assumes that you want to execute that query. Ad Hoc is available by dropping down the Query box and finding it in the list.

Note

Your default query result format is the one used to display the information. Also note that you have no choice; the Query Result Format drop-down box is empty. See the section "Creating a Query Result Format" for details on creating and setting a default format.

2. To proceed, click the OK button in the upper-right corner. The Query Properties dialog appears.

3. You now change architectures and add expressions and groups as needed. Refer to the section "Creating a Query" for more details.

4. Once your query is defined, click the OK button. Unlike a saved query, your ad hoc query executes when you click OK.

Figure 16.8.
Ad hoc query
dialog.

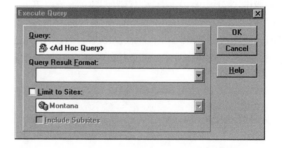

CREATING AN AD HOC QUERY FROM AN EXISTING QUERY

This feature affords you the opportunity to take a previously defined query, make modifications, and execute without affecting the original query. This is particularly useful when creating a complex query that does not seem to work the way you planned, but you do not want to foul up the logic by experimenting. You can base an ad hoc query on the original saved query to experiment to your heart's content without changing the original.

16

To create this special ad hoc query, you perform the following steps:

1. First, you must pick a query from which you build your ad hoc query. You then execute that query. Refer to the section "Executing a Query" for details.

2. After the query is executed, the Query Results window appears as shown in Figure 16.9.

Figure 16.9.
Query Results
window.

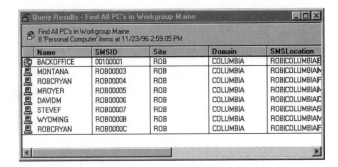

3. Double-click the Query Name Panel. This is the section at the top that displays both the query name and a brief description of the query results. The Query Properties dialog appears.

4. Modify the original query as necessary. Note that you are not changing the original query. Your changes remain in effect as long as you keep the Query Results window open. Furthermore, you may modify and build upon previous changes as long as you keep the Query Results window open.

5. Click OK in the upper-right corner. Notice that you execute the query instead of save it.

Tip

After several modifications, you may find the query that suits your needs. Rather than recreate the query from scratch, you can select all the expressions and click the Copy button. You then create a new query and use the Paste button to paste the expressions. Name, add a comment, and save as usual.

EXECUTING A QUERY

Once you create a query, it does no one any good taking up database and screen space. You need to execute it, if for no other reason, to find out if it works.

The query you defined is executed against a database. Keep in mind that SMS is, in this instant, merely a front end used to extract data based on your criteria. You may, even at this stage, limit the search to a particular site with or without its subsites. Finally, the data retrieved displays in a window. Using a query results format, as discussed later in the chapter, you can modify how results data displays.

To execute a query, perform the following steps:

1. Choose File | Execute Query from the menu or the Execute Query button on the toolbar. The Execute Query dialog appears as depicted in Figure 16.10.

Figure 16.10.
Execute Query
dialog.

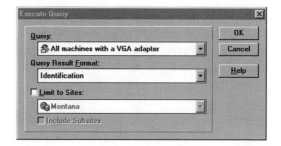

2. Choose the query you want to execute from the Query drop-down box.
3. Choose the query results format you want to use from the Query Result Format drop-down box.

Note

If you choose anything other than ad hoc for the query, the default query results format is displayed. This does not preclude you from choosing another format.

4. Next, you may choose to limit your query to a specific site and further include or exclude a subsite. To limit to a site, click the Limit to Sites checkbox and then choose the site from the drop-down list. By default, subsites are not included. To include them, you may click the Include Subsites checkbox. This is particularly useful when you have multiple sites in your SMS domain with many PCs. You can limit the sites and therefore limit your results and speed up the query.

5. Click OK in the upper-right corner to execute the query.

Figure 16.11 shows the Query Results window for a query I executed. Your query may vary in number of returned records and format, but the results are always displayed in the Query Results window.

Figure 16.11.
Query Results
window.

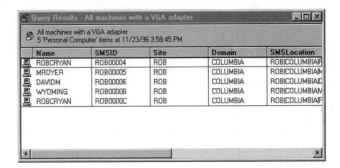

Tip

To view the properties of any object in the results window, point with your mouse or pointing device and double-click. The Personal Computer Properties [Computer Name] window appears.

Caution

You can also delete from the Personal Computer Properties [Computer Name] window. Although you are prompted with a dialog to confirm, there is a chance you can delete a record from the database. This action permanently deletes from the database, so all historical data for that PC is lost.

CREATING A QUERY RESULT FORMAT

As you explore the nuances of SMS queries, it becomes apparent that each function and feature of queries builds upon or complements each other. The query result format is no different. Once you define a useful query, you undoubtedly want to display the results in an appropriate format.

Each architecture, when you initially set up SMS, has a query result format called Identification. This format lists only attributes in the Identification group of a particular architecture. Not only do you have the ability to create your own formats, but you can create multiple formats for each architecture. Further, each architecture can have its own default.

Because the more suitable method is to include only those attributes that you queried against, the query result format becomes essential to querying effectively.

To create a query result format, perform the following steps:

1. From the menu, choose File | Define Query Result Formats, or click the Define Query Result Formats button on the toolbar. The Define Query Result Formats dialog appears, as shown in Figure 16.12.

Figure 16.12.
Define Query
Result Formats
dialog.

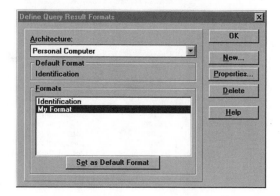

2. Choose the architecture. You should choose the architecture that you are querying against. Note that the default is Personal Computer. For more information on architectures, refer to the section "Creating Queries."

Note

The Default Format frame just below Architecture displays the default for the current architecture. Changing the architecture changes the default, although with a new installation, you do not notice it because all formats are called Identification.

3. Click New to create a new format. This opens the Query Result Format Properties dialog as shown in Figure 16.13.

4. Your cursor flashes in the Name text box. Make the name something that at least partially describes the format's purpose. Descriptive names help identify it for yourself and others.

5. The bottommost portion of the dialog, Available Columns, coincides with attributes within the architecture you chose in the previous steps. Choose those attributes that are appropriate by finding the attribute, highlighting it, and clicking the button Add to Format.

16

*Figure 16.13.
Query Result
Format Proper-
ties dialog.*

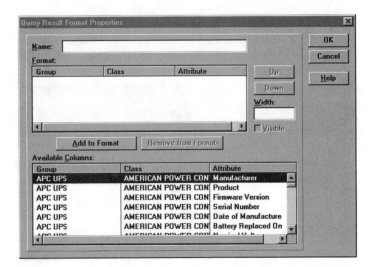

Note

Notice that as you choose the attributes, they appear in the Format box. Also notice that after your first addition, the Remove from Format button is available.

Highlight the format item and click Remove from Format to delete from the Format box.

Also note that there are two options, Visible and Width, associated with each attribute column you choose. Visible determines whether the column is displayed in your query results. Width, in pixels, determines the column width.

6. To the right of the Format box are the Up and Down arrows. These buttons change the order in which the columns appear in the Query Results window itself.

Notice in the Format box in Figure 16.14, the order, from top to bottom, is LogOn Name and Site. Now view Figure 16.15 and observe the column order. The format order directly coincides with the results column order.

7. Click OK to save the format you created.

Figure 16.14.
Order of attribute
entry.

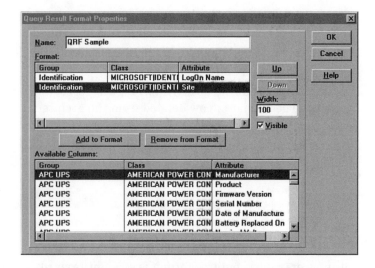

Figure 16.15.
Column order as
defined by the
query result
format.

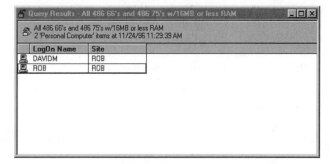

DELETING A QUERY RESULT FORMAT

There are a few steps to deleting any format:

1. From the menu, choose File | Define Query Result Formats, or click the
   Define Query Result Formats button from the toolbar. The Define Query
   Result Formats dialog appears as shown in Figure 16.12.

2. Choose the architecture where the format resides.

Caution

> Remember that each architecture has its own set of formats. Some
> architectures may use the same name. Be sure you delete a format
> from the correct architecture.

16

3. From the Formats box, choose the format you want to delete. You may select only one at a time. Although this is inconvenient, I am inclined to think that this feature prevents unwanted deletions.

4. Click the Delete button to the right.

5. A confirmation box, as shown in Figure 16.16, appears. Click Yes to confirm. The format is now deleted from the architecture.

Figure 16.16.
Delete format
confirmation box.

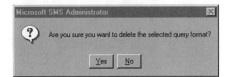

EDITING A QUERY RESULT FORMAT

Editing a previously entered format is straightforward, but there is a shortcut that can speed things along. Follow these steps to edit your format. The shortcut is discussed later.

1. From the menu, choose File | Define Query Result Formats, or click the Define Query Result Formats button from the toolbar. The Define Query Result Formats dialog appears as shown in Figure 16.12.

2. Choose the architecture where the format resides.

Caution

Remember that each architecture has its own set of formats. Some architectures may use the same name. Be sure you edit a format from the correct architecture.

3. From the Formats box, choose the format you want to edit.

4. Click the Properties button to the right. The Query Result Format Properties dialog appears, as shown in Figure 16.17. Notice that unlike a new query, there is a name and format criteria.

5. From this dialog, edit the format by changing the name, adding or deleting format criteria, or setting a particular format item to visible or not visible.

6. Click OK when finished.

When you execute a query using your query result format, you run the risk of obtaining output that includes unnecessary columns or columns that are poorly ordered. You need not edit the properties from scratch just to see how it displays differently. You can instead use a shortcut to a dialog with some limited editing capabilities.

Figure 16.17.
Editing a
previously saved
format.

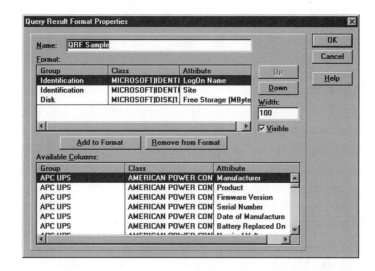

Caution

You can only edit the Query Results window display. The actual query result format is not changed.

From the Query Results window, double-click the column header bar, shown in Figure 16.18. The Partial Details dialog appears as shown in Figure 16.19.

Figure 16.18.
Shortcut to
editing a query
results format.

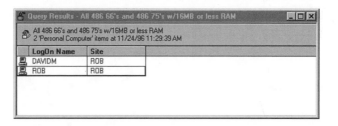

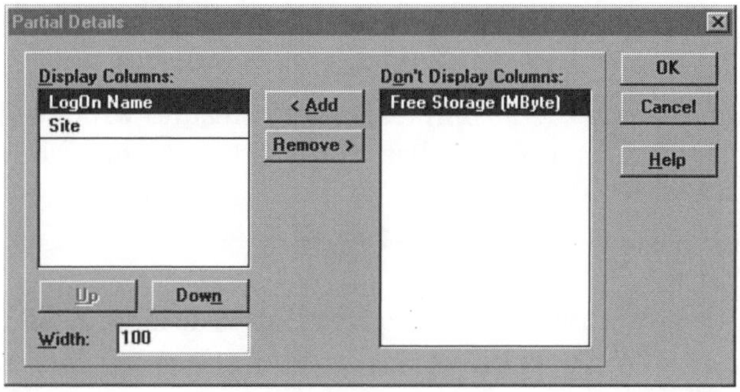

Figure 16.19.
Partial Details
dialog.

16

QUERIES

The Partial Details dialog is a hidden tool that can speed things up for you. From here, you can manipulate those columns that you chose when creating the query results format by deleting, changing the display order or column width, or excluding them from display. Essentially, the only thing that you cannot do is add new columns.

The Display Columns box lists all the attribute items you chose when creating the original format. They are in order of display from top to bottom. The buttons below, Up and Down, change the order of display for the item selected.

The Add and Remove buttons located between Display Columns and Don't Display Columns move columns from one box to another. For example, suppose you want to keep the column but remove it from display. You select that column and click the Remove button. The reverse is true for a non-displayed column you want to display.

Another feature of Partial Details is Width. Although you can drag a column to adjust width, specifying pixels in the Width column is more precise (as precise as adjusting by number of pixels can be).

Finally, the key benefit is that when you click OK, you see the updates immediately.

CANCELING A QUERY

Querying a large database may take some time. Fashioning a query improperly and unleashing it will delay fixing the problem. You need not wait until the query is finished. To cancel a query, follow these steps:

1. From the menu, choose Edit | Cancel Query. A dialog appears to confirm the cancel, as shown in Figure 16.20.

Figure 16.20.
Cancel query
confirmation box.

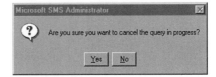

2. Click Yes to cancel the query in progress.
3. To close the incomplete Query Results window, press Ctrl+F4, or for Windows NT 4.0, click the X in the upper-right corner of the window.

DELETING A QUERY

You might want to delete a query that is no longer useful. For example, suppose that you created a query that helped determine upgrades and then you performed those upgrades. You might not need that specialized query any longer, nor do you want it to take up screen space. Delete the query with the following steps:

1. From the menu, choose File | Open and choose Queries from the list, or click the Queries button on the toolbar. The Queries window appears, as shown in Figure 16.21.

Figure 16.21.
Queries window.

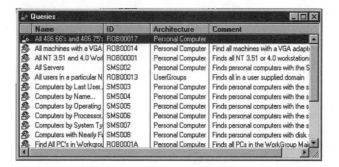

2. Using your mouse, select the query you want to delete. You may select multiple queries.

3. From the menu, choose Edit | Delete or press the Delete key. You are prompted to confirm the delete, as shown in Figure 16.22.

Figure 16.22.
Delete query
confirmation box.

4. Click Yes to confirm. You see a second dialog, as shown in Figure 16.23, demonstrating the serious nature of deleting. Clicking Cancel aborts the present operation without deleting.

Caution

There are multiple cautions here. First, be sure that you delete the correct query or queries. Second, this is a permanent delete from the SMS database. You must recreate from scratch a query that is inadvertently deleted. Third, both pending jobs and alerts based on your query or queries will fail.

16

5. Click Yes to confirm. The confirmation box clears, as shown in Figure 16.23, and the query is deleted. Clicking No clears the confirmation box and aborts the present operation without deleting.

Figure 16.23.
Second confirma-
tion box.

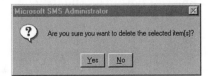

VIEWING AND MODIFYING A QUERY

Viewing and modifying queries are both closely related. You modify a query by performing the steps to view. Both have specific uses to aid in administering SMS.

VIEWING A QUERY

From time to time, you may need to check the logic of a query and subsequently modify it. If you are unfamiliar with some of the components, refer to the earlier section "What Is a Query?". Otherwise, follow these steps to view your query:

1. From the menu, choose File | Open and choose Queries or click the Queries button on the toolbar to open the Queries window, as shown in Figure 16.24.

Figure 16.24.
Queries listed in
the Queries
window.

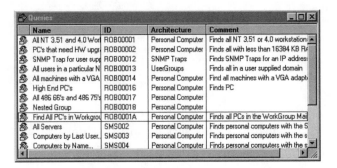

2. You should see all saved queries listed, usually in alphabetical order unless you changed it. From those listed, select the query to view.

3. From the menu, choose File | Properties and then press Alt+Enter or double-click the selected query. The Query Properties dialog appears, as shown in Figure 16.25.

Figure 16.25.
Query Properties
dialog.

The expressions, the heart of the query, are visible in the large text box in the lower left corner. The action of opening for review a query does not, in and of itself, change the query. You are only viewing content. There is a fine line between viewing and modifying in that the same steps as in "Viewing a Query" apply. From the dialog shown in Figure 16.25, you can make changes.

MODIFYING A QUERY

Modifying a query really means changing or deleting the name, comment, an expression, grouping, or architecture. Although you can change the query's architecture, making that change means you must deal with a completely different set of attributes. The query's expression, on the other hand, has a multitude of changes available. For example, you could change the comparison value, logical operator, relational operator, wildcard, or attribute, or you could delete the expression altogether. The following steps detail the various changes and deletions that are available:

1. From the menu, choose File | Open and choose Queries, or click the Queries button on the toolbar to open the Query window, as shown in Figure 16.24.

2. You should see all saved queries listed, usually in alphabetical order unless you changed it. From those listed, select the query to modify.

3. From the menu, choose File | Properties and then press Alt+Enter or double-click the selected query. The Query Properties dialog appears, as shown in Figure 16.25.

16

QUERIES

> *Note*
>
> The preceding three instructions apply to any change to the query. Other than deleting the entire query, you must make your changes from the Query Properties dialog.

NAME AND COMMENT FIELDS

To change the title or comment boxes, simply point to the text box with your mouse and click. Modify or delete at will. Remember to apply the rules of naming and commenting mentioned earlier in this chapter.

EXPRESSIONS

Modifying an expression requires only the knowledge of what constitutes an expression. In addition to understanding the discussion earlier in this chapter, you should also know that the logical operator immediately preceding an expression and the expression itself are both considered, by SMS, to be as one. Therefore, you are required to highlight both.

Given this requirement, highlight the expression and, if applicable, the logical operator using your mouse or pointing device by pointing and clicking with the left button. To highlight both, the key is to employ some basic Windows-style tricks. Hold the Ctrl or Shift key while clicking, in any order, the expression and logical operator.

A wealth of new opportunities open up to you in the form of buttons whose labels were previously grayed out (unavailable). You should see the Properties, Copy, and Delete buttons change from gray labels to black labels (available).

DELETING AN EXPRESSION

Deleting is especially useful if you have an expression where the basic logic is correct, but an expression no longer applies. Equally useful is the ability to remove an expression in the middle of a group. You can substantially change the expression without starting over. The following rules discuss the caveats of deleting an expression.

The first caveat is that you delete a clause or subclause that implies you must include the logical operator immediately preceding an expression. Conversely, you do not, and cannot, delete any individual part of a clause or subclause such as the logical operator. You must highlight the expression and its logical operator for removal. If you highlight an expression and omit its logical operator, you cannot delete. In fact, the Delete button remains unavailable.

Note

The exception to the adjacent operator rule is a single expression. For example, a single expression in a query does not have an adjacent operator, so removal is possible. All others must include the adjacent operator. SMS does not allow dangling operators, which are operators that precede or follow expressions that have no link to another expression or group.

COPYING AN EXPRESSION

Copying a useful expression can make your life quite a bit simpler when working with a complex query. Some complex queries may use the same or a slightly modified expression in several places. Rather than reinvent the wheel each time, you copy and paste. Copying introduces some caveats you should be familiar with before you start. The next two figures demonstrate these concepts.

Figures 16.26 and 16.27 show valid selection of single and multiple expressions, respectively. These are not the only valid selections for a copy, but they do demonstrate the most common application. Notice that you can include the logical operator BETWEEN in a multiple expression selection, whereas you do not include it in the single expression selection. Also note that you only include the logical operators if they join two expressions.

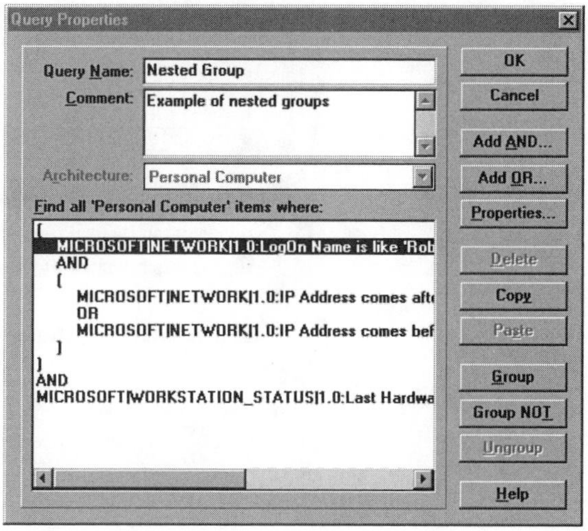

Figure 16.26.
Valid single
expression
selection for a
copy.

16

Figure 16.27.
Valid multiple
expression
selection for a
copy.

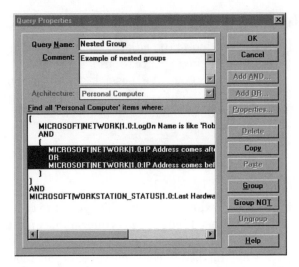

You cannot copy an expression and a single logical operator. Figure 16.28 shows an example of what happens if you include the adjacent operator. Notice that the Copy button is disabled. SMS considers this selection to be invalid and does not let you complete the task. Notice that you are allowed to delete. Refer to the section "Deleting an Expression" for more details.

Figure 16.28.
Attempt to
include the
adjacent operator.

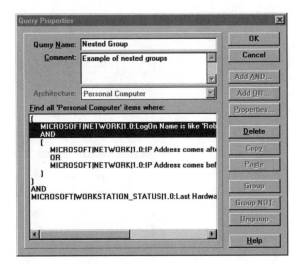

PASTING

A copied clause or subclause is immediately available through the Paste button. Only after completing a successful copy does SMS make the Paste button available. Where your cursor or selection is in the Find all [architecture] where text box determines where your copied expressions are pasted. Expressions are pasted immediately after the expression selected. Further, the pasted clause is separated from the other clauses by an AND operator. SMS uses this operator to link to the rest of the query. Operators included within a clause, however, are not changed.

Caution

SMS disables the standard Windows clipboard function. Your only option is to select the clause or subclause and use the Copy and Paste buttons provided for you.

MODIFYING ATTRIBUTES, RELATIONAL OPERATORS, AND COMPARISON VALUES

Modifying the expression is slightly simpler than copying or deleting. Your selection includes only the expression itself. Clauses and subclauses cannot be modified as a whole. Each component of a clause is addressed individually. To modify an expression, use the following two steps:

1. First, you select the expression itself. Do not include an adjacent operator or the Properties button will not become enabled, as shown in Figure 16.29.

Figure 16.29.
Valid expression
selection for
properties
modification.

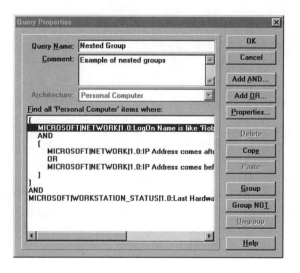

16

2. Click the Properties button. The Query Expression Properties dialog appears, as shown in Figure 16.30.

Figure 16.30.
Query Expression
Properties dialog.

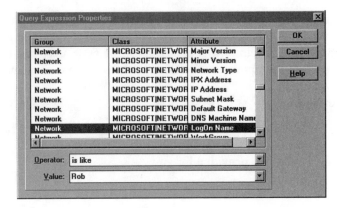

This is the same dialog you see when creating an original expression. You can change any aspect of the expression including the relational operator, comparison value, or attribute. By default, changing the attribute requires a change in relational operator and comparison value. You can change the relational operator and comparison value, on the other hand, without affecting the attribute.

Changing the relational operator dramatically changes the expression. For example, an expression seeking all computers with 16MB or less RAM looks like the following:

```
MICROSOFT¦X86_PC_MEMORY¦1.0:Total Physical Memory (Kbyte)
➥ is less than or equal to '16384'
```

A slight change to your expression in the relational operator such as using is less than does not include any computer with 16MB of RAM—only those with less.

Using is more clearly shows what a simple change does to the final output. In that case, only those computers with exactly 16MB of RAM meet the criteria.

The preceding example is a perfect demonstration of how a change in comparison value causes your query to return seemingly bizarre results. Suppose you want to find all computers with 16MB of RAM or less, but you enter 16000 instead of 16384 for your comparison value. This attribute has a numeric data type and requires you to enter the size in kilobytes. Given those two criteria, you must be sure that you enter only numbers and the numbers correspond to an actual RAM amount (2 to the nth power). Therefore, your query results, using 16000, do not include any computers with 16384 (16MB).

TOGGLING A LOGICAL OPERATOR

One sure way to change the entire results of a query is to toggle the logical operator from AND to OR or vice versa. It can be particularly useful when, like most of us, you clicked Add AND when you really meant to click Add OR.

The rules for toggling a logical operator are much like some of the other rules previously mentioned. You can only select the operator itself, as shown in Figure 16.31. Including the adjacent expression or parenthesis is considered invalid for the purposes of toggling. The Toggle button is enabled only after you make the valid single operator selection. Once the button is enabled, you simply click to change between the two operators.

Figure 16.31.
Valid logical
operator toggle
selection.

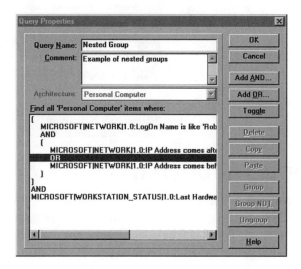

CHANGING OR UNGROUPING A GROUP

Often you have an existing group that you want to change or remove altogether. As in creating a group, you have to highlight the expressions and perform the operation. You do, however, need to include the parentheses and, if applicable, NOT IN. To change or ungroup a group, follow these steps:

1. Select the first part of the group (that is, NOT IN or open parenthesis).

2. Holding the Shift key, click the close parenthesis. Note that you see all parts of the group or group NOT highlighted, including open and close parentheses and NOT IN if applicable, as shown in Figure 16.32.

3. Using the buttons to the right, you have the option to change the group from a group to a group NOT or vice versa or ungroup as needed.

Changing from a group to a group NOT or back is especially useful to obtain a list of computers that do not match your criteria. For example, you may find yourself obtaining results from a query that includes a high percentage, say, 90 percent. Oftentimes, someone wants to see the short list. More often, you create a query that gives you a list with 900 out of 1000 machines. The exact opposite, listing only the 100, may be more appropriate and easier to examine and use.

16

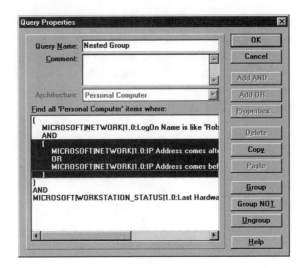

Figure 16.32.
Valid group
toggle selection.

TROUBLESHOOTING

The most common problem to troubleshoot is query logic. You will find that most of your erroneous results relate directly to improperly implemented logic. The caveats and rules discussed earlier, especially the rules of precedence, usually play a significant part in unraveling problematic queries.

Classically, the more complex queries with nested or multiple groups will trip you up. However, simpler queries misread can cause headaches. To remedy this, remember that order of precedence is much like the order of operation in mathematics. Remember "Please Excuse My Dear Aunt Sally" for parentheses, exponents, multiplication, division, addition, and subtraction? In the world of queries, it is slightly simpler: parentheses, AND, and OR.

Assuming that you have a nested group query, you need to look at the query as SMS does. This means that you walk through the query in a mathematical manner. This process looks like you are entering a tunnel.

Start from the top of the expression list and scan for the first open parenthesis as SMS does. Then, look at that group as a whole, scanning it for any other groups. Once you are at the heart of the query (that is, there are no more groups), you look for the first AND. Evaluate that clause and then the ORs and then back out of the tunnel.

Simpler queries without groups require only that you look at the logical operators. AND is always before OR—always. SMS needs to compare two expressions. If you have an AND, look closely at the expressions immediately before and after it. That is the clause.

Understanding what makes up a clause and how SMS looks for operators will provide you with the tools necessary to troubleshoot logic problems.

Additionally, you should check the following items if query problems arise:

◆ Are you querying against the correct architecture?

◆ Is the logic correct? Remember to write the query in pseudo-query language to clarify what you mean.

◆ Are you using the correct relational operator? Remember that `is` and `is like` are different and give you different results.

◆ Have you entered the correct data type? Attributes are either numeric or string data types. Numeric in a string or string in a numeric cause the query to fail.

◆ Did you enter the data type in a format that SMS understands? RAM, for instance, is in kilobytes, not megabytes. 16 and 16384 are vastly different.

◆ Are there records in the database? In the Sites window, do you see any machines? If not, you may have a problem with the inventory.

These questions are some basics to narrowing in on a problem. There is also the possibility that your site is not talking to the database correctly or some corruption exists. Including more details about SQL Server troubleshooting is best left to *Microsoft SQL Server 6.5 DBA Survival Guide,* also published by Sams.

SUMMARY

SMS, among other tasks, gathers information. The query simply retrieves that information. The subsequent results provide the information from which sound business decisions can be based. The one caveat is that the query itself must be accurate for the returned information to be relevant. This chapter provides the tools necessary for accurate queries that return useful information.

As discussed in the very beginning of this chapter, the power of SMS is the query. Throughout the chapter, the intricacies, tips, cautions, and notes have demonstrated the power of asking SMS the right questions. Although there are numerous examples in this chapter, they are not all inclusive of what can and is being done in this arena. The various aspects of a query, such as the myriad of operators, expressions, and clauses, are used to tailor queries to meet the needs of a particular organization.

16

CHAPTER 17

Machine and Site Groups

Systems Management Server is an excellent tool for managing computers, and its value is greatest in organizations with large numbers of machines. However, large numbers of items are difficult to administer in any situation, even with an attractive GUI interface. SMS provides machine groups to enable administrators to create collections of machines from the SMS database. These collections can represent any subdivision of machines that may be required, even across sites or domains. For instance, you can form machine groups of all Windows NT workstations, all accounting department computers, all servers, or all computers with less than 5 percent free disk space. Machine groups can even include other machine groups, allowing you to create a hierarchy of machine groups. You can then use machine groups as input to SMS jobs.

Because a large SMS installation has many machines, it may also have many SMS sites, depending on how the installation is organized. Companies with many physical sites may make each physical site an SMS site. Similarly, machines may be assigned to different SMS sites according to departments or other organizational subdivisions, even if all the departments reside in the same building. However, there may be similarities between SMS sites that make it appropriate to apply the same operations to each of them. In this case, grouping the similar sites together may make operations more efficient, so SMS provides site groups. You can then use site groups as input to jobs, queries, and alerts.

MACHINE GROUPS

Machine groups can contain both machines and other machine groups. Including machines in groups has several benefits. Including another machine group in a machine group makes it easier to maintain groups that have a relationship with each other. An example is different machines that are included in different levels of testing of SMS packages. You might perform the first series of tests with machines in a lab. Once the package is performing properly on these machines, then you might do another series of tests on these machines and the machines of the technical staff. The final level of testing might involve all the machines in the department. You could set up machine groups for testing level 1, testing level 2, and testing level 3. By making level 3 include level 2 and level 2 include level 1, you only need to include a new lab machine once in level 1. It is then included in testing that is done at any level.

MANAGING MACHINE GROUPS

Machine groups are simple containers with only a name, comment, and contents. To create an empty machine group, just open the Machine Groups window in SMS

Administrator (see Figure 17.1) and click the New button on the taskbar. Alterna-
tively, you can select File | New or you can press Ctrl+N. This displays the Machine
Group Properties dialog, in which the you can enter a machine group name and a
comment.

Figure 17.1.
The Machine
Groups window.

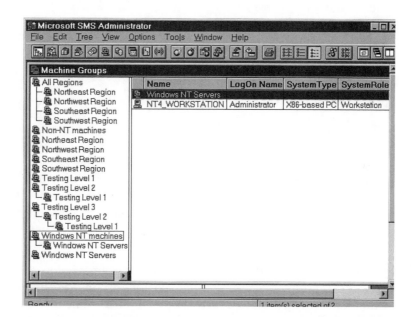

Tip

Because you have only the comment field to record additional information, it may be appropriate to describe the group and include the date
it was created and your name, in case questions arise in the future.

You can delete machine groups at any time by selecting the group and then hitting
the Delete key or using the Edit menu's Delete option. A simple prompt is displayed
to confirm the request. If the request is confirmed, then the group is deleted,
including any reference to the group in other groups. You can disable deletion
confirmation prompts by selecting the appropriate options in the Confirmation
dialog, which is available from the Options menu.

Later in this chapter, you will see that you can use machine groups as input to SMS
jobs in order to determine which machines the jobs are applied to. Deleting a
machine group does not affect such a job once it becomes active because the machine
list is recorded at the time the job becomes active, regardless of where it came from.

The job does not refer back to the machine group at any later time. Therefore, any changes to the machine group, including deleting the group, do not affect the job. This is also true for adding machines to the machine group—a job that has already been created and that is based on that group is not also run on the newly added machines.

You can edit machine groups at any time. Simply select the group and double-click it. Alternatively, you can choose File | Properties or press Alt+Enter. You can then change the group's name or comment.

MANAGING MACHINE GROUP CONTENTS

The easiest way to add machines or machine groups to machine groups is to simply drag and drop them. From any of the windows that display machines (the Sites, Query Results, or Machine Groups windows), select a computer and drag it to the Machine Groups window, either over the name of a machine group or if the appropriate group is currently selected, into the right pane. Drop the machine and it is added to the group. You can do the same thing for multiple machines selected using the Ctrl or Shift keys and the mouse, as in any other Windows application.

Similarly, you can add a machine group to another machine group by simply selecting it in the left pane of the Machine Group window and dragging it over the name of the other machine group. If machine groups are already in a machine group, then you can select them from the right pane of the Machine Group window and drag and drop them on the name of another machine group. You can do this with multiple machine groups at once, just as with multiple machines.

If you prefer keyboard commands, then you can use the File menu's Add to Group menu option, which displays the Add to Machine Group dialog (see Figure 17.2). This dialog displays the currently selected machines and allows you to select the machine group to which they should be added.

Figure 17.2.
The Add to
Machine Group
dialog.

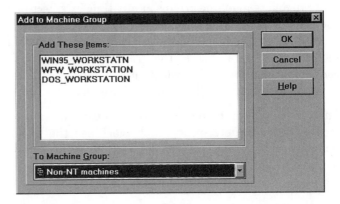

With large sites, it is very tedious to manually select machines for inclusion in machine groups. In this case, it is more appropriate to use queries if at all practical. Execute a query, as discussed in Chapter 16, "Queries," and in the Query Results window, use the mouse or the Edit menu's Select All option to select the machines. Then, simply drag and drop the selection to the appropriate machine group in the Machine Groups window. (See Figure 17.3.) As previously discussed, you can also use the File menu's Add to Group menu option.

Figure 17.3.
Dragging selected
machines from a
query's results to
a machine group.

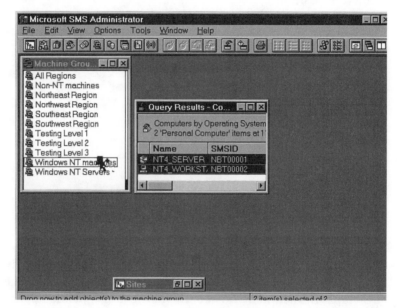

You can remove machines from a group by simply selecting the machines and hitting the Delete key or choosing the Edit menu's Delete item. As with deleting groups, removing machines does not affect any outstanding jobs. Removing machines from machine groups only removes the machine from the machine group—it does not delete the machines themselves.

DISPLAYING OR PRINTING MACHINE GROUP INFORMATION

You can manipulate the SMS Administrator's Machine Groups window to present the machine group information in different ways by selecting the View menu's Partial Details option. You can change the order of the columns, their width, and which columns are displayed. These changes are used for all future SMS Administrator sessions if the Options menu's Save Settings Now item is executed or if the

Save Settings on Exit item is checked and the SMS Administrator is closed. You can also display the Partial Details dialog (see Figure 17.4) by double-clicking the column headings in the Machine Groups window. Single-clicking a column heading sorts the list in ascending order of that column, and single right-clicking the column sorts it in descending order. You can also adjust column widths by moving the mouse to the divider between column headers and manipulating it. Similarly, you can move columns by selecting and holding their column headers and dragging them to another position.

Figure 17.4.
The Partial
Details dialog.

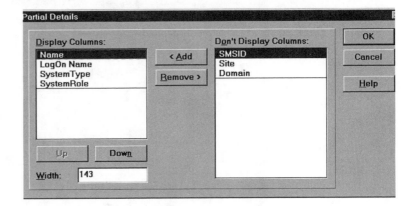

While displaying the machine groups, you can expand a group that has subgroups by one level in the left pane by double-clicking the group. Double-clicking the group again collapses it. Alternatively, you can use the Tree menu's Expand One Level or Collapse Branch menu items or their keyboard equivalents, + and –. A single branch can be completely expanded by using the Expand Branch item or the * key. To expand all branches at once, use the Tree menu's Expand All item, or use the Ctrl+* keys. You can collapse all branches with the Collapse All menu item or the Ctrl+– keys. Note that for most of these keyboard options, you can use the keys from the main keyboard or the keypad. However, for the Ctrl+* and Ctrl+– sequences, you can only use the * and – from the keypad.

You can print machine group details by selecting a group and then choosing File | Print or by pressing Ctrl+P. The report includes all the machine details for the selected group, with the same formatting as the group in the Machine Groups window. Unfortunately, the report does not include the machine group comments, and only one group is included in each report. To generate more sophisticated reports, you must use other tools.

USING MACHINE GROUP INFORMATION IN OTHER APPLICATIONS

It may be necessary to use machine group information in other applications. For instance, you might need to communicate the information with a manager to ensure that all his staff's machines are included in the appropriate group. The machine group data could be extracted from the SMS database, using an appropriate SQL-oriented tool and ODBC, but a much easier technique is to simply copy and paste it. With the appropriate group selected in the Machine Groups window, choose Edit | Select All, followed by the Copy Table option. In an appropriate Windows application, use its Edit | Paste option and the data is copied into that application. If the application is table-oriented, such as Microsoft Excel, then the data continues to have separate columns. Otherwise, the data is dumped as text with spaces between columns, one line of text per record.

USING MACHINE GROUPS WITH JOBS

There may be some benefit in creating machine groups in order to have a sense of order for the SMS inventory, but their greatest benefit comes from using them with jobs. You can use jobs to distribute packages to machines or to share applications. You can also use jobs to send packages to distribution servers for these purposes.

Usually, it is not appropriate to send jobs to all machines. Some computers might have incompatible CPUs, some might already have the applications, some might not be properly licensed, and so on. When creating jobs, you can specify certain machines in response to a query or by giving a specific machine path (domain/site/machine name). However, queries can be very expensive in terms of resource usage, paths can be too specific, and neither method allows for complete flexibility. You can set up machine groups once and use them many times with no further effort. Machine groups can cross multiple domains and sites and can include any combination of machines. Therefore, using machine groups is the most powerful option available for jobs when it comes to selecting targets.

You can select the machine group when creating a new job by using the Machine Group drop-down list box, as shown in Figure 17.5. You can also select a machine group from the Machine Groups window and drag it onto a package in the Packages window, which automatically starts the job creation process, displaying the Job Details dialog.

Figure 17.5.
The Job Details
dialog with
Machine Group
drop-down list
box expanded.

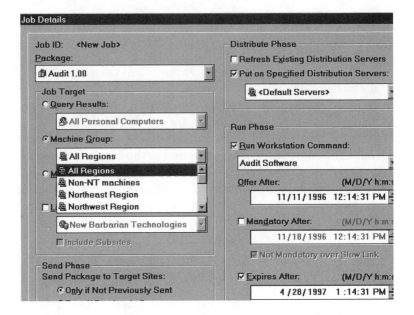

Similarly, if you need to send a package to distribution servers, then you can use the drop-down list box in the Distribute Phase section to determine which machine group the package is distributed to.

Caution

There is a known problem (see Microsoft Knowledge Base Article Q140051) that prevents packages being sent to distribution servers if the machine group is changed and the package is resent. However, this problem affects only Run Command on Workstation jobs, not Share Package on Server jobs. The simple workaround is to also check the Refresh Existing Distribution Servers checkbox when resubmitting the job.

SITE GROUPS

Like machine groups, site groups can contain both sites and other site groups. Putting sites in groups allows you to readily restrict SMS jobs, queries, and alerts to certain sites, with complete flexibility about how those sites are determined. Including another site group in a site group makes it easier to maintain groups that have a relationship with each other. For instance, you can base sites on organizational subdivisions, with divisions being site groups. In such a situation, vice presidents may have several divisions reporting to them, so you could create site groups for each vice president and the division site groups could be included in the VP site groups. If reporting relationships change, it is a simple matter to move a site or a divisional site group from one VP's site group to another.

Managing site groups is much like managing machine groups. There are some subtle management differences between the two, but the most significant differences are in terms of where the groups are used and why.

MANAGING SITE GROUPS

Site groups are simple containers with only a name, comment, and contents. To create an empty site group, just open the Site Groups window in SMS Administrator (see Figure 17.6) and click the New button on the taskbar. Alternatively, you can choose File | New or press Ctrl+N. This displays the Site Group Properties dialog, in which you can enter the site group name and a comment.

Figure 17.6.
The Site Groups
window.

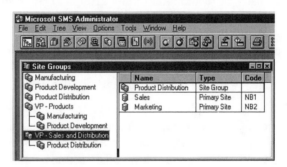

Tip

Because you have only the comment field to record additional information, it may be appropriate to describe the group and include the date it was created and your name, in case questions arise in the future.

You can delete site groups at any time by selecting the group and then pressing the Delete key or using the Edit menu's Delete option. A simple prompt is displayed to confirm the request. If the request is confirmed, the group is deleted, including any reference to the group in other groups. You can disable deletion confirmation prompts by selecting the appropriate options in the Confirmation dialog, which is available from the Options menu.

You can use site groups as input to SMS jobs, queries, and alerts in order to determine which sites the jobs are applied to or which sites the queries and alerts include. Deleting a site group does not affect a job once the job has become active, because the site list is recorded at the time the job is created, regardless of where it came from. The job does not refer back to the site group at any later time. Therefore, any changes to the site group, including deleting the group, do not affect the job. This is also true for adding sites to the site group—a job that is already based on that group is not also run on the newly added site. Queries are executed right away, so they use the site group in the form that it appears in at the time.

You can edit site groups at any time. Simply select the group and double-click it. You can also choose File | Properties or press Alt+Enter. You can then change the group's name or comment.

Managing Site Group Contents

The easiest way to add sites or site groups to site groups is to simply drag and drop them. From either of the windows that display sites (the Sites or Site Groups windows), select a computer and drag it to the Site Groups window, either into the right pane or over the name of a site group. Drop the site and it is added to the group. You can do the same thing for multiple sites selected using the Ctrl or Shift keys and the mouse, as in any other Windows application.

Similarly, you can add a site group to another site group by simply selecting it in the left pane of the Site Groups window and dragging it over the name of the other site group. If site groups are already in a site group, you can select them from the right pane of the Site Groups window and drag and drop them on the name of another site group. You can do this with multiple site groups at once, just as with multiple sites.

If you prefer keyboard commands, the File menu has an Add to Group menu option, which displays the Add to Site Group dialog. This dialog displays the current items selected and enables selection of the site group to which they should be added.

Displaying or Printing Site Group Information

You can manipulate the SMS Administrator's Site Groups window to present the site group information in different ways by selecting the View menu's Partial Details option. You can change the order of the columns, their width, and which columns are included. These changes are used for all future SMS Administrator sessions if the Options menu Save Settings Now item is executed or if the Save

Settings on Exit item is checked and the SMS Administrator is closed. You can also display the Partial Details dialog by double-clicking the column headings in the Site Groups window. Single-clicking a column heading sorts the list in ascending order of that column, and single right-clicking the column sorts it in descending order. You can also adjust column widths by moving the mouse to the divider between column headers and manipulating it. Similarly, you can move columns by selecting and holding their column headers and dragging them to another position.

While displaying the site groups, you can expand a group that has subgroups by one level in the left pane by double-clicking the group. Double-clicking it again collapses it. Alternatively, you can use the Tree menu's Expand One Level or Collapse Branch menu items or their keyboard equivalents, + and –. You can completely expand a single branch by using the Expand Branch item or the * key. To expand all branches at once, use the Tree menu's Expand All item or use the Ctrl+* keys. You can collapse all branches with the Collapse All menu item or the Ctrl+– keys. Note that for most of these keyboard options, you can use the keys from the main keyboard or the keypad. However, for the Ctrl+* and Ctrl+– sequences, you can only use the * and – from the keypad.

You can print site group details by selecting a group and then choosing File | Print or by pressing Ctrl+P. The report includes all the site details for the selected group, with the same formatting as the group in the Site Groups window. Unfortunately, the report does not include the site group comments, and only one group is included in each report. More sophisticated reports must be generated using other tools.

USING SITE GROUP INFORMATION IN OTHER APPLICATIONS

You might need to use site group information in other applications. For instance, it may be necessary to communicate the information with another administrator to ensure that all his sites are included in the appropriate group. You could extract the site group data from the SMS database, using an appropriate SQL-oriented tool and ODBC, but a much easier technique is to simply copy and paste it. With the appropriate group selected in the Site Groups window, choose Edit | Select All, followed by the Copy Table option. In an appropriate Windows application, use Edit | Paste, and the data is copied into that application. If it is table-oriented, such as Microsoft Excel, then the data continues to have separate columns. Otherwise, the data is dumped as text with spaces between columns, one line of text per record.

USING SITE GROUPS WITH JOBS

You can use site groups with several SMS facilities, including jobs. You can use jobs to distribute packages to sites or to share applications. You can also use jobs to send packages to distribution servers for these purposes.

Sometimes, it is not appropriate to send jobs to all sites. Some sites might be administered by other departments, or they may be test sites, where certain jobs are not required. When creating a job, you have an opportunity in the Job Details dialog (see Figure 17.7) to limit the job to particular sites. This can be a particular site from the Sites window or a sites group. You can expand this option to include the sites that report to these sites by checking the Include Subsites checkbox.

Figure 17.7.
Using sites when
creating a job.

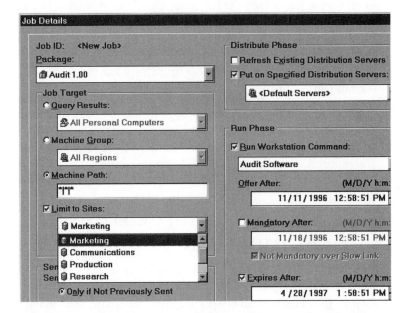

Caution

For SMS version 1.1, limiting a job to a specific site but not including child sites does not work—it will still go to the child sites. Microsoft advises setting up a machine group to include the same machines as the desired sites and then using that group. See the Microsoft Knowledge Base Article Q153205 for more details.

USING SITE GROUPS WITH QUERIES OR ALERTS

It may be appropriate to limit the execution of a query to specific sites. For instance, a manager interested in data for his sites might not want to see information for other sites as well. When executing a query, you can limit the query in the Execute Query dialog (see Figure 17.8) to a site in the Sites window or a site group from the Site Groups window. You can further extend the query to include subsites reporting to those sites.

Figure 17.8.
Using site groups
when executing a
query.

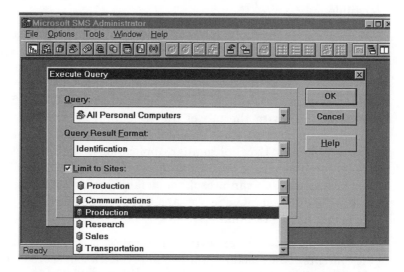

Alerts are strongly based on queries; alerts are really just scheduled queries with actions that are executed depending upon the results. You might want to limit an alert to particular sites. You can specify this in the Alert Query dialog (see Figure 17.9) while creating the alert.

Figure 17.9.
Using site groups
when creating an
alert.

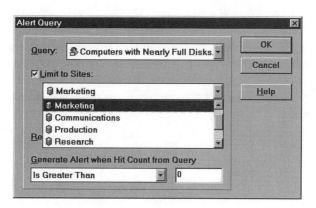

BETTER MACHINE GROUP AND SITE GROUP INFORMATION COPYING

Earlier in this chapter, you saw that SMS Administrator does have some nice options to copy and paste machine group and site group information to other applications. Copying groups is a good idea, but you can only do it with one group at a time. In more complex environments, you might need to copy the information more efficiently. Fortunately, SQL Server provides a simple facility to make this possible.

You can find BCP.EXE (bulk copy) in the \MSSQL\BINN directory of an SQL Server server. At the command prompt, if you enter **BCP SMS.dbo.MachineGroups out TEST.TXT -t, -r\r\n -U sa -P** *password*, a dump of the MachineGroups table is created in a text file called TEST.TXT. The MachineGroups table contains all the machine groups and their comments. With the use of the -t parameter, as specified, the fields will be comma-delimited, and with the use of the -r parameter, the lines will be terminated appropriately for a Windows environment. As a result, you can import the information to Microsoft Excel or similar applications. Note that case and spacing are important in the use of the BCP command. Also, BCP prompts for the field terminators and so on. You can accept the defaults because BCP generally gets correct column details from SQL Server, and the command already specified the appropriate values for the terminators.

By substituting MachineGroupDetails for MachineGroups, you can extract information for the contents of the machine groups. However, the correct response to the prompt for the storage type of the MachineID column is smallint. This table shows which machines and machine groups (in separate columns) are contained in each machine group. Formatting this information in a useful form might take some programming, especially if details relating to the machines are required, because you must extract those details from other tables.

It may be appropriate to use SQL Server views in order to get all the MachineGroups and MachineGroupDetails data at once and appropriately merged using the BCP command. You can even extend this concept to include machine details, especially from the machine views provided by SMS's SMSVIEW.EXE program. Some programming may still be necessary to display the hierarchies nicely and do other formatting, but at least all the appropriate data is included. To create a view for this purpose, it is necessary to use SQL Server's Enterprise Manager program. Drill down to the SMS database on the appropriate server and then use the Manage menu's Views item. Then, enter the following:

```
CREATE VIEW vMachineGroups AS SELECT MachineGroups.Name MachineGroupsName,
➥ MachineGroupDetails.Name MachineGroupDetailsName, Comment, SubGroupName,
➥ MachineID FROM MachineGroups, MachineGroupDetails WHERE MachineGroups.Name
➥ *= MachineGroupDetails.Name.
```

You only need to enter this once. You can then execute the BCP command whenever necessary using the vMachineGroups view in place of the MachineGroups table.

You can use the same techniques to extract information from the SiteGroups and SiteGroupDetails tables. Working with the SiteGroupDetails table is a little easier than working with the MachineGroupDetails table because site groups don't contain machines, so there is no need to refer to the machine tables or views.

BETTER MACHINE GROUP AND SITE GROUP REPORTING

SMS Administrator does have some nice options to print site group or machine group information. However, you can only print one group at a time, and the output does not include the machine or site group comments. In a large organization with many groups and many staff who may be interested in such details, this facility is certainly not sufficient.

A tool such as Microsoft's Visual Basic can do wonders to improve SMS machine group and site group reporting. Other tools, such as Microsoft Access, might be even easier to use, but in its simplest form, Access depends strongly upon SQL SELECT statements to collect its data. In this case, the SELECT statement must be very complex. By using the vMachineGroups view created in the previous section, it is easy to select the data required. However, when creating reports, it is necessary to have all columns in a readable form. In this case, it is necessary to replace the MachineID column with something more useful, such as computer name. As a result, it is best to join the vMachineGroups view with the vIdentification view (produced with SMS's SMSVIEW.EXE program). Unfortunately, the inner and outer joins required to join these two views conflict with each other. You can do the SELECT on the original tables, but then you lose the desired simplicity. Therefore, a more procedural approach, such as what is possible with Visual Basic, is more appropriate. A sample program (MACHGRPS.EXE) to accomplish this goal is provided with this book. The program's output is shown in Figure 17.10. The main source code is shown in Listing 17.1. The full source code is provided on the CD-ROM.

Figure 17.10.
The SMS Ma-
chine Groups
program.

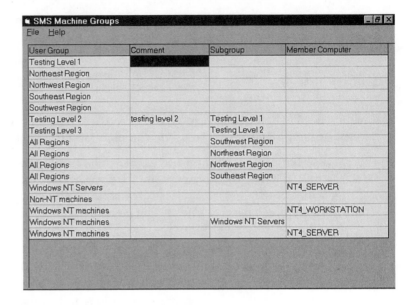

LISTING 17.1. MACHINE GROUPS REPORTING PROGRAM.

```
'setup ODBC connections to the SMS database
Data1.Connect = "ODBC;DSN=SMS;DATABASE=SMS;"
DBGrid1.DataSource = Data1.Recordset
DBGrid1.Refresh
Data1.RecordSource = "SELECT * FROM vMachineGroups"
Data1.Refresh
Data2.Connect = "ODBC;DSN=SMS;DATABASE=SMS;"
DBGrid2.DataSource = Data2.Recordset
DBGrid2.Refresh
'set column widths
Grid1.ColWidth(0) = Grid1.Width / 4
Grid1.ColWidth(1) = Grid1.Width / 4
Grid1.ColWidth(2) = Grid1.Width / 4
Grid1.ColWidth(3) = Grid1.Width / 4
'set column header
Grid1.Row = 0
Grid1.Col = 0
Grid1.Text = "User Group"
Grid1.Col = 1
Grid1.Text = "Comment"
Grid1.Col = 2
Grid1.Text = "Subgroup"
Grid1.Col = 3
Grid1.Text = "Member Computer"
'figure out number of records
Data1.Recordset.MoveLast
Rows = Data1.Recordset.RecordCount
```

```
'transfer data records to display grid
Grid1.Rows = Rows + 1
Data1.Recordset.MoveFirst
For i = 0 To Rows - 1
    Grid1.Row = i + 1
    Grid1.Col = 0
    Grid1.Text = DBGrid1.Columns(0).Text
    Grid1.Col = 1
    Grid1.Text = DBGrid1.Columns(2).Text
    Grid1.Col = 2
    Grid1.Text = DBGrid1.Columns(3).Text
    Grid1.Col = 3
    'change machine ID to machine name, if there is one
    If DBGrid1.Columns(4).Text <> "" Then
        Grid1.Text = "test"
        Data2.RecordSource = "SELECT * FROM vIdentification WHERE dwMachineID="
➡ + DBGrid1.Columns(4).Text
        Data2.Refresh
        Grid1.Text = DBGrid2.Columns(1).Text
    End If
    Data1.Recordset.MoveNext
Next I
```

The main routine for MACHGRPS.EXE is executed when the main form for the program is loaded. It connects to the SMS database, associating a couple of DBGrid controls with the vMachineGroups and vIdentification views. A little formatting is done, and then the program works through the DBGrid associated with the vMachineGroups view. When it comes across MachineIDs that aren't NULL, it uses the other DBGrid to look up their names. As this is done, the columns are transferred to a grid control, which is used to present the information in an attractive fashion.

Note that this program connects to the SMS database by using ODBC. ODBC is easy to use for this kind of situation; however, a quick bit of setup is required to establish how the link is made. You use the ODBC Control Panel for this purpose. Its System DSN button must be clicked, showing the System Data Sources dialog. Clicking the Add button presents a list of ODBC drivers, and of course for SMS you need the SQL Server driver. Then the ODBC SQL Server Setup dialog is shown, as in Figure 17.11 (after hitting the Options button). If SQL Server is not a listed option for ODBC drivers, reinstall the ODBC component and select this driver when presented with the opportunity. If a separate ODBC setup is not available, run the setup for an application that includes it, such as Access or Visual Basic.

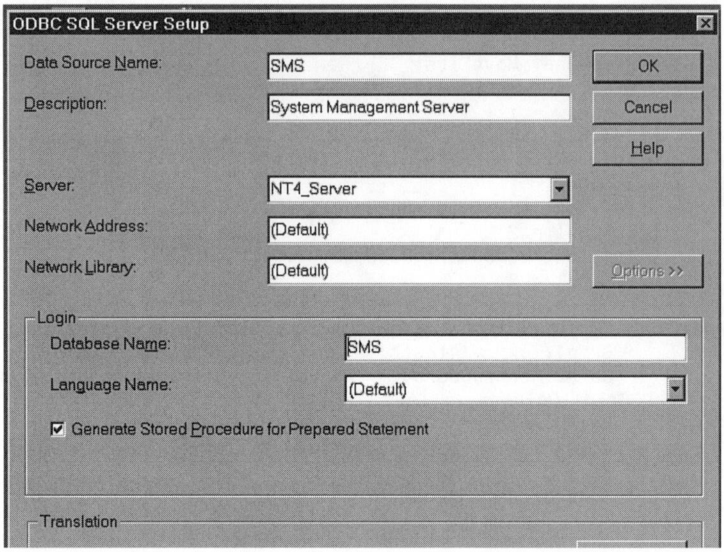

Figure 17.11.
ODBC setup
details.

SUMMARY

SMS's machine and site groups are a powerful yet simple and flexible facility to make SMS administration much more practical. With judicious use of machine groups, you can direct jobs to only the appropriate machines, regardless of how difficult it is to determine which machines are appropriate. Furthermore, you can create machine groups once and use them repeatedly with no further effort. Site groups are also easy to use but allow jobs, queries, and alerts to be restricted to appropriate sites so that you can tailor operations to an organization's needs. Copying and printing the group details is very easy but limited; however, with a little effort, it is easy to implement better solutions.

CHAPTER 18

Packages

Several studies have been done by the Gartner group and others that show that most of the costs for a machine are not the purchase and upgrades to hardware, but, rather, the software maintenance required for it. Consider this scenario: a medium-sized network of about 2,400 machines needs a single driver upgraded. The upgrade requires only a 10-minute visit to each machine. 10 minutes times 2,400 machines comes to roughly 400 hours to upgrade the driver. 400 hours times about $40 an hour comes to roughly $16,000. As you can see, this can be very tedious, time-consuming, and can become a costly effort. Consider the implications if the upgrade requires a 60-minute upgrade, as well as the frequency of other routine upgrades (such as virus updates, service packs and patches that require upgrades to the workstations). The impacts can add up exponentially. The real key is to automate the installation as much as possible, and to take advantage of SMS's packages as a delivery mechanism. This chapter will guide you through the process of creating packages for distribution to the client PCs. Chapter 19, "Jobs," discusses the second part of the process, creating jobs for the distribution of the package. In this chapter, I will discuss the following:

◆ Software distribution in general

◆ Set user expectations

◆ Creating source files

◆ Storage considerations

◆ Scripts

◆ Types of packages

◆ Creating Run Command on Workstation packages

◆ Creating shared packages

◆ Creating inventory packages

◆ Administrative installs

SOFTWARE DISTRIBUTION IN GENERAL

The distribution mechanism of SMS enables an administrator to set up multiple distribution points within an SMS hierarchy. SMS uses the concept of *packages*. A package is merely a set of files with instructions. Once the distribution points are configured, the administrator can send packages that the client pieces, the Package Command Manager (PCM) or Program Group Control (PGC), can interpret and execute. What can be distributed to the client? In general, anything that can be installed or run at the client can be distributed through SMS. Items that can be distributed to clients include

◆ Off-the-shelf applications

◆ Data files

- Custom applications
- Routine maintenance (such as virus scans)
- Software removal
- Inventory of client files
- Registry updates
- Stop/start/installation of services
- Service packs
- Operating system upgrades

This chapter will guide you through the configuration process for SMS to perform these functions, as well as show you how to avoid many pitfalls.

First and foremost, a note about testing and staging: It is strongly encouraged that a lab be installed that replicates the production environment as closely as possible, and that extensive testing is performed on anything to be distributed to the SMS clients. SMS is a very powerful tool. Just as an administrator can upgrade an application for the entire enterprise with a single package, a single detail overlooked can wreak havoc on the entire enterprise. SMS does not have a native "undo" button. Be prepared to roll-back or uninstall any packages distributed to the client PCs; this will be discussed in more detail in the section "Scripts," later in this chapter.

Also consider the use of SMS's machine groups and site groups. These groups can be configured by geographic location, application, business lines, and so on. These features enable the administrator to perform a "phased" installation. In short, if there is a problem, it is much better to have it happen on a small scale rather than a larger one.

STRANGER THAN FICTION

I recall a two-by-four in the corner of a crowded computer room with the words "Crowd Control" written on it. I wondered what was going on at the time this device was created. Fortunately, I never had to use it!

SETTING USER EXPECTATIONS

Quite often, end users are forgotten in the march to technical superiority. It is, however, the end user who eventually evaluates administrators' performance and keeps them employed. It is a difficult concept for the end user to relinquish control of his or her machine and have it managed as a corporate asset. If SMS is installed on a new deployment, it is not very difficult to implement procedures with SMS because the end user is familiarized from the first logon. In an existing installation, it is best to forewarn users and provide instructions on how to use the SMS client. One thing you don't want to happen is to have users flooding the help desk with calls about "This thing just popped up on my screen! What am I supposed to do?"

The control provided by SMS can be quite a culture shock to the end user. For example, SMS can be configured to search a machine for the presence of unauthorized files or software. When the violation occurs, SMS can be configured to collect the files suspected of violation, delete a random directory, and send an e-mail to the responsible party and his or her boss informing them of the violation. SMS can also make a package available for a set period of time. After this period of time has expired, SMS can make the package mandatory and force it to the client or make it no longer available. The release of SMS 1.2 also takes advantage of native SNMP traps that can forward specific events from the Windows NT event logs, such as an unsuccessful logon to a console for proactive troubleshooting. It is quite rewarding when a call to an end user is answered with the question "How did you know I did that?"

The point is that the amount of control applied by SMS can be very granular. SMS can be configured as "Big Brother is Watching" or as a silent observer.

CREATING SOURCE FILES

The first thing to do is install source files for the package. The source files are a directory or share on a server volume that will be used as a template to be copied to several distribution points within the SMS infrastructure. As with any software to be installed, you must research the installation procedures, switches, .INF files, answer files, and so on. When preparing to install a third-party application, the vendor may provide extended installation features, such as variable substitution for IP addresses. In particular, look for indications of network installs that require decompression of source files, administrative installation requirements, such as registry alterations or common program groups, as well as quiet installation options. You may want to contact the third-party vendor for Software Developer's Kits (SDK) to customize the standard installation code.

For example, Windows 95 had two separate installation procedures for installation. You could install from the .CAB files or from a network setup. The network setup installation used previously extracted files for installation and optimized the installation time.

In general, these options propose many advantages to be exploited. Install the source code on a server and apply the appropriate file- or share-level permissions. Figure 18.1 displays the permissions for a shared Solitaire folder. Read rights are required for packages to see the files, and write rights are required if the installation is required to write to the source directory.

Figure 18.1.
Applying
permissions.

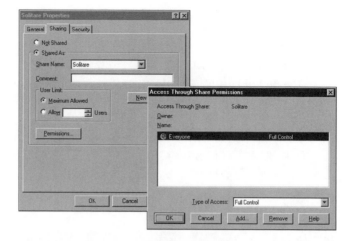

Caution

Avoid using directory, file, and share names that exceed the 8.3 character format. Clients that do not support long filenames have problems that can be very cryptic to figure out with some setup routines.

Another thing to consider is where you install the source files. You usually want to install the source files on the machine designated as the central, or primary, site server. Security problems can arise if you install the source code on a machine that is not part of a Windows NT 3.5 to 4.0 trusting or trusted domain. This is also true with Microsoft's LAN Manager, IBM's LAN Server, or Novell's NetWare Servers. The SMS service account requires at least read access to the locations where it copies files. SMS also requires full access to the location where the source files are distributed.

Caution

You must create a separate account without security restrictions to the servers that distribute applications but do not participate in a domain. Take great caution with expiration dates, synchronizing passwords, and applying appropriate permissions. These culprits can cause underlying problems with package distribution that can send you chasing ghosts. I recall spending nearly a day trying to figure out why a package was not being distributed to other distribution servers, only to find that I had loaded the source files on a server that was not part of a trusting or trusted domain.

In a Novell NetWare 4.*x* environment, bindery emulation must be set on the context that SMS distributes software. Specifically, NetWare 4.02 allows up to 16 bindery emulations for individual contexts, instead of running bindery emulation on the whole server. If bindery emulation is not available on the context targeted for distribution, SMS cannot access the resource.

By default, SMS installs itself on the volume with the most free space. This can be configured through the Site Properties | Domains | Domain properties option of the SMS Administrator. (See Figure 18.2.)

Figure 18.2. Configuring destination volumes.

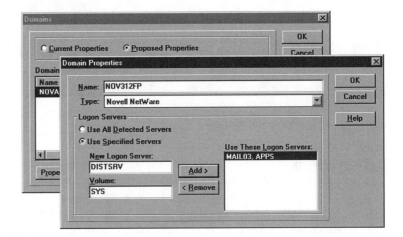

Caution

Avoid using the Use All Detected Servers option shown in Figure 18.2. If you select this option, SMS will locate all servers that it has access to and install itself on the largest volume SMS can detect. I have had SMS install itself on the SYS volume of a NetWare server and take up nearly all the volumes' space. This did not allow the clients to print because there was not enough space to spool the print job.

STORAGE CONSIDERATIONS

Because of the compression routines performed by SMS, distribution to a server might require up to four times the original package's source directory if the site server is also a distribution server, and only three times the original source files if it is not a distribution server. This can be significant if the storage capacity is limited. Monitoring and troubleshooting the distribution process is discussed in detail in Chapter 19.

Caution

> SMS gives an error saying that it cannot copy or decompress files only if there is not enough disk space to do either. Because monitoring the error logs doesn't tell you that you are out of disk space, an administrator might be looking in all the wrong places, trying to figure out why packages are not being delivered to distribution servers and clients.

SCRIPTS

Quite often, custom and commercial software requires scripting of some sort to alleviate user intervention. Automation is the key to success with any software distribution mechanism. Scripting can involve a simple batch file or a complex Visual Basic or Microsoft C++ script.

There are many misconceptions about the capabilities of SMS. SMS is merely a distribution mechanism that makes a package available to the client. What happens when the client invokes a process is entirely dependent on the instructions of the script and the context of the logged-on user. As mentioned before, SMS does not have an undo button. For this reason, you should always make available an uninstall script that can undo what the package has done. Consider this when creating the install scripts for items such as backing up files, instead of overwriting them should you need to roll back the installation.

Another item of consideration is creating different scripts for different client platforms.

What is done at the workstation is as important as how it is done. When sending a package to a client, a couple of questions should be asked, "How much memory does the application require? How much storage is available?" Fortunately, you can answer the physical questions with the use of queries. The inventory and only the machines meeting those requirements receive the package, as shown in Figure 18.3.

Figure 18.3.
Querying inven-
tory properties.

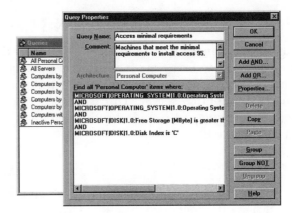

Querying the SMS database's inventory can also be an excellent tool when doing operating system upgrades, as you can specify certain requirements that must be met prior to an installation.

Note

All operating system upgrades require a reboot, which could result in possible loss of data for the end user.

SMS also provides different clients for different operating systems. When SMS detects a different OS, it automatically upgrades the client to the appropriate client. This can, however, produce strange results on multiboot systems because SMS does not "downgrade" the client pieces.

When deploying the SMS client in a new environment, you should communicate with the end user about what is going to happen. Effective communications prepare the end user for what is going to happen to the machine. Kixstart, a utility from Microsoft, is an excellent tool that can place a logon message that warns the end user what is going to happen to the machine and the process involved. It can also be used to inform the end user what software will be altered, indicate whether rebooting the machine is required, or even provide a phone number to call if things aren't quite right after an installation. Ineffective communications are the cause of many "user revolts" to the introduction of a new component. I have seen packages sent out that rebooted the machine after installation. In one particular case, a mandatory package was installed that rebooted the machine, causing the client to lose a 22-page document. This obviously was a great inconvenience to the end user (who was not very happy), and also caused the local administrator to be leery of installing new packages.

Several scripting packages, from simple to complex, are available for sending instructions to the client. Seagate's WinInstall has the capability to run a discover process prior to installing software. After the discover process is complete, you can install software and make any other alterations to the machine, and then run the discover process again. The discover process will detect all the changes made to the client (files updated, registry entries, and so on), and automatically create the script for you. Kixstart provides some simple scripting features as well.

PACKAGE DEFINITION FILES (PDFs)

Another way to set up a package is with package definition files (PDFs). PDFs are text files that pass instructions to setup command lines. Other scripting products, such as Seagate's WinInstall, can also create PDFs for use with SMS for Microsoft and non-Microsoft applications. Microsoft includes PDFs for several of their products. You can import a PDF file to an application that will predefine several settings for a package. The following steps show how to import a PDF file:

1. From the Packages window, select File | New. Click the Import button in the Package Properties dialog. (See Figure 18.4.)

Figure 18.4.
Select the Import
button to import
a PDF.

2. The File browser window appears. (See Figure 18.5.) Select the `SMS\PRIMESITE.SRV\IMPORT.SRC\ENU` subdirectory. You will see several PDF files. Selecting one of these files feeds SMS the parameters it requires to configure most of the package.

Figure 18.5.
Selecting PDF
files.

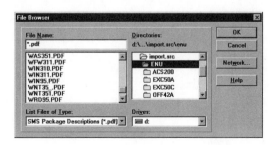

18

3. Select a PDF and click OK. SMS fills out most of the information. As shown in Figure 18.6, the PDF file also passes information to the package properties about various types of installation that can be performed. Keep in mind that the PDFs are only used to manipulate the setup routine. Custom installs often require scripting beyond a simple setup switch.

Figure 18.6.
Setup package for
workstations.
Using PDFs to
configure a Run
Command on
Workstation
package.

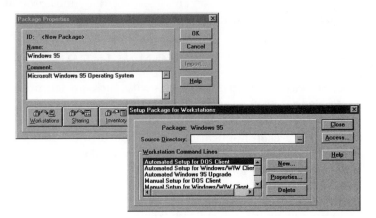

4. Set up the source directory and hardware platforms for the package to be installed from, and the package is complete.

Note

If you have not specified the source directory or hardware platforms, you receive an error stating "This package is only partially set up for workstations" or "You have not configured hardware platforms for this package."

PDFs are merely a way to inform SMS of package properties. PDFs are used by the runtime version of Microsoft Test that is included with SMS.

Note

The runtime version is included with SMS, but the full Microsoft Test product to create scripts and compile the code must be purchased separately.

Listing 18.1 is an example of a PDF that comes with SMS for Access 95.

Listing 18.1. An example of a PDF file for Access 95.

```
[PDF]
Version=1.0

[Package Definition]
Product=Microsoft Access 95
Version=7.0
Comment=Microsoft Access 95
SetupVariations=Compact, Typical, Complete, Custom, Uninstall

[Compact Setup]
CommandLine=setup.exe /Q1 /B2
CommandName=Compact
UserInputRequired=FALSE
SupportedPlatforms=Windows95, Windows NT 3.1 (x86)

[Typical Setup]
CommandLine=setup.exe /Q1 /B1
CommandName=Typical
UserInputRequired=FALSE
SupportedPlatforms=Windows95, Windows NT 3.1 (x86)

[Complete Setup]
CommandLine=setup.exe /Q1 /B3
CommandName=Complete
UserInputRequired=FALSE
SupportedPlatforms=Windows95, Windows NT 3.1 (x86)

[Custom Setup]
CommandLine=setup.exe
CommandName=Custom
UserInputRequired=TRUE
SupportedPlatforms=Windows95, Windows NT 3.1 (x86)

[Uninstall Setup]
CommandLine=setup.exe /Q1 /U
CommandName=Uninstall
UserInputRequired=TRUE
SupportedPlatforms=Windows95, Windows NT 3.1 (x86)

[Setup Package for Sharing]
ShareName=acs95ash
ShareAccess=UserRead, UserWrite, GuestRead, GuestWrite

[Program Item Properties 1]
CommandLine=msaccess.exe
Description=Microsoft Access 95 Install
ConfigurationScript=smsacm32.exe acs95a+install setup.stf
➥   "SETUP.EXE /B4 /Q1" "SETUP.EXE /U /Q1"
RegistryName=acs95a+install
DefaultINIFile=
RunMinimized=FALSE
RunLocalCopyIfPresent=FALSE
DriveMode=UNC
```

continues

18

PACKAGES

LISTING 18.1. CONTINUED

```
SupportedPlatforms=Windows95
SetupIcon=ACS95A01.ICO
DisplayIconInProgGroup=TRUE

[Setup Package for Inventory]
InventoryThisPackage=TRUE
Detection Rule Part 1=File 1
;Detection Rule Part 2=AND
;Detection Rule Part 3=File 2

[File 1]
FILE=MSACCESS.EXE
COLLECT=FALSE
Checksum=
DATE=9,28,95
SIZE=2839552
TIME=00, 00
```

The PDF calls on several setup switches for various types of installations, as well as SMS-specific information such as platforms supported, comments, exit routines, and so on.

Note

> Other items of interest are the entries for BYTE size, DATE, and so on. These items will be reviewed in further detail in the section, "Creating Inventory Packages."

Much of this information is also used for jobs. The next step is to create a job, which gives instructions on how to distribute the package. See Chapter 19.

TYPES OF PACKAGES

Packages are defined by a combination of packages, jobs, and queries. These components will be reviewed in more detail in the following sections. SMS can perform three basic types of packages at the workstation:

◆ Run Command on Workstation

◆ Share Package on Server

◆ Inventory Package

RUN COMMAND ON WORKSTATION

A Run Command on Workstation package is, basically, launching an executable at the workstation. A common misunderstanding is that SMS should provide miracles at the desktop. Actually, SMS only provides the PCM or PGC with the command line to execute at the client, and can only invoke a process that is predetermined by the scripting process. Any switches usually used with the executable can also be passed through to the installation code.

THE SHARE PACKAGE ON SERVER

A Share Package on Server enables an administrator to share source code on distribution servers. Based on the group an individual belongs to, SMS can build custom program groups on the desktop when the user logs in. Because the groups are dependent upon the user and not the desktop, an administrator creates roving software.

Another nice feature is the capability to place networked applications on multiple distribution servers. If the client portion of SMS cannot locate the server, it tries the next distribution server that the application was distributed to. This provides a level of fault tolerance that does not leave the client machines unusable in the event of a server crash.

Tip

> Another feature to take advantage of with shared packages is the capability to update multiple distribution servers simultaneously from a single point. This means the administrator can update files to an application or image in one location and allow SMS to do the work of updating multiple distribution points in the enterprise.

INVENTORY PACKAGE

An inventory package gives an administrator the ability to monitor files at the workstation level with great accuracy. You can configure an inventory to monitor what versions of what software are installed on the client's machine. You can also track different versions of DLLs or network drivers, for example. Another option allows you to collect files and forward them to the SMS console, as well as keep a history of the files when they change.

For example, you can collect the AUTOEXEC.BAT file from the workstations and keep a history of the file. A client calls the help desk and explains that he or she can no longer execute Office applications. You ask if the client has done anything to the machine and, of course, the client says, "No." From that point, you can pull up an inventory history from the SMS Administrator and point out the changes to the path, showing that the user installed DOOM. You can now create a package to install the old AUTOEXEC.BAT file back to the client.

18

Creating Run Command on Workstation Packages

Creating a Run Command on Workstation package is actually a two-part process: creating the package and creating a job. Creating a package is merely passing information such as source directory, setup switches, and so on to the SMS system. Some of the instructions for creating a job for the distribution process are where, when, and how to install the package. Creating the package is discussed in this chapter, and creating a job for the package is discussed in Chapter 19. The following steps show how to configure a run command on a workstation package:

1. Click the Packages button and select the File | New menu option. The Package Properties dialog appears. (See Figure 18.7.)

Figure 18.7.
The Package
Properties dialog.

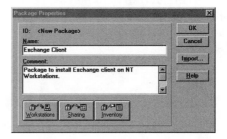

2. Enter the name of the package as well as additional comments. The client sees these comments when he selects Details from the Package Command Manager.

Tip

By clicking the help button displayed in Figure 18.7, the Help window appears. (See Figure 18.8.) The Help window is easily accessible here and is a good source for basic SMS references and their functions.

3. In the Package Properties dialog, click the Workstations button to configure the package. You are prompted for the source location of the files. Click the Ellipsis button to browse the location. You are presented with a window that allows you to browse local or network connections. (See Figure 18.9.) You can also select the Network button to browse other network resources.

Figure 18.8.
The Help win-
dow.

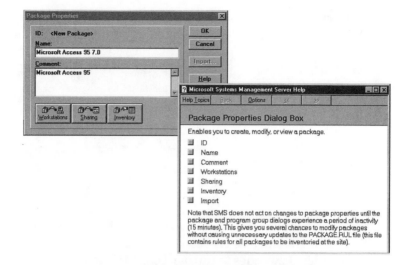

Figure 18.9.
The Directory
Browser window.

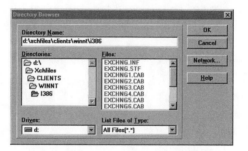

4. Click the OK button after selecting the source directory and the Setup Package for Workstations window appears again. (See Figure 18.10.)

Figure 18.10.
The Setup
Package for
Workstations
dialog.

5. Click the New button and the Command Line Properties dialog appears. (See Figure 18.11.) The command name and command line are required.

Figure 18.11.
The Command
Line Properties
dialog.

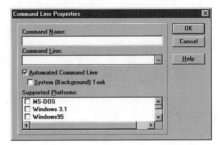

6. Enter the command name or select the Ellipsis button to browse for the command line to be executed at the client. (See Figure 18.12.) Enter any additional switches to further define the setup instructions. For example, SETUP.EXE /M is often used for a minimal install or SETUP.EXE OPTIONAL.INF specifies an information file for setup to read.

Note

If you use a PDF, the command name is automatically configured after you select the type of install (minimal, maximum, custom, and so on).

Select OK to finish configuring the package.

Figure 18.12.
Setting up the
command line to
be invoked at the
client.

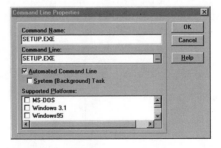

7. The Automated Command Line option is used for packages requiring no end-user intervention. The System (Background) Task option is intended for "quiet" installations that require no screen output. This option allows the install to run as a background task on Windows NT if Package Command Manager is running as a service. In this scenario, if nobody is logged

on, an administrator can pass commands to run in the background. If someone is logged on, the package is invoked with the token of the logged-in user as opposed to a local system account.

8. The last option in the Command Line Properties window (refer to Figure 18.12) is to select the supported platforms. This option is very important. SMS only makes the package available to selected operating systems.

Caution

If a package was sent to an NT (*x*86) client without selecting Windows NT (*x*86), SMS never shows this as an available package to an NT (*x*86) client. When troubleshooting, this is something to keep in mind when packages do not reach to the client.

9. Select OK when finished and you return to the Setup Package for Workstations dialog. (See Figure 18.13.)

Figure 18.13.
The Setup
Package for
Workstations
dialog.

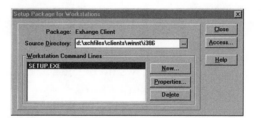

10. Selecting the Access button allows the administrator to define read and write access of the files after distribution to the distribution servers. (See Figure 18.14.)

Figure 18.14.
Assigning access
rights.

11. Assign read and write permissions for the distribution share. Users and guests are referring to domain users and domain guests.

When you close the Setup Package for Workstations dialog, you might receive the warning message shown in Figure 18.15.

Figure 18.15.
Warning
message.

The warning in Figure 18.15 appears when the source code is local to the server on which you are configuring the package. As long as the server remains online and has appropriate security access, this error message is not a concern. Keep in mind that this is a problem in untrusted domains, as in Microsoft's Lan Manager/Workgroups, IBM's LAN Server, or NetWare servers that have not been configured with proper security access.

12. When finished configuring the package, select OK from the Package Properties dialog. SMS sends a message indicating it will update the package at all sites. (See Figure 18.16.)

Figure 18.16.
Update message.

13. The package then shows up in the Packages window and is ready for deployment. (See Figure 18.17.)

Figure 18.17.
The Packages
window with
package defined.

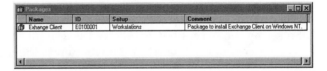

CREATING SHARED ON SERVER PACKAGES

As with the Run Command on Workstation packages, creating a Share Package on Server is also a two-part process: creating the package and creating a job to distribute the package.

The following steps show how you set up a Share Package on Server package by importing a PDF file for Access 95:

1. From the Packages window, select File | New. Select the Sharing button to configure the Shared package on Server. Click the Import button and in the File Browser dialog (see Figure 18.18), select the

SMS\PRIMESITE.SRV\IMPORT.SRC\ENU directory. This example uses a PDF shipped with SMS 1.2 for Access 95. There are several predefined PDFs for Microsoft products. Many third-part installation scripts write their own PDF's for SMS. Contact the third-part vendor to find out if they have written a PDF for the product to be installed. All the information entered with the PDF can be altered to meet your specific requirements.

Figure 18.18.
Importing a PDF
file.

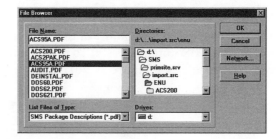

2. Select the ACESS95A.PDF file and click OK.

3. The Setup package for Sharing window appears. Click the Sharing icon to begin configuring the shared package. (Refer to Figure 18.7.)

4. Enter the source directory and share name of the source code, as shown in Figure 18.19.

Figure 18.19.
Setting up shared
package proper-
ties.

Caution

Never use an administrative share such as C$, D$, or ADMIN$. When SMS is instructed to remove the package, it attempts to delete all the files and subdirectories of the share.

5. Select the New button to set up the program items. The Program Item Properties window appears. (See Figure 18.20.)

Tip

As mentioned earlier, shared packages can be a mechanism to update multiple distribution servers from a single point. Simply type the Universal Naming Convention (UNC) or `\\servername\volumename` for NetWare, and SMS updates these distribution servers from a single location. You avoid copying source files to multiple distribution points each time an image is updated.

6. Click the Properties icon. Many of the entries from the PDF file were imported to SMS automatically. To review the settings in the Program Item Properties dialog (see Figure 18.20) and their purpose, see Table 18.1.

Figure 18.20.
The Program
Item Properties
dialog.

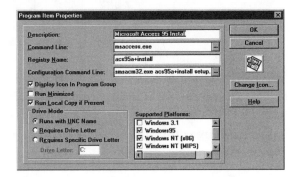

In the example in Figure 18.20, everything except the source directory and share name has been filled in by the PDF. Any of the entries can be altered to meet custom requirements.

TABLE 18.1. OPTIONS IN THE PROGRAM ITEM PROPERTIES DIALOG.

Option	Definition/Comments
Description	Description of the package. This entry is seen by the end user.
Command Line	Command line to be executed.
Registry Name	Registry entry to be used for associating the application for another application to call.
Configuration Command Line	Command line or script used to configure the local workstation the first time the application is run. This is useful for

Option	Definition / Comments
	making required Registry or .INI edits for a network-based application. Some applications do not have a true network-based installation and require local system files. This is another way to use the option to install the local files.
Display Icon in Program Group	Icon to be displayed at the client.
Run Minimized	Application is minimized when launched.
Run Local Copy If Present	This instructs the client to search for a local installation. If a local copy is present, that copy is run. If no local copy is present, the network-based installation is used.
Drive Mode	By default, the Runs with UNC Name radio button is selected. Some applications do not run with a UNC name, so you have the option of using a drive letter or requesting a specific drive letter. If the specific drive is already in use, the client is prompted before it is redirected.
Supported Platforms	Select the platforms to which you want the package made available. Keep in mind that the package never appears at the desktop if the desktop's platform is not selected.
Change Icon	Change the icon to be displayed.

18

PACKAGES

Caution

If a client requires access to files stored locally on a system or Registry modifications, the shared package might run incorrectly if it runs at all.

Much of the information entered in the Program Properties window is also used for jobs. The next step is to create a job, which gives instructions on how to distribute the package.

CREATING INVENTORY PACKAGES

Inventory packages are a mechanism that audits the local machine for files that meet certain criteria. An inventory package can be configured to collect these files and forward them up the SMS hierarchy. SMS can also keep a history of these files. (See Figure 18.21.) For example, an end user reports that the machine can't run a particular application any more. Of course, the end user never did anything to the machine. The administrator can look at the machine properties of the client and identify changes made to the AUTOEXEC.BAT file. The administrator can review the history of the last time it was edited (see Figure 18.21) and see that the user installed a game that overwrote the path to his or her applications. Because the file was forwarded to the console, the corrections can be made, and the file can be sent back out to the client in the form of a Run Command on Workstation, and all is well again.

Figure 18.21.
The Personal
Computer
Properties dialog
showing collected
files.

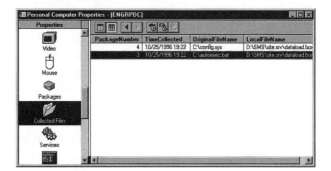

Another use for the inventory package is configuration management and version control. Files can be identified by the date, size, Cyclic Redundancy Check (CRC), and so on. Once the rules are defined, a query can be performed to identify which machines have what version of a particular DLL, for example. Once the criteria is defined, SMS will create new records in the SMS database that can be queried. Figure 18.22 is an illustration of a query that is available after the Inventory System Files package is created.

Figure 18.22.
The Query
Expression
Properties dialog.

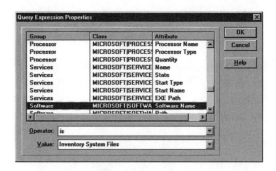

The following steps show how to set up an inventory package:

1. From the Packages window, select File | New. Click the Inventory button. The Setup Package for Inventory dialog appears. (See Figure 18.23.) In the example, the inventory package is configured to inventory, and it collects system files from the client. See Table 18.2 for a full explanation of the options in this dialog.

Figure 18.23.
The Setup
Package for
Inventory dialog.

18

PACKAGES

TABLE 18.2. OPTIONS IN THE SETUP PACKAGE FOR INVENTORY DIALOG.

Option	Description
Add AND	Adds a logical AND operator. Use this when you only want to inventory the files if all criteria are met.
Add OR	Adds a logical OR operator. Use this when you want to inventory the files if any criteria are met.
Properties	Opens the properties for the selected files.
Delete	Deletes the selected file.
Copy	Is supposed to copy the entries to the clipboard but does not work. Only works in the context of the current setup inventory packages window.
Paste	Is supposed to copy the entries to the clipboard but does not work. Only works in the context of the current setup inventory packages window.
Toggle	Toggles between AND and OR expressions. Only displayed when the operator is highlighted.
Group	Groups the logical expressions with parentheses. Use this when creating a complex inventory package.
Ungroup	Removes parentheses from the grouped expressions.

Note

> Package rules prioritize from the first logical operator down. For
> example, if using an AND criteria that is not met at the top of the file
> list, the query would stop and not look for any other conditions en-
> tered after it. Also, group expressions take a higher priority than a
> single logical operator.

2. Check the Inventory This Package box.

3. Click the Add AND button. The File Properties window appears as shown
   in Figure 18.24.

Figure 18.24.
The File Proper-
ties dialog.

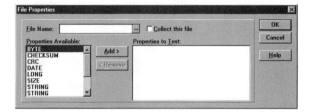

4. Type the filename or click the Ellipsis button to browse.

Note

> If the file is selected from the Browse button, you can make SMS
> retrieve the more advanced properties with the Retrieve option, such
> as file size, date, checksum, and so on. (See Figure 18.25.)

Figure 18.25.
Properties to
test for.

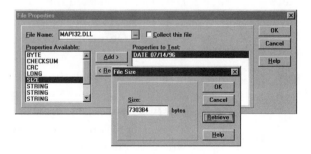

5. Select the Collect This File checkbox if you want to collect a copy of the file.
   (Refer to Figure 18.24.)

Caution

When collecting files, consider the size of the files collected. Collecting a large file from all clients in the enterprise can fill up disk space very quickly. Usually, you want to collect only small text files.

6. Add any additional properties and select OK. A message indicates that the inventory rules will be updated at all sites. (See Figure 18.26.)

Figure 18.26.
Update message.

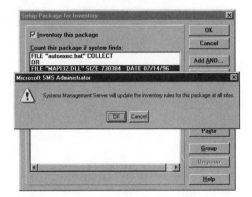

7. Enter a name and comments to identify the inventory package and click OK. The inventory instructions are updated at the current site and all child sites. The inventory criteria is then updated in a file called PACKAGE.RUL in the SMS\SITE.SRV\MAINCFG.BOX\PKG.RUL directory. Listing 18.2 displays the modifications made to this file for the previously defined rules.

LISTING 18.2. THE PACKAGE.RUL FILE.

```
PACKAGE 1 "Inventory System Files" FILE "autoexec.bat" COLLECT
  OR
  FILE "MAPI32.DLL" SIZE 730384    DATE 07/14/96
  OR
  FILE "config.sys" COLLECT
```

The AUDIT.RUL file is used for inventory packages and will be discussed in more detail in Appendix D, "Extending Inventory Collection."

ADMINISTRATIVE INSTALLS

The installation that requires administrative rights for Windows NT Workstation poses an entirely different problem. If an application needs administrative privileges to be installed and the user that is logged on only has domain user privileges, this presents a problem. By default, PCM is installed as a service on all servers. Figure 18.27 displays the PCM installed as a service.

Figure 18.27.
Package Com-
mand Manager
NT as a service.

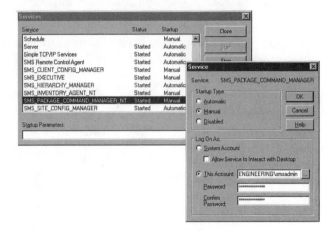

This service can also be installed as a service on Windows NT Workstation client with the INSTSRV utility included on the SMS CD-ROM in the SUPPORT\DEBUG*PLATFORM* directory. Figure 18.28 displays the options presented for the service installation utility.

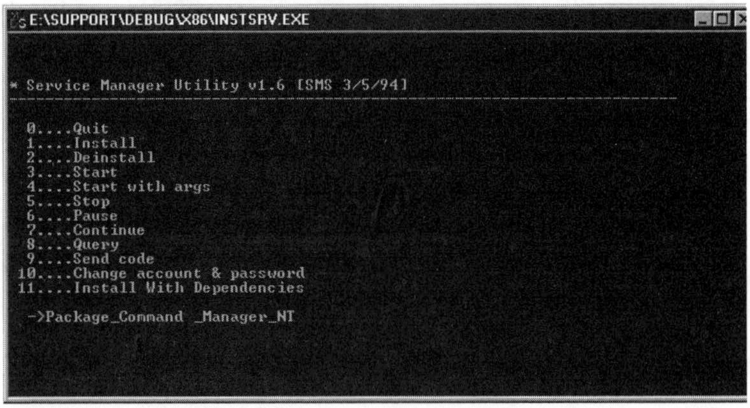

Figure 18.28.
The Service
installation
utility.

> *Note*
>
> The service installation utility can be used to install the service remotely.

Keep in mind that packages to be installed must require no screen output and the package must be automated requiring no user input. The PCM as a service can install packages with nobody logged on, but if someone is logged on when the package arrives, it is installed by the regular PCM with the context of the logged-on user instead of PCM running as a service with access to the local system account.

SUMMARY

Once the inventory and Share Package on Server packages are defined, a job must be submitted to send the packages out to the distribution points and eventually to the clients. Inventory packages automatically create jobs to update the inventory process. Extending inventory is discussed in more detail in Appendix D. Much thought, planning, and testing should be performed when distributing software to the client. This work up front can save extensive time and resources. Time and resources saved are capital saved, especially when a distribution can be automated instead of having to visit all the clients in the enterprise every time an update is performed.

18

PACKAGES

CHAPTER 19

Jobs

Systems Management Server uses jobs to send instructions to site servers, distribution servers, and clients of the SMS infrastructure. Jobs also contain scheduling information and a package or other data that needs to be distributed. There are basically four different types of jobs that the SMS system uses:

◆ Run Command on Workstation job

◆ Share Package on Server job

◆ Remove Package from Server job

◆ System job

The Run Command on Workstation, Share Package on Server, and Remove Package from Server jobs are initiated by the administrator from the user interface of the SMS system. System jobs are used primarily for status, inventory, and synchronization instructions. This chapter focuses on these types of jobs and how to take advantage of several attractive features.

TYPES OF JOBS

The following sections show the types of jobs that the SMS system uses and their purposes.

RUN COMMAND ON WORKSTATION

A Run Command on Workstation job is used to distribute packages to SMS clients to be initiated by Package Command Manager (PCM). The job contains information such as when to make the package available, who will receive the package, and where to place the distribution files.

SHARE PACKAGE ON SERVER

A Share Package on Server job is used to place the networked applications on distribution servers. Configuration information about shared applications is made available through the Program Group Control (PGC) at the client.

PGC can be configured to "follow" the user. Based on the groups a user belongs to, the shared package appears on whatever machine the user logs onto, if the SMS client is installed.

A Share Package on Server job can also be used to keep multiple servers' software updated on shares or volumes from a single point. This is a great tool for ensuring consistent software updates.

REMOVE PACKAGE FROM SERVER

A Remove Package from Server job is used to remove a workstation package or shared package from distribution servers. After a distribution of client files, the administrator should remove the packages to free up system resources. Consider setting up alerts to monitor disk space usage. The administrator can configure SMS to send an SNMP-based trap to the administrator and even execute a predefined set of instructions such as initiating an e-mail or paging an administrator. Refer to Chapter 15, "Using Help Desk Utilities and Diagnostic Tools," for more details.

Note

> Canceling or deleting a job does not remove the files from distribution servers. The administrator must use a Remove Package from Server job to remove the files once they have been distributed. The same is true for collected files.

SYSTEM JOBS

System jobs are not initiated by the administrator. System jobs are used to distribute system instructions and collect inventory information. System jobs are also used to synchronize system information. For example, a system job is automatically generated when you create an inventory package or change the frequency with which a client is inventoried.

JOB PROCESSES

SMS uses three primary processes to move information throughout the SMS infrastructure:

◆ Scheduler

◆ Sender

◆ Despooler

These processes create files, use compression algorithms, make connections, and monitor the distribution of data and files. It is important to understand how and where the SMS system moves the data and files within the infrastructure when troubleshooting configuration problems or package distribution. As illustrated in Figure 19.1, these processes are the delivery mechanism for the distribution process.

19

JOBS

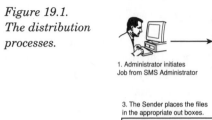

Figure 19.1.
The distribution
processes.

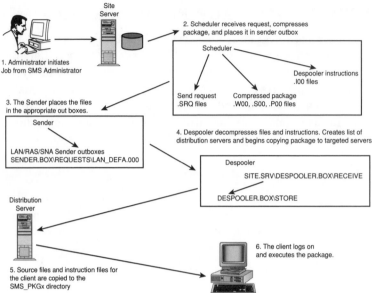

1. Administrator initiates
Job from SMS Administrator

2. Scheduler receives request, compresses
package, and places it in sender outbox

Scheduler

Despooler instructions
.I00 files

Send request   Compressed package
.SRQ files   .W00, .S00, .P00 files

3. The Sender places the files
in the appropriate out boxes.

Sender

LAN/RAS/SNA Sender outboxes
SENDER.BOX\REQUESTS\LAN_DEFA.000

4. Despooler decompresses files and instructions. Creates list of
distribution servers and begins copying package to targeted servers

Despooler
                 SITE.SRV\DESPOOLER.BOX\RECEIVE

DESPOOLER.BOX\STORE

Distribution
Server

6. The client logs on
and executes the package.

5. Source files and instruction files for
the client are copied to the
SMS_PKGx directory

SCHEDULER

Scheduler monitors the SMS database for the activation of a job from the SMS Administrator console. Scheduler then compresses the package and places the compressed file in a sender outbox, which is the \SITE.SRV\SENDER.BOX\TOSEND directory. The files have different extensions, depending on the type of job created (.WXX for Workstation, .SXX for Shared, and .PXX for System). Scheduler also creates Despooler instructions (.I00 instruction files) in the same directory and issues a send request to the senders.

The Send Request files (.SRQ) are created and placed in the appropriate outbox for the sender to be used. The outbox for the LAN sender is the SMS\SITE.SRV \SENDER.BOX\REQUESTS\LANDEFA.000 directory. There are also directories for the RAS and SNA outboxes. The SRQ files contain information to connect and copy the files to the other site servers. Figure 19.2 displays the directory structure after the package job has completed.

The Scheduler also monitors the status of the jobs and passes this information to log files and the SMS Administrator Console. Monitoring the status of a job can be very helpful when troubleshooting. The various job status settings are explained in Table 19.1.

Figure 19.2.
Directory struc-
ture of completed
job.

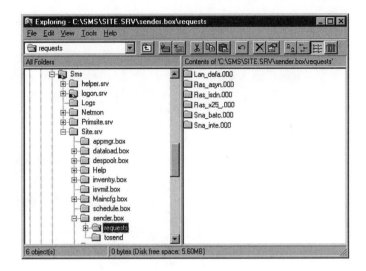

TABLE 19.1. JOB STATUS.

Job Status	Meaning
Pending	Job has been initiated by the administrator but has not started initiating the distribution process.
Complete	The job has completed the instructions.
Retrying	This is the one to worry about. If SMS cannot connect, insufficient disk space and the License Manager are a few items to check. I have seen instances where License Manager was set too low and refused connections from a site server.
Canceled	Someone has canceled the job from the SMS User Interface. Canceled jobs no longer appear as available packages to the client.
Failed	After a job has been in retry state for 48 hours, the job is marked "failed" and does not attempt to execute.

Caution

Scheduler uses several real-time parameters to execute instructions. It is very important to synchronize the time on SQL, NT, OS/2, and NetWare servers as well as their clients. Strange results can appear, such as incorrect time stamps on inventory or packages not being

19

JOBS

delivered to clients, because the client is a day ahead of the available time. This can also be confusing when reading error logs.

Figure 19.3 shows the workstation status properties. If the last hardware scan and last software scan times are different, suspect time synchronization problems.

Figure 19.3.
The Personal
Computer
Properties
window.

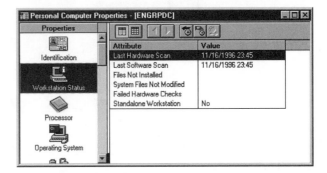

If multiple senders are defined, Scheduler determines which sender will move data to the targeted sights fastest and coordinates the sending order by their priority and the start time. Figure 19.4 displays the Job Schedule window where you configure the Start After time, and the Priority and Repeat settings.

Figure 19.4.
Job priority.

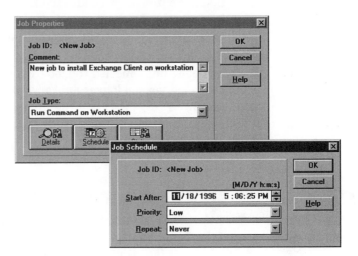

SENDERS

The sender copies the compressed files and instruction files to the targeted site in the SMS\SITE.SRV\DESPOOLER.BOX\RECEIVE directory. Six types of senders can be configured through the site properties Senders option, as illustrated in Figure 19.5.

Figure 19.5.
Configuring
senders.

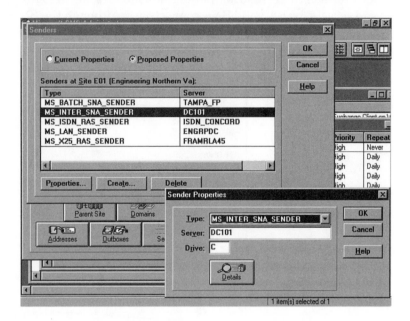

The following are three categories of senders:

- ◆ LAN sender. Installed by default, it is always used to send jobs to itself.
- ◆ RAS sender. Utilizes Microsoft's Remote Access Server for communications. RAS must be configured on both networks to communicate, but does not necessarily have to be on the site server itself.
- ◆ SNA sender. Uses SNA for communication. As with RAS, Microsoft's SNA server must be installed on both networks that will be communicating. Note that Microsoft's SNA server is a separate product and does not come with SMS.

Both the parent and the child site must meet the physical, data link, and network requirements in order to implement the appropriate senders. This may require the purchase of additional hardware or software such as modems, data lines, SNA Server, or specific NICs (Network Interface Cards) for the service to be installed. Keep in mind that parent sites and their child sites must be using the same protocol frame types.

19

JOBS

In most larger organizations, T-1 through T-3 links are available and can be utilized as "local" sites. Others aren't so fortunate and have to consider link speeds as low as 28.8Kbps. Figure 19.6 shows how to take advantage of redundant paths for communications and software distribution. If one sender is unavailable, SMS uses an alternate route. Also notice that the configuration in Figure 19.6 does not use the site servers for RAS and SNA connectivity. Although the SMS site server can also be the SNA or RAS server, you can use different servers to offload some of the work.

Figure 19.6. LAN, RAS, and SNA configurations.

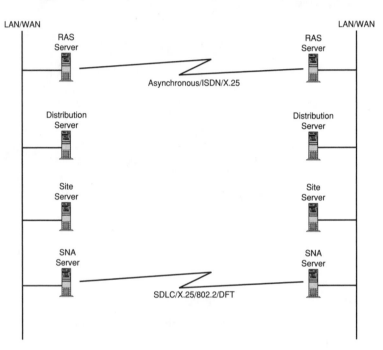

If bandwidth is an issue, Sender Manager can be set to minimize traffic or deny access to a particular sender at certain times of day. As illustrated in Figure 19.7, Sender Manager can be configured to consume a predetermined amount of bandwidth at designated times during the day. From the SMS Administrator, select Tools | Sender Manager. In the example, Sender Manager has been configured to use less bandwidth during the peak utilization periods, such as when users log on and perform most of their work at the WIDS company.

Note

Sender Manager was not implemented in SMS until version 1.1. After the problem with SMS utilizing all available bandwidth in 1.0, Microsoft provided a Sender Manager tool, separate from the SMS user interface. Even in version 1.2, it is still not fully integrated. You can have one session of SMS running, and if you select Sender Manager from the Tools menu of the SMS Administrator more than once from a single session, you may have multiple sessions running concurrently, which can be confusing.

Figure 19.7.
Sender Manager.

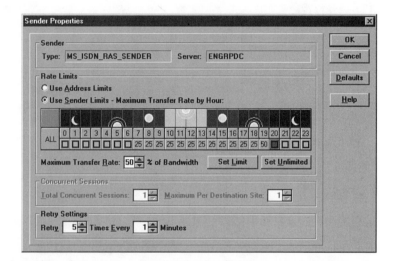

Note

Sender Manager has a Sender Properties option and an Address Properties option. Both contain a maximum transfer rate setting to configure the maximum percentage of bandwidth SMS can use during the distribution process. The setting for a sender overrides the setting for an address.

Warning

If you have multiple senders defined, you must also ensure that the other senders are configured in the same manner. SMS recognizes that one sender is unavailable and attempts to use other senders that are installed. Although this is great for redundancy and avoiding high long-distance charges, SMS by default uses all available bandwidth and can cause an impact on normal remote communications.

19

Jobs

LAN SENDER

During installation, the LAN sender is installed by default. All jobs targeted to the local site use this sender. The LAN sender is used by locally accessible devices, including high-bandwidth WAN links. Both ends of the communicating sites must be using the same protocols. Any Windows NT protocol such as TCP/IP, IPX, or NetBEUI can be used for communications.

Warning

Do not remove the LAN sender, because it is used to manage the local site as well as to make connections to remote sites. Also, when using IPX to communicate between sites, make sure that the frame type 802.2 or 802.3 is being used at both ends. By default, an NT server uses the autodetect selection for protocols. If Windows NT does not detect a frame type on initialization, it defaults to 802.2. If a GSNW (Gateway Services for NetWare) or NetWare Server is using 802.3, the sites will not be able to interact. As illustrated in Figure 19.8, each sender has its own outbox.

Figure 19.8.
Outboxes.

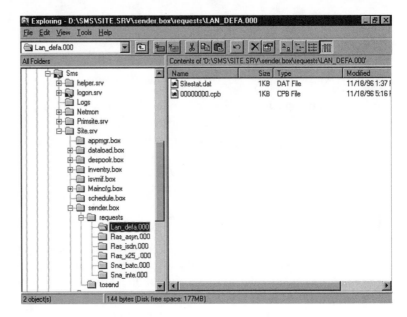

RAS SENDER

Utilizing Windows NT Remote Access Service (RAS), sites can communicate over normal asynchronous phone lines with standard modems, ISDN, or over a frame relay. Remote access must be installed at each end of the remote networks but not necessarily on the SMS server. You may also need to configure servers on both ends of remote sites with similar hardware, software, and protocols. This is also true for the other two RAS communication methods, ISDN and X.25.

Note

Make sure that NetWare and OS/2 account names and passwords are synchronized and have read/write access to the volumes that will be accessed. RAS phone book entry and the user ID that RAS uses must also be synchronized. Table 19.2 describes the different settings for the RAS sender and their meanings.

TABLE 19.2. RAS ADDRESS PROPERTIES.

Property	Meaning
Phone Book Entry	RAS phone book entry on the remote server.
User ID	User ID for remote RAS account.
Password	Enter the password for the remote RAS account. The password is case sensitive.
Server Name	The site server for the destination site.
Domain	Remote site server domain.
Username	Windows NT user account to be used to access the remote site server. This account must have read and write privileges to the sms_SITE share. The same writes are required for a NetWare or OS/2 server.
Password	Password for the remote Windows NT account.

Note

As illustrated in Figure 19.9, when using the RAS sender to connect to sites, you must configure a phone book entry for all receiving sites from the site properties options as well as RAS Administration. Also, be sure that the accounts have adequate rights on the user account and the server is set up to accept incoming calls at all receiving sites.

19

JOBS

Figure 19.9.
RAS addresses.

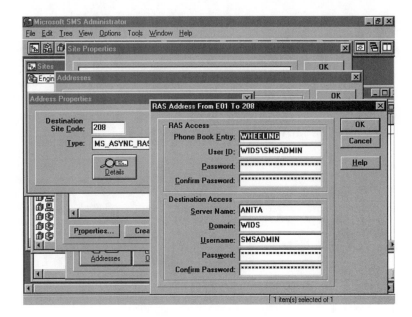

SNA SENDER

The SNA sender uses Advanced Program to Program Communications (APPC) LU 6.2 to communicate between sites. In order to utilize the SNA senders, Microsoft's SNA Server must also be installed at both ends of the WAN link to enable communications by SNA. SNA senders can be either interactive or batch mode. As with RAS, you may also need to configure servers on both ends of remote sites with similar hardware, software, and protocols. Figure 19.10 shows the dialog used to configure the SNA sender.

Figure 19.10.
SNA address
properties.

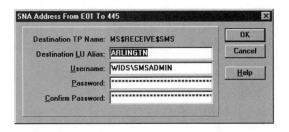

Table 19.3 lists the different settings and meanings for the SNA sender.

TABLE 19.3. SNA ADDRESS PROPERTIES.

Property	Meaning
Destination LU Alias	Destination LU 6.2 alias configured on the remote site.
Username	User account to be used to access the remote site. This account must also have read/write access to the SMS_SITE share of the remote server.
Password	Case-sensitive password for the account entered in the Username entry.

Note

You can use only one of these senders between sites, interactive or batch. You can utilize one but not both between sites.

DESPOOLER

The Despooler process copies the files in the SMS\SITE.SRV\DESPOOLER.BOX\RECEIVE directory and copies the package and instruction files to the SMS\SITE.SRV \DESPOOLER.BOX\STORE directory. Despooler then creates a temporary directory on the root of the SMS drive and begins decompressing the files on the site server. After the decompression is complete, this directory is deleted. The decompressed files are placed in the SMS\LOGON.SRV\PCMPKG.SRC directory of the designated distribution servers for the site.

Tip

Exclude the site server from being a distribution server. Use the site server to distribute files to the locally based file and print servers. These servers are usually beefed up to easily perform the local distribution process, which takes advantage of the fan-out architecture of SMS. Keep in mind that SMS is a synchronous mechanism when planning the infrastructure.

Figure 19.11 displays a poorly planned SMS infrastructure. In this example, one server must distribute the software asynchronously to each of the participating distribution servers.

19

JOBS

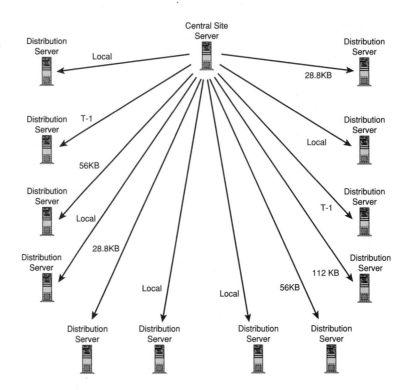

*Figure 19.11.
Inefficient design
for distribution
and communica-
tions.*

As illustrated in Figure 19.11, if a site server has 15 servers to update a 200MB package, it could be quite a while until it reaches server number 20, especially if you are dealing with low bandwidth and overutilized distribution servers.

Note

There is also a bug in SMS 1.0 and 1.1 that stops distribution to more than 20 servers per site. Real-world experience has shown that placing a limit of about 7 distribution servers per site and a maximum of 500 users per distribution server is a good general rule. This achieves acceptable distribution time frames at minimal load to the distribution servers. Also set up geographically local distribution servers to avoid sending packages over slow WAN links. Figure 19.12 displays an efficient design for distribution.

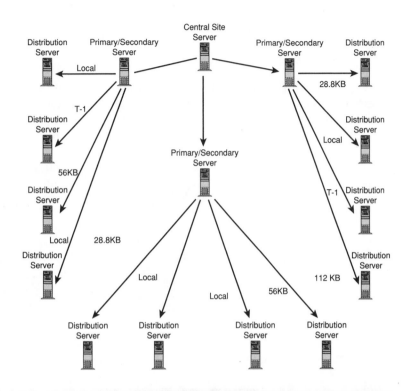

Figure 19.12.
Efficient design
for distribution.

Note

If any distribution servers are NetWare servers, you must configure Gateway Services for NetWare on the server that the Despooler service is running.

Compression can be tuned in the Windows NT Registry under HKEY_LOCAL_MACHINE \Software\Microsoft\SMS\Components\SMS_Despooler. The value can range from the default of 1 (the fastest using the least compression) to 7 (the slowest with maximum compression). Consider changing this on the site server if packages are to be sent over slow links.

Note

This entry is not placed into the Registry until a package is sent to the distribution server. You can also make this entry manually.

CREATING A RUN COMMAND ON WORKSTATION JOB

There are two ways to create a Run Command on Workstation job. From the Jobs menu, you can select File | New, or you can drag the package and drop it on the targeted machines. Figure 19.13 displays the initial dialog for the Run Command on Workstation job. Add a comment to identify the job.

Figure 19.13.
Job Properties
dialog.

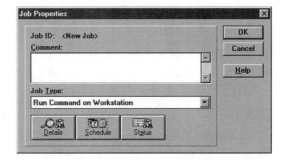

After you select the Details button, the Job Details dialog appears, as shown in Figure 19.14. From the Package drop-down list, select the package to be distributed.

Figure 19.14.
The Job Details
dialog.

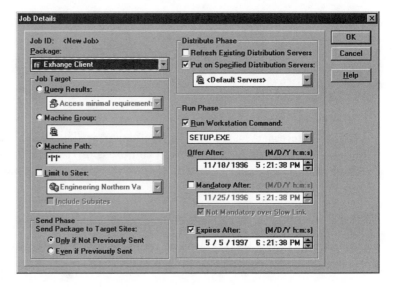

Next, you configure the job target. There are three ways to configure the targeted clients:

Query Results. The targeted machines can be based on a predefined query. This is useful if you want to be sure the targeted machines meet specific hardware or storage criteria.

Machine Group. A predefined machine group as described in Chapter 17, "Machine and Site Groups."

Machine Path. The machine path is the user-defined path of a site, domain, and machine name separated by the | symbol. The asterisk can be used as a wildcard. For example, to send a package to all machines in a particular site, the machine path is *sitename|domainname|**.

Caution

The asterisk also includes any servers in the domain. If you deliver a package that reboots the machine, you may inadvertently reboot a server.

The job target can also be narrowed down to specific sites containing the target computers:

Limit to Sites. The Limit to Sites option distributes only to a specific site. The Include Subsites option is used with the Limit to Sites option.

Selecting the Include Subsites option distributes the package to all the child sites of the site selected in the Limit to Sites option.

CONFIGURING THE PHASES

Next, you configure the phases. The three different phases SMS utilizes to control distribution to the SMS servers and clients are the Send, Distribute, and Run phases. The Run Command on Workstation job does not have to use all phases. There are certain advantages to breaking up the job phases.

SEND PHASE

In the Send Phase group of the Job Details dialog, you configure the send phase. The send phase is used to control the distribution of the compressed package. The following options are available:

Only if Not Previously Sent. Selecting this option sends the package only to sites that the package has not been sent to previously. This option is handy if you want to save time during the distribution process. SMS only sends the instruction files instead of compressing and copying the entire source directory to the distribution servers.

Even if Previously Sent. Select this button to force an update of the source files. For example, if you were testing a script file and made changes to it in the original source directory, you could use this option to refresh the source files of targeted distribution servers.

Note

A confirmed bug in SMS 1.0 and 1.1 exists if a package was sent from a parent site to a child site. If the administrator tries to create a job to send the package from the child primary site through the SMS Administrator, you get an error saying that the package type is incorrect. The workaround is to resend the package from the parent site with only the send phase selected.

DISTRIBUTE PHASE

In the Distribute Phase group in the Job Details dialog, the following options are available:

Refresh Existing Distribution Servers. Use this option to overwrite the package source directory on the distribution server.

Put on Specified Distribution Servers. By default, the Default Servers option is selected. This machine group targets all servers that have been defined as default servers from the site properties Servers option, as shown in Figure 19.15. You may want to define custom machine groups if distribution servers are added and you only want to send the package to the new servers.

Figure 19.15.
Default servers.

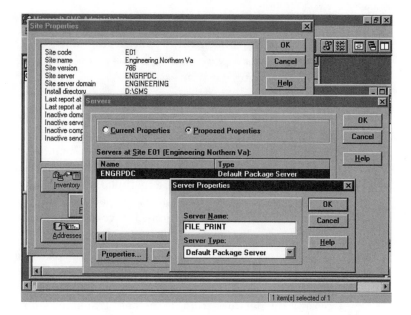

Run Phase

The run phase is useful if you have already distributed the package. This option can speed up the distribution process when a job is repeated and the source files do not need to be updated. The following options are available in the Run Phase group of the Job Details dialog:

Run Workstation Command. Select this option and use the drop-down list box to select the command line to be invoked at the client. These command-line options are defined when the package is originally created. If this box is cleared, the package is not available to the clients. This is useful if you only want to refresh distribution server source files.

Offer After. Enter the date and time that the package is to be made available. When this time is reached, the client's PCM presents it as an available package.

19

JOBS

Caution

The package is made available according to the client's date and time. If you send out a package and it never appears at the client, suspect the client's date and time settings.

Mandatory After. You can configure a package to be optional to the client for a week and then force the package to be installed. Enter the date and time that the package becomes mandatory. When this time frame elapses, the package becomes mandatory. The client's PCM displays a window to the client, "This package will be installed in 5.00 minutes," and counts down the five minutes and installs the package. (Be careful using reboots in combination with mandatory jobs. I have seen end users lose a whole day's worth of work when a mandatory job reboots a machine.)

Not Mandatory over Slow Link. Choosing this option does not install a package over a slow link such as RAS. When the client is inventoried, SMS uses the `netspeed.com` file to determine the type of connection the client is accessing the network from. If the data transmission rate is considered slow, the package is not forced to the client. For example, you do not want to push an office install to a client dialing into a 28.8 RAS server.

Expires After. Select the expiration date for the package. The package no longer appears in the client's PCM after this time frame passes. Once again, this setting is dependent on the client's time.

Note

Expiring a package does not remove a package from the servers. You must use a Remove Package from Server job, which is discussed later in this chapter.

Click the OK button to return to the Job Properties window.

Click the Schedule button. Figure 19.16 displays the Job Schedule dialog.

Enter the Start After parameter for when the job is to start. Select the priority: low, medium, or high. Higher priority jobs are processed before jobs of a lower priority.

Select the Repeat option. The Repeat option can be never, daily, weekly, biweekly, or monthly. This is particularly useful when you want the same job, such as a virus scan, to be repeated at the client.

Select the OK button when finished to return to the Job Properties dialog.

Figure 19.16.
Job Schedule
dialog.

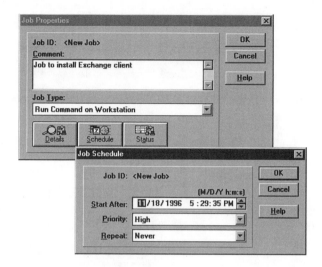

Select the OK button in the Job Properties dialog to finish creating the job. The job is displayed as pending in the Jobs dialog, as shown in Figure 19.17.

Figure 19.17.
Pending jobs.

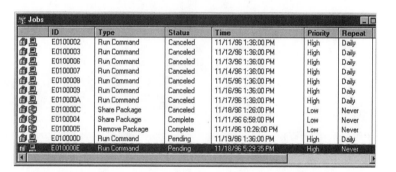

CREATING A SHARE PACKAGE ON SERVER JOB

Providing networked applications has several advantages, such as centralized administration and reduced hard disk space usage. Creating a Share Package on Server job sends the package source directory to the targeted distribution servers and creates a share. This share can then be accessed by the clients, depending on the group they belong to.

In Chapter 18, "Packages," a shared package was created. Two additional steps are required to make the package available to the client: creating a program group and creating a Share Package on Server job.

Note

SMS 1.2 now supports Share Package on Server for Windows 95
clients.

To finish configuring the Share Package on Server, complete the following steps:

1. Create a program group. From the Program Group window, select File |
   New. The Program Group Properties dialog appears, as shown in Figure
   19.18.

Figure 19.18.
Program Group
Properties dialog.

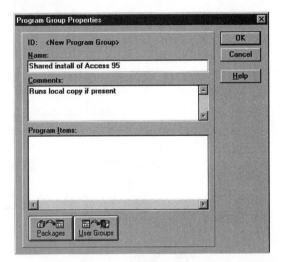

Caution

Do not use a forward slash (/) or a full colon (:) in the program group
description. Windows 95 and Windows NT PGC do not interpret these
characters and, as a result, PGC fails to create the program group
shortcut. The PGC.LOG file will contain an error message, "Failed to
create program group."

2. Enter the program group name and optional comments. Select the Packages button to open the Program Group Packages dialog. Here, you can add
   a package, as shown in Figure 19.19.

Figure 19.19.
Program Group
Packages dialog.

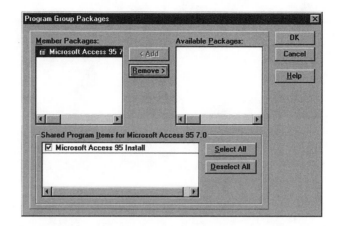

3. Select any of the predefined available shared packages, and click the OK button.

Note

Multiple packages can be selected to appear in the user's personal program groups.

Caution

Any user-added icons altered or added are removed to ensure that the desktops are managed consistently. This also holds true for any icons that are altered or deleted; they are rebuilt fresh the next time the user logs on.

4. From the Program Group Properties dialog, click the User Groups button. The User Groups dialog appears, as shown in Figure 19.20.

Because this package is based on user groups, a user can have a roving desktop that follows him from workstation to workstation. For example, if a user belongs to a group named Sales that has a package to share Excel, when that user logs in to a machine, the shared package builds the program groups, icons, and path to available servers automatically. When this user logs off and another user logs on who is not a member of Sales, the program no longer exists.

19

JOBS

Figure 19.20.
User Groups
dialog.

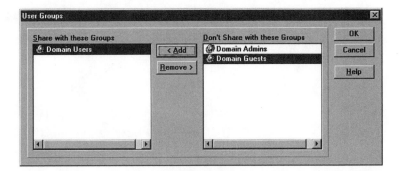

Note

If GSNW is installed, you can select NetWare groups to share the package with.

5. When finished, select OK. The message shown in Figure 19.21 appears, reminding you that a job must be created to distribute the package.

Figure 19.21.
SMS update
message.

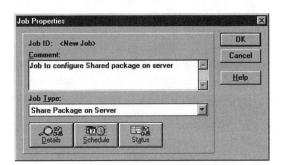

6. From the Jobs menu, select File | New. The Job Properties dialog appears. Select the Share Package on Server option for the job type, and enter comments to identify the job, as shown in Figure 19.22.

Figure 19.22.
Selecting the
Share Package on
Server job type.

7. Click the Details button, and the Job Details dialog appears. (See Figure 19.23.)

Figure 19.23.
Share Package on
Server Job
Details dialog.

From the Job Details dialog, select the package to be shared.

CONFIGURING THE JOB DETAILS

As with the Run Command on Workstation job, you must configure the job details. The three groups in the Job Details dialog are

- ◆ Job Target
- ◆ Send Phase
- ◆ Distribute Phase

JOB TARGET

The job target can be narrowed down to specific sites containing the target computers:

Limit to Sites. The Limit to Sites option distributes only to a specific site. The Include Subsites option is used with the Limit to Sites option.

Selecting the Include Subsites option distributes the package to all the child sites of the site selected in the Limit to Sites option.

SEND PHASE

The send phase is used to control the distribution of the compressed package. The following options are available to configure the send phase:

Only if Not Previously Sent. Selecting this option sends the package only to sites that the package has not been sent to previously. This option is handy if you want to save time during the distribution process. SMS only sends the instruction files instead of compressing and copying the entire source directory to the distribution servers.

Even if Previously Sent. Select this button to force an update of the source files. For example, if you were testing a script file and made changes to it in the original source directory, you can use this option to refresh the source files of targeted distribution servers.

DISTRIBUTE PHASE

The following options are available to configure the Distribute phase:

Refresh Existing Distribution Servers. Use this option to overwrite the package source directory on the distribution server.

Put on Specified Distribution Servers. By default, the Default Servers option is selected. This machine group targets all servers that have been defined as default servers from the site properties Servers option. You may want to define custom machine groups if distribution servers are added and you want to send the package only to the new servers.

Click the OK button when finished. Click the OK button in the Job Properties dialog, and the package appears as pending. You are finished setting up the Share Package on Server.

CREATING A REMOVE PACKAGE FROM SERVER JOB

Deleting or canceling a job only deletes the compressed package files at the sending site servers; the instructions in the SQL database and the package are removed from the Package Properties window. However, this does not remove the decompressed files of the packages' source directory or the packages that have already been installed at the client. A Remove Package from Server job removes the packages' compressed and decompressed files stored at the server.

Note

> The Remove Package from Server job does not remove the source files that are used for the original distribution on the originating server.

To create a Remove Package from Server job, complete the following steps:

1. From the Jobs window, select File | New. The Job Properties window appears. Enter comments to identify the package.

2. As illustrated in Figure 19.24, the Job Details dialog appears. Select from the drop-down list box the package to be removed.

Figure 19.24.
Job details.

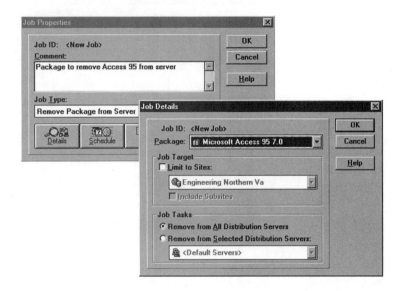

Limit to Sites. The Limit to Sites option only removes the package from a specific site. The Include Subsites option is used with the Limit to Sites option.

Selecting the Include Subsites option removes the package from all the child sites of the site selected in the Limit to Sites option.

3. Click the OK button, and the Job Properties dialog appears. Click the OK button again to submit the job and it enters pending status, as shown in Figure 19.25.

The Remove Package from Server job has been submitted and displays a pending status.

Caution

Never set up a package to use a Windows NT hidden administrative share such as C$ or ADMIN$. If you send a Remove Package from Server job in that situation, SMS 1.0 and 1.1 attempt to remove all the files in that share even if it is the root of a drive or the system root. SMS 1.1 will not allow a share with $ as the last character.

19

JOBS

Figure 19.25.
Pending package.

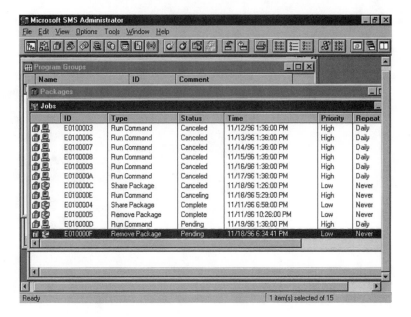

SYSTEM JOBS

System jobs are jobs initiated by the SMS system. Generally, they are used to send instructions for inventory collection, secondary site creation initiation, synchronization events, and updates to site server properties. For example, changing the inventory frequency for the clients generates a system job.

Tip

If a system job fails during the creation of new secondary site servers, check for the BOOTSTRAP.EXE file on the root of the machine to be installed as well as the SMS subdirectory. The BOOTSTRAP.LOG file can also be monitored for site creation status.

Monitor system job status for connectivity problems as described in the following section.

VIEWING JOB STATUS

Tracking the job as it moves throughout the SMS system is important when troubleshooting the distribution process. The SMS processes report information back to the SMS administrator to track the status of the job. The overall status information reported to the SMS administrator can be viewed by double-clicking the job from the Jobs window, as shown in Figure 19.26.

Figure 19.26.
Job status.

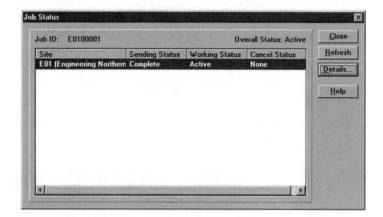

Table 19.4 is a summary of the different job status entries for sending, working, and cancel status.

TABLE 19.4. OVERALL JOB STATUS.

Status	Meaning
Pending	Scheduler is waiting to activate the job and has not started yet. You can still delete the job before it starts or modify the job's properties.
Active	Indicates that Scheduler has received the job instructions and is in the process of carrying out the job at the site.
Retrying	Indicates that the job has failed in its initial attempt to carry out the instructions but will retry to carry out the instructions. This state is indicative of connectivity, disk space, or License Manager problems.
Complete	The job has completed successfully and has been executed at all the targeted clients. Note that this only indicates that all the targeted clients executed the package; however, it is not an assurance that the package installed correctly.
Canceling	The job is in the process of being canceled. A job in the canceling status cannot be deleted.

continues

TABLE 19.4. CONTINUED

Status	Meaning
Canceled	The job has been successfully canceled, and SMS performs no further action. The job can now be deleted.
Failed	After retrying the job several times, the job is marked "failed." View the SMS event log and the destination server's event log. Also use SMSTRACE.EXE to view the SMS logs, as described in the next section, "Troubleshooting."

By selecting the Details button, you can view more detailed information, as shown in Figure 19.27.

Figure 19.27.
Detailed job
status.

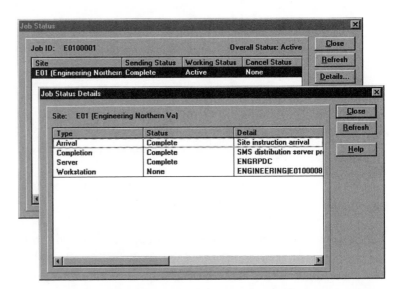

> *Note*
>
> The Job Status Details dialog tracks the job status per machine by domain name and unique SMS ID. This is helpful in determining which workstations have and have not received the package.

The different job status settings and their meanings are listed in Table 19.5.

Table 19.5. Viewing detailed job status.

Status	Meaning
None	The sender has not processed the send request .srq file.
Pending	Job has been initiated by the administrator, but the job has not started to send the package and instructions to the target sites.
Active	Indicates that the sender is processing the job but has not completed.
Complete	The job has completed the instructions for that phase of the distribution. For the Workstation type, this indicates that the client has executed the package.
Retrying	This is the status to worry about. If SMS cannot connect, insufficient disk space and License Manager are a few items to check. I have seen instances where License Manager was set too low and refused connections from a site server.
Canceled	Someone has canceled the job from the SMS user interface. Canceled jobs no longer appear as available packages to the client.
Failed	After a job is in retry state for 48 hours, the job is marked "failed" and does not attempt to execute.

Note

System jobs also display these status entries. This is helpful when troubleshooting where the job is failing, for example, during a site creation process.

DISTRIBUTION CONSIDERATIONS

An SMS package can use up to four times its original size by the time the package is completed:

The original source directory (1)
Sender box (1/2)
Despooler master copy (1/2)
Temporary directory (1)
Final distribution copy (1)

> ## *Note*
> You can remove the package in the \SENDER.BOX\TOSEND directory after the package has been sent to the distribution sites.

Exclude the site server from being a distribution server. The final source directory is not created.

Also, use the Remove Package from Server job after successful distribution, which frees up the space used by the package.

Use Sender Manager to control the times and the amount of bandwidth to be used. You may only want distribution to occur late at night or early in the morning to minimize network traffic.

Keep in mind that some clients access the network via RAS dial-in.

TROUBLESHOOTING

SMS is designed to report information, warnings, and error events to the Windows NT application log. Figure 19.28 displays an event detail from the Windows NT event log about SMS being out of licenses.

Figure 19.28. Windows NT application event log.

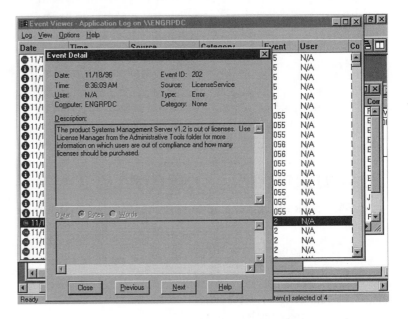

License Manager is the single largest culprit I have run into. Unless you know where to look, you may never figure out why a job cannot complete. Keep in mind that SMS can use up to 20 connections when creating a site. When License Manager reaches its limit, it merely refuses connections for that product. Check License Manager settings for SQL, SMS, Windows NT, and BackOffice settings.

SMS also logs errors to the SMS database. To view the SMS events, open the Event window from the toolbar. Figure 19.29 displays the error that License Manager created by refusing connections.

Figure 19.29.
Viewing the SMS
event log.

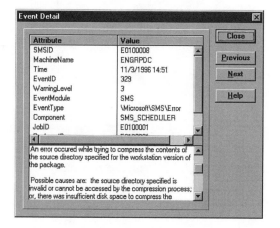

Along with the capability to write log information to a file, Systems Management Server includes the Trace (SMSTRACE.EXE), which you can use to review these diagnostic log files. By default, tracing will be enabled for the Windows NT service components of Systems Management Server but can easily be deactivated for performance improvements with the SMS Service Manager, as shown in Figure 19.30. From the Tools menu, select SMS Service Manager.

Once tracing is enabled for a particular component, you can use the SMS trace utility, SITE.SRV\(ARCHITECTURE).BIN\SMSTRACE.EXE to open the log file and monitor it in real time.

Note

SMS 1.2 does not install this file by default. It can be located on the original CD-ROM in the \SUPPORT\DEBUG\(ARCHITECTURE) directory.

Figure 19.30.
Service Manager.

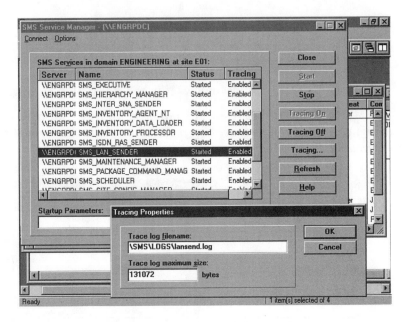

Log files are located in the SMS\LOGS directory. You can use SMS Service Manager to set log file locations and maximum sizes. Table 19.6 lists the SMS components and the relevant log files for monitoring job information.

TABLE 19.6. LOG FILES TO MONITOR.

Process	File
Job Scheduler	DESPOOL.LOG
Despooler	SCHED.LOG
Senders	LANSEND.LOG, RASASYNC.LOG, and so on
PGC	SMSLOG.TXT
AppStart	SMSLOG.TXT
PCM	No log file; must use /debug switch

Tip

If the PGC.LOG file contains an error message, "Failed to create program group," on NetWare clients, check the version of NWCALLS.DLL, as well as the other client .DLLS.

Information in a log file usually includes the time of day, error codes, a description, and identification of the component and thread ID. If you want to see what is happening with a particular component, you can check the log files to see how things are progressing. Figure 19.31 shows the SMSTRACE utility as it monitors the log files.

Figure 19.31.
Monitoring log
files with the
SMSTRACE *utility.*

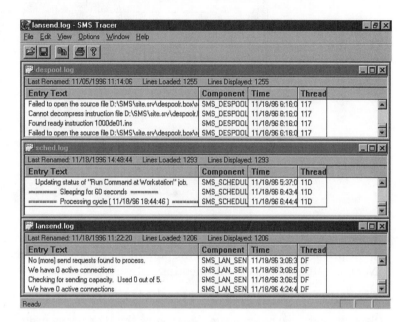

Another useful tool is the DUMPSEND utility included with the SMS CD-ROM. With it, you can view detailed contents of the send request, such as destination site, priority, job name, job ID, outbox location, job status, sender record, and so on.

If the package doesn't show up at some clients but does show up at others, suspect the time and date settings of the client PC.

Monitor the package directory to see if it is created. The directory these files are stored in is the \\DISTRIBUTION SERVER\SMS_PKGx\PACKAGEID directory. Figure 19.32 compares the directory structure with the package ID.

Figure 19.32 illustrates that the package was generated at site code EO1 and that the package ID is the same as the directory structure. This is particularly useful in identifying package locations by their directory names. Also monitor the files in the following directories that are used to compress and decompress files during the distribution process:

```
SMS\SITE.SRV\SENDER.SRV\TOSEND
SMS\SITE.SRV\DESPOOLER.BOX\RECEIVE
SMS\SITE.SRV\DESPOOLER.BOX\STORE
```

19

Jobs

Figure 19.32.
Package ID /
Directory struc-
ture comparison.

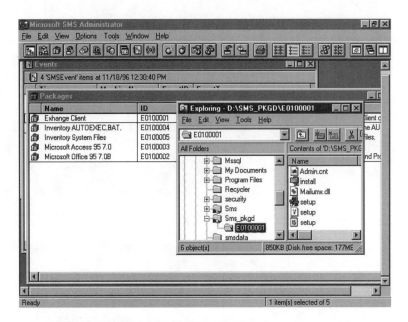

Errors can occur in the different areas that SMS moves the data across the network. If the problem can be isolated to the point in a process that a job fails, consider using Network Monitor for troubleshooting network problems.

Check that enough disk space is available to receive and decompress the package.

Security can also be an issue. Make sure that the passwords for the accounts used for the senders are synchronized. Make sure you differentiate the SQL sa account and passwords from the SMSADMIN passwords. Also make sure the accounts are valid and that the password has not expired.

Use caution when using long filenames in excess of 8.3 character format. For NetWare servers, the OS/2 name space NLM must be installed on the server. Even with this NLM running, there are a lot of reported problems doing this. As a general rule of thumb, avoid using long file names and directory structures when distributing to non–Windows NT distribution servers.

When scripting with InstallShield3, use the -SMS switch with SETUP.EXE on the command line of an SMS package. Without this switch, SMS may close the network connection before the package is complete.

Summary

You will probably spend more time troubleshooting jobs than any other component of the SMS system. Because jobs use so many components of SMS and NT, there are several points that can cause a job to fail. Careful planning and attention to detail can prevent many of these problems from occurring.

CHAPTER 20

Making the Software Distribution

Delivering software to client computers is one of the most powerful and fundamental features of System Management Server. In previous chapters, you saw how packages are put together and managed and how jobs are created to send those packages where they can be used. In this chapter, you will see how the packages are used at the clients' sites and how SMS handles the packages along the way.

When packages arrive at SMS clients, they can be used for a variety of purposes. Installing or upgrading applications, or even operating systems, are certainly some of the more obvious purposes. Packages can also cause software that is already on the client to be executed, such as virus checks, disk scans, or software deinstallation.

Keeping software on end-user computers is not always desirable. There are benefits to putting the software on a server and allowing the user to run it from there. Some benefits are that the software can be secured against unauthorized modifications; it won't be stolen or lost if the end-user computer is stolen or lost; disk usage is minimized; and concurrent usage limitations can be easily enforced. SMS greatly facilitates using applications in this fashion by getting the software to the server and by making it easy for the users to access it. In fact, SMS enhances this kind of usage by also providing load balancing and by allowing you to remove a server from production, and yet still let the users access the application (on another server).

Given these powerful options, this chapter will describe how you can use Package Command Manager to handle packages that arrive at the client. It will also look at how the applications are made available at the SMS package distribution servers, both for installation on the end-user computer and for use off the server (through the network). Packages made available for use off a server are called shared applications. (They are called *shared* because they are offered through file shares, as opposed to true client/server applications, which are more message-oriented.) How SMS facilitates using applications off the server is discussed in a review of network applications. Both program groups and user groups are reviewed in detail. Who gets each program group is determined through the use of user groups. Finally, the chapter will conclude with an overview of the flow of the packages and related files, with an eye to aiding in troubleshooting.

PACKAGE COMMAND MANAGER

Package Command Manager (PCM) is the SMS program that checks for packages that should be installed on the client and gives the user the opportunity to execute them. Package Command Manager is provided in various forms, one for each of the different supported client platforms. Microsoft provides Package Command Manager for Windows 95, Windows, Windows for Workgroups, Windows NT, DOS, Macintosh, and OS/2. See Figure 20.1 for an example of PCM for the Windows platforms, and see Listing 20.2 for an example of PCM on DOS. When PCM is run on OS/2, it must be run as a Windows program, and helper processes are available to make connections. (See the SMS documentation for more details.) The Windows NT and Windows 95 version of PCM is PCMWIN32.EXE, the version for Windows or Windows for Workgroups is PCMWIN16.EXE, the version of MS-DOS is PCMDOS.EXE, and the version for Macintosh is PCMMAC. Vendors can write package command managers to support other platforms. In fact, Computer Associate's AssetWORKS, discussed in Appendix C, "Third-Party Integration—Making the Job Easier," includes such programs for UNIX, OpenVMS, and NetWare Server platforms.

Figure 20.1.
Package Com-
mand Manager.

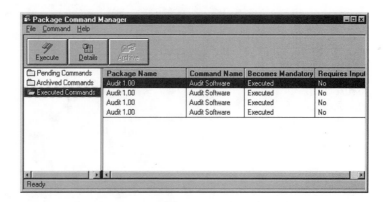

To the end user, PCM is not visible unless packages are available to install, or the user invokes it from the SMS Clients program group. When the user's machine first becomes an SMS client, it displays the PCM welcome screen, by default, as shown in Figure 20.2. If there are packages available, the user will see the Package Command Manager window with the package name, the command name to be used, when the package will become mandatory (if ever), and whether or not input is required. Buttons and menu items are available to give the user an opportunity to get more details about the package (see Figure 20.3), to execute it if the user wants to use the package, or to archive it if the user wants to save it for later. The user can also choose to see previously executed or archived commands. An Options dialog is provided under the Commands menu to enable the user to adjust some settings. (See Figure 20.4.) By default, PCM checks for new packages once an hour, but the user can adjust this to be more or less frequent. The Commands menu does have a Refresh option to initiate an immediate check if the user is anticipating a package. Other options allow the user to set the default user name and company name to be used when setting up applications that require this information. These are stored in the Local section of the hidden C:\SMS.INI file on each client as UserName and CompanyName.

20

MAKING THE SOFTWARE DISTRIBUTION

Figure 20.2.
The Package
Command
Manager welcome
screen.

Figure 20.3.
The package
Details window.

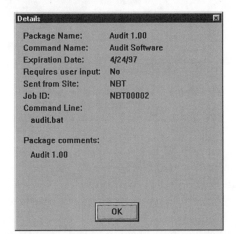

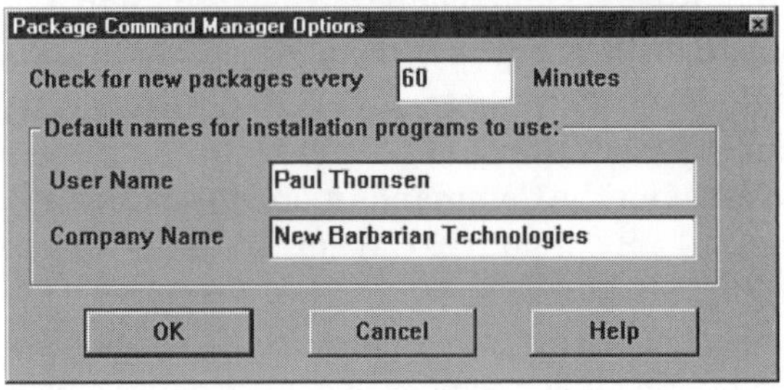

Figure 20.4.
The Package
Command
Manager Options
dialog.

PACKAGE COMMAND MANAGER FOR WINDOWS AND WINDOWS NT

PCM is started as soon as Windows (in any of its forms) is started, when SMSRUN (SMSRUN16.EXE or SMSRUN32.EXE) is executed. SMSRUN is usually included on the load line of the WIN.INI file (or the \HKEY_CURRENT_USER\Software\Microsoft\Windows NT\CurrentVersion\Windows\LOAD Registry key, in the case of Windows NT), and it checks the C:\MS\SMS\DATA\SMSRUN.INI file. This file usually tells SMSRUN to start PCM. When the user exits or closes PCM, the program simply closes its window. PCM can't actually be stopped except by special programs that can see background processes and that have an option to kill them. Such programs include the Windows 95 Close Program window (displayed by hitting Ctrl+Alt+Delete), PVIEWER.EXE from the Windows NT resource kit, or PVIEW.EXE from the Win32 Software Developer's Kit or Visual C++. A program for viewing and killing processes for Windows and Windows for Workgroups, WPS.EXE, is provided in the SUPPORT directory tree on the SMS CD-ROM. (See Figure 20.5.) Usually, it is not necessary to fully stop the Package Command Manager. However, stopping PCM is necessary in order to restart it in debug mode (to be described later), for testing start-up situations, and to prevent a mandatory job from executing when its time has come.

Figure 20.5.
WPS *program from the SMS support tools.*

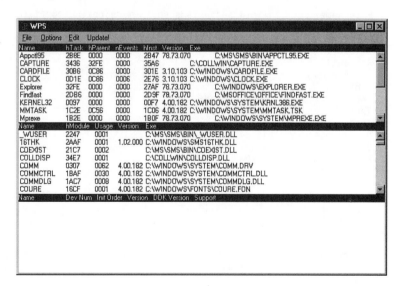

When not visible, PCM is still running (on a normal SMS client), allowing it to routinely check for new packages. As it starts, PCM checks the SMS.INI file, which has a Package Command Manager section. There it finds out where to look for new packages (InstructionSharePoint), where to report back the results (ResultSharePoint), where to keep a history of packages (LocalRegistryLocation), and how often to do the checks (PollingInterval). PCM double-checks the InstructionSharePoint value every time it checks for instructions. For each newly arriving job, the SMS site server puts a new record in a file whose name is the SMSID of the machine that is the job's destination. The file's extension is .INS. You can find this file in the PCMINS.BOX (by default) directory of the SMS_SHR shares of all logon servers. You could find the file as \\NT4_SERVER\SMS_SHR\PCMINS.BOX\NBT00001.INS. If the file does not exist, it is created automatically when the first job arrives. You can read these files by using an unsupported program called PCMDUMP.EXE, located in the SUPPORT directory on the SMS CD-ROM. Among other things, the output of this file indicates exactly where the package can be found, as shown in Listing 20.1.

Listing 20.1. PCMDump output.

```
PCM Instruction File Dump Utility v1.0a
Copyright 1994-1995 Microsoft Corporation

File Name        : \\nt4_server\sms_shr\pcmins.box\nbt00001.ins

PCM Version      : Beta 455
SiteID           : NBT
RequestID        : NBT0001
PackageID        : NBT00001
JobID            : NBT00002
Install Flag     : Unspecified
Install By Date  : 00/00/00 00:00:00
Install By Full  : No
Display Date     : 11/07/96 12:38:00
Display Full     : Yes
Expiration Date  : 04/24/97 13:38:00
Expiration Full  : Yes
User Input Flags : Unspecified
Operating System : MS-DOS Windows Windows95 WindowsNT(x86)
   WindowsNT(MIPS) WindowsNT(Alpha)
Disk Usage       :
Run Command      : audit.bat
WCL Name         : Audit Software
Server(s)        : \\NT4_SERVER\SMS_PKGC\NBT00001\ Type: 2 Zone:
Package Name     : Audit 1.00
Comments         : Audit 1.00
Domain Name      :
Reserved         : 00 00 00 00 00 00 00 00 00 00 00 00 00 00
   00 00 00 00 00 00 00 00 00 00 00 00 00 00
   00 00 00 00
```

On Windows NT, the functionality for checking for new packages is also included in a service, usually called SMS_PACKAGE_COMMAND_MANAGER_NT. Using this service allows packages to be installed on the Windows NT machine even when no one has logged onto it (as long as user intervention is not required and no windows are displayed). This service is automatically installed and started on logon servers, but for other Windows NT machines, you must do this manually. This is done by copying the service program (PCMSVC32.EXE) onto the computer and using a service management program, such as INSTSRV.EXE. You can find the PCM service program on the \\site_server\SMS_SHRx share in the \SITE.SRV\X86.BIN directory. You can find INSTSRV in the SUPPORT directory tree on the SMS CD-ROM. INSTSRV is an interactive program that allows manipulating services on Windows NT computers, even remotely. This includes installing services. You must use INSTSRV to install the service, and you can also use it to start and stop services, change accounts, and so on. You can also do these latter tasks in a more GUI fashion by using the Services Control Panel.

Package Command Manager for Macintosh

The Macintosh Package Command Manager looks much like the Windows versions, except that the menu is at the top of the display, as opposed to appearing the PCM window (as in all standard Macintosh applications). The Mac PCM also works the same as the Windows versions, except that it is started by the inventory collection program, which in turn must be in the Startup group for the Macintosh.

Package Command Manager for DOS

For DOS clients, you must manually invoke PCM. This must be done after the client's networking components are started, so including it as part of the network logon is ideal. However, you can invoke it later as well. When PCM is closed on a DOS client, it stops altogether, so it is not watching for the arrival of new packages. The DOS version of PCM has a command-line-oriented interface, which is very different from the Windows versions in that it is character-based. (See Listing 20.2.) There are commands to show pending packages (see Listing 20.3) or details of packages (see Listing 20.4), as well as the other basic PCM functions, such as executing and archiving packages. Note that there is no command to set options; this is appropriate for the frequency of checking for new packages because PCM can't run in the background for DOS clients. The other two options (user name and company name) must be set by directly editing the SMS.INI file.

LISTING 20.2. PACKAGE COMMAND MANAGER ON DOS.

```
Microsoft (R) Package Command Manager for DOS 1.2 (Build 786)
 Initializing...

Microsoft (R) Package Command Manager for DOS 1.2 (Build 786)
(P)ending Commands, (A)rchived Commands, (E)xecuted Commands,
A(r)chive [#], E(x)ecute [#], (D)etails [#], (H)elp, (C)lose
Choice:
```

LISTING 20.3. PCM ON DOS SHOWING A PENDING PACKAGE.

```
Microsoft (R) Package Command Manager for DOS 1.2 (Build 786)
 Initializing...

Microsoft (R) Package Command Manager for DOS 1.2 (Build 786)
(P)ending Commands, (A)rchived Commands, (E)xecuted Commands,
A(r)chive [#], E(x)ecute [#], (D)etails [#], (H)elp, (C)lose
Choice: Show (P)ending Commands

Pending Commands:
Num Package Name     Command Name      Becomes Mandatory   Requires Input
 0 Audit 100         Audit Software    Never   No          No

Microsoft (R) Package Command Manager for DOS 1.2 (Build 786)
(P)ending Commands, (A)rchived Commands, (E)xecuted Commands,
A(r)chive [#], E(x)ecute [#], (D)etails [#], (H)elp, (C)lose
Choice:
```

LISTING 20.4. PCM ON DOS SHOWING PACKAGE DETAILS.

```
Microsoft (R) Package Command Manager for DOS 1.2 (Build 786)
 Initializing...

Microsoft (R) Package Command Manager for DOS 1.2 (Build 786)
(P)ending Commands, (A)rchived Commands, (E)xecuted Commands,
A(r)chive [#], E(x)ecute [#], (D)etails [#], (H)elp, (C)lose
Choice: Show (D)etails for a Command: 0

Details for: Audit 1.00
  Expiration Date: 4-25-97
  User Input Required? No
  Sent from site code: NBT
  Job ID: NBT00006
  Command Line: audit.bat
  Package Comments: Audit 1.00

Microsoft (R) Package Command Manager for DOS 1.2 (Build 786)
(P)ending Commands, (A)rchived Commands, (E)xecuted Commands,
A(r)chive [#], E(x)ecute [#], (D)etails [#], (H)elp, (C)lose
Choice:
```

PACKAGE COMMAND MANAGER DEBUG MODE

On the Windows platforms, you can start PCM with a /DEBUG switch that starts the Package Command Manager normally, except that an extra window is also displayed, as shown in Figure 20.6. Messages are shown when any PCM action occurs. You can only invoke PCM with the /DEBUG option by killing the currently executing PCM and then starting it from the command line. The initial invocation causes PCM to run in its background mode. If you want to use the PCM interface, you have to invoke it a second time.

Figure 20.6.
Debug Messages
for PCM.

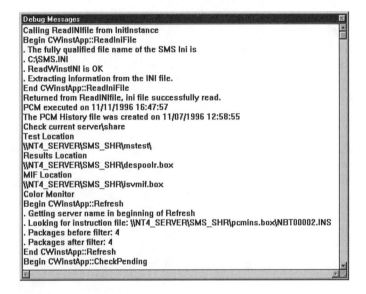

```
Debug Messages
Calling ReadINIfile from InitInstance
Begin CWinstApp::ReadIniFile
. The fully qualified file name of the SMS Ini is
. C:\SMS.INI
. ReadWinstINI is OK
. Extracting information from the INI file.
End CWinstApp::ReadIniFile
Returned from ReadINIfile, ini file successfully read.
PCM executed on 11/11/1996 16:47:57
The PCM History file was created on 11/07/1996 12:58:55
Check current server\share
Test Location
\\NT4_SERVER\SMS_SHR\mstest\
Results Location
\\NT4_SERVER\SMS_SHR\despoolr.box
MIF Location
\\NT4_SERVER\SMS_SHR\isvmif.box
Color Monitor
Begin CWinstApp::Refresh
. Getting server name in beginning of Refresh
. Looking for instruction file: \\NT4_SERVER\SMS_SHR\pcmins.box\NBT00002.INS
. Packages before filter: 4
. Packages after filter: 4
End CWinstApp::Refresh
Begin CWinstApp::CheckPending
```

SHARED APPLICATION MANAGEMENT

Shared applications are applications that are available over the network from a server (or multiple servers) on a share (or shares). If the network and servers are reliable and fast, then the user might not even realize that the applications he or she is using are not on his or her own computer. The systems administrator, however, can find it easier to maintain the application on the servers, can maximize uptime, can control usage, and can reduce the possibility that the application will fall into the hands of unauthorized people.

Getting the applications to the server is a job to which SMS is well suited. It is already set up to send packages to user computers. To get there, they must be placed on servers. Adjusting the process a little to stop at the server is not difficult. To initiate such a job, the administrator need only change the job type when creating the job from the default Run Command on Workstation to Share Package on Server.

When creating a Share Package on Server job, it is only necessary to determine which sites and which distribution servers will be used. (See Figure 20.7.) The actual clients that benefit from this package are determined by the use of program groups. Generally, it is best to put the application on as many distribution servers as possible in order to maximize its availability. However, you might not do this in order to save disk space or for other reasons. If some distribution servers are not used, you must give some thought as to whether all the appropriate kinds of servers are included at each site. In particular, if there are clients who can only connect to NetWare servers, the package should be made available on at least one NetWare server that is available to them. Similarly, if the sites have users in multiple domains, the package should be put on a distribution server in each domain. In this case, trust relationships do not help because the clients will only check distribution servers in their own domain—they will not look beyond it to find other servers they may have access to.

Figure 20.7.
Shared package
job details.

A shared package is also given a share name, which is offered on all the distribution servers so that the users can access the application. Allowing for the lowest common denominator, the share name must be in the 8.3 format. Security for the share is determined by using the Access button in the Setup Package for Sharing dialog when setting up the package for sharing. (See Figure 20.8.) The package is placed in a top-level directory tree with the same name as the share name. If guests are given read and write access when setting up the package, the share gives full control access to members of the domain guests group. The same is true for the domain users group.

Figure 20.8.
Package sharing
options.

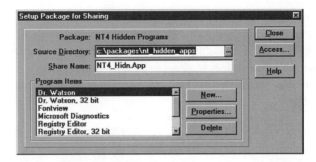

Tip

Changes to a shared package's access rights are reflected only when the package is redistributed. Be sure to create a new job if a change in the package access rights is necessary.

When creating a package that is intended to be used as a shared application, you must give some thought to the application's requirements. Many applications simply involve opening and executing files, and all files are expected to be found wherever the first one is. In such a case, the exact placement of the files is not important. More sophisticated applications may require important files to be on the local hard disk, may set up and use Registry entries and OLE information, may depend on related applications, or have similar considerations. In these cases, it is necessary to run a setup program of some sort on each client computer, even though most of the application is already set up on the server. Some applications have a specific network install option. For others, the administrator might have to analyze the application's requirements and provide a script to provide the necessities.

Good examples of sophisticated applications with special considerations are the Microsoft Office applications. They share various programs for some common features, such as graphing and spell-checking. They are also very strongly OLE-based and use the Registry and other Windows features extensively. To handle the common applications problem, the common applications (located in the MSAPPS directory tree) must be considered separately from the other applications and distributed as a job in its own right. Furthermore, different combinations of Office applications result in different configurations of the MSAPPS directory tree, so it might be necessary to have several MSAPPS packages. To handle the OLE requirements and so on, a setup program must be run on each client to ensure that all the appropriate configuration details are handled.

As time goes on, a shared application will eventually become unneeded. New versions will be set up, users' requirements will change, better products will be developed, and so on. Eventually, you can remove shared applications from the servers, providing room for others. You can do this by using the third kind of SMS job, Remove Package from Server (as shown in Figure 20.9). Remove Package from Server jobs have essentially the same options as Share Package on Server jobs, in that the package can be removed from all sites and servers or from appropriate subsets.

Figure 20.9.
Remove Shared
Package job
details.

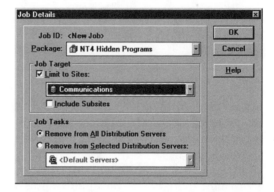

Caution

Remove Package from Server jobs accomplish their goal by simply deleting the entire directory tree where the application is shared. It is important to be sure that there are no other applications or other files also sharing that directory tree and that any data residing in those directory trees has been moved if it's still needed. Note that nothing is removed from the client PCs, so it may also be necessary to remove the corresponding program groups or to run a job on each client to make other changes.

NETWORK APPLICATIONS

Getting packages to servers is important, and in some cases, that is all that is required. The users may be able to find the files on the server and use them appropriately. Most users would rather not be bothered with such details, so SMS provides a facility called network applications to make shared applications easier to access. Network applications provide icons to appropriate users, and SMS takes care of finding a server with the application.

Note

Network application functionality is not available for DOS, Macintosh, or other non-Windows platforms. These systems may be able to access shared applications directly, but they can't take advantage of the SMS network application features.

USER GROUPS

SMS provides an easy way to provide users with access to shared applications, using what are called program groups. Not all programs, however, may be appropriate to all users, and so to make the right program groups available to the right users, SMS uses user groups.

SMS user groups are based on domain global user groups in a Windows NT environment, NetWare user groups in a NetWare environment, and both, when both are present. Each site server checks for user groups, and when it finds them, it sends MIFs to update the inventories.

Collecting user group information is done only once per day, by default, but if there are many sites and many user groups within an SMS hierarchy, this activity can be significant. If a domain is used over multiple site servers, it may be unnecessary for each of them to send updates about the user group information. A program called SETGUG.EXE is provided in the SUPPORT directory tree on the SMS CD-ROM to control whether a site server collects such information and if so, how often. SETGUG (set global user group enumeration) is a particularly unfriendly program in the sense that it provides no feedback or command-line help. It is briefly documented in the TOOLS.WRI file in the SUPPORT directory. Normally, this program is used as either SETGUG /E Off or as SETGUG /E On /I 2 to turn enumeration off or to turn it on with enumerations once every two days, respectively.

If you want a printed listing of SMS user groups, the easiest approach is to create a query (or use an ad hoc query) in SMS Administrator, based on the user groups architecture, without any conditions. This provides a Query Results window with all the SMS user groups, which you can print using the File menu's Print item.

If changes are made to domain user groups and you want to implement these changes right away, then another program in the SUPPORT directory tree, UGMIF, is useful. This program can check a given domain for user group changes and then produce a MIF file reflecting these changes. Once the MIF file has been processed, the user groups show up in the SMS databases.

PROGRAM GROUPS

Once a shared application is at a server, the system administrator will want to make it easy for the users to access it there. Microsoft Windows users usually access applications using Program Manager or in the more recent variations of Windows, through the Start menu's Programs item. In both cases, programs can be subdivided into groups to make them easier to find. SMS provides a simple facility to manage these groups, using what it calls program groups.

Program groups are created by the system administrator by opening the Program Groups window in the SMS Administrator program and then clicking the New button. This invokes an empty Program Group Properties dialog, as shown in Figure 20.10. The group should be given a name that the users will relate to and a comment to make the use of the group clear to administrators at a later date. The Program Items control will fill as packages are added to the group, using the Packages button, which displays the Program Group Packages dialog. (See Figure 20.11.) Note that only packages that are set up for sharing are available to this window. Clicking the User Groups button displays the User Groups dialog (see Figure 20.12), allowing selection of the SMS user groups that should have this package available to them.

Figure 20.10.
The Program
Group Properties
dialog.

Alternatively, you can add all of a package's icons to a program group by choosing the package in the Packages window and then choosing the File menu's Add to Group menu item.

*Figure 20.11.
The Program
Group Packages
dialog for adding
shared packages
to a Program
Group.*

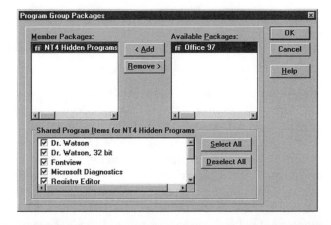

*Figure 20.12.
The User Groups
dialog for
specifying who
can use the group.*

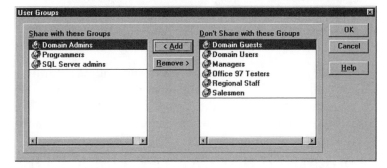

SETTING UP A PACKAGE FOR USE AS A NETWORK APPLICATION

Applications used as network applications are shared applications. Therefore, the considerations for shared applications do apply. However, there are also some additional considerations for such applications.

Programs that require secondary programs will want those secondary programs distributed as shared applications and made available using the same techniques as the primary shared applications. It may not be appropriate, however, to display icons for these programs (they are invoked from functions within the main programs). Therefore, when preparing the shared secondary application package, it is important to uncheck the Display Icon in Program Group option.

20

MAKING THE SOFTWARE DISTRIBUTION

Another consideration may be the working directory. By default, SMS network applications use the c:\ directory as the working directory. If this is not considered appropriate, you can set an environment variable, SMS_WORKING_DIR, on each client to indicate a more appropriate location.

When creating packages, you can manually add details that cannot be specified using the SMS Administrator. Among these is an option that is appropriate for network applications. As with shared applications, network applications may require some client-side setup before they can be executed properly. The SMS network application components include a program called DOSETUP.EXE. If the package includes a reference to this program with a command to run any kind of setup program or script, it is run, and when properly completed, the normal program is put in its place in the program group. DOSETUP also maintains a status field in the Registry entry for the program so that the SMS program group components can tell if the setup was successful the last time it was attempted and whether or not it needs to be retried. See Chapter 18, "Packages," in this book for further details, or the SMS Resource Kit.

A Registry entry can be set up when the package is installed in order to facilitate the deinstallation of the package when it is removed. The Registry entry is HKEY_CLASSES_ROOT\SMS\Applications\app_registry_name\Info\Deinstall_App. This program is run prior to removing the share and deleting the files in the directory tree.

PROGRAM GROUPS AT THE USER'S DESK

On the other end of the process at the user's desk, a program is run whenever Windows is started, namely APPCTL16.EXE or APPCTL32.EXE (more easily referred to as APPCTL). It determines which user groups this user belongs to and checks the network application database for applications available to users in those groups and on this platform. It then creates Program Manager program groups (or Start Menu Programs program groups, as the case may be). Each program item in the new program groups actually points to a program called APPSTART.EXE, with a parameter that is the Registry name when the program group was created. When the icons are actually clicked, APPSTART looks up the Registry entry and finds out which servers the application can be found on and which actual program should be run. As APPCTL creates the program groups, it displays progress messages in a small window, as shown in Figure 20.13, but very briefly.

Figure 20.13.
The Program
Group Control
window.

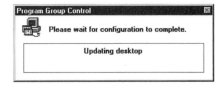

With the new program groups, the user can start the programs the same as any other program. If the program requires a special script or setup program to complete any appropriate client-side setup, then this is executed the first time the user clicks the icon. However, after that point, only the program is executed.

APPCTL is started as soon as Windows (in any of its forms) is started, when SMSRUN (SMSRUN16.EXE or SMSRUN32.EXE) is executed. SMSRUN is usually included on the LOAD line of the WIN.INI file, and it checks the C:\MS\SMS\DATA\SMSRUN.INI file. This file usually tells SMSRUN to start APPCTL, among other things.

Once APPCTL has done its initial setup of appropriate program groups, it becomes a background process, providing services for the applications started from the program groups that APPCTL provided. One of the options with SMS's shared packages is that the program items can each have a drive letter associated with them. Some programs, especially older ones, do not understand the universal naming convention and therefore must be given a drive letter. If the program keeps a record of where its files are found, then it will probably expect to find them in the same place every time it is run, so it may require a specific drive letter. You can specify these details when setting up the package, and APPCTL is the component that makes them happen. APPCTL is processing in the background, watching for execution of these programs. If a network connection is required, APPCTL sets it up, and when the program is completed, the connection is dropped.

Occasionally, a specific network drive is required for the program item, but APPCTL won't be able to provide it. The drive letter may already be in use, the LASTDRIVE parameter may be too low, or there may be other problems. In this case, APPCTL displays a message to the user, asking if he wants to use the next available drive letter instead. The user can accept this or cancel the operation altogether.

APPCTL also takes care of other considerations that were specified when the shared package was set up, such as whether their icons are to be displayed, whether they are to run minimized, and whether an attempt should be made to find a local copy.

If you do not want to see the APPCTL window, you can hide it by including /hide as a switch when starting APPCTL. The current APPCTL can be stopped using the /stop switch. If the SMS program groups are no longer required on this client, they can be removed by invoking APPCTL with /delete. You can disable Program Group Control as a whole for any given client by using the /disable:yes switch.

An important consideration to keep in mind is that the program groups should not be made available to users prior to the arrival of the shared applications. Otherwise, the programs will certainly fail.

Network or Shared Application Tools

Sometimes it is necessary to dig a little deeper when trying to use shared application features to access network applications. Files become corrupted, things can be misconfigured, and other problems can arise. SMS comes with four tools that an SMS administrator will find very handy in such situations. All these tools can be found in the SUPPORT directory tree on the SMS CD-ROM.

NADUSER.EXE (see Figure 20.14) is a Windows application that shows which groups the current user is a member of. It also looks at the network application databases. It requires a few DLLs that may not be available on the client you are currently checking out, in which case you should be able to find them at \\site_server\ SMS_SHR\X86.BIN or the equivalent. The DLLs required are NADAPI16.DLL, SMSNET.DLL, and SMSNETMS.DLL, and you can place them wherever you want, as long as you can find them when running NADUSER.

Figure 20.14.
NADUSER.

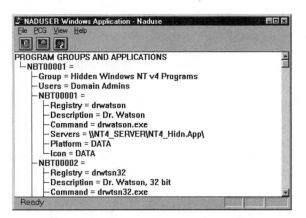

A very similar program to NADUSER, but command-line–oriented, is VIEWNAD.EXE. It provides output as shown in Listing 20.5.

Listing 20.5. VIEWNAD.EXE output.

```
INTERACTIVE
LOCAL
Domain Admins
Administrators
Users
Everyone
Domain Users
NBT00001
```

```
Program Group ======= NBT00001 ==========
  Group         Hidden Windows NT v4 Programs
  Users         Domain Admins
  +- NBT00001
  |  Registry    drwatson
  |  Description Dr. Watson
  |  Command     drwatson.exe
  |  Platform    WindowsNT(X86)
  +- NBT00002
  |  Registry    drwtsn32
  |  Description Dr. Watson, 32 bit
  |  Command     drwtsn32.exe
  |  Platform    WindowsNT(X86)
  +- NBT00003
```

If you have reason to suspect that the network application databases are corrupted, it is a fairly simple matter to reset them with RSAPPCTL.EXE. This program is command-line-oriented, and it deletes the current database and initiates a refresh from the site server. You can do this for this site, all its child sites, or a particular child site. If this command is done on the site server itself, then its parent must be specified so that it can know where to get the refresh. Run RSAPPCTL with the /? switch for the specific details. RSAPPCTL requires various DLLs, but these can all be found in the SITE.SRV\X86.BIN (or equivalent) directory on the server or SMS console.

NADRESET.EXE is a handy program to clear the network application database of any unneeded items. This may occur if a site had a parent site but then became independent or was given a new parent. In this case, NADRESET removes the old parent's records.

TROUBLESHOOTING SOFTWARE DISTRIBUTION

There is always the possibility that something will break when there are so many options and facilities for software distribution. This is especially true in a large, complex environment.

Troubleshooting can often be readily accomplished by following the process from beginning to end and seeing if anything is amiss. Once something is found to be out of place, further investigation can focus on that area, attempting to determine where things ended up and why. This chapter reviewed the major steps along the way from the administrator's and user's points of view, but a behind-the-scenes understanding is also important.

Being comfortable with the various programs involved in the process and knowing which tools are available to aid in troubleshooting is also a great help.

20

MAKING THE SOFTWARE DISTRIBUTION

PACKAGE FLOW

Software distribution with SMS is basically a matter of distributing packages, so how they flow from point to point is critical. Microsoft's SMS Resource Kit is a wealth of information on these processes. The volume of information, however, may be overwhelming, if not intimidating. This overview may provide a good starting point.

When an SMS job is activated, the site server at the originating site puts the package into a compressed file that it uses to send the package to all sites (unless it has been told to limit the job to certain sites). At those sites, the site server distributes the package to all distribution servers, unless certain logon servers were specified. If a site has subsites and the job was told to include subsites, then the receiving site servers also pass the package along to those sites.

It is actually the SMS Scheduler that checks the SMS database for new jobs. When the Scheduler does its periodic check for jobs and finds a job whose start time has come, it creates a compressed package file (named package#.W* for Run Command on Workstation jobs or package#.S* for Share Package on Server jobs) containing the directory tree for the package, and puts it in the TOSEND directory. At the same time, the Scheduler creates despooler instruction files (each named job#,Itarget site_code) to be sent to the target sites (also put in the TOSEND directory) and sender request files (*.SRQ) to be used by the sender on the same machine as the Scheduler (put in SENDER.BOX\REQUESTS\LAN_DEFA.000, for instance).

Like the Scheduler, the SMS senders periodically check for work to do. When they find it, they read the sender request file in order to determine which destinations to send to and which files should be included from the TOSEND directory. The files are sent to the Despooler's RECEIVE directory on the destination computers.

At the target computers, the SMS Despooler service watches for newly arrived packages and instructions, and when it finds them, it deals with the packages according to the instructions. In all cases, they are moved from the Despooler's RECEIVE directory to its STORE directory, and they are decompressed to a temporary directory tree. The Despooler then continues its work by copying the temporary directory tree's contents to the distribution servers at the site, as specified in the instructions, and by deleting the temporary directory tree. Finally, if the job is a Run Command on Workstation job, the Despooler creates Package Command Manager instruction files (named machine#.INS) and puts them in the appropriate Maintenance Manager service's PCMDOM.BOX for the destination domain. If the job is a Share Package on Server job, however, the Despooler offers the distribution servers' directory trees as shares.

To finish the process for Run Command on Workstation jobs, the SMS Maintenance Manager service copies the PCM instruction files to the appropriate logon servers, where the Package Command Managers on all the clients can find them.

Note that in some cases, various parts of SMS may be separated among various servers, or combined in one server, depending on performance considerations, site requirements, and so on. In all cases, however, the package flow is the same.

Figure 20.15 shows a simplified overview of the package flow process. For details beyond what this section presents, refer to the SMS Resource Kit, which goes into much more detail. This chapter gives you a "big picture" on which you can build your knowledge.

Figure 20.15. A simplified overview of package flow.

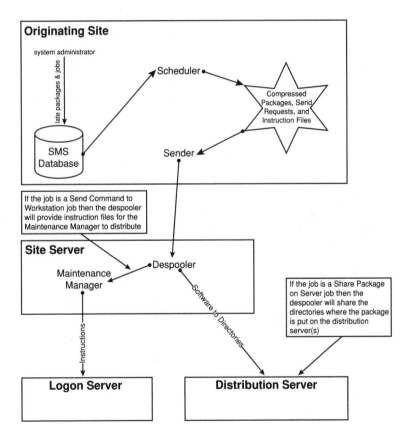

NETWORK APPLICATION INFORMATION FLOW

Users need to access the applications once they have gotten to the server, and SMS's program groups are a particularly powerful and appropriate way to do this. When the administrator sets up the program group details, the information must flow through the systems so that it can be available at the user's desk.

The SMS Application Manager service at each site periodically checks the SMS database for network application information. When it finds details, it uses them to create configuration files for program items and program groups (files with extensions of .HAF and .HAG, respectively, stored in the MAINCFG.BOX\APPCTL.SRC\DATABASE directory).

The SMS Maintenance Manager service ensures that the configuration files are copied to all the logon servers, where the application control program can find them.

Note that network application information always flows down, so if extra applications are added midway in the hierarchy of SMS sites, then it is the lowest sites and clients that have the possibility of getting all the applications.

POTENTIAL PROBLEM AREAS

Given our understanding of SMS software distribution, various points at which the process can fail will be evident. To begin with, the package and job must be properly defined, with the files readily available to be formed into the compressed package files that are sent down the line. Each of the appropriate options must be correctly specified, in order to ensure that the job does not appear in the wrong form at the end destination.

At each of the servers, including the originating server, the required SMS services must be started. This can be verified with the SMS Service Manager. The senders must also be able to make their connections, in order to get the files to the destination servers. This includes ensuring that the addresses and related details for the site servers are correct.

Given the central importance of SQL Server to SMS, it is critical that it is operating normally, especially for the initial aspects of software distribution. Similarly, each of the SMS servers must be functional. If there are intermediate servers between where the job is initiated and where it ends up, then those servers must be checked as well.

At the clients, the Package Command Manager or application control programs must be running. They must have the capability to access the shares on the server, and the appropriate files must be available there.

USEFUL TOOLS

This chapter discussed many tools that are useful for troubleshooting problems. These include PCMDUMP, PCM's debug facility, NADUSER, VIEWNAD, RSAPPCTL, and NADRESET. Other tools should not be overlooked, however.

Among the most significant tools is the capability to log the activity of the SMS services and especially to view this in real time. Tracing is usually turned on and off using the SMS Service Manager (otherwise it is done using Registry editing, but the effect is the same). With tracing turned on, lines are written to various log files in the \SMS\LOGS directory. Each log's filename makes it fairly clear which service it contains information for. You can watch these files by running SMSTRACE.EXE (see Figure 20.16), which is found in the \SMS\SITE.SRV\X86.BIN (or equivalent) directory.

Figure 20.16.
SMSTRACE.

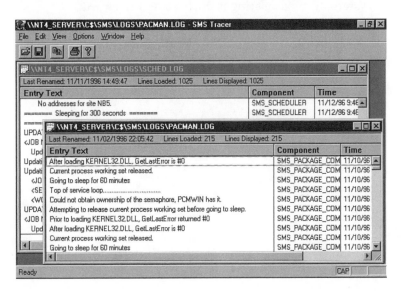

Otherwise, it is important for the SMS administrator to use the standard SMS and Windows NT tools when troubleshooting problems with package distribution. The SMS Administrator may record events, and there will be job status information when reviewing the jobs, both of which are very valuable. The Windows NT Event Viewer may also have some details.

SUMMARY

System Management Server's facilities for making software distributions are easy to use at each step, yet as a whole, they are quite powerful and flexible. Packages

20

MAKING THE SOFTWARE DISTRIBUTION

containing software for any purpose can be readily distributed to end users, who have a simple and flexible interface in the form of Package Command Manager to manage these packages. Packages can also readily be created to share applications from a server, and this facility even provides for automatically offering shares.

Applications offered from servers can be utilized by users on Windows-based computers through Program Manager or the Start menu's Programs tree in the usual fashion. SMS, however, can provide behind-the-scenes processing that allows these applications to be offered from multiple servers, making it possible to balance workload among servers or to take a server out of production during working hours.

SMS provides a variety of tools to watch the processing of jobs and to analyze the files that make all this functionality possible. With an understanding of the flow of the system, troubleshooting is fairly straightforward.

CHAPTER 21

Using the Network Monitor

The Network Monitor gives an SMS administrator an easy way to determine and resolve network problems. It is used to collect information in real time off the network so that the administrator can analyze what problems might be occurring on the network. It uses protocol parsers to parse the protocols that travel on the network. SMS version 1.2 supports over 20 different protocol parsers. The Network Monitor has been included with SMS since the very first version. It interoperates with the Network Monitor agent in the Windows NT computer. By using SMS inventory management options, you can go straight to the Network Monitor and monitor a specific machine. Network Monitor is especially great for monitoring network applications and their operations in terms of moving data across the network. This gives an administrator a troubleshooting mechanism for finding out if the network applications are communicating in the right manner.

REQUIREMENTS FOR THE NETWORK MONITOR

There are some key requirements in setting up a network environment to facilitate the Network Monitor. The Network Monitor is a software-based product that does not have any hardware dependency. The only hardware requirement is a network card that supports promiscuous mode, meaning that the network card intercepts all network activity.

What makes the Network Monitor a real beauty is that it is not dependent on any specific network card. As long as the network card is NDIS-compliant, you can use the Network Monitor. The Network Monitor requires that Windows NT–based machines run the Network Monitor Agent to monitor traffic on machines that exist on other subnets. This allows the Network Monitor to manage those machines and view information about the network statistics on the segment that the machine operates on. Figure 21.1 shows the Network Monitor Agent being installed. To install the Network Monitor Agent, you must do the following:

1. Click the Start button.
2. Go to the Settings menu and select the Control Panel.
3. Double-click Network.
4. Click the Services tab.
5. Click the Add button.
6. Scroll and select Network Monitor Agent.
7. Click Network Monitor Agent and click OK.
8. Enter the path of the distribution files and click OK.
9. Click OK.

After you have installed the Network Monitor Agent on a Windows NT–based computer on each subnet, the Network Monitor can be used on all subnets.

Figure 21.1.
The Network
Monitor Agent.

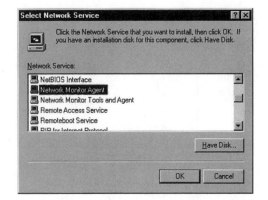

FEATURES OF THE NETWORK MONITOR

The Network Monitor offers a vast number of features. It mainly allows remote monitoring of machines in the network. This monitoring deals with the amount of network traffic that moves in and out of the machine. Some of the features of the Network Monitor include

◆ Automatically finding routers

◆ Determining the top users

◆ Resolving all addresses to NetBIOS name

◆ Protocol distribution

With these features, the Network Monitor enables the administrator to find out where the most frequent frames are traveling and which protocols are most often used on the network. It also offers the capability to automatically interoperate with the routers in the organization's environment. It also offers information about the frequency of occurrence of certain frames by certain clients, which enables you to find out if a network board is chatty on the network. Network Monitor helps the administrator to know the NetBIOS names of the protocol addresses of the computers in the environment. This makes it easier for the SMS administrator to know which machine is having problems talking to other machines. These features can simplify for an administrator what might look like a complex task. Figure 21.2 shows the Network Monitor option in the inventory of a Windows NT–based computer.

Note

Some older network interface cards do not support promiscuous mode. Make sure when buying a network interface card that you buy one that supports promiscuous mode.

Figure 21.2.
The Network
Monitor, shown
in the SMS
Administrator in
the inventory of a
computer.

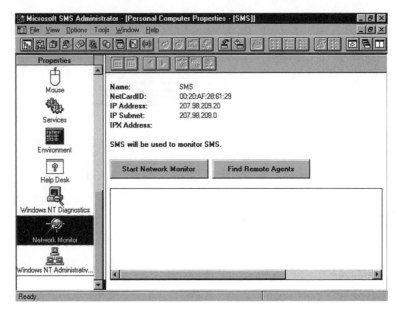

STARTING THE NETWORK MONITOR

You can start the Network Monitor in two locations. The first location is underneath the client's inventory. If you scroll to the bottom of the inventory, you see an option to start the Network Monitor. If the machine that you select is a Windows NT computer, it requires the Network Monitor Agent to be installed. The second method of starting the Network Monitor is underneath the SMS Administrator's Program menu. It gets installed with all the other SMS administration tools on the client. When doing a custom install, you can choose to not install the Network Monitor by deselecting it and removing it from the list of things to be installed.

There is a difference in the two ways that you start the Network Monitor. If started under the client's inventory, it monitors that specific client; however, if started in the SMS Administrator's group in the Program menu, it monitors all clients on the network. The way you start the Network Monitor plays a vital role in how it runs. If you want to monitor information that is organization-wide and deals with all the machines in your environment, it's important to start the Network Monitor in the SMS Program menu. If you simply want to look at a specific client under the client's inventory, you can exit the Network Monitor.

SECURITY

You can put security on the Network Monitor at several different levels. The possible configurations that are started when the Network Monitor starts are the following:

21

- ◆ Full access for capturing and displaying data
- ◆ Partial access that allows for just displaying data
- ◆ Full access

These configurations are set underneath the Control Panel Network Monitor Agent icon. You can select passwords for these specific configurations. Figure 21.3 shows the Network Monitor Agent configuration in the Control Panel.

Figure 21.3.
The Network
Monitor Agent
configuration in
the Control Panel.

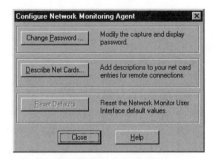

USING THE NETWORK MONITOR

When using the Network Monitor, you have several different options that enable you to operate with the Network Monitor in several different capacities. Some of the functions you can perform with the Network Monitor include the following:

- ◆ Capture packets directly off the network
- ◆ Display and filter captured packets
- ◆ Edit and retransmit captured packets on the network to reproduce problems and test resources
- ◆ Capture packets off local computers to look at different information over specific intervals

Once the Network Monitor is started, you see the Network Monitor window, which is shown in Figure 21.4. The Network Monitor's interface is split into four separate sections. These sections are the bar graph, session statistics, station statistics, and summary statistics.

BAR GRAPH

The bar graph displays the current activity on the network. It uses several different headings to display statistical information:

- ◆ Percent Network Utilization
- ◆ Frames Per Second

- ◆ Bytes Per Second
- ◆ Broadcasts Per Second
- ◆ Multicasts Per Second

With these functions, you can figure out how much activity exists on your network. If this utilization seems high, you know that there could be a problem with your network infrastructure.

Figure 21.4.
The Network Monitor window.

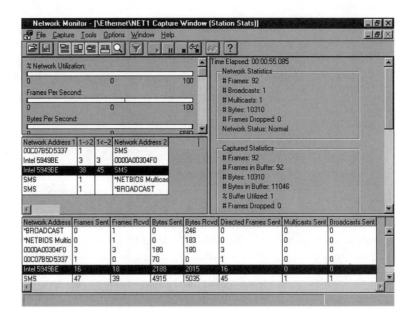

SESSION STATISTICS

Session statistics gives you information about person-to-person conversation on the network. It gives information about each combination of two machines talking, giving you information about the number of frames per second that are sent.

STATION STATISTICS

Station statistics gives information about the conversation of one station on the network, generally providing information such as the total number of broadcasts sent.

SUMMARY STATISTICS

Summary statistics gives graphs of total network utilization, frames, broadcasts, multicasts, and other types of statistics.

CAPTURING DATA

The key element to utilizing the Network Monitor is capturing data. This allows you to capture the number of packets during a given time. At the same time, you can filter what type of information you want to capture. This information is put into memory and can be written to a disk to be viewed at a later date. Some network analysis programs call this a trace file, because you can trace what problems have occurred on the network. To start capturing the data, go to the Capture menu in the Network Monitor, shown in Figure 21.5, by doing the following:

1. Start the Network Monitor.

2. Proceed to the Capture menu and select Start.

Figure 21.5. The Capture menu.

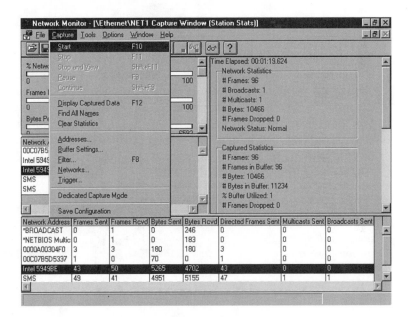

You see the four sections of your Network Monitor monitoring and providing data to your console. All the friendly names are displayed in the session statistics with what communication is going on between each of the stations. Before capturing, you can do what is called filtering. You can filter information according to several different criteria. Generally, you do this according to address patterns. Figure 21.6 shows the Capture Filter. To get to the Capture Filter, you must do the following:

1. Start the Network Monitor.

2. Proceed to the Capture menu and select Filter.

Figure 21.6.
The Capture
Filter.

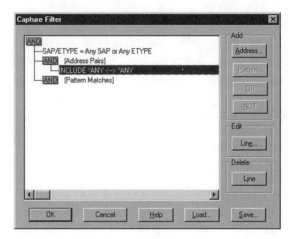

You can select what addresses you want to add to filter. At this point, all station addresses are added. If you look at Figure 21.7, you see the address expressions displaying the station-to-station communication between the machines so you can provide specific filters on what machines you want to see communicate. The filter provides one of the most beneficial things for a Network Monitor because you can provide a specific range of what you want to monitor on the network, which gives the SMS administrator a close look at what is going on to solve problems and monitor resources. The filter can be one of the most powerful features of the Network Monitor.

Figure 21.7.
Address expres-
sions displaying
station-to-station
communication
between ma-
chines.

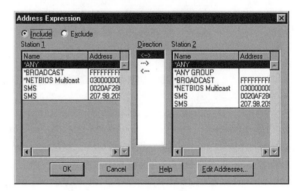

STOPPING AND VIEWING THE PACKETS

Once you have captured the information in the Network Monitor, it is important to be able to stop and view this information. You can do this by accessing the Capture menu again. To stop and view data, you need to do the following:

1. Start the Network Monitor.
2. Go to the Capture menu and select Stop and View.

Once you have stopped and viewed, Network Monitor pulls up the information about the packets you have received. Figure 21.8 shows the view for the packets received. Once you see this summary of all the frames captured, you can use what is called a display filter to filter what information you want to see in the summary of all the capture packets. To do this, you want to do the same thing you did when you filtered the captured packet. After you look at a specific packet that has gone across, you can look at its details. The details are broken up into three different categories and three panes on the window. In Figure 21.9, you see the three panes listed:

◆ Summary pane

◆ Detail pane

◆ Hex pane

These panes are listed in this order from top to bottom. With these panes, you can look at three different views of what the packet is about.

Figure 21.8.
A list of packets
sent and received.

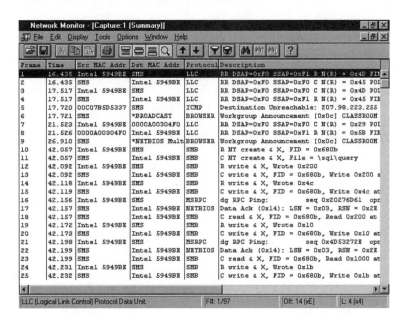

Figure 21.9.
Three panes on
the window.

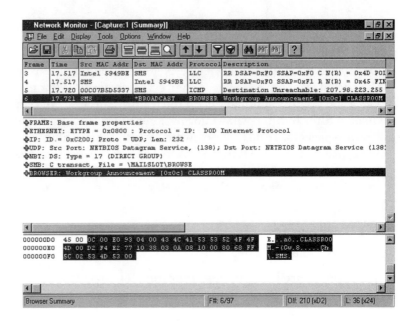

SUMMARY PANE

The Summary pane lists all the frames that are included in the captured data. Table 21.1 lists the columns for these frames. With this pane, you can look at several different things, such as the frame numbers, which are assigned in sequence according to when they actually occurred.

TABLE 21.1. COLUMNS IN THE SUMMARY PANE.

Time	Displays the time relative to when you first started the capture process.
Source MAC Address	Displays the hardware address of the computer that is sending the frame.
Destination MAC Address	Displays the hardware address of the computer receiving the frame.
Protocol	Shows the protocol that is used to transmit the frame.
Description	Gives a brief description and summary of what exists in that frame.
Source Other Address	Identifies another address that is given to the workstation, generally either an IP or IPX address.
Destination Other Address	Another address for the destination of the frame, usually an IP or IPX address.

With these options, you can view the summary of information sent while capturing data.

DETAIL PANE

The Detail pane in the middle of the screen gives specific details on the frame. This information is generally variable depending on what type of information you have captured, although it generally describes the different levels of what has happened on the network layers when communicating. It identifies what protocols were used in helping this frame get to its destination, and it can cover a wide spectrum. Generally, it covers whether you are on an EtherNet network or a Token Ring network. It also covers information specific to what transport protocol and addressing scheme were used to communicate this information.

HEX PANE

The Hex pane is at the bottom and shows you two things. First, it shows you a hexadecimal dump of the information that was gathered in the capture. At the same time, to the right of the hex dump is an ASCII dump of what actually has happened. Note that when you have an unencrypted network, you can see items such as passwords in this dump being transmitted across the network, which definitely helps people in spoofing certain networks.

SAVING YOUR INFORMATION

Once you have looked at this information, you can save it for future reference or to send it to a colleague. To save information in the Network Monitor after viewing it, you must do the following:

1. Go to the File menu.
2. Click Save As.
3. Enter the filename for the trace file you will create and click OK.

Now you have saved the information from your captured session. This information is saved in the SMS/Netmon/X86/Captures directory. This directory contains all the captured information, which you can then copy to disk.

Note

You can also print this information. Just go to the File menu and select Print to print this information to the designated printer.

SUPPORT FOR OTHER NETWORK ANALYSIS SYSTEMS

Network Monitor also supports other network analysis tools. Export files from these tools can be brought into Network Monitor. Network Monitor supports all the Network General trace files that you create.

SOME NEW PROTOCOL PARSERS, STARTING WITH SMS VERSION 1.1

SMS version 1.1 added new protocol parsers, because of the Internet support. The popularity of the Internet has made some new protocol parsers necessary. The following parsers are new to Network Monitor, starting in SMS version 1.1:

- ◆ HTTP
- ◆ IPXCP
- ◆ IPCP
- ◆ NBTFCP
- ◆ CBCP
- ◆ CCP
- ◆ PP PAP
- ◆ SNMP
- ◆ Netlogon Broadcast
- ◆ SPX2

These new parsers are used for Internet protocols and other specific protocols that have been recently added.

SHOWING THE TOP USERS

Showing the top users that send information on the network is very simple. This feature enables you to find out which users are using the network most often and why. Figure 21.10 shows the Find Top Users dialog, in which you can select several different settings:

- ◆ Amount of Users to Display
- ◆ Base List Upon
- ◆ Apply Current Display Filter to List

Figure 21.10.
The Find Top
Users dialog.

These options enable you to configure how many users you can display if you are going to display the list, based upon data link layer addresses or MAC addresses, and if you want to apply the display filter to the list that you are looking for with the top users. To get the Network Monitor to start finding the top users, you must do the following:

1. Go to the Tools menu.
2. Select Find Top Users.
3. Configure the Find Top Users dialog to your needs.
4. Click OK.

Once you do this, Network Monitor displays the Top Users dialog. Figure 21.11 shows the Top Users dialog, which gives you the top senders and the top recipients. The top senders list is located at the top of the dialog, and the top recipients list is located at the bottom.

Figure 21.11.
The Top Users
dialog.

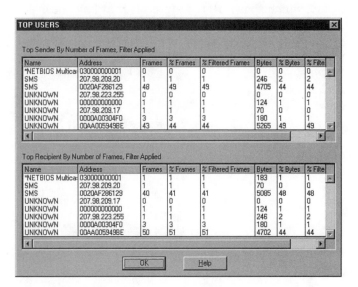

PROTOCOL DISTRIBUTION

Another tool that the Network Monitor gives you is very important: Protocol Distribution. Protocol Distribution gives you statistical information on what protocols and the amount of these protocols that have been used in communicating stations in the network. Figure 21.12 shows the Protocol Distribution dialog, which gives you statistical information on what you can base the Protocol Distribution on. You can base this list upon several different criteria:

◆ Last Protocol in Frame

◆ First Effective Protocol in Frame

◆ All Protocols in Frame

Figure 21.12.
The Protocol
Distribution
dialog.

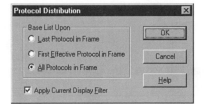

Once you select one of these options, it gives you the total number of frames that have been captured and the total number of bytes that have been captured, broken down on a protocol-by-protocol basis. Figure 21.13 shows the Protocol Distribution Report, which shows all the protocols that have been sent and the percentage and number of bytes sent.

Figure 21.13.
The Protocol
Distribution
Report.

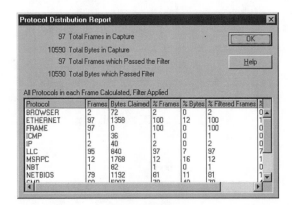

Note

Just as you could apply the Find Top Users selection to the display filter, you can also compare it to the Protocol Distribution selection.

RESOLVING NETWORK ADDRESSES

You can resolve network addresses from a name very easily. This allows you to not be so confused by all the addresses and NetBIOS names in your network. Go to the Tools menu and select Resolve Addresses from Name. Figure 21.14 shows the Find Network Addresses From Name dialog, which enables you to run a query to resolve addresses according to a name that you specify.

Figure 21.14.
Find Network
Address From
Name dialog.

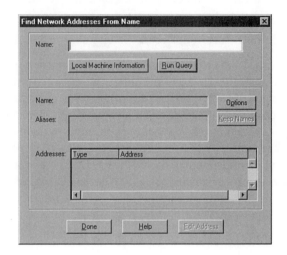

TOOLS SUMMARY

The Network Monitor tools give administrators a great deal of power in managing specific information about their networks and collecting information on troubleshooting and capacity planning. You can make sure that the network infrastructure can support the SMS environment you want to foster. This becomes increasingly important when communicating not only with the site servers to the logon distribution servers but also with the client logon servers. You should maintain some kind of history on what type of information is being transmitted and the amount. This inspires a great deal of confidence for the network administrator who has to help maintain much of what has to happen.

SMS ROLES WITH THE NETWORK MONITOR

It becomes very important to use the Network Monitor in an SMS environment, because the SMS environment deals with a lot of communications with many servers and a lot of data movement. Imagine the amount of data discussed in the previous chapters that moves across the network to let site servers communicate with logon servers, logon servers communicate with clients, site servers communicate with distribution servers, and distribution servers communicate with clients, with the addition of all the other communication on your network. It is important for an administrator to make sure that he or she can maintain the amount of traffic that his or her network can provide. This can be done, of course, by using the Network Monitor. In SMS, you need to monitor the following keys:

◆ Communication between the SMS Server and SQL Server

◆ Communication between the clients and the logon server

◆ Communication between the site server and distribution server

These three areas are important because they deal with a lot of heavy communications between all three roles. With the packages sent from the site server to the distribution server, you can imagine a lot of communication taking place. This package being sent can cause a network halt, especially when you do not take into consideration some of the other tasks that are done on the network. It is important to use the Network Monitor to your advantage in your SMS environment to make sure that specific clients do not have chatty network cards or a network problem occurring with their protocol. The Network Monitor also gives a clear definition for SMS to deal with networking information and statistics.

NETWORK MONITOR SDK

The Network Monitor provides the flexibility of adding protocol parsers. You can customize the protocol parsers by using the Network Monitor Software Developer's Kit (SDK), which comes with the BackOffice SDK. The SDK is a software developer's kit that allows programmers to extend the capabilities of the Network Monitor itself. If you run a specific custom protocol in your organization (for example, some manufacturing organizations create specific protocols to communicate with machinery), you can add these protocols to the Network Monitor database by creating an extension using the SDK to create a protocol parser. To explore this subject further, refer to the BackOffice SDK.

SUMMARY

Network Monitor is a tool to contend with, because it offers the robust capability of monitoring and gathering information about your network environment. You can save this information and use it at a later time. Some of its greatest benefits, of course, are the logon capabilities of the Network Monitor and the capability to filter some of the information about your network infrastructure. SMS offers a great add-on tool that can adapt to any environment, which enables you to monitor either a single client or an entire network. With the flexibility of the Network Monitor utility and its development with the software development kit, an administrator has every opportunity for maintaining and controlling the network environment he or she has to manage.

21

CHAPTER 22

SMS on the Internet

The Internet has certainly caught the imagination of the world. A large part of the excitement may be the marketing hype of the vendors who stand a chance to make a profit off the whole thing. However, the Internet does indeed have some great virtues that make it worth consideration in relation to any computer system. Especially in the forms Internet technologies take within organizations (as an intranet), they can help to maximize the benefits of a System Management Server installation.

When people talk about the Internet, they usually mean the World Wide Web, which is a wonderful method to present and obtain information in a variety of forms. SMS is strongly based on a large source of information: the machine and software inventories and other tables that are stored in SQL Server. Therefore, SMS and the Web are a natural match, in that various people need to be able to readily access information that SMS can provide. Managers want to know what their investment in computers has bought them. Systems analysts want to know what their users' computers can support. System administrators want to ensure that only licensed software is installed on the company's computers. Network administrators want to verify who's using which addresses. The combinations of people and needs are endless. Giving sophisticated query tools to all these staff may not be appropriate. They probably already have World Wide Web browsing capabilities, so why not have them just browse on over to the SMS server?

Even without the World Wide Web, the Internet is still many things. At a basic level, it is a network like any other, so if sites on either side of the country (or world) are both connected to it, then why not have them communicate through the Internet? The classic answer has been security—who knows who between the sites will have a chance to grab the network traffic and the information contained in it? Fortunately, Microsoft has provided a solution to that issue, so the possibility is worth considering.

A very popular application on the Internet is electronic mail, based on the standard SMTP (Simple Mail Transfer Protocol). E-mail can be used to great benefit with SMS if it is used as the action that is executed when an alert occurs. That way, if an SMS site has a remarkable event occur, it can send a message anywhere in the world. This is especially handy if the person receiving the message is at a place where he cannot otherwise access the SMS systems, but he can access his e-mail.

The problem of managing many computers or many network devices has been with us long before SMS came along. A standardized, if limited, solution is a TCP/IP protocol called SNMP (Simple Network Management Protocol). SMS version 1.2 includes SNMP facilities, so SMS can be used to collect intranet management information through SNMP, and it can send some of its information to intranet management tools through SNMP.

As technical specialists, we shouldn't forget that the Internet is a great source of one of our favorite commodities—information, including information about SMS. Whether obtained from Web sites, newsgroups, or mailing lists, SMS information from the Internet is invaluable, as well as often extremely timely.

Finally, the SMS and the Internet (or intranet) can be thought of in another direction—SMS can help manage Internet and intranet components. Upgrading client or server software, solving problems, watching for problems—SMS does it all. SMS even includes a network monitor, which can be very handy when digging deeply into Internet problems.

THE WORLD WIDE WEB AND SMS: A SIMPLE SOLUTION

The World Wide Web is a great means to communicate information to anyone who may be interested. No up-front work must be done, in terms of account setups, application installation, and so on, and the interface can be changed as requirements and opportunities change. This is a great opportunity for SMS in that the inventory that SMS collects is one of its most valuable features, and therefore making this available to users through WWW technology can be quite powerful.

The number of tools for providing information on the World Wide Web is probably uncountable, given that new products come on the market daily. For this reason, any given solution is probably not ideal for all situations. For purposes of discussion, this chapter uses an unsupported product from Microsoft called dbWeb.

dbWeb is intended to be a simple interface between ODBC data sources and the Internet Information Server, which comes with Windows NT Server version 4.0. SMS stores its data in an SQL Server database, which is easily interfaced with using ODBC. dbWeb is a great solution for SMS administrators who want to make SMS information available on their intranet but don't want to be bothered with a lot of programming and other setup. dbWeb simply requires that dbWeb be installed, the ODBC database connection be set up, and the desired tables and columns be defined. Additional options are provided for more complex needs or formatting, but these are all readily used when the time comes.

You can find dbWeb at `http://www.microsoft.com/intdev/dbweb/`, along with various forms of documentation to answer most questions. You can download the software as several disk-sized files or as one large file. All of these files must be executed, and if you downloaded them as several files, you can place them in a temporary directory where the setup program can be run. If you download them as one large file, running the file performs the whole setup. The dbWeb setup shuts down the Internet Information Server, so it is necessary to use the Internet Service Manager to start it again. The dbWeb service itself is also not started automatically, so it is necessary to use the Services Control Panel to start it.

ODBC 3.0 is installed as part of the dbWeb installation, and several sample databases are set up. These are useful for seeing what dbWeb can do and for testing that the setup was successful. You must add a system data source for the SMS database using the Add button displayed in the Data Sources dialog (see Figure 22.1), which you can display by using the System DSN button in the ODBC Administrator (or Control Panel).

Figure 22.1.
ODBC Adminis-
trator.

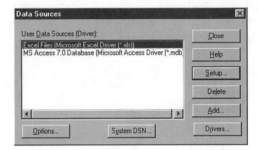

From the Add Data Source dialog, select the SQL Server ODBC driver, and the ODBC SQL Server Setup dialog is displayed. (See Figure 22.2.) You can use this dialog to specify which server the SMS database is served from, that the database name is SMS, and that the name for the data source is SMS.

Figure 22.2.
ODBC SQL
Server driver
setup with the
Options button
selected.

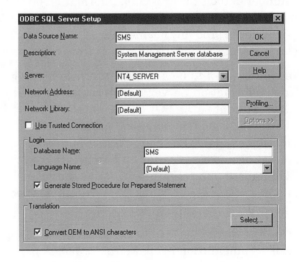

Once ODBC is set up, it's necessary to run the dbWeb Administrator (see Figure 22.3) to define how some SMS Web pages should be created.

Figure 22.3.
dbWeb
Administrator.

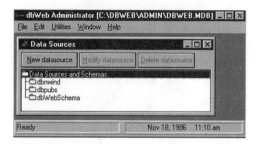

Clicking the dbWeb Administrator's New datasource button displays the Data Source dialog (see Figure 22.4), where you can use the Ellipsis (...) button on the Data Source Name field to select the SMS ODBC data source that was previously set up.

Figure 22.4.
dbWeb Data
Source details.

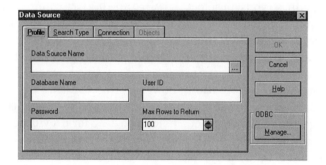

In addition, the database name must be specified as SMS, and a valid SQL Server user name and password are required. Clicking OK returns you to the dbWeb Administrator main window. Clicking the line in the list box that was added for the data source changes the New datasource button into a New Schema button. *Schemas* are the details regarding what information dbWeb should make available and how, so they are critical to the whole process. Clicking the New Schema button provides an opportunity to run a wizard or to create it manually. To start, it's a good idea to use the wizard. It allows the selection of which tables to use, which columns to display, and so on. Manual creation, or at least modification, is required in order to set up more complex queries, assign column properties (such as names), use more sophisticated output, and so forth, as shown in Figure 22.5. However, this can wait for the moment—it will be discussed later in this chapter.

Figure 22.5.
dbWeb schema
options.

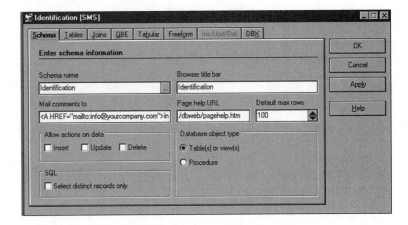

For an example of using the wizard, you can select the dbo.vIdentification view when asked for a table. This view shows basic information about all the machines in the SMS database. Useful ways to select machines might be by computer name or domain, so you can select the Name0 and Domain0 columns when asked for the columns to query. When they are selected from the list of available fields, you must click the > button to display them when the query-by-example page is shown. On the next wizard page, you can select the name and domain fields again to be displayed when the results of the query are shown. Selecting more fields is tempting (to give the user more initial information); however, the resulting Web page will soon become very wide if you do this, forcing the user to do a lot of horizontal scrolling. The next wizard page allows you to select a field to be used for providing more details. The Name0 field should be appropriate for this purpose because names are unique and easy for users to relate to. Finally, you must give a name to the schema, and in this case, Identification seems appropriate.

dbo.vIdentification is one of the views created by SMS's SMSVIEW.EXE program. SMS's database is based on a fairly complex set of tables. Using these tables for reporting purposes can be very tricky, so Microsoft provided the SMSVIEW program to create these views. If this program has not been run on the SMS server that is being used for the dbWeb work, then the views will not be available. Therefore, you should run this program prior to trying this work. It is available in the SMS directory tree and requires no input.

You can test the schema created by the wizard by using a Web browser and entering the appropriate URL, which takes the form `http://web_server_name/scripts/dbweb/ dbwebc.dll/schema_name?getqbe`, substituting the appropriate Web server name and schema name, as shown in Figure 22.6. The Web server name is the same as the name of the SMS server where Internet Information Server and dbWeb are installed. The schema name is the name given at the end of the wizard—Identification in this example. Of course, this kind of URL may be rather unwieldy for end users, so it is probably appropriate to set up a simple traditional Web page listing the options for the users, and that page can include links to the dbWeb URLs. The traditional Web page could be referred to with an URL such as `http://web_server_name/ SMS_Info`.

Figure 22.6.
Internet Explorer
is used to call up
the query-by-
example page.

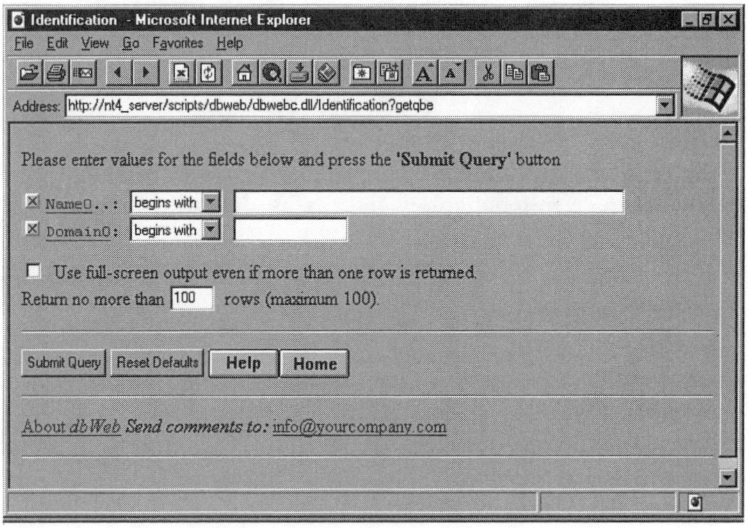

Entering the URL causes a page to be displayed that allows selecting specific machines by name or domain. When you click the Submit Query button, a page of rows of the data requested is returned. For the purpose of this discussion, the selection won't be limited in this example. The results are something like those in Figure 22.7.

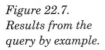

Figure 22.7.
Results from the
query by example.

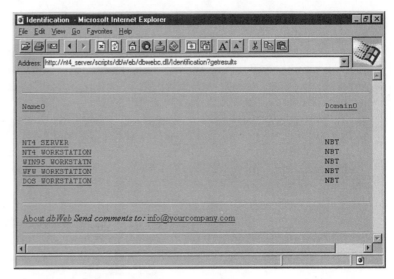

You can use the name field to provide complete information on any single machine, so clicking a name displays details as shown in Figure 22.8.

Figure 22.8.
Further details.

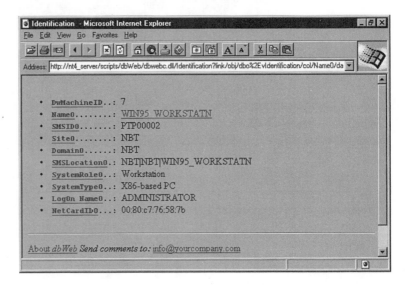

EXPANDING THE SOLUTION

dbWeb has a variety of options that you can specify when manually setting up or modifying schemas. If you select a schema in the dbWeb Administrator, the Modify datasource button changes to Modify schema. This opens the schema modification dialog, as shown previously in Figure 22.5. Details that can be changed include whom comments should be e-mailed to, the page's title, and column headings.

You can also set up more sophisticated schemas using the schema modification dialog. For instance, many SMS reports involve using the views provided by SMS's SMSVIEW program. However, these views provide details for each machine ID, which is not too meaningful to users. Bringing in vIdentification details would be very helpful. By manually creating a new schema that is similar to the Identification schema created in the earlier section but also including the vDisk view, you can create a useful schema for disk information, as an example.

The schema name for the disk example will be called Disks, as will its browser title bar. The tables will be dbo.vDisks and dbo.vIdentification, both of which must be added to the Tables Used in This Schema control under the Tables tab. A new join must be created under the Joins tab to join the dbo.vDisk's dwMachineID with dbo.vIdentification's (a regular = join will serve this purpose). For the query-by-example fields, you can make appropriate choices under the QBE tab, such as dbo.vDisk's Free_Storage__Mbyte_0, Disk_Index0, Storage_Tyep0, and File_System0. For the columns to be displayed on the results page, the query-by-example pages should be included as well as Serial_Number0 and some from dbo.vIdentification, such as Name0 and Domain0. The final page will display all the fields included under the Freeform tab, one line per field, so adding all fields may be appropriate. However, the freeform is only used if a query finds only one record (thus the need to include the serial number on the tabular tab).

You can specify additional options while setting up the schema. For instance, if the end user will never care about disk drives, then a constraint could be created on the Joins tab to ensure that dbo.vDisk's Disk_Index0 is always greater than B. On the other hand, this field could be included among the query-by-example fields, and the user could decide whether to include diskette drives or not. On the Tabular tab, you can specify the properties for each column, allowing adjustment of column labels, column widths, sort priorities, column positions, and so on. One property that should be particularly useful at this point is the Automatic Link property, which could be specified on the dbo.vDisk Disk_Index0 field, for instance. This should be set with a criteria of dbo.vDisk.Serial_Number0 being equal to the current value. When the Column Properties window is open, you can change the category of properties from Column Properties to All Properties (meaning they apply to the whole page). This allows you to set a page header and footer. The end result with all these changes looks something like Figure 22.9.

Figure 22.9.
A more sophisti-
cated dbWeb
schema.

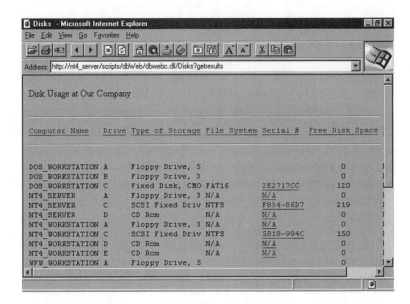

You can modify the query-by-example pages much like the tabular output pages. They can be given more useful column labels, the control types can be specified, value operators can be provided, and so on. This allows selection of data in whatever manner may be appropriate.

dbWeb's use of automatic links can provide a wide variety of functionality that users may expect from Web pages. dbWeb also includes a facility, DBX files, to use HTML tables, background and foreground graphics, various fonts, and so on. Read the dbWeb documentation for details on how to use these facilities.

Using Forms

dbWeb allows SMS data not only to be displayed but also to be entered. For most SMS data, this may not be appropriate—the software and hardware inventory programs do this in a much more objective and complete manner than humans could hope to. However, some information cannot be obtained by programs directly. Examples are the computer user's name, phone number, physical location, and so on. For this reason, every SMS client usually has a MIF entry program, which is primarily intended to allow entry of such information. The MIF entry program works nicely enough, but it doesn't have a lot of sophisticated options to ensure that all users enter all fields, especially in a consistent manner. For this reason, the SMS administrator or operator could review this information in the SQL Server database and make changes, but they wouldn't be reflected back at the users' desks when they change the information. A better solution may be required—one that allows both the user and the administrator to see and modify the user information back at the SQL Server database. Using WWW forms is a particularly appropriate solution in that the user already knows how to do such things, the process is reasonably intuitive, and the user already has the program (the browser) to do the job.

dbWeb facilitates setting up such forms in almost exactly the same way that it allows setting up SMS Web pages. The main difference is that on the Schema tab of the schema modification dialog, the actions must be enabled. In the case of SMS user information, it is only appropriate to allow updates—deleting or inserting machines shouldn't be done in this way. When the update action is selected, the Ins/Upd/Del (insert/update/delete) tab is enabled. There, the columns to be updated can be specified with appropriate properties.

In order to use the dbWeb form, the user must drill down to the appropriate computer, as was done with the dbWeb pages seen in the previous sections. However, when the user gets down to the freeform page, there is a Submit button at the bottom with the possible actions that can be selected. When the user clicks this button, a WWW form is displayed, as shown in Figure 22.10, allowing data to be entered.

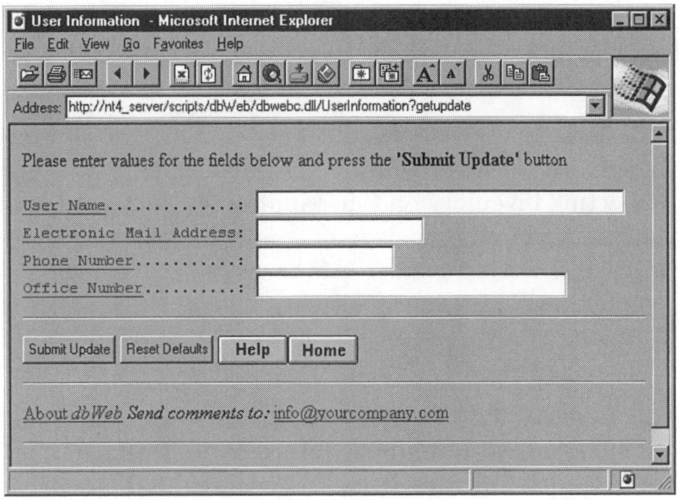

Figure 22.10.
A dbWeb form to
enter some SMS
user information.

One consideration that makes the use of dbWeb forms a little tricky is that there can be columns from only one table at a time. However, SMS often separates data into specific and common tables, so you must give some thought to setting up the forms appropriately.

SMS SITE COMMUNICATION THROUGH THE INTERNET

The popularity of the Internet has made it extremely pervasive. Throughout all the technologically advanced countries, connection services are available, and even in less advanced countries, pockets of service can be found. At the same time, the huge volume of activity supported by the Internet and the subsidies received in the past from government mean that the service is relatively cheap. Therefore, a company's SMS sites are likely to be at locations where Internet connectivity is an option and where that option is much cheaper than any other WAN option—a very attractive combination.

Why wouldn't everyone use the Internet as their WAN? The first reason is irregularity of service—given that the Internet isn't under your control, you can't guarantee that bandwidth is available when you need it. Another is security—who knows who has access to your packets as they flow through the Internet? A more philosophical question is that of intent—the Internet was originally intended to share information for scientific and education purposes. Does your transfer of SMS data qualify, or in fact, does it make it more difficult to achieve the original purpose in that you'll be using bandwidth that otherwise could be used for those purposes?

Solutions to each of these problems may not be acceptable for all situations. Irregularity of service may not be important if real-time response is not important. Collecting inventory and distributing packages can be done overnight, and with sufficient planning, delays of a few days may be acceptable. The intent of the Internet could be considered to be evolving along with its technologies. The biggest problem may be that of security. Fortunately, Microsoft has introduced a new solution to this problem with version 4.0 of Windows NT—namely, Point-to-Point Tunneling Protocol (PPTP).

PPTP allows TCP/IP, NetBEUI, or IPX packets to flow from one site (point) to another but encapsulated within other TCP/IP packets. The encapsulated packets are encrypted, so even if someone does grab copies of the PPTP packets, he or she won't be able to read anything of significance from them.

Microsoft's implementation of PPTP with Windows NT version 4.0 is very dependent on RAS, so when it's used with SMS, the RAS sender must be used. RAS can go over ISDN, X.25, or multiple modems, so the link can be very fast. On the originating SMS server, the RAS sender dials to a local RAS server to get onto the Internet. The RAS client then sees that it has a PPTP RAS entry, and so it refers to it to find where it should find the PPTP-enabled server, which is the remote SMS server. The TCP/IP traffic communicated between the RAS client and the remote server is all encrypted, with the encryption automatically based on the logon security.

E-Mail and SMS

Among the fundamental technologies of the Internet are the standardized network protocols that it is built on. The more mechanical protocols, such as TCP and IP, take care of getting network packets from one site to another. On these are built higher level protocols that provide a service. One of the most important of these is for electronic mail, and it is called Simple Mail Transfer Protocol (SMTP).

SMTP makes it possible for mail servers and clients from a huge number of vendors and individuals to work together, making Internet mail one of the easiest to use and most popular applications of the Internet. Anyone who can connect to the Internet can have e-mail service, and wherever he or she goes, he or she can connect through the Internet to his or her mail server and collect or send mail messages. In this manner, Internet e-mail can be a powerful option for communicating SMS status reports to whomever may be interested. This can be done by simply e-mailing reports or more powerfully, by having SMS initiate e-mails when necessary.

The easiest way to automate using e-mail with SMS is to use SMS alerts. Alerts are queries that are repeated on a regular basis and that can execute a command if the query results indicate that it is appropriate to do so. All that is needed is a command-line oriented e-mail interface. Then, you can easily set up an SMS alert to regularly check for servers whose disk drives' free disk space drops to less than ten percent. When any server is found that meets this criteria, the e-mail notifies the administrator to correct the problem before it turns into a real problem.

Tip

If your current e-mail solution doesn't provide a facility to send e-mail from the command line of a Windows NT server, you may want to check out VanceMail!, a nice little shareware program. You can find it at `ftp://ftp.digital.com/pub/micro/pc/winsite/winnt/netutil/vmail104.zip`. It is not a Digital Equipment Corporation product. Refer to the included help file for details on using it in a command-line mode.

SNMP AND SMS

Like SMTP, SNMP is an application-oriented protocol provided as part of the TCP/IP family of protocols. SNMP stands for Simple Network Management Protocol, and as such, it provides management options. These options are available not only for traditional computers, but also for the various intelligent devices that make up a network, such as bridges and routers. SNMP is primarily notification oriented, in the sense that machines can notify SNMP tools of events that occur. SMS can collect SNMP notifications, and it can send them to other SNMP-based tools. SMS can even translate Windows NT events into SNMP messages. How SNMP is used with SMS is covered in Chapter 23, "Housecleaning in SMS."

SMS TECHNICAL INFORMATION ON THE INTERNET

The Internet was originally set up for distributing technical information among scientists and educators. Computer professionals soon found that it was a wonderful facility for sharing their information as well. Newsgroups were the original tool for informal, rapid exchanges of ideas. FTP (File Transfer Protocol) was the tool for transferring files. The World Wide Web came along much later and proved to be a great method for sharing information and making files available, but in a more formal, thought-out manner. The WWW technologies have even been extended to provide discussion forums. Other Internet tools, such as e-mail and IRC, are also useful for communicating technical information, but they don't tend to be used for SMS information. No discussion of SMS and the Internet is complete without mentioning these wonderful possibilities.

The independent newsgroup for SMS information is `comp.os.ms-windows.nt.software.backoffice`. It is carried by most news servers, so talk to your Internet provider for details on where you can find one. Microsoft has numerous SMS newsgroups on its news server, `msnews.microsoft.com`, such as `microsoft.public.sms.misc` and `microsoft.publc.sms.admin`.

Microsoft's Web site (`www.microsoft.com`) is the ultimate source of information on SMS, providing up-to-date product details, various files, white papers, and, most importantly, the SMS Knowledge Base. Other WWW sites with SMS information include ComputingEdge at `www.computingedge.com/` (it seems to be involved in the most important SMS add-ons) and the jrh Group Ltd. at `jrhgroup.com`. In an effort to inspire the academic community to contribute to the world of Windows NT in the same way that they have to UNIX, Microsoft set up the European Microsoft Windows NT Academic Centre, which can be found at `emwac.ed.ac.uk/`. There are a few sites, such as `www.bhs.com`, that claim to have SMS coverage, but these do not seem very actively supported. Various trade magazines include SMS information, such as *BackOffice Magazine* (www.backoffice.com). *PC Week* (www.pcweek.com) is a good source for up-to-date news and analysis on system management and other topics, but SMS is rarely mentioned.

SMS MANAGING INTERNET COMPONENTS

System Management Server is all about managing computers. The Internet wouldn't be possible without computers. SMS can contribute to the Internet in that it can manage those computers. Web browsers are one of the most competitive software arenas, and as a result, new versions come out on a frequent basis. Distributing these upgrades to users is an ideal application of SMS packages. The same is also true, if to a lesser degree, of server software. Clients and servers also have all the usual problems that any computers have, so SMS's capabilities to watch for problems, provide hardware and software details, and remotely control computers are invaluable.

SUMMARY

The Internet (or its technologies used as an intranet) can be valuable with SMS. Information can readily be published, intersite communications can be facilitated, alerts can be sent by e-mail, management information can be collected and distributed, and technical information about SMS can be found. In addition, you can use SMS to manage clients and servers that are used for the Internet.

These options require using various technologies, such as the World Wide Web, dbWeb, PPTP, SMTP, SNMP, and newsgroup readers. They involve using various SMS features, such as the SMS database, senders, alerts and queries, and SNMP traps and event-to-trap translators. Despite the diversity of elements, each is relatively easy to set up and use, and the power they offer make them well worth the effort.

- Housecleaning in SMS

- Optimizing SMS
  Performance

PART V

Performance Tuning and Optimization

CHAPTER 23

Housecleaning in SMS

As you have seen, SMS is an animal to contend with. It involves gathering a great deal of information and organizing that information in a certain fashion. An important key in doing this is making sure that the integrity of the database is maintained and that there are certain mechanisms to maintain the database. This chapter covers the different tools and operations that an administrator can implement to make sure that his or her SMS environment is constantly cleaned and the integrity of the data is valid. This chapter also discusses the features that notify the administrator or trigger certain actions when specified criteria have been met.

SQL SERVER DATABASE OPERATIONS AND MAINTENANCE

One of the key elements of the SMS environment is SQL Server. It offers a service to the SMS site server as a depository for all of the SMS information. Due to the size and importance of the information, it is important to make sure that the SQL Server is properly maintained. There are several operations and maintenance tasks for the SQL Server to make sure that it runs optimally and the integrity of the data is maintained. Many of the tools are given to you on the SQL Server, although SMS itself offers some tools to monitor and manage the SQL Server. These tasks will facilitate two things. The first is fault tolerance, which is a key to being able to maintain information and not have to worry about losing it. The second is performance, which is an issue that everyone is worried about. If certain aspects are maintained and certain tasks are done on a timely basis, performance need not become a concern.

There are many rules on how to set up the SQL Server, many of which are discussed in Chapter 24, "Optimizing SMS Performance." This chapter covers the features that will enable an administrator to maintain and manage the SQL Server in the SMS environment.

DBCC (DATABASE CONSISTENCY CHECK)

The Database Consistency Check is a tool that is provided with the SQL Server. It allows the administrator to check the physical and logical consistency of the database. It is important to run this check once a month. The two key things that you need to check are the SMS database and the log. The time to run this check is prior to ever running a backup on the database or if you are restoring the database. If a problem exists, you receive an error. In that case, it may be important to restore the last clean backup.

Caution

Before running the Database Consistency Check, make sure that no copies of the SMS Administrator are running. It is also recommended that you shut down the SMS Executive and SMS Hierarchy Manager Services.

There are three commands that are important to use when running the DBCC. They are as follows:

◆ DBCC Newalloc—checks database extents
◆ DBCC CheckCatalog—checks system tables
◆ DBCC CheckDB—checks all tables in a database, for consistency between tables and indices, and so on

Note

The command Newalloc is new to SQL Server 6.5. It replaces the command Checkalloc that was in SQL Server 6.0.

MAINTAINING SQL SERVER DEVICES

The SQL Server devices are the components that interface with the SMS site server to deposit data. These components play an important role in storing the SMS data. There are several guidelines and rules for checking these devices. The three devices that need to be checked are as follows:

◆ SMS Database
◆ Tempdb Database
◆ Transaction Logs

SMS DATABASE

The SMS database is the most important component. It is where the SMS site server places all information for the SMS site. One of the key rules for the SMS database is to keep it below 80-percent full. To check the status of the database, use the SQL Enterprise Manager to go in and look at the properties of the database to see what amount of the database has been used. Once you have exceeded 80-percent full, it is important to expand the database. If you can't expand the database, make sure you expand the device. That might involve adding another hard drive to the SQL Server.

Caution

> Do not exceed the limits of the SMS database. If this happens, detrimental problems could occur. Consult SQL Server documentation for further details.

TEMPDB DATABASE

The Tempdb database is where all temporary tables are stored. This database can change in the amount of space that is used. It is important to make sure that this database stays below 60-percent full. Many times this database is heavily used when queries are made. Large queries can easily make the Tempdb database exceed its limit. If it exceeds 60 percent, it is important to expand the database for Tempdb.

Tip

> If you are using SQL Server 6.5, you can use Performance Monitor to monitor the space used by the database, using the object SQLSERVER and the counter MaxTempdbSpaceUsed.

TRANSACTION LOGS

If you need to monitor the transaction logs, it is important that you use Performance Monitor. You can use the object SQLSERVER-LOG and the counter LOG SIZE. If the log size exceeds 60 percent of capacity, you will need to expand the transaction log.

Tip

> The SQL Server messages window inside the SMS Administrator can be an important tool in monitoring the communication of the SMS site server and SQL Server. Keep this window open at all times. If it is not open, messages will not appear.

BACKING UP THE SMS DATABASE

In any environment, it is important to offer some type of fault tolerance. One of the key elements in providing fault tolerance is backing up the system in which you are operating. In the SMS environment, there are several things that need to be backed up. One is the SQL Server environment and the other thing is, of course, the SMS site server. This section covers the backup on the SQL Server. The following section discusses backing up the key SMS components. When backing up, it is important that you shut down the SMS services on the SMS site server.

The first thing to do when you are going to back up on a SQL Server is to create a backup device. In Figure 23.1, you see the Database Backup/Restore window where a backup device is created. The steps are as follows:

1. Open up the SQL Enterprise Manager.
2. Click on the Tools menu option.
3. Select Database Backup/Restore.
4. Click on New, which will bring up the New Backup Device dialog box.
5. In the Name box, put in the logical name to reference the backup device.
6. Select Backup Device type, either disk backup device or tape backup device.
7. Click on Create, which will close the New Backup Device dialog box and bring you back to the Database Backup/Restore dialog box.
8. Click on Initialize Device.

Figure 23.1.
The Database
Backup/Restore
window.

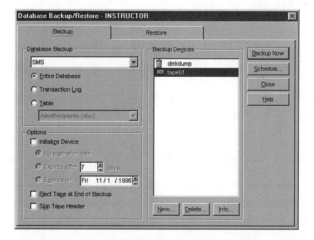

Note

In Step 4, there are two backup types. Disk backup device would save information to disk, whereas tape backup device would save information to tape.

Tip

> It is recommended that you first back up to the site server directory, and from there, back up to tape.

The backup device has now been created. You are ready to back up. If you stay in the same window where you created your backup device, you simply click on Backup Now, and it will back up the SMS database.

Restoring the SMS Database

Using the same utility that you used to back up the SMS database, you can restore the SMS database. When restoring the database, you want to make sure that the helper server and the services on the SMS site server are off and that none of the SMS Administrator programs are running. This will help to ensure a clean restore. If you are restoring a database because you had to reinstall SQL, it is wise to restore the master database also, because of some of the changes SMS might have made to the master database.

Caution

> It is important when restoring the SMS database that you restore on the SQL Server with the same database configuration that you backed up the database.

Moving the SMS Database

If, for some reason, the SQL Server computer has failed and you need to move the SMS database to another SQL Server, it is important to do the following:

1. Make sure that you have backed up the existing SMS database from the SQL Server.
2. Install the SQL Server or use an existing SQL installation.
3. Create the devices for the new database at the same size or larger than the previous database.
4. Shut down all of the services for the SMS site and helper servers, making sure that the SMS Administrator is not running.
5. Restore the database onto the new SQL Server.
6. If the name of the server database login has changed on the SQL machine, make sure that you run the SMS setup, click on Operations, and make the changes under the SMS database option.

7. When running the SMS Administrator, change the database name at the logon screen.

SMS HOUSECLEANING AND MAINTENANCE

The housecleaning of SMS deals with several different tools and operations. It is important to make sure that you maintain not only the integrity of the database on the SQL Server, but the actual directories and structure of the site server. To maintain the site server, several tools are available, which are discussed in this section. It is important to use these tools at the right times and perform these tasks on a regular basis. This is the key to maintaining and documenting all of the operations done with the SMS site server. For instance, if you were going to leave the organization, or one of your staff members was, it would be detrimental to the company if there is no information on the operations done on the SMS site.

DATABASE MANAGER

When maintaining the SMS database, there are times when a lot of unused information is left on the SMS database. Some of the obsolete and unused data represents active jobs, events, SNMP traps, and computer history that stays in the SMS database and needs to be removed on a constant basis. It is good to create a schedule of when you are going to run the Database Manager. If you look at Figure 23.2, you will see the Database Manager. As time passes, the SMS database can be left with information that has to be released as soon as possible to maintain and control the amount of space taken. There are several operations that you can do in the SMS Database Manager.

Caution

When running the Database Manager, make sure that there are no other instances of the SMS Administrator running. Use care when doing any database operations with the SMS Database Manager.

Note

In SMS version 1.2, there have been some enhancements to the Database Manager. You now have the ability to display a list of the duplicated computers that will be deleted from the database. You can delete the information from the database or merge the two computers together. There is also a new option to delete old collected files, based on a specific date.

23

HOUSECLEANING IN SMS

To run the specific operations of the Database Manager, do the following:

1. Start the SMS Database Manager.

2. Go to the Tools or Machine menu option.

3. Select the operation that you want to run.

Figure 23.2.
The Database
Manager
(DBClean.EXE)
when selecting
Delete Collected
Files from the
Tools menu.

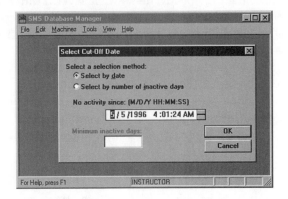

MERGING DUPLICATE COMPUTERS

One of the options in the Database Manager is for merging duplicate computers. When deleting the sms.ini file on the client, a new SMS ID will be created so the second computer will show up. You can merge the information of both computers so that you can keep the historical data on the old computer while maintaining the new information taken from the last inventory.

DELETING DUPLICATE COMPUTERS

You are given another alternative for duplicate computer results. The alternative is to delete the record. If this is selected, it will delete the selected computer record while maintaining the other computer record. Deleting duplicate computers becomes important for making sure that you don't keep a number of instances of the computer's history in the SMS database. This can take some unused space that you will never need or use.

DELETING GROUP CLASSES

There is an option to delete the information for groups that exist in the database. The results of any custom group or audit information that SMS has performed can be removed from the database by deleting the group classes. It is up to the administrator to select what group class he or she wants deleted. For example, if there was a specific group, such as operating systems, and you used the Database Manager, you could remove all of the information about all of the operating systems for all of the machines and the site of the SMS database.

DELETING COLLECTED FILES

SMS gives you the option to collect files from the machines in the environment. When these files are collected, there has to be a mechanism to get rid of them when the administrator does not need to maintain them any longer. The location and information about the collected file is put in the SMS site database. The file itself is actually put onto the site server. Deleting collected files will allow both of these to be purged.

DELETING UNUSED COMMON OR SPECIFIC RECORDS

Often, people customize the information that is pooled from the computers in the SMS environment and put this information into the site database. Much of these specific records and unused common information can be purged from the SMS database by using this option. There are two ways that you generally view information in the SMS database. One of the views is in a table to see the specific record. The other way of viewing information is in columns where you can see values that apply to multiple computers or multiple information. Using this option of setting machine groups, you can change what way you would like to view information. You can set the machine group preferences according to what architecture you would like to view.

MAINTAINING AND MONITORING THE DIRECTORY STRUCTURE OF THE SITE SERVER

There are several directories in the SMS site that can cause the SMS site to become bogged down. To monitor these directories becomes a very key function. Though much of the maintenance on these directories can involve actually deleting or moving files, it is most important to monitor them. Many of the SMS processes and operations that go on actually do these mechanisms or allow these mechanisms to happen. Table 23.1 lists the SMS directories that can contain files that will be generated as SMS performs its functions. These should be monitored for stale files that can be deleted. If large numbers of files begin to accumulate in any of these directories, the associated services should be checked to ensure that they are processing properly.

TABLE 23.1. SMS SITE DIRECTORIES.

Directory	Usage
`sms\logon.srv\pcmins.box\:`	Job instruction files for each machine
`sms\logs\:`	Services logs
`sms\site.srv\dataload.box\deltamif.col\:`	MIFs to be loaded
`sms\site.srv\dataload.box\files.col\:`	Files collected from machines
`sms\site.srv\siterep.box\:`	Files to be sent by the site reporter
`sms\site.srv\despoolr.box\receive\:`	Files to be despooled
`sms\site.srv\despoolr.box\store\:`	Packages that have been distributed
`sms\site.srv\inventry.box\:`	Inventory files to be processed
`sms\site.srv\inventry.box\history\:`	Inventory details for all the machines at this site
`sms\site.srv\maincfg.box\pcmdom.box\:`	Instructions for each machine
`sms\site.srv\schedule.box\:`	Jobs to be processed
`sms\site.srv\sender.box\requests\:`	Requests for sending activity
`sms\site.srv\sender.box\tosend\:`	Packages to be sent
`e:\sms_pkge\:`	Packages

SMSTRACE

SMSTRACE is the utility that comes with SMS that enables you to log and monitor the information about the services running on your SMS site. This information can be configured in the type of view that you want. You can change the view according to columns, you can filter messages, and you can ignore certain lines. All of this information runs in real time. A nice thing about SMSTRACE is that all of the log files are produced in ASCII text. You can use this information to track down what services might not be operating the way they should. As an example, one circumstance that warrants using SMSTRACE is if a job gets stopped, you can check the logs of the different services involved to see where the problem has occurred. Table 23.2 lists the services and the log files that these services correspond to.

TABLE 23.2. LOG FILES PRODUCED BY **SMSTRACE**.

Service	Log Files
SMS Alerter	ALERTER.LOG
Applications Manager	APPMAN.LOG
Bootstrap	BOOT.LOG (in SMS root directory of Secondary Site Servers)
Inventory Dataloader	DATALODR.LOG
Despooler	DESPOOL.LOG
Site Hierarchy Manager	HMAN.LOG
Inventory Agent	INVAGENT.LOG
Inventory Processor	INVPROC.LOG
LAN Sender	LANSEND.LOG
RAS Sender	RASSEND.LOG
RAS Sender [async]	RASSYNC.LOG
RAS Sender [ISDN]	RASISDN.LOG
RAS Sender [X.25]	RASX25.LOG
SNA Sender	SNASEND.LOG
SNA Sender [Batch]	SNABATCH.LOG
SNA Sender [Interactive]	SNAINTER.LOG
SNA Receiver	SNARECV.LOG
Maintenance Manager	MAINTMAN.LOG
Package Command Manager	PACMAN.LOG
SMS Scheduler	SCHED.LOG
Site Configuration Manager	SCMAN.LOG (in root directory of SMS drive)
Site Reporter	SITEREP.LOG
SMS Executive	SMSEXEC.LOG
SMS Administrator	UI.LOG
SNMP Trap Filter Log	TRAPFLTR.LOG

23

HOUSECLEANING IN SMS

Tip

It is wise to minimize the number of services that are traced, in order to minimize the impact on performance.

TASKS TO DO ON A PERIODIC BASIS

There are several operations that should be done on a periodic basis. You can break these operations into three categories of when they need to occur.

◆ Daily tasks

◆ Weekly tasks

◆ Monthly tasks

The daily tasks are as follows:

◆ Reset logs so that old events are not retained.

◆ Check the SQL Server messages when viewing the different SMS Service messages.

◆ Back up the SMS database along with the master database.

◆ Use Network and Performance Monitors to make sure performance is adequate for the environment.

The weekly tasks are as follows:

◆ Check duplicate machines and use the Database Manager to either merge or delete the duplicate computers.

◆ Monitor the drive space on both the SQL Server and the SMS Server, making sure that the SMS Server has adequate disk space.

◆ Check the SMS database and make sure that all devices and logs are not close to full.

The monthly tasks are as follows:

◆ Restore the backup to make sure that your backups are working properly.

◆ Use the DBCC utility to check SQL Server, to make sure the SMS database is consistent.

◆ Check unused records and abandon collected files using DBClean.

AREAS TO BACK UP

An earlier section discussed backing up the SQL Server. There are several components on the SMS site server that are important to back up to enable you to restore an SMS site server if a failure occurs. There are only a few key areas that you have to monitor and back up to be able to reconstruct the configuration of your SMS database. Much of this can be backed up to a very small media type. Key components to back up are as follows:

- Site Control File (`SiteCtrl.CT0`)
- Registry Entry — `HKEY_LOCAL_MACHINE\CurrentControlSet\Services\SMS`
- Registry Entry — `HKEY_LOCAL_MACHINE\SOFTWARE\Microsoft\SMS`
- `SMS.INI` File
- Site Server SMS Directory
- `SMSLS.INI`

Using Alerts, Events, and SNMP Traps

These operations give the administrator an additional way to understand what is going on in the SMS environment. They are *event-driven tasks* that, when a certain condition is met, will generally offer a result. This result can be in the form of a message, an execution of a program, or some type of statistical information. The main key with these components is to use them to the best of your advantage to monitor the activity of your systems environment on a periodic basis. This section deals with the mechanisms in which these operations take place and how the results are read.

Alerts

Alerts are one of the most informative tools that the SMS site server can offer an administrator. They allow the administrator to set a condition, and if this condition is met or exceeded, it will then provide a result. This result can be in the form of a message, a command line, or an event. There are two key characteristics of an alert. These characteristics are

- Queries
- Actions

These two characteristics are what make an alert work. A query allows you to set an alert on the basis of queried information that makes up the inventory of machines. For example, all machines with hard drives that exceed 80-percent full can be set up as an alert from the query on hard drives that exceed over 80-percent full. Once this criteria is met, you can allow an action to take place. That is the second characteristic of an alert. The action, of course, might be to send a message to users to clean up their hard drives. Figure 23.3 shows the Alert Properties dialog.

Figure 23.3.
The Alert Prop-
erties dialog in
the SMS Admin-
istrator.

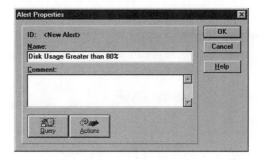

THE ALERTER

This service allows the alert to happen by watching the alert in the database kick off a query. When the condition of the query is made, an action occurs. This action is kicked off by the Alerter. This is all configured when creating the alert.

QUERY

The query is one of the most important elements for the alert. It enables you to specify the query condition that has to be met before the alert will respond. You are prompted when selecting the query to determine what query you want this alert to ride upon. The query also asks what sites you want to run this alert on. You can limit this alert to specific sites or you can include all subsites underneath the primary site you choose. One of the options is to actually repeat the query after a certain number of minutes. The default is 120 minutes. The final configuration for the query is to actually select when you want the query to be met. This means you can generate an alert whenever it hits a certain hit count. This hit count is met with several different conditions. The following conditions can be used:

◆ Is greater than

◆ Is less than

◆ Is equal to

◆ Increases by at least

◆ Decreases by at least

◆ Changes by at least

With these conditions, you can select what hit count the query has to reach before the alert will appear. Then the action will be triggered.

In Figure 23.4, the query window for the alert is shown.

Figure 23.4.
The query
window in
creating an alert.

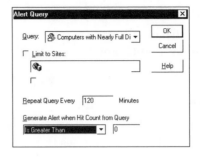

ACTION

Once the query is met, it triggers an action. This action can be selected underneath the Actions button in the Alert Properties dialog when creating an alert. The action response will trigger an action by three different methods. These methods are as follows:

- ◆ Log an Event
- ◆ Execute Command Line
- ◆ Notify Computer or Username

With these methods, you can select either just one of the methods or more than one of the methods to actually act once the alert is met. This action, of course, is triggered by what is called the Alerter. Although it is repeating its queries, once it meets its hit count, it will not run the action again. It only runs the first time the alert is met. In Figure 23.5, the Alert Actions dialog is shown for the alert. These three methods of action will determine how the administrator finds out if the alert is met.

Figure 23.5.
The Alert Actions
dialog for the
alert.

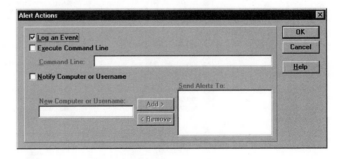

LOG AN EVENT

This method will show an event in the Windows NT Event Viewer and in the SMS Administrator underneath the Events window.

EXECUTE COMMAND LINE

This option will actually run a command once the alert is hit. However, this command cannot launch any type of application that will require a window or a console.

NOTIFY COMPUTER OR USERNAME

This method will notify the specific computer or usernames you add when the alert is met. The computer or usernames then become instantaneously aware, while on the network, that the hit count has been met.

EVENTS

SMS keeps track of the ongoing operations by using a mechanism called an event. Events allow the administrator to find out at what stage SMS is working on various operations. The Event Log logs events in three ways: warnings, information, and errors. These messages are sent to two different places. The first place is the Windows NT Event Viewer, which can be found under the Administrative Tools menu option under the Start menu. The other place that events are sent is the Events window in the SMS Administrator. Figure 23.6 shows the Events window in the SMS Administrator.

Figure 23.6.
The Events
window in
the SMS
Administrator.

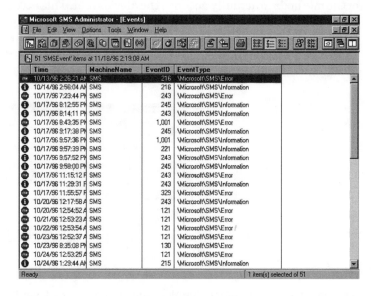

You will see that the events are all logged in the order that they have occurred. The specific time is shown. There are several different types of events. There is a stop event and an information event. Stop events generally mean that there is a serious problem with the SMS site server. An information event is just information to let the administrator know that something has occurred. These events are also recorded in the Windows NT Event Viewer. They are broken up and categorized in many different groups.

These groups are as follows:

◆ Time

◆ Machine Name

◆ Event ID

◆ Event Type

Using these categories, you can categorize events. The following are the columns for the events:

◆ Time. The time the event actually occurred.

◆ MachineName. The name of the machine where the event occurred.

◆ EventID. The event ID describing the event.

◆ EventType. The type of event that occurred, either an error or information event.

◆ Event details. When you want to pick a specific event, you can double-click it. This will allow you to look at the event details of that particular event.

In Figure 23.7, an Event Details dialog is shown for an SMS error. The event details show several different attributes. These attributes have different corresponding value types. The attributes are as follows:

◆ SMSID

◆ MachineName

◆ Time

◆ WarningLevel

◆ EventModule

◆ EventType

◆ Component

These attributes can tell you specific information about where, when, and how the event occurred. The box underneath these attributes and value types will describe the event in a comment that is sent from the SMS server describing what actually has happened. With this, the administrator can figure out why the problem has occurred. It is important for the administrator to sometimes look at events to see if they are too old to be worth keeping. To delete events, use Delete Special from the Edit menu on a specific event ID or events dated before a specific date. This enables you to clean up your Events window for old events or events that may be insignificant with certain types of event ID.

Figure 23.7.
Event Detail
dialog for an
SMS error.

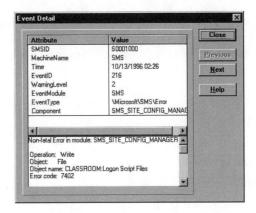

SNMP TRAPS

SNMP Traps is a new function for SMS version 1.2. It allows SMS to integrate with several SNMP Managers and to help provide information for certain events that happen in the SMS environment. It integrates with the events that Windows NT offers with integration set into the Windows NT SNMP service. The SMS event to trap the translator translates events to traps, which can then be sent to the Windows NT SNMP Service. The service then sends the trap to its destination, which is generally an SNMP Manager. An SNMP Manager is a product that allows SNMP traps to come in so that information can be provided about a specific device or a specific event. You can specify the events that you want translated into an SNMP trap on several different criteria:

◆ The source of the event

◆ The event ID

◆ Number of occurrences of a certain event

◆ Number of occurrences of a certain event and a specified time

Note

SNMP traps can be forwarded only over LAN connections. SNMP traps cannot be forwarded over RAS connections.

EVENT TO TRAP TRANSLATOR

This feature is underneath the Administrator Tools of the properties of a Windows NT computer. The Windows NT computer must be running the SNMP service for this to actually start sending traps. You can go in and modify the trap translator prior to running the SNMP service so it will be set. This operation takes specific events that you can customize to send as traps to the SMS database. These traps can be queried later on to find out if certain criteria are met on the Windows NT computer. The Windows NT computer has four management information bases (MIBs) to view for information. This information can be used for looking up SNMP information. This information can later be forwarded to a management system if needed. These four MIBs are as follows:

- ◆ Internet MIB II
- ◆ LAN Manager MIB II
- ◆ DHCP MIB
- ◆ WINS MIB

These are the actual bases for information to be pulled for SNMP traps to be driven. Information based on these bases can be put into an SMS database or forwarded to an SNMP Management System. Figure 23.8 shows the Event to Trap Translator in the SMS Administrator. Two selections can be made: custom and default. If you select custom, there are certain settings that you can define for what events get sent as traps. You can select the Settings button at the bottom, which opens the window shown in Figure 23.9. These are the event sources for what logged events will be sent as SNMP traps. Once this has been set up, there is a Settings button, which allows you to select what you see in Figure 23.10 (which is the settings for the traps). This dialog offers several different configurations. These configurations are the following:

- ◆ Limit Trap Length. Mechanism for restricting the length of bytes for the trap.
- ◆ Trap Throttle. Mechanism for the throughput of traps within a number of seconds.

You have a choice of either stopping the forwarding of traps or allowing the trap throttle to be disabled.

Note

The SNMP Event to Trap Translator requires the Windows NT machine to have loaded the SNMP service.

23

HOUSECLEANING IN SMS

Figure 23.8.
The Event to
Trap Translator
in the SMS
Administrator.

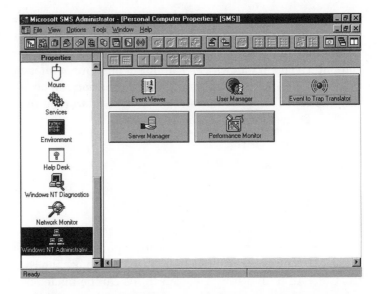

Figure 23.9.
The event source
for what logs will
be forwarded as
traps.

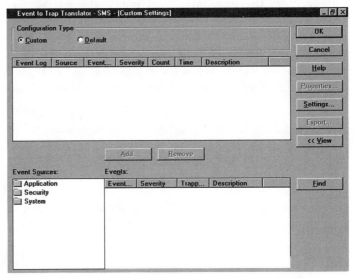

Figure 23.10.
The Settings box
for the traps.

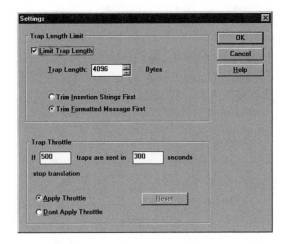

SNMP TRAP RECEIVER

The SNMP Trap Receiver exists on the site server. It gathers SNMP traps that have been translated from events to match those traps to the filters that you have specified. This allows the other traps to be discarded. There is a log file that has all of the information for this, SMS/Logs/Trapfltr.log.

SUMMARY

This chapter discussed the ways of maintaining the day-to-day operations of an SMS environment. Many elements of the environment are discussed, from the SQL Server and the SMS Server to the different tools that are provided to integrate both. As the versions have succeeded, more tools and more functionality have been provided for cleaning up sites. These tools give you a mechanism for your day-to-day, week-to-week, month-to-month tasks, and for reducing the amount of trouble in your environment. As you move forward, you can try to find answers to the questions of performance and fault tolerance while making a process of doing these tasks seamlessly.

23

HOUSECLEANING IN SMS

CHAPTER 24

Optimizing SMS Performance

Imagine an application that enables desktop management for 3 to 40,000 clients by providing inventory management, application management, troubleshooting, and diagnostics per client. An application of this magnitude would be, as you might expect, very complicated. This chapter discusses the optimization of your SMS environment as well as the SQL servers in your environments. It also discusses the Sender Manager and Performance Monitor, and how their use may help you with this task. Generally, you can break up optimizing SMS into two categories, hardware and software. Hardware and software work together to create an optimal environment. Some of the same key techniques and issues involved in optimizing a Windows NT Server are also relevant to the optimization of an SMS server.

HARDWARE CONSIDERATIONS

Hardware is the core element of a computer. At times, the applications in your environment might not be running as optimally as they should be. Often, this can be directly related to the hardware configuration. Evaluating your hardware configuration really boils down to determining how efficiently it can deliver data to different parts of the computer. Furthermore, if these parts aren't running at optimal speed, it can sometimes cause an application to run slowly or not operate at all. The primary areas to consider are memory, processor, disk I/O, and network I/O.

MEMORY

Memory is important, because it creates a temporary repository where applications and services reside while running. SMS contains many services that take a large amount of memory. You can generally expect somewhere near 18MB of memory to be used while SMS is running on your primary site server. On the secondary server, you can look at somewhere near 16MB. These memory usages are at startup, and they are only considering the SMS services—not any other services or the operating system itself. Each logon server will need somewhere near 8MB of RAM. In running the SMS Administrator, you can also assume 4MB of memory to be needed. If you will be using the more complex tools of the SMS Administrator, you are looking at somewhere near 16MB of RAM.

On the site server, you generally have more active SMS services than on the secondary site server and logon server. Because of this, your primary site server generally needs to be beefed up with more memory than the other two server types. It is strongly recommended to buy servers in the environment for SMS only, and not to use them for file and print services or user and logon authentication. The minimum memory requirement for an SMS server is 24MB. If SQL Server coexists with SMS on the same server, you should allot at least 32MB of RAM for these products alone. This, of course, is a minimum requirement. The recommended amount of memory is 48MB of RAM. It is suggested that if you have over five servers in the SMS environment, you should configure the SMS primary site server with no less than 64MB of RAM in order to run at optimal speed. Although you could run with 48MB of RAM, the performance difference is noticeable, so more megabytes are suggested.

PROCESSOR

One of the key areas that is generally thought to cause degradation to an SMS server is the processor. A processor usually does not pose much of a bottleneck in most medium-sized SMS environments. Generally, disk I/O and memory are the areas that directly affect performance. However, it is recommended that you use a Pentium. The minimum requirement for a server is a 486 DX2/66. SMS takes advantage of multiprocessor machines, so if you are running in a large environment, it is generally suggested to get multiprocessor machines, SMP (Symmetric Multi-processing Machines), to run your SMS site service. SMP is a very efficient choice when you are running a SQL server on the same server as the site server.

DISK I/O

It is suggested that disk devices are at least SCSI-2 fast wide or SCSI-3. Consider fault tolerance and performance your primary goals by implementing a RAID level 5 subsystem served by a bus-mastered SCSI-2 fast wide or SCSI-3 controller. Additionally, intelligently partition your data on multiple drives by grouping related data and files on the same drive.

NETWORK I/O

Network I/O poses a great deal of concern, especially when the SMS environment is first created. The communication that takes place between the SMS site server, SQL Server, logon servers, distribution servers, and other secondary site servers can initiate a lot of traffic at initial startup. One key suggestion for eliminating problems locally is using, on the backbone where the site server and other SMS servers communicate, a 100Mbps EtherNet or some other high-speed backbone. Communication with clients is very minimal. However, when a client first logs in, generally one to two megabytes can be transferred when gathering inventory information. Thus, a network overload is possible when clients log on to an SMS logon server for the first time. This may warrant having the users log on in shifts the first day after an SMS environment is implemented. For example, one shift would come in at 8:00 a.m., another at 9:00 a.m., and the final shift at 10:00 a.m. The number of shifts and clients per shift would depend on your environment.

SOFTWARE CONSIDERATIONS

The software components that consume the most memory on an SMS server are the following: SMS Services, SMS Administrator, and operations and tasks done with the Administrator tools. You've already learned about the large amounts of memory needed for the SMS-related servers. This section covers what is actually using the memory and how you can justify that amount of memory in a site server. The SMS services and the Administrator tools encompass many operations that consume large amounts of memory. All of these services and tools can be monitored by the Windows NT Performance Monitor, which is discussed later in the section "Using NT Performance Monitor to Tune."

Note

One quick optimization scheme is simply to not allow other applications to exist on your SMS servers. In this type of environment, all SMS servers are devoted to SMS only.

SMS SERVICES

When setting up SMS on a site server, all of the services are installed on the site server. This enables SMS to operate and manage its communication with other sites. This section covers the different services and their primary operations. These services all require a certain amount of memory, which, in turn, is the reason SMS performance is partly based on having ample memory.

SMS_EXECUTIVE

The SMS_EXECUTIVE service is the core service for most of SMS's operations. Several different components are integrated into the SMS_EXECUTIVE. These components are

- ◆ Maintenance Manager
- ◆ Inventory Processor
- ◆ Site Alerter
- ◆ Reporter
- ◆ Scheduler
- ◆ Despooler
- ◆ Inventory Data Loader
- ◆ Senders
- ◆ Applications Manager

Although these components comprise the Executive, the resources involved in their individual tasks are quite different. The Inventory Data Loader will initiate transactions for storing data into the database. The Maintenance Manager is more network I/O bound, as it converses with the logon servers. If using an RAS sender, you are going to need the RAS Communication service. If you are using the SNA sender, you are going to need an SNA server on the site server. These options will take additional amounts of resources. Two components that are going to be key to software distribution, and therefore communicating with the distribution servers, are the Despooler and Scheduler. These components are going to cause a lot of processor-intensive operations and additional disk I/O. Because the Scheduler and Despooler are extremely resource-intensive, it is generally good to move these services onto another server. This topic is covered later in the section "Adjusting Your Design."

Hierarchy Manager

The Hierarchy Manager's main job is to manage different site configurations. If you go into the properties of a site and make proposed changes to the site configuration, you will initiate the Hierarchy Manager. The Hierarchy Manager will then create what is called a *control* file. When it creates this control file, it sends it to the site for implementation. The Hierarchy Manager's other task is monitoring the SMS database. In doing this, it sometimes initiates transactions against the SMS database. Overall, the Hierarchy Manager does not require a great amount of resources. You should assume some level of disk and network I/O, but most of the Hierarchy Manager's tasks are relatively small, so the impact on system resources is minimal.

Site Configuration Manager

Once the Hierarchy Manager has created a control file, the Site Configuration Manager uses this control file to propagate the changes. Because the Site Configuration Manager is going to propagate changes, it is important to assume that a substantial amount of disk I/O will be required for local site server changes. Additionally, any remote site server changes will involve substantial network I/O because the Site Configuration Manager also deals with secondary sites. Much of what the Site Configuration Manager does can be further controlled by setting an interval. This interval is the time that it takes to actually propagate the change, and you can adjust this. The site control file that is picked up by the Site Configuration Manager exists in the SMS/Site.SRV/Sitecfg.box. You can expect the Site Configuration Manager to require both disk I/O and network I/O in executing its tasks. As it also operates as a site monitoring tool to monitor other site configurations, network I/O may be more of a consideration for SMS optimization.

Package Command Manager

The Package Command Manager is a service that runs on all Windows NT servers that are installed in the SMS site. Its main job is to handle the unattended execution of packages from the distribution servers. It constantly polls for new packages at a configurable interval. It involves some amount of I/O with the distribution server and use of the processor on the end user's PC.

Inventory Agent

The Inventory Agent handles the inventory of the servers in the SMS environment. The Inventory Agent activates every 24 hours and looks at the hardware and software inventories of all of the servers in the environment. Because it is a 24-hour interval, you can adjust this so that it is done at night, or when no operations are taking place in the environment. This is a very manageable service.

SMS Administrator Tool

The SMS Administrator takes somewhere near 4MB of RAM, and this is just "vanilla" SMS Administrator. Many operations, depending on the number of machines, will cause SMS Administrator to use an additional—often substantial—amount of RAM. You may wish to give some thought as to whether you want to run the SMS Administrator on another Windows NT computer instead of your site server. The SMS Administrator typically takes about 40MB of disk space when installed on a machine.

When running the SMS Administrator, it will be communicating with your SQL server. When opening the Sites window, you are initiating what is called a *background query*. This query will return a minimum of 726 bytes per site machine. So, opening up your Sites window to look at all of your machines takes 726 bytes of memory for each machine shown. Additional queries could easily double the amount of memory needed. It is important to understand the memory, network, and disk I/O requirements for the SMS Administrator tool. It is generally suggested to run the SMS Administrator tool on a server or machine other than the site server itself, usually on an administrator's work desk with a large amount of memory. This allows you to maximize the amount of memory that the site server can use for the other services discussed earlier. This scenario also allows the SMS Administrator to run optimally on the administrator's workstation or wherever the administrator chooses to install it.

CLIENTS

Up to this point, much thought has been given to server optimization, but there are equal considerations from the clients as well. Some SMS operations require use of client resources. For example, when a client first logs on to the domain of the site server, it immediately copies one to two megabytes from the logon server upon execution of the SMSLS login script. This operation, as discussed earlier, can directly affect network performance and should be implemented in a controlled fashion. Generally, a client will need to store 3MB of information locally (on disk) to be able to operate as an SMS client.

You should run DEFRAG and SCANDISK on your clients before deploying SMS to your workstations. After SMS is installed, it will be easy to automate these processes and to automate other diagnostic tools and virus scans. As with any install, be prepared to properly test—in your lab—all client configurations prior to SMS deployment.

SQL SERVER OPTIMIZATION

A SQL Server database is used to store all of the SMS information. SQL Servers have always been known to carry large amounts of data in their databases. Because of this, it is generally a good rule to make sure that the SQL Server has been provided the proper amount of resources. Several questions arise when considering the amount of resources needed on a SQL Server. These include whether the SQL Server will share the same computer as the SMS site server, how large is the SMS database, what is the network I/O requirement between the SQL Server and the SMS server, and do any other databases exist on the SQL Server that maintains the SMS database. The answers to these questions can give you enough information to determine the amount of resources needed. Because SQL Server optimization involves all computer resources, there are several guidelines that will be described in this section. These guidelines will be presented as two different categories: hardware requirements and software configuration.

HARDWARE REQUIREMENTS

SQL Server's hardware requirements are generally associated with the size of the database. The expected size of a database will influence the determination of storage space, memory, disk I/O, and network I/O requirements. Establishing a global hardware requirement minimum does not translate well, as the hardware requirements vary, depending on the size of the SMS database. This section looks into some of these guidelines.

Note

SQL Server can run on the same machine as the SMS site server. This, however, is not recommended. Because of the amount of resources needed to be able to run the SQL Server appropriately, it is generally good practice to install SQL Server on a separate server and let the SMS server run separately.

STORAGE SPACE CONSIDERATIONS

It is safe to say that for SQL Server, at least a one-gigabyte hard drive is needed. This, of course, would be for a minimal SMS site. On SQL Server, you create a device where the SMS database will reside. With the database, there is a corresponding transaction log. The transaction log is used to journal the transactions executed against the database. The SMS database is updated by an MIF (Management Information File). For each machine, one MIF is used to actually update the machine's database records. When a user first logs in, an MIF is loaded into the database. This takes the SQL server approximately one to two minutes. To process 500 MIFs would take half a day, somewhere near ten hours, at optimal speed. The minimum requirement for the data and log devices is around 10MB. For each machine put into the database, assume somewhere near 25KB to 35KB per machine. If you add 20,000 machines to your environment, your SQL Server would need somewhere near 700MB just to hold the data of the machines. The log device is generally 10 percent of this number, so if the data device is going to be 700MB, you need to allocate at least 70MB for the log device itself.

There is also a data and log device called Tempdb. Tempdb is used as a temporary workspace for SQL Server. When a query is executed, SQL Server will use Tempdb to store intermediate result sets. The Tempdb data device should be at least 20 percent of the SMS data device, and the Tempdb log device should be somewhere near 20 percent of the Tempdb data device itself. Therefore, in the 700MB scenario, your Tempdb data device would be 140MB and your Tempdb log device would be somewhere near 28MB.

Caution

Be aware that the size of the data device and the size of the database need to be monitored. Check the amount of the space used by the SMS database on the data device. If this number exceeds 80 percent, it would be a wise idea to expand the database. If the Tempdb device exceeds 60-percent usage, you need to expand Tempdb.

Tip

It would be a good idea to monitor Tempdb during peak hours so you will get a realistic idea of the overall usage required of Tempdb.

SQL SERVER MEMORY

SQL Server is one of the most memory-intelligent applications that runs in the Windows NT environment. The minimum requirement for a SQL Server is 16MB, although I recommend that you start with at least 32MB on a SQL Server machine. The more memory you allow SQL Server, the faster your SMS operations will go. Adding memory to SQL Server generally speeds up SMS a great deal. It is safe to say that putting the same amount of memory in your SQL Server as in your primary site server would be an appropriate amount for the SQL Server machine. For example, if your primary site server has 64MB, you can probably look at putting 64MB in your SQL Server machine. This might sound like a lot of memory, but SQL Server will use this memory and enable the SMS operations to run much faster.

As mentioned previously, another consideration is whether SQL Server is operating on the same server as the SMS primary site server. If this is the case, the primary site server is generally going to need double the amount of memory that it would need if the SQL Server was on a separate box. Therefore, if the SQL Server has 64MB and the SMS server has 64MB, and both operations are to be done on one server, that one server would need approximately 128MB of RAM. However, it is recommended to run SQL Server separately from the SMS server.

SQL SERVER DISK I/O

Many of the same considerations discussed regarding the SMS server's disk I/O can be applied to SQL Server. The only difference is that if the SMS primary site server and SQL Server are running on the same machine, it becomes important to put the SMS site server information on a separate disk from the SQL Server. You should also put NT server on a separate disk so that all drives can sequentially write and read at the same time. It is generally wise to also use separate controllers for these disks, while making sure that you use a bus-mastered controlled SCSI-2 fast wide or SCSI-3 controller.

SQL SERVER NETWORK I/O

It is important to make sure that you have substantial network bandwidth capabilities between the SMS site server and the SQL Server. This, of course, relates to the scenario where the SMS and SQL Servers are on two different machines.

> *Note*
>
> Processors have become very important to SQL Server. If you are running other databases on the SQL Server, you might consider adding a second processor. With the addition of a processor on SQL Server, you will incur a notable increase in performance.

THE SQL SERVER CONFIGURATION PARAMETERS

There are some additional configuration parameters for SQL Server that need to be configured to allow the SMS server to run at optimal speed. These parameters directly affect how well SMS server operates. The next few sections will discuss these parameters:

◆ User Connections

◆ Open Objects

◆ Memory

USER CONNECTIONS

This configuration parameter sets the maximum number of users that can simultaneously access the SQL Server. After this number is reached, no further connections will be granted to the database. Each instance of an SMS Administrator needs at least five user connections; the SMS server itself needs around 20 user connections. These 20 connections are used for services in other SMS operations. You should set the user connections at 10 connections above and beyond what SMS needs. So, a safe estimation for supporting just one instance of the SMS Administrator would be 30 to 35 user connections.

OPEN OBJECTS

This parameter determines how many views, tables, or store procedures you can have open at any time. The default setting for this is 500. It is generally advisable to set this number at 5,000 or greater for the SMS server.

SQL SERVER DEDICATED MEMORY

The memory setting determines how much total memory is allotted to SQL Server. This value is broken up into 2,048-byte units. The default value for this is 4096 (= 8MB), and needs to be increased. If you increase this number, it will allow the SQL Server to operate at a much higher performance level, although it does take this memory away from other processes and applications running on the same box.

SENDER CONFIGURATION

The sender is a component that runs under the Executive service. Its main job is to provide site-to-site communication. There are three main types of senders: LAN sender, RAS sender, and SNA sender. The RAS sender can be categorized into three different subtypes: asynchronous, ISDN, and X.25. The SNA sender can be categorized into two different subtypes: interactive and batch. Note that a RAS sender requires the use of Remote Access Service, and an SNA sender requires the SNA Server product.

The sender process is somewhat complex because it involves many different components. The first component is the Scheduler. The Scheduler prepares packages to be deployed to another site. It then stores the package, with instructions, in what is called the outbox. The outbox is basically a directory from where the Sender retrieves the package for deployment to the addressed site. The Sender is involved in site-to-site communications, and its performance is largely based on network bandwidth.

OUTBOX

The outbox is an area that is used by the Scheduler. The Scheduler processes the package and puts it into the outbox to be sent to another site. The sender then picks the package up and deploys it to another site using one of its senders. This outbox can have several configurations. One, it can be scheduled. You can schedule the outbox to operate only at certain times. Two, it can be prioritized. You can specify the job priority necessary for the outbox to accept it. You should also allow the outbox to be a backup outbox. If one of the outboxes you have set is not functional or not operating, and a job has not been sent, and if on the destination site you have addressed a backup outbox, a job can then be sent via that outbox. If you look at Figure 24.1, you will see the Outbox Schedule dialog, which allows you to schedule job specifics.

Figure 24.1.
The Outbox
Schedule dialog.

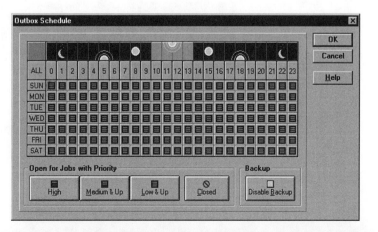

Scheduler

The Scheduler's main job is to select and monitor an appropriate sender. The Scheduler uses several criteria in determining which sender is chosen to send a job. After determining what senders are installed, it then calculates what jobs are being processed and how long those jobs will take to finish processing. It uses what is called a sender capability file (.CPB) to calculate this information. It also accounts for the outbox schedule and the priority of the job. Overall, it determines which outbox/sender will process the job fastest using these criteria methods and then monitors the sender after the job has been scheduled. The Scheduler plays an important role in site-to-site communication because it is what initiates the operation of the outbox and sender.

Sender Manager Tool

Once the outbox and Scheduler have done their job, it is now the sender's job to transfer the information to the other sites. The Sender Manager function allows you to configure the way the sender utilizes the communication link between sites. The Sender Manager is new to SMS version 1.2. It provides the ability to configure different parameters, allowing you to control the bandwidth utilization across a communication link. You can also set the number of active sender connections. Figure 24.2 shows the Sender Manager; note the configurable parameters: estimated bandwidth, concurrent sessions, maximum transfer rate, and retry counts. In SMS 1.1, these settings were configured via the Registry because there was no Sender Manager function within SMS.

Figure 24.2.
The Sender
Manager tool.

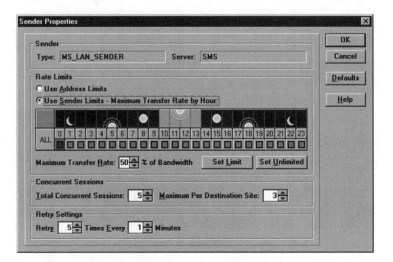

RATE LIMITS

There are two selections for rate limits when configuring the sender. You specify the transfer rate and transfer times this sender should operate within. You can set it for different times at different maximum transfer rates. The first rate limit is the address limits. The address limits give you the ability to use the default transfer rate, which is set in your Address Properties dialog for the sender properties. Because this is not a very flexible selection, I recommend that you use the sender limits. This gives you full control of the transfer rate when transferring jobs to other sites. You can configure the time and rate for the transfer, using this option. So, between the hours of 8:00 p.m. and 6:00 a.m. (when the network is free), you can set the maximum transfer rate at a higher percentage.

CONCURRENT SESSIONS

The total current sessions are the number of threads the sender can utilize on the machine in performing sender operations. If you raise this number, it gives the sender more threads and more system resources to utilize. Maximum Per Destination Site specifies the maximum concurrent sessions that the destination site can utilize.

RETRY SETTINGS

Any attempt to send a package that fails will have to be retried. Retry Settings allows you to set how many times you wish to resend the package. Leaving this number at its default is generally acceptable.

MULTIPLE SENDERS

Using multiple senders is a very wise decision. This is because multiple senders allow a certain amount of tolerance and load balancing. When using multiple senders, if one fails, you always have the others as a backup. This is a fault tolerance mechanism, and it also provides load balancing. Although only one job can be sent per sender, if you have multiple jobs, you can load balance between the senders when sending the jobs to the other site. This is an advantage if you are running site-to-site communication. I recommend setting up multiple senders using your primary link. If your primary sender is LAN-based, then a secondary (backup) link could be configured as a dial-up RAS connection using a RAS sender.

USING NT PERFORMANCE MONITOR TO TUNE

The Performance Monitor is one of the greatest gifts that Microsoft could have ever given an NT administrator. It offers a robust view of different components of the operating system, as well as other services and applications that use system resources. Much of the data that you receive from a Performance Monitor can be used for capacity planning, trend analysis, foresight of growth, and troubleshooting. The Performance Monitor becomes a key player in an SMS administrator's job. You can use the Performance Monitor to zoom in on the amount of resources that the SMS is taking from the NT Server. Using that information, you can decide on configurations that will create a more optimal environment for its SMS site server. Figure 24.3 shows the Performance Monitor chart. There are several ways to view information in the Performance Monitor. You can use charts, logs, and reports, and there are several ways of monitoring. You can monitor what are called objects and counters.

Figure 24.3.
The Performance
Monitor.

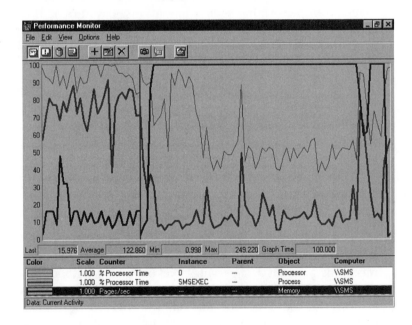

CHARTS

Charts are one way of looking at information and deciphering how different parts of the system are working. The way this view works is that you see a line being generated on the screen that varies up and down, depending on the value that is brought back from the object or counter that you are monitoring. Charts are good for looking at things immediately, to see if there is a problem. They are very convenient and easy to use. However, charts might not be a good documenting solution, because it would be very difficult to print them out and maintain them.

Reports

Reports are another view that give you the same information a chart would, but in report form. This is an excellent way of being able to provide documentation so that you can file hard copies of trend analysis. Reporting is probably one of the most unused capabilities of the Performance Monitor. It is recommended, in an SMS environment, that you monitor via reporting and log this information to track any changes in your SMS environment.

Logs

Logging entails monitoring several objects and counters over time, and then viewing that information via a chart or report. Be aware, however, that logging too much information can affect system response time.

Objects and Counters

Objects are components that you use to monitor in Performance Monitor. With each object, there are several counters or attributes. For example, the processor object has a counter of Percent Processor Usage. The processor is a part of the machine and is therefore an object that can be monitored by the Performance Monitor. There are certain key objects in SMS that should be monitored on a constant basis to allow you to pool information per the performance of your SMS site server and other servers.

The Key Areas to Monitor

There are several key areas to monitor on an SMS Site Server. All of the areas discussed in this section are available in the Performance Monitor and they deal with several objects that are NT-dependent.

Object: Thread

A thread is an object that executes instructions for the processor. Each running process gets at least one thread.

Counter: %Processor Time

When looking at this object, the first counter that shows up is `%Processor Time`, the most important counter for this object. Once this is shown, there is a box that lists the instances of the different threads that are being used by various services and operations that are running on the machine. If you scroll down this box, you will see several different SMS services. You can see several SMS threads that are part of a service. You can monitor each individual thread. The most important thread would be the Executive services thread (SMS_EXEC). Pick the SMS_EXEC thread you want, remember the number of the thread, and monitor it. Convert that decimal instance number that you have to a hexadecimal number. This will be used to go into the registry to find the registry entry for that thread. Start the Registry Editor and then go to subtree `localmachine/software/Microsoft/SMS/Components/SMS_EXECUTIVE/Threads`. Compare the hexadecimal number that you got from converting the decimal instance number to hex and there you will find the thread component responsible for the thread and `%Processor Time` counter. You can use this in conjunction with SMS Performance Monitor windows by tiling the windows horizontally or vertically and figuring out which processes are working.

Counter: `%User Time`

This shows you what threads are running in user mode, which is ring three. Ring three is the non-protected ring. It is where most applications run in non-critical operations.

Counter: `%Privilege Time`

As mentioned, ring three is where applications run, and threads running at this level cannot cause any integrity problems for the operating system. The operating system kernel and device drivers run in what is called ring zero. Ring zero is a protected ring and `%Privilege Time` monitors the threads that run in this ring. This ring is generally called OS-protected.

> *Note*
>
> Ring protection is a standard used by Intel. It allows the operating system device drivers and kernel to be protected by application failures or any other type of ring three operation. Protection mode began as an architectural implementation after the 80386 processor. Windows NT takes full advantage of ring zero versus ring three protection.

Object: `Process`

The `Process` object is the collaboration of all of the threads. When monitoring an instance of one of the processor objects under a specific counter such as `%Processor Time`, you will see a collaboration of all of the threads you saw under the thread object.

The same counters that apply to the thread apply to the process; it is just a collaboration of all of the threads instead of looking at each thread individually.

OBJECT: Processor

The Processor is one of the key components in the machine. As discussed earlier, a processor generally does not cause a bottleneck in SMS environments, but you do need a means to be able to monitor the processor. If you monitor the processor, you can also get information about other things such as disk I/O, network I/O, and memory. Sometimes your processor readings do not come out correctly and you think that it is time to upgrade the processor. This is not always true. Sometimes a bottleneck in memory disk I/O or network I/O can cause the processor to perform badly.

COUNTER: %Processor Time

This counter gives you the elapsed time that the processor has been busy. It is expressed as a percentage. This is one of the most important counters. As you look into this counter, you need to follow the amount of processor time that is utilized. This number needs to stay below 80 percent. If it stays consistently above 80 percent, you either have a problem with memory disk I/O or network I/O or it might be time to upgrade your processor. This counter is going to take all operation services and applications into consideration when monitoring, so not only will it monitor what happens with SMS, but also the NT operating system and whatever functions and services you put on this server.

Note

> Processor spikes are very common. Sometimes you will see percent processor time at 100 percent, but only for a short period of time. This is called a processor spike, and it does not need to be considered when you analyze or monitor any information about a possible bottleneck. As long as the processor doesn't run above 80 percent on a consistent level, you are safe.

OBJECT: Memory

You learned earlier how SMS utilizes memory and how it is very intensive on memory. Because of this, it is important to be able to monitor memory and make sure that you have the appropriate amount of memory service on your SMS site server. The memory object allows this to happen. It is an object that includes both real and virtual memory. When memory is used, it is broken up into what are called pages. These

24

pages can be drawn from either real memory or virtual memory that is stored on disk. The following are some counters to monitor when monitoring memory on an SMS server:

◆ Counter: Pages/Sec

◆ Counter: Pages Input/Sec

COUNTER: Pages/Sec

This counter is the sum of pages that are read and written from disk. This includes the sum of both pages input/sec and pages output/sec. If this number seems to be increasing, you are suffering from excessive paging, which means you need to add memory in the computer.

COUNTER: Pages Input/Sec

This counter registers the number of pages that are read from disk. These pages cannot have been referenced by real memory. If this number seems to increase, you are suffering from excessive paging and would need to add more memory.

Note

Intel and MIPS processors generally use 4KB pages (4096 bytes). The DEC Alpha AXP uses 8KB (8192 bytes) pages.

ADJUSTING YOUR DESIGN

As you bring up your SMS site the first time, you will notice, over a period of time, that you are going to have to do certain things to make your SMS site run in a more optimal fashion. By offloading some of the tasks that SMS has to do on the site server, several things can be done to allow SMS to operate in a much better fashion. These include using a helper server, or several other recommendations that I will detail in the "Recommendations" section.

HELPER SERVER

A helper server is a server that can take over some of the SMS site server tasks. The minimum requirement for this operation to happen is, at least, a Windows NT 3.51 domain controller, which takes over some of these services. As seen in Figure 24.4, this is how you actually allow helper server operations to be moved to other servers. The services that can be offloaded are the Scheduler, Inventory Data Loader, Inventory Processor, and the Despooler. When moving these operations to a helper server, the entire SMS executive services move over. Only certain processes can be moved over. Here are some suggestions when moving things to the helper server:

◆ If you are thinking about running multiple senders, put the senders on a helper server.

◆ If the site server is processing MIF files and seems to be busy, possibly move the Inventory Data Loader to the helper server.

◆ If you feel the site server is busy accessing the SQL Server, move the Inventory Data Loader and Scheduler to a helper server.

Figure 24.4.
The Services
dialog under the
site properties.

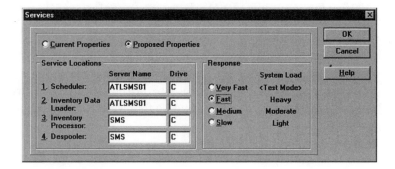

RECOMMENDATIONS

The following are some general suggestions for performance management for Systems Management Server:

◆ Constantly check network traffic to determine if an SMS site needs to be broken up into multiple sites.

◆ If the SMS site server looks as if it is being impacted by SQL Server and the other SMS services operations, consider moving those services to a helper server.

◆ Constantly look at the event logs and find and fix problems as they occur. Be proactive!

◆ Schedule jobs at off hours, generally at night when users are not on the system.

◆ Do not send mandatory installs to all workstations at the same time; schedule them at different times.

◆ Do not enlarge environments with a large number of user groups, forcing user group MIFs to be constantly generated. You can use the set global user groups program (SMSGUG.EXE) to change the user group MIF interval.

◆ Consider exactly what you are going to log—try not to log everything. Log only the most important operations you need information for.

◆ Do not use too many alerts, especially if they involve very complex queries.

◆ Beware of the files which are inventoried. If you select too many files, you could cause a large amount of disk space to be copied through the SMS site server.

SUMMARY

Performance tuning of SMS is a very complex task because it involves several different areas. Additionally, these areas span hardware and software. Understand that without optimizing your SMS environment, you could cause some serious and detrimental problems for yourself. Be sure to use all the tools available to manage your SMS environment. It is important to log pertinent information and keep a historical analysis of your SMS site. Although no SMS site is perfect, there are important guidelines that should be followed in the management of SMS.

SMS Reference

There have been many companies involved in the success of SMS as a desktop management platform. The ability to easily snap in a third-party extension to SMS has also drawn a lot of attention to third-party companies. The complexity of the SMS architecture has also drawn the attention of several Microsoft Solution providers for consulting services. Some of the consultants, participating vendors, Web sites, and newsgroups for useful information are as follows:

Microsoft Supplemental Order Center
(800) 360-7561
SMS Installation and Configuration
SMS Administrator's Guide
SMS Concepts and Planning
Microsoft BackOffice Resource Kit
Systems Management Server Software Developer's Kit (SDK)

Stream International, Inc.
(703) 522-0820 x343
1700 North Moore Street, Suite 1705
Arlington, VA 22209-1904
URL: www.stream.com
Consulting/integration services, product sales

Computing Edge
(206) 844-6435
(800) 844-7184
13125 Odell Road
Duvall, WA 98019
URL: www.computingedge.com
Proxy domain services
Asset management and NetWare integration

ASI Corporation
6 Antares Drive
Ottawa, ON K2E8A9
URL: www.assetpro.ca
AssetPRO
Asset management

Netlabs
(415) 961-9500
(415) 961-9300 (fax)
4920 El Camino Real
Los Altos, CA 94022
Asset Manager

Anderson Consulting
5901 Tilbury Road
Alexandria, VA 22310
(703) 901-7046
Consulting services

Janus Technologies
Robinson Plaza Three, Suite 210
Pittsburgh, PA 15205-1018
(412) 787-3030
Argis
Asset management

Tally Systems
PO Box 70
Hanover, NH 03755-0070
(603) 643-1300
URL: www.tallysys.com/products/smspromo.htm
NetCensus, Cenergy, Centameter
Metering, software inventory, asset management

Desktop Management Task Force
(503) 696-9300
JF2-51
2111 Northeast 25th Street
Hillsboro, OR 97124
DMI specifications

Express Systems
(206) 728-8300 x414
(206) 728-8301 (fax)
2101 Fourth Avenue, Suite 303
Seattle, WA 98121-2314
URL: www.express-systems.com
Express Meter
Metering products

BateTech Software
(303) 763-8333
(303) 985-0624 (fax)
7500 W. Yale Avenue, B100
Denver, CO 80277
Customer One
Help desk management software

Vycor
(800) 888-9267
(301) 220-0727 (fax)
5411 Berwyn Rd.
College Park, MD 20740
DP Umbrella
Help desk management

Apsylog
(415) 812-7700
(415) 812-7707 (fax)
1900 Embarcadero Rd.
Palo Alto, CA 94303
PC Galaxy
Help desk management

Seagate (formerly OnDemand Software)
1100 Fifth Ave. S., Suite 208
Naples, FL 33940-6407
WinInstall
Software distribution and scripting
URL: www.ondemand.com

Network Managers, Inc.
73 Princeton Street, Suite 305
North Chelmsford, MA 01863
NMC 4000
Network management

BackOffice Magazine
URL: www.1fw.com

Microsoft SMS 1.2
URL: www.microsoft.com/smsmgmt

Microsoft SMS Resource Kit
URL: www.microsoft.com/smsmgmt/reskit.htm

Microsoft Knowledge Base
URL: www.microsoft.com/kb

APPENDIX B

Managing the Enterprise

Although this book is devoted to Microsoft Systems Management Server (SMS), the current release of SMS provides only a subset of the tools necessary for managing the entire enterprise. The basic hierarchy of enterprise management includes not only systems management (where SMS fits very well), but also the additional disciplines of network and applications management. SMS does offer some functionality for performing rudimentary network protocol monitoring and analysis, but it was not designed for managing the various network elements, such as hubs and routers. Likewise, SMS can now capture and forward SNMP traps, but it doesn't currently offer any built-in functionality to handle these traps itself. Therefore, SMS is generally used in conjunction with other network management tools such as HP-OpenView or CA-Unicenter.

This appendix is intended to provide a look at the bigger picture of enterprise management as a whole. I define the discipline of enterprise management and describe the base requirements for managing a distributed computing environment. Although not intended to be all-inclusive, some general guidelines are offered for implementing a full enterprise management strategy.

These guidelines are then followed with a brief description of how you can use the basic management features of SMS in an enterprise management context. Also, I provide a quick scan of some emerging trends in the enterprise management arena, along with a brief discussion of the new Microsoft Management Console (MMC).

ENTERPRISE MANAGEMENT STRATEGY

Managing the enterprise is the necessary discipline of ensuring the security and reliability of the network communications fabric, the systems connected to that network, and the critical applications running on those systems. It is more important than ever to implement the right set of tools and methodologies to successfully manage these interdependent layers in a distributed systems environment. Figure B.1 illustrates the relationship between network, systems, and application management. Each management layer is shown as being dependent on the strong foundation of the layers below it.

The network foundation is generally the most critical layer in terms of enterprise management, because all the systems and applications are dependent on the underlying communications fabric. If a failure occurs in the network, all the dependent systems and applications are affected. The systems that are connected to the network are, in turn, the supporting layer for business applications. If a particular server crashes, all applications and users dependent on that system are unable to continue working. Likewise, an entire organization can also be significantly impacted if a particular mission-critical application fails.

*Figure B.1.
Typical enterprise
management
layers.*

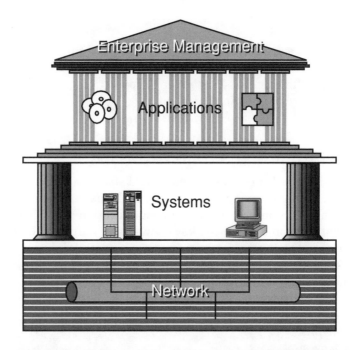

Note

High availability has become the latest battle cry among corporate CIOs in their attempt to reduce financial losses attributed to network and system down time. However, just throwing more money at bigger and better hardware is not the answer. A complete enterprise management strategy that encompasses the full hierarchy of network, systems, and applications management is required to provide real end-to-end service assurance.

To maintain a healthy distributed computing environment, you must develop a well thought-out strategy that addresses network, systems, and application management. You must implement the right management tools and practices to provide remote diagnostics, automatic statistics and trending, and event alerts that are generated when any component needs attention. Enterprise management is simply a disciplined methodology that provides controls and preventative measures to reduce cost and proactively prevent troubles before a major failure occurs. Of course, the extent to which a corporation chooses to implement a full-blown enterprise management strategy depends largely on available resources and the opportunity cost associated with investing in such a strategy.

Management Components

A full-fledged enterprise management strategy includes specific criteria to address each of the following components: fault management, operational management, performance management, and configuration management. These four management components are the key elements in reducing the total cost of ownership in today's distributed computing environment. As shown in Figure B.2, these four components permeate all three layers of the enterprise management hierarchy (network, systems, and applications).

Figure B.2.
Enterprise
management
components.

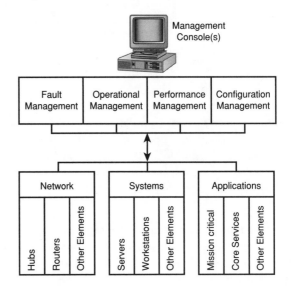

The following lists outline the basic functionality required within each of the four management components:

Fault Management

Problem/event management (fault detection)

Automatic event and alarm notification

Remote diagnostics

Operational Management

Remote administration

Reporting and scheduling

Routine backup and maintenance

Performance Management

Performance monitoring

Tracking specific thresholds

Configuration Management

Automated software distribution and upgrades

Maintaining consistent operating system patches on all systems

Software and hardware inventory

Monitoring and control of software licensing

MANAGEMENT TOOLS

Several competing tools on the market today provide varying levels of functionality for managing these components. (See Table B.1.) Some tools are designed to address a particular segment of the problem space (for example, Microsoft Systems Management Server concentrates primarily within the systems management layer). Other tools attempt to be all-inclusive by bundling everything into one platform. Most of the one-size-fits-all management tools fall short of their promises. These mega-management tools are often less efficient in some categories than the best-of-breed type tools that are focused on managing the elements within a certain management layer. However, as technology advances, there is hope that a single-tool, single-platform solution is not far off. (See the sections "Emerging Technologies" and "Microsoft Management Console (MMC)," later in this appendix.)

TABLE B.1. MAJOR SYSTEM MANAGEMENT PRODUCTS.

Tool Vendor	Product
Microsoft	Systems Management Server (SMS)
Hewlett-Packard	OpenView
Computer Associates	CA-Unicenter
IBM	NetView
Tivoli	TME 10
Boole & Babbage	Enterprise Automation Suite
Open Vision	AXXiON family of products

B

MANAGING THE ENTERPRISE

Several of the products listed in Table B.1 do in fact interoperate. For instance, SMS integrates with some of the higher-end enterprise management tools (such as HP-OpenView, CA-Unicenter, and NetView). Microsoft has also worked with a number of other vendors to provide hooks for SMS so that third-party products could extend its functionality. The following lists some of the types of third-party add-on tools that are currently available to work with SMS.

Add-on Product Types

Asset management	Performance monitors
Backup and recovery	Report generators
Batch schedulers	Server hardware management
Billing systems	Software distribution
Enterprise management platform integration	Software license metering
Help desks	UNIX desktop management
NetWare server administration	UNIX server administration
NetWare and UNIX primary site SMS server proxies	UPS monitoring
Network automation	Virus checkers
Network management systems	Windows 95 Registry management

The following lists some of the Independent Software Vendors (ISVs) currently marketing products that integrate with SMS.

Vendors

ABC Systems & Development	Great Plains Dynamics
Accent Technologies	Hewlett-Packard
American Power Conversion	Infonet
Apsylog	Intel Corporation
Arcada Software	Janus Technologies
Argent Software	Legent
ASI Corporation	McAfee
AT&T GIS	Micro Design Specialists
BateTech Software	NEC Corp
Cabletron Systems, Inc.	NetSoft

Vendors

Candle	OnDemand
Cheyenne	OpenVision
Comma Soft	Querisoft
Compaq Computer Corp.	Saber Software Corporation
Computer Associates (CA)	Siemens Nixdorf
Computing Edge	Software Spectrum
Cornerstore	Stirling Software
Corporate Software, Inc.	Tally Systems
Creative Interactions, Inc.	Tivoli Systems, Inc.
Crystal Services	Tripp Lite
DCA	VisiSoft
Digital Equipment Corporation	Vycor
Express Systems	Wave Research
Frye Computer	Workgroup Systems
Fujitsu	XNet Technology

SECURITY POLICIES

An enterprise management strategy is not complete without a meticulous information security policy. A corporate security policy should provide sufficient protection to secure all information assets from risk associated with tampering or unauthorized access. You should provide security controls in the following basic areas:

- Authentication: Who are you? (proof of identity)
- Authorization: What systems or data are you authorized to access? (explicit permission)
- Data protection: Is the data legitimate and secure? (integrity and confidentiality)
- Non-repudiation: Is access to the data undeniably tracked by individual user account? (non-disputable acknowledgment)
- Audit trail: Is a record maintained to trace who did what and when? (activity log)

You should implement standard security policies for all user accounts in an organization. You can then establish an account template that automatically sets the default properties required whenever a new user account is created. Figure B.3 shows the parameters set in a typical account policy.

Figure B.3.
Account policy
parameters set
within NT User
Manager.

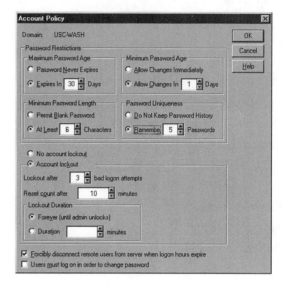

Figure B.4 illustrates the panel used to set individual user properties on a user account within NT User Manager. This utility defines individual security parameters such as group membership, user profiles, logon hours, server access, and dial-in privileges.

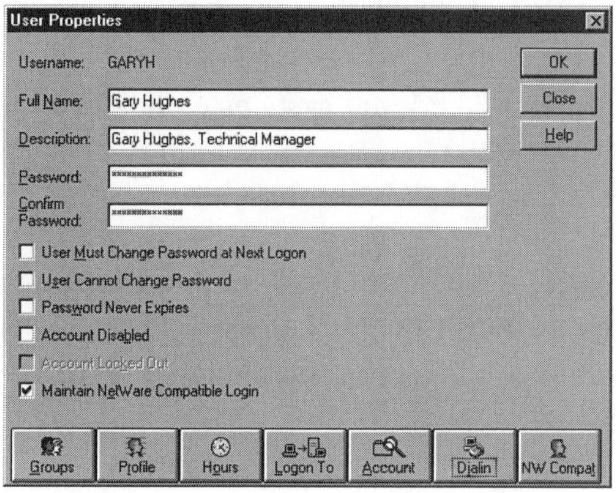

Figure B.4.
User Properties
window in NT
User Manager.

There are six minimum requirements for securing the network communications fabric itself:

◆ All network elements should be physically secured.

◆ All remote access to network elements for management purposes should be authenticated and authorized.

◆ Dial-in and dial-out access must be authenticated.

◆ The network management tool should be highly secure.

◆ The network elements should be sufficiently intelligent to protect themselves from denial of service attacks (intrusion detection).

◆ Link level encryption should be provided on every hop between all the network routers.

You should implement proper monitoring of the systems to audit security-related activities to ensure compliance with the stated security policies. (See Figure B.5.) Additionally, I recommend that you implement NTFS file access permission on all NT servers to more adequately protect the data stored on those machines.

Figure B.5.
Setting up an
audit policy
in NT User
Manager.

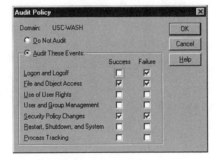

DISASTER RECOVERY PLANS

Every business should regularly evaluate its disaster recovery plan to assess its effectiveness within the context of the current environment and emerging technologies. A disaster recovery plan should identify the redundancy and fault-tolerance provisions within the systems and networks that will protect against most disruptions. The plan should also detail a complete, tested process for restoring the systems or data in the event of a complete server or site failure.

Testing the capability to quickly recover from a failure is just as important as testing all the backup procedures and other preventative measures. Unfortunately, too many organizations fail to give the recovery piece the attention it deserves. Failure recovery within a distributed computing environment is usually part of a hardware recovery strategy. The software restoration piece, including restoring application programs and data, requires a robust backup and restore program.

Tip

It is better to implement NTFS file permissions on critical directories and data; the associated security information is then backed up along with the files. On the other hand, share-level permissions are not stored with the files themselves, and you might have to recreate the security context if you ever have to recover the data from the backup media.

A good disaster recovery plan should also include provisions for storing backup tapes in a fireproof safe or at an off-premise site. You must also keep a log of backup operations to validate that a successful backup has occurred as scheduled.

On a yearly basis, the backups should be restored to a blank machine in order to verify the capability to completely recover both operation and data. You should perform the first such test very shortly after installing a new machine.

In addition to the built-in backup utility in NT (see Figure B.6), there are several good third-party backup utilities now available for NT-based systems. The exact product you choose will depend on how well the backup utility satisfies your requirements for features, functionality, scaleability, and price.

Figure B.6.
The NT Backup
utility.

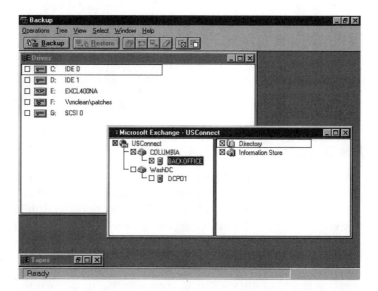

Warning

Don't wait until a disaster occurs to test your restore process!

Clearly identify application data, source code, and other elements critical to the business. The disaster recovery plan should include protections for all mission-critical information assets. You should implement a rigorous change control process to ensure that any additions or modifications to the environment comply with established guidelines. The change control process should cover both hardware and software installations and upgrades. All changes should also be audited and logged.

Training

When developing an enterprise management strategy, be sure to include training for the support personnel who will implement the strategy, particularly if you use SMS.

Because the core components of SMS run on the Windows NT Server operating system and SMS uses the SQL Server database environment as its data repository, be sure to get the proper training on these products as well. Table B.2 lists the minimum recommended training for implementing SMS.

TABLE B.2. RECOMMENDED MICROSOFT TRAINING.

Microsoft Course Title	Duration
Support Fundamentals for Microsoft Windows NT Workstation	Five days
Support Fundamentals for Microsoft Windows NT Server	Five days
Supporting Microsoft Systems Management Server	Five days
System Administration for Microsoft SQL Server	Five days

Network Management

Network management procedures monitor and maintain the health and welfare of the enterprise network communications fabric. As described earlier, the network layer is the foundation on which all the distributed systems in an organization depend. A failure within the network layer can put whole business units out of commission for hours, a very costly proposition. As part of an overall enterprise management strategy, you must give proper attention to network management, in order to minimize any network down time.

Network Discovery

Using the appropriate tools (for example, HP OpenView or CA-Unicenter), you can automatically discover and map network devices to provide the most up-to-date view of both the physical and logical networks.

PERFORMANCE MONITORING

Network management tools can also track performance. The tools can monitor specific operating criteria so they can generate an early warning when these measures exceed defined thresholds. You can also use the performance monitoring tools for trouble analysis.

FAULT DETECTION

Tools are also available to graphically display any faults detected within the network. Most of these tools can automatically trigger alerts or other events, and some tools can even generate automatic trouble tickets.

REMOTE CONFIGURATION

Network management tools should also allow remote configuration on network devices. Most of the tools available in this category can at least browse network components for information to produce reports and inventories. However, with the more sophisticated network management tools, you can also remotely reconfigure most network devices as needed, without dispatching a network engineer to visit the physical device.

SYSTEMS MANAGEMENT

The following sections present some general guidelines for implementing a systems management scheme. The items listed in these sections address some areas that deserve consideration but are often overlooked. Again, these guidelines are not meant to be all-inclusive but simply provide a framework to get started with developing an overall enterprise management strategy.

SOFTWARE RELEASE PROCEDURES

Any good software quality program includes provisions for change management. However, the actual software release and distribution procedures are not always given the attention they deserve. With the introduction of rapid application development (RAD) techniques and the trend toward more frequent software updates, the release and distribution procedures are now more important than ever. The following items listed should be considered when developing a sound and effective software release procedure:

◆ Review current release procedures to ensure that no unauthorized distributions can be initiated without going through the established process.

◆ Implement a strict procedure for moving all software releases through a rigorous testing and quality assurance cycle before anything is moved into a production environment.

◆ Inform and train the user community well in advance of the intended release to prevent any unnecessary disruptions to critical business routines.

◆ In distributed environments, check directory replication settings to ensure software builds and patches are synchronized at each application server.

◆ Document all aspects of the software release procedure. When using SMS as the software distribution tool, be sure to document the details of creating packages and package distribution jobs. The complete procedural flow, including everything from receiving a software update for distribution, to the development team, to actually sending the distribution package out to the clients, should be documented as part of an overall software quality assurance program.

Tip

In distributed computing environments, make sure that all software releases are tested on a clean machine (one that is not used for development but is configured as a typical end-user desktop) to ensure that all required DLLs and so on are properly packaged with the release. Also, test thoroughly to make sure that a new software release does not adversely overwrite a shared DLL used by another application.

After the software release has passed the clean machine test, it is also prudent to test the software distribution process itself. Create a software distribution package in SMS and run a job that sends the new release to another clean machine on a different network segment. After sending the package, have someone test the software thoroughly again on the other end to make sure everything still works correctly before the final release to the end users.

Although taking these steps might seem like overkill, you will save yourself a lot of trouble in the long run. You will also buy yourself a lot more client appreciation by taking these extra steps to minimize any disruptions.

COMPUTER ACCESS PROCEDURES

Security and system access procedures are critical components of an overall enterprise management strategy. The following items are suggested as additional considerations when developing standard corporate computer access procedures:

- Evaluate upgrading current desktops to a 32-bit platform (either Window 95 or Windows NT Workstation, as appropriate). These systems help enable a single login strategy in mixed environments.
- Revise or create new forms for requesting and granting user access. Place the responsibility for establishing login IDs and user accounts with a central security group.
- Consider implementing server-based user profiles to lock down the desktop environment and prevent inadvertent tampering with system files.

Note

Security is always weakened when there are multiple login IDs and user accounts required for the same individual to access different systems. Many users resort to posting their list of login IDs and passwords somewhere on their desks, because it becomes a burden for them to remember them all. Furthermore, having multiple user accounts stored in multiple systems makes security administration much more complicated and costly. Also, security can be compromised when there is a delay between the time an employee leaves a company and when all their multiple user accounts are revoked. Take steps to develop and implement a single-login strategy.

Backup Procedures

Good, reliable file backups are your safety net in case of system failures. Be sure to consider the following items when developing your backup procedures:

- Implement a central backup process that ensures that all system files are properly backed up.
- Implement additional SQL Server or other DBMS backup procedures, as required.
- Establish backup and restore policies, tape retention guidelines, and set up an audit to ensure the backups are performed.

Systems Monitoring Procedures

Continual monitoring of the systems in your network will provide early warning whenever a particular system's health begins to decline. Your system's monitoring procedures should include the following basic items:

◆ To protect equipment from surges, spikes, noise, and power fluctuations, provide Uninterruptible Power Supplies (UPSs) for all systems not currently protected.

◆ Establish a centralized management console so that all critical systems can be administered remotely.

◆ Set up alerts and monitor performance in order to receive early warning before a major failure occurs.

You can watch specific system counters with Performance Monitor in order to generate an alert if a certain threshold is exceeded. Figure B.7 illustrates the window for setting alert options in NT's Performance Monitor.

Figure B.7.
Setting alert
options with
Performance
Monitor.

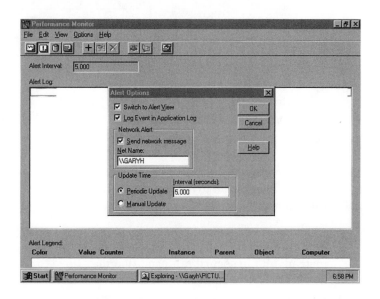

The NT Event Viewer (shown in Figure B.8) is also useful for keeping a record of when and if certain events occurred.

Figure B.8.
The NT Event
Viewer.

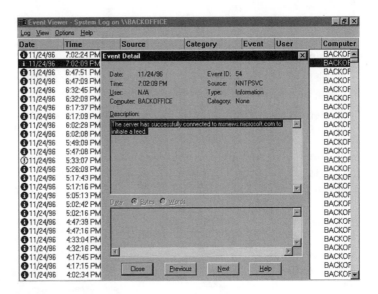

NT SERVER DIRECTORY STRUCTURE RECOMMENDATIONS

File storage on an NT server requires some special considerations for optimal performance. In addition to normal server hard drive management techniques, the following items should also be considered:

◆ Implement NTFS security to ensure security context is saved with the files (and therefore backed-up with the files). If you rely on share-level security instead, all file security information may have to be recreated if the files have to be restored from backup.

◆ Increase the system partition to 500MB or more to allow room for growth for future NT versions.

◆ Increase the swap file space to twice the memory to allow room for a system dump if ever necessary.

◆ Move the print spool to another physical drive separate from the system, to prevent I/O contention for the drive spindles.

◆ Avoid using NT server software-based RAID implementations. Hardware-based RAID solutions, although more expensive, are much safer and better suited to an enterprise environment.

MANAGING WITH SMS

SMS provides the basic tools needed to manage the systems (server, workstations, and so on) within a distributed systems environment. SMS is tightly integrated with NT, but you can also use it to manage NetWare and (with add-on products) UNIX platforms. The basic features of SMS are

◆ Asset inventory (both hardware and software)

◆ Software distribution

◆ Help desk support and remote control

◆ Network protocol analysis

◆ Integration with other network management tools

Note

Microsoft System Management Server is a robust but complex tool. Implementing SMS in an enterprise of any magnitude requires careful and thorough planning. At a minimum, your implementation plans should address where to install the central SMS site, where to install other primary and secondary sites, specific database storage requirements, additional server and network loads, user group/organization structure, and how SMS will be integrated into your overall enterprise management strategy. Refer to the earlier chapters of this book for more planning considerations and an in-depth explanation of all the features and functionality of SMS.

B

MANAGING THE ENTERPRISE

ADMINISTRATION

Microsoft's System Management Server was designed to help ease the burden of administering large, geographically distributed computing environments. The primary function of SMS is to make it possible to remotely manage the servers and desktop machines connected to the corporate network, without resorting to physically visiting the machine each time it needs attention. This dramatically cuts the total cost of ownership on these systems, which is conservatively estimated to be approximately $1280 annually. (See Figure B.9.)

The SMS Administrator tool allows you to remotely manage and monitor the systems in your environment. In addition to performing functions inherent to the features of SMS itself (asset inventory, software distribution, remote control, and network protocol analysis), the SMS Administrator tool also allows you to remotely operate the normal Windows NT Administration tools. Figure B.10 illustrates the view within the SMS Administrator that provides this functionality.

Figure B.9.
Desktop systems
total cost of
ownership.

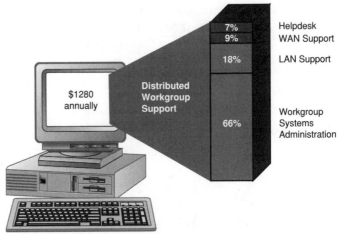

Figure B.10.
SMS Administra-
tor for Windows
NT administra-
tion.

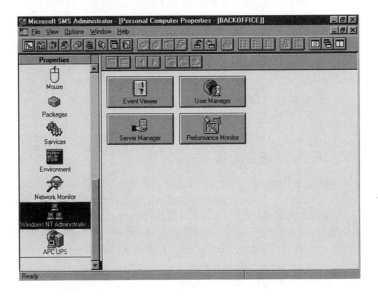

The SMS Administrator also allows you to perform administrative tasks for a particular primary site and all the subsites beneath it. Figure B.11 illustrates the basic concept of an SMS site hierarchy. Logging in as the SMS Administrator at a central SMS site allows you to administer every system in the hierarchy.

Figure B.11.
SMS site
hierarchy.

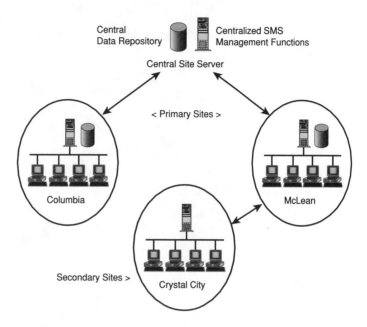

Within an SMS site, you can use the SMS Administrator tool to view and manage all the software and hardware assets defined to SMS. Figures B.12 and B.13 show the Sites window within the SMS Administrator and provide examples of the type of information available about each managed system.

Figure B.12.
System network
properties within
a Sites window.

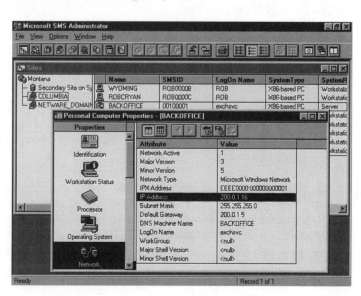

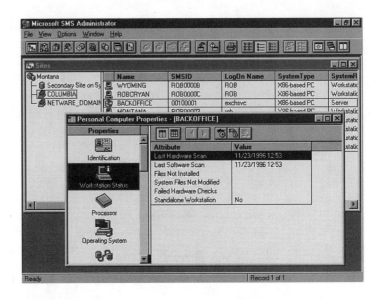

Figure B.13.
Workstation
status properties
within a Sites
window.

As illustrated in Figures B.12 and B.13, simply double-clicking any machine name listed in the SMS Sites window allows you to view all the properties associated with that particular server or workstation. The information that is collected and stored in SMS about each managed system allows the administrator to accurately plan for machine and software upgrades. Having this information handy is also tremendously helpful when trying to diagnose a problem.

MONITORING

The NT Performance Monitor, which can be executed from the SMS Administrator (refer to Figure B.10), provides the capability of tracing various counters associated with each managed system. Numerous objects and counters are exposed to Performance Monitor (the number of monitoring objects available depends on the software applications that are installed).

SMS also provides a Network Monitor that you can use to watch general network traffic. It is useful for determining network utilization and for performing basic protocol analysis.

SYSTEMS

The NT Performance Monitor is illustrated in Figures B.14 and B.15. These illustrations are meant to show how easily you can establish a remote monitoring session to watch critical parameters on a specific machine.

Figure B.14.
The Add to Chart
dialog box of the
Performance
Monitor.

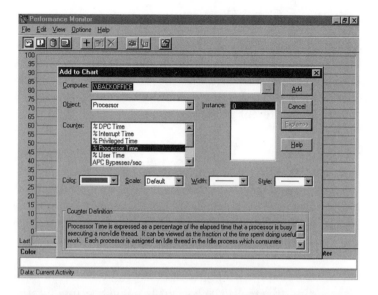

Figure B.15.
A Performance
Monitor trace.

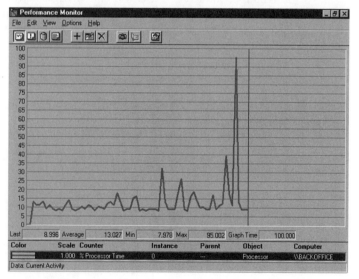

Figure B.14 presents the screen used to select a computer and the various objects and counters to monitor. In this case, %Processor Time is selected and added to the chart. As the Counter Definition indicates, %Processor Time is a percentage of the elapsed time that a processor is busy.

Figure B.15 illustrates the trace produced for the selected counter. You can also save these traces to a file for later replay and analysis.

NETWORKS

The SMS Network Monitor is an excellent tool for remotely watching network traffic associated with a particular managed system. This monitoring tool allows you to watch the transmitted frames, capture various network statistics in real time, and then play them back later for analysis. The SMS Network Monitor also supports nearly fifty different protocols.

Note

Although the SMS Network Monitor is certainly easy to use, it does require that the operator have a basic understanding of network protocols in order to effectively use the information gathered. For instance, in order to filter on specific protocol packets or effectively analyze the statistics that are captured, you need to know what you are looking at.

However, with minimal instruction, even the networking novice will find this tool to be a great troubleshooting aid. It's terrific for the help desk person who is trying to diagnose a trouble call. He or she can quickly see whether a client's machine is actually talking across the wire and make a basic determination on whether the client's problem is network- or application-related.

Figure B.16 shows the SMS Network Monitor in action and illustrates some of the statistics that are collected.

Figure B.16. The SMS Network Monitor.

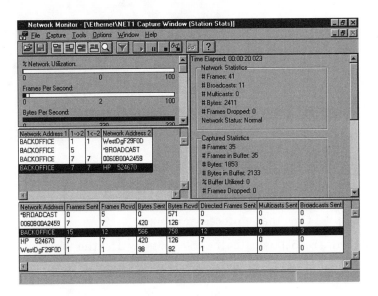

Figure B.17 shows the dialog box used in Network Monitor to enter a name for saving the network trace file.

Figure B.17.
Saving a trace
file in SMS
Network Monitor.

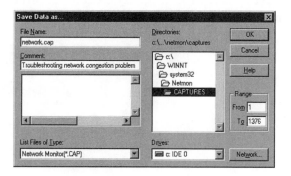

ALERTS

SMS provides the capability to generate alerts for specific events. An alert event occurs when a specified result set is returned from a query executed against the SMS database. You must first define the query and then associate it with an alert. Figures B.18 through B.23 illustrate the required sequence for establishing an alert in SMS Administrator.

Open the Queries window in SMS Administrator (see Figure B.18) and define a new query that you wish to associate with an alert. Refer to Chapter 16, "Queries," for more details on creating SMS queries.

Figure B.18.
Step 1: Create
an SMS query
in SMS Admin-
istrator.

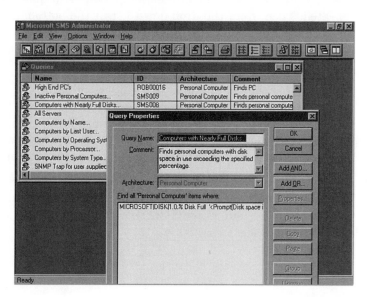

Open the Alert window in SMS Administrator (see Figure B.19) and define a new alert. Enter a name for the alert and a short description or other comment. To associate the alert with the query created earlier, choose the Query button on the bottom of the Alert Properties dialog box.

Figure B.19.
Step 2: Define a
new alert in the
Alert Properties
dialog.

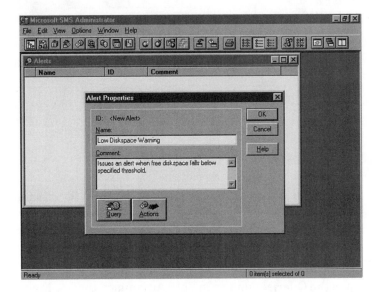

On the Alert Query dialog box (see Figure B.20), select a specific query from the drop-down list. Enter a value, in minutes, for how often the query should be automatically repeated. Then, from the drop-down list at the bottom of the dialog, choose the criteria for generating an alert based on the results of the query. Optionally, you can specify whether to limit the query to a specific SMS site. Once you have completed entering the alert information, press OK to return to the Alert Properties dialog.

After creating the query and associating it with an alert, you need to specify the action to take when the alert conditions are encountered. On the Alert Properties dialog (refer to Figure B.19), press the Actions button. This will display the Alert Actions dialog shown in Figure B.21, where you can specify any or all of the following actions: log the event, execute a particular command line, or notify a certain user or computer console.

The Alerts window within the SMS Administrator lists all alerts that have been defined for the system. Figure B.22 shows the new alert that was created following the preceding Steps 1 through 4.

Figure B.20.
Step 3: Associate
the query to the
new alert.

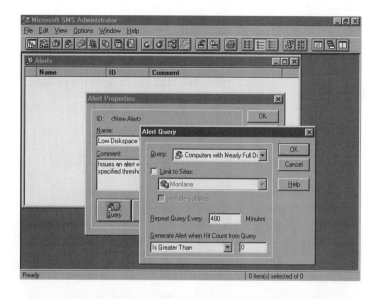

Figure B.21.
Step 4: Specify
the alert actions.

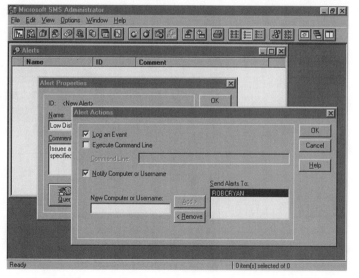

Figure B.23 shows the results returned after executing the Low Diskspace Warning query that was defined previously. The results window identifies a particular workstation that has less free diskspace than the threshold specified in the query.

Figure B.22.
Alerts dialog with
the newly defined
alert.

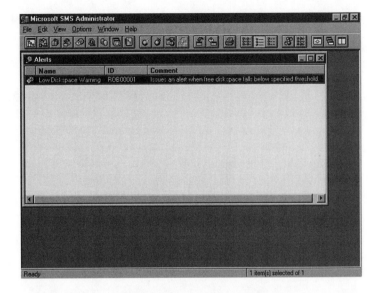

Figure B.23.
Query results
displayed after
executing the
query.

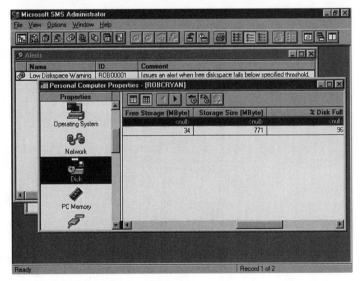

SOFTWARE DISTRIBUTION

Of course, SMS also makes it easy to electronically distribute software to the servers and desktops within an organization. Figure B.24 shows how you can manage with the SMS Administrator the various distribution packages, the jobs created to deliver them, and the various machine queries that have been defined.

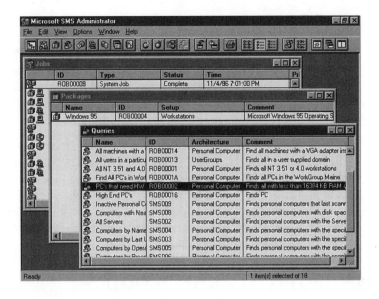

*Figure B.24.
SMS Administra-
tor showing SMS
jobs, packages,
and queries.*

APPLICATION MANAGEMENT

Application management is another discipline intended to detect and recover from application failures in a timely manner. The focus should be on providing optimum service to the end user with minimal down time. You can implement application management in varying degrees, depending on the nature of the application in question and the cost to the business if there is a failure.

APPLICATION MANAGEMENT INFORMATION BASE (MIB)

For mission-critical applications, you should develop application management facilities as an integral part of the system. The required SNMP agents and Management Information Base (MIB) should be implemented to monitor appropriate application error, performance, and security data. Any pertinent alarm information can then be forwarded to a central management console.

In large organizations where there are typically multiple mission-critical applications deployed throughout the enterprise, the process of developing custom MIBs must be coordinated carefully. Each application group should not have to reinvent the wheel over and over again to develop an appropriate application MIB. The corporation should standardize a common set of application management criteria and develop a core MIB that is suitable across the entire organization. You can then extend this core MIB as needed by the individual application groups to add additional application-specific management criteria.

SNMP AGENTS

You must load an SNMP agent locally on each machine that requires application management services. An SNMP agent acts as an interface to the application MIB and responds to requests (get, get-next, and set operations) received from the SNMP manager program. The only time that an SNMP agent initiates a conversation with the manager program is when a fault is detected in one of its managed objects.

The Windows NT–based SNMP service (which you can install along with the TCP/IP network protocol) includes an SNMP agent. The Windows NT Resource Kit also includes several SNMP-related utilities. These utilities include an MIB compiler, a utility for using Performance Monitor counters with SNMP, and an SNMP monitor utility that can log results into any ODBC database. For more information on working with SNMP agents, refer to the "NT Server 4.0 Networking Guide" available on Microsoft's October 1996 TechNet CD-ROM.

EMERGING TECHNOLOGIES

Several new developments are taking shape with regard to managing the enterprise, and Microsoft is heavily involved in all of them. Microsoft recently launched a new program called Zero Administration Initiative for Windows that is aimed at supporting the new NetPC. Microsoft has also joined with other major software companies to develop tools for the new Web-based enterprise management schema that is quickly taking shape. To round it out, Microsoft released a beta version of its new Microsoft Management Console at the 1996 Professional Developers Conference in Long Beach, California. These emerging technologies are too new to cover in much detail in this book, but they are certainly important developments and deserve a mention in a discussion on enterprise management.

Tip

Be sure to check Microsoft's new Web page that is devoted to management tools and technologies, http://www.microsoft.com/management.

ZERO ADMINISTRATION INITIATIVE FOR WINDOWS (ZAW)

Microsoft's Zero Administration Initiative for Windows was launched in support of the new NetPC, and it is designed to reduce the total cost of administering standard Windows-based systems. The major goals of ZAW are to increase the manageability of client systems and to automate such tasks as operating system updates, application installation, and desktop system lock-down. Users will be able to roam between PCs and automatically maintain their personal desktop look and feel. The Zero

Administration initiative will also enable application software developers to more easily develop and deploy applications. There is a bit of crossover in this area with SMS, but Microsoft maintains that it is not intended to replace SMS but extend it.

The following are specific features of the Zero Administration Initiative for Windows:

◆ The operating system will update itself when the computer is booted, without user intervention. The latest code and drivers will be automatically pulled from a local server, the corporate intranet, or the Internet, if available. The Automatic Desktop feature will also automatically install all available applications when invoked.

◆ Users' data can be automatically mirrored on the PC and the server, providing fault tolerance and allowing mobile users to have access to information, whether connected to the network or not. Additionally, users will be able to roam between PCs while maintaining full access to their data, applications, and customized environment.

◆ A central administrator will be able to control all aspects of the client systems across the network. The client systems can be "locked down" to maintain controlled, consistent, and secure configurations across sets of users.

◆ The full Active Platform (including key client and server Internet technologies) will provide the flexibility to deploy both Web-style "thin client" applications and the full wealth of personal productivity and client-server applications. Using the lock-down feature, administrators will be able to tune the client environment to the exact needs of each user, and be able to change these as business needs dictate.

These new ZAW functions will be built into forthcoming releases of Windows 95 and Windows NT Workstation operating systems. IT managers will soon have increased flexibility and control for managing their Windows-based environments.

WEB-BASED ENTERPRISE MANAGEMENT (WBEM)

Another very interesting development is the emerging WBEM technology, which appears to be close to producing some actual product. The WBEM initiative is intended to provide a framework for interoperability between the many disparate management tools, protocols, and APIs. It promises to unify management data (SNMP, DMI, HTML, and others) collected from various object providers and translate it to a common Hypermedia Management Protocol (HMMP). A new Hypermedia Management Schema (HMMS) is being developed to facilitate this translation and to allow any number of management applications to communicate with the managed objects.

MICROSOFT MANAGEMENT CONSOLE (MMC)

The new Microsoft Management Console (formerly code-named Slate) is another important development to note. This new tool provides a single host for integrating many different administration and management applications. Microsoft intends to integrate all the administration tools for their BackOffice products into MMC. It has also released the MMC Software Developer's Kit (SDK) and is encouraging other vendors to develop new management utilities to work within MMC. The primary goal of MMC is to provide a common, easy-to-use interface that serves as a single, integrated console for complete enterprise management. MMC was designed as an object-oriented container to host various snap-in modules. MMC does not have any functionality of its own, but provides the framework for snap-in modules built by Microsoft and other third-parties. MMC does not require the use of any specific protocol or proprietary object repository because each snap-in module is responsible for this functionality. MMC is built using Component Object Model (COM)-based interfaces, and all snap-ins are implemented as COM in-process server DLLs. The snap-in components can inherit properties from the MMC host and can work independently of each other or interoperate with other snap-in components. The most important aspect of MMC is the "node manager," which includes the code required for the snap-ins to function within the console's environment. Additionally, MMC's "snap-in manager" provides the means of identifying available snap-in modules and allowing the user to select and manipulate objects within a snap-in.

The visible parts of MMC are typical of any Windows-based application: a title bar, a menu bar, a toolbar, and, optionally, one or more client windows. Each client window has two view panes in which the various snap-in modules can place objects and implement the capability to manage these objects. It is too soon to tell, but it is likely that many vendors will develop utilities to plug into MMC. Regardless, MMC is going to be an important tool to anyone involved with administering Microsoft BackOffice products.

SUMMARY

This appendix examined the discipline of enterprise management from a holistic approach, including network, systems, and application management. I offered some general guidelines and considerations for developing an enterprise management strategy. Some of the specific administration and management functions of SMS were also discussed in the context of the various enterprise management disciplines.

The last few sections of this appendix discussed emerging trends and the evolving Web-based management tools. I also briefly reviewed the new Microsoft Management Console (MMC).

- +Plus Pack

- AssetWORKS

APPENDIX C

Third-Party Integration— Making the Job Easier

Even more than a product, Microsoft's System Management Server is an architecture. It's easy to say that SMS is weak in terms of the machine details collected, that it doesn't have any license management, that it doesn't do useful reporting, that non-PC devices are ignored, or that it lacks other critical system management functions. Such criticisms have some merit, but they overlook SMS's great beauty—its architecture. SMS is very modular, very scalable, very tolerant to failures at any given point, and basically easy to use. Microsoft has made certain that SMS is a great architecture and that it provides the important functionality that system managers require. Organizations that use SMS can readily build on SMS to suit their own needs. Other vendors (third parties) can build on SMS by applying their expertise to produce products that solve the big problems companies have with their machines. SMS makes it all possible.

Many products have some integration with SMS, and I encourage you to review and research these to ensure that you make the best use of SMS. However, some products are particularly significant in terms of how tightly integrated they are with SMS and how the system management function is particularly well served when they are used with SMS. Several of those products will be described in this appendix.

Technical analysts owe it to their employers and clients to be well aware of the products available in their areas of technical expertise. In order to survive, vendors of third-party products must solve problems that are worth paying to solve. Those problems may well affect the people who pay you to do your job. SMS helps to solve the problems, as does your expertise, but buying an additional solution is often an important part of the equation.

Microsoft encourages the process of getting SMS customers and third parties together by listing all the SMS-related (or complementary, as Microsoft says) products it knows at its Web site (http://www.microsoft.com/smsmgmt). Otherwise, SMS customers can become aware of potentially useful third-party products by searching the Web, reading trade magazines, reading books such as this one, and conferring with fellow SMS technical specialists.

SMS technical analysts will find third-party SMS-related products available for various tasks. These tasks include license management, software metering, management of non-PC or non-Microsoft devices, reporting, enhanced software or hardware auditing, help desk functions, and software installation.

Many third-party products integrate with SMS by using the SMS database as a base from which to initiate their tasks. From there, they can get details about machines that allow the products to determine how they should execute. Other third-party products integrate with SMS by producing SMS-compatible MIF files. These files are then uploaded by SMS, enhancing the database or allowing standard SMS reporting techniques to be used. Still other products replace SMS-provided components.

This appendix examines two third-party SMS products: +Plus Pack from Computing Edge and AssetWORKS from Computer Associates (previously from Digital Equipment Corporation). Administrator +Plus provides various important SMS enhancements, including use of the SMS Administrator on Windows 95 consoles, enhanced inventory collection, and the use of Novell NetWare servers. AssetWORKS provides a large number of SMS functions, including enhanced reporting, inclusion of UNIX, and OpenVMS.

+Plus Pack

+Plus Pack is a product from Computing Edge, which is one of the premier SMS third parties. Some of the key people at Computing Edge were previously on the SMS team at Microsoft, so they have excellent knowledge of SMS and the requirements of those who use it. You should check out their Web site at `http://www.ComputingEdge.com` to get the latest details on this and other products, as well as to get evaluation copies of the software.

+Plus Pack is a consolidation of several products, each licensed separately, called Administrator +Plus, Inventory +Plus, and Package Command Manager +Plus for NetWare Servers. Administrator +Plus allows the SMS Administrator program (and the Security Manager) to run on Windows 95 PCs. Inventory +Plus allows the enhancement of the SMS inventory by including anything that can be found in the Windows 95 or Windows NT Registries. Package Command Manager +Plus for NetWare Servers provides a Package Command Manager for NetWare servers, allowing them to receive jobs for execution on the NetWare servers, and it also allows collection of inventory information about NetWare servers.

Administrator +Plus

SMS administration is mostly done, appropriately, with the SMS Administrator program. You can use the SMS Administrator to initiate remote control or network monitoring functions, or you can use it to check on inventory details, use queries, create packages, initiate jobs, monitor alerts and events, modify site characteristics, and so on. However, in an organization of any significant size, these functions are most likely done by a variety of staff. Senior SMS staff change site configurations and check on the state of the system. Operational staff put together packages and send them to the appropriate machines. Help desk staff check on client details or use remote control. Some of these staff members are happy to use Windows NT on their desks, so running the SMS Administrator is not a problem. However, others may require Windows 95, either for applications that are compatible only with Windows 95 or because the users are standardized on Windows 95 and the technical staff must be able to reproduce the user situations exactly. Administrator +Plus solves this problem nicely by allowing the SMS Administrator program to run on Windows 95.

Administrator +Plus has its own setup program, providing various files to make its tricks possible. However, it also prompts for the SMS CD-ROM so that it can grab most of the necessary files (including SMS Administrator itself). Once installed, the SMS Administrator runs very much as it does on Windows NT (see Figure C.1). The only significant limitations are that you cannot use Network Monitor, you must re-enter the logon details each time you execute the Administrator, remote control of Windows NT Workstations may not be possible, and some event details may not be available.

Figure C.1. SMS Administrator and Security Manager on Windows 95.

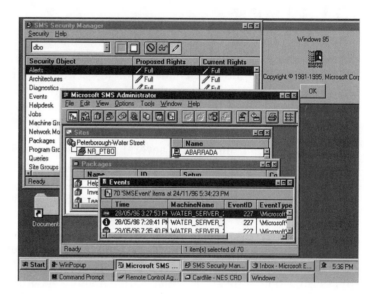

INVENTORY +PLUS

One of the best reasons for investing in SMS is that it allows collection of details on all the PCs that an organization owns. One would hope that as a company buys machines and software, it keeps track of these details and has this information readily at hand. However, this is not nearly as practical as it sounds. Despite standardization, machines are bought as budgets and priorities allow, and given the fast pace of the computer industry, there is a great chance that the machines bought in the last batch are superseded by better, cheaper models. PCs are also relatively inexpensive (compared with other kinds of machinery), so it is easy for a manager to avoid the standardized purchasing procedures. Furthermore, as machines come into the company, some details are recorded, but often these don't include details that only later prove to be important. Software is even more prone to these difficulties. Finally, machines and software are moved and reconfigured as needed or at the whim of individual users or technical specialists. Therefore, any knowledge of the state of a company's machines is good for only a small period of time. It must be continually updated, and SMS is great at this function.

However, it is not wise for SMS to collect all information about everything for everybody. The databases would become huge, and the load on the network and servers would be prohibitive—not to mention concerns about privacy. Therefore, it is appropriate that an organization's SMS administrators extend the SMS inventory collection process according to their organization's needs. Creating MIF files is not at all difficult. Generally, the information put in those MIF files can be readily obtained by simple programs. However, one of the most valuable sources of information on Windows 95 or Windows NT machines is the Registry, as is Microsoft's intent, but obtaining information from it can be very tricky.

The Registry is very flexible, allowing for the needs of any variety of programs. You might need information about networking protocols, for instance, which is available in the Registry's `LOCAL_MACHINE\System\CurrentControlSet\Services\Class\NetTrans` tree. However, it won't have a TCP/IP subtree but rather will contain keys such as `0000`, `0003`, `0004`, and so on. The order varies, depending on which protocols are installed, which is the default, and so forth. The way to find out which is which is to check each one for known values, such as `DriverDesc`. Once you find the right subtree, it is easy to collect the right keys. Fortunately, Computing Edge took the hard work out of dealing with these complexities by providing Inventory +Plus. It is largely based on scripts, which are used to specify which Registry entries should be collected and how they can be found. The scripting is somewhat like the MIF files themselves, so an SMS administrator should be able to start developing them very quickly. Figure C.2 shows the icons for the default inventory details that Inventory +Plus provides.

Figure C.2.
Inventory details
provided by
Inventory +Plus.

Inventory +Plus runs as an agent on the clients, collecting information from the registries according to the scripts. There are different packages for Windows NT and Windows 95; the main differences are that the NT agent runs as a service (as opposed to a hidden application), and the sample scripts are different because the registries contain different information. Windows NT has a Registry entry for the speed of the CPU, for instance, whereas Windows 95 doesn't. The Windows 95 sample scripts collect a wide range of useful information, including desktop details; time zone and TCP/IP details; a huge variety of hardware details; ODBC, basic network, and Office 95 details; and various general Windows 95 details. The Windows NT samples provide much the same information but also collect details on Exchange Server, Internet Information Server, and Proxy Server. The sample scripts may have their limitations, but they are often a good place to start. As an example, the Windows 95 TCP/IP information doesn't account for Dynamic Host Configuration Protocol (DHCP), so if DHCP is used, misleading results are returned.

PACKAGE COMMAND MANAGER +PLUS FOR NETWARE SERVERS

As discussed in Chapter 20, "Making the Software Distribution," SMS provides Package Command Managers for various platforms, and other vendors can provide them for others. Computing Edge provides a Package Command Manager for NetWare servers. NetWare servers have been very popular over the years for providing file, print, and other services, so an organization is likely to have many of them. Like other servers, they tend to require a fair amount of maintenance, and yet it is unlikely that each one has its own dedicated administrator. The ideal situation is to have experts performing administrative functions from a central location, and SMS is a great tool for making this possible. However, out of the box, SMS doesn't provide the option to run jobs on NetWare servers. The NetWare servers can be used as package distribution servers, but they don't have a PCM and thus can't run the packages themselves. This is where PCM +Plus for NetWare Servers comes in.

Package Command Manager +Plus for NetWare Servers (PCM++/NW) is an NLM (NetWare Loadable Module) serving as a Package Command Manager. If the jobs must execute without delay or intervention, then they must be set up to not require any input, and they must be made mandatory. PCM++/NW also enhances the inventory information available about NetWare servers on which it is installed by picking up MIF files that are in the SYS:\MS\SMS\NOIDMIFS directory.

PCM++/NW supports version 3.11 and higher NetWare servers, and the server must be configured as a logon server in a domain of type NetWare in the SMS site or as a NetWare proxy domain server. The PCM++/NW NLM uses the server it is running on as the distribution server for the job, so it must be set up accordingly.

ASSETWORKS

Digital Equipment Corporation has long been one of the premier companies in the computer industry. It has a large number of popular products and has great strengths in a variety of technologies. To continue its viability in the fast-changing world of computers, Digital embraced Microsoft's technologies, including Systems Management Server. This has led Digital to produce AssetWORKS. AssetWORKS extends SMS facilities to UNIX, OpenVMS, and PATHWORKS clients, all of which are Digital products. (UNIX is also sold by many other companies, of course, and AssetWORKS includes support for many of those versions.) In addition, AssetWORKS improves SMS features such as reporting, and includes new features such as software metering, health monitoring, and DMI (Desktop Management Interface) support. Digital also worked with Computing Edge, and this led to the inclusion of support for NetWare servers, among other things. Recently, Digital sold AssetWORKS to Computer Associates, but Digital and Computing Edge continue to be involved with it. You can contact Computer Associates for more details (http://www.cai.com), but Digital and Computing Edge should also be able to help.

Although features such as software metering, health monitoring, and improved reporting are important, AssetWORKS's support for non-PC machines is bound to be its most important feature. In today's cost-conscious environment, computer support staffing is bound to grow less slowly than the complexity of the environments they are trying to support. Therefore, most organizations are bound to have fewer people dedicated to supporting minicomputers, despite their importance. Providing SMS tools to help them with their job is a necessity.

For UNIX and OpenVMS computers, AssetWORKS can provide inventory collection and job execution services, much as it does for personal computer or Macintosh clients. Inventory collection includes a wide variety of hardware and operating system details, and default packages are provided to find installed software. Later sections in this appendix give good examples of how detailed the inventories of the UNIX and OpenVMS clients can be. Inventory collection can be extended to include your own software definitions or anything else that can be made into an MIF file. Job execution can install patches, application software, licenses, and data files of various sorts.

UNIX seems to be better supported by AssetWORKS than OpenVMS, reflecting Digital's expectation that UNIX will continue to be a growth area for many years to come. On UNIX, AssetWORKS also provides health monitoring and file collection facilities.

As with SMS packages intended for PCs, preparation of packages for UNIX or OpenVMS clients requires considerable effort and testing. However, for organizations with numerous minicomputers, this effort is easily justified.

Like Computing Edge's +Plus Pack, AssetWORKS's components are licensed on an individual basis so that customers can pay for what they use. The central functionality that is added to an SMS server requires a Server license, but this also allows use on as many SMS consoles as desired. The features that involve software on PCs

C

THIRD-PARTY INTEGRATION

and Macintoshes require a PC client license for each client. Features involving OpenVMS or UNIX require an Enterprise Client license for each such client. NetWare Inventory Plus clients require an Inventory Plus client license for each NetWare server. Finally, Proxy Domain client licenses are required for each NetWare server providing this functionality.

UNIX CLIENTS

AssetWORKS includes support for the following:

> Sun's Solaris, v2.3 or 2.4
> Sun's SunOS, v4.1.2
> IBM's AIX, v3.2.x or 4.1.x
> Hewlett-Packard's HP-UX, v9.x or v10.x
> Digital's Digital UNIX, v2.0 or higher
> Digital's ULTRIX, v4.3 or higher

Inventory collection for UNIX clients provides details in a variety of machine groups, as shown in Figure C.3. Figure C.4 shows UNIX software inventory details and Figure C.5 shows user account details.

Figure C.3.
AssetWORKS's
UNIX inventory
groups.

AssetWORKS's UNIX inventory collection provides details in a huge variety of useful categories, such as users, hosts, file entries, disks, licenses, networking, and so on. Being able to check these details from a central location for all a company's UNIX machines, regardless of where they are, is very valuable.

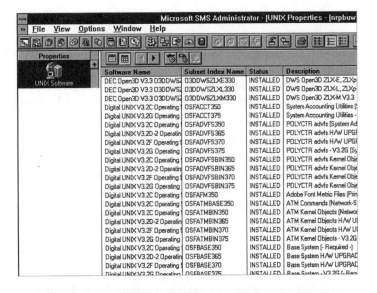

Figure C.4.
Details of
AssetWORKS's
UNIX Software
group.

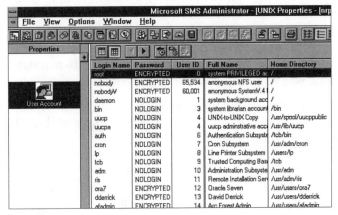

Figure C.5.
Details of
AssetWORKS's
UNIX User
Account group.

C

UNIX software installation packages must run unattended (due to the way the Package Command Manager works) and thus must use installation autoanswer capabilities. Autoanswer files must be created during a manually executed test installation, using the script command. Another consideration is that text files (such as scripts) that are created on Windows NT probably do not use the same kind of line terminators as UNIX or OpenVMS. Digital provides utilities such as avmscript to correct for this issue.

Given that most UNIX systems are often used by multiple concurrent users, the concept of a Package Command Manager must be different from that with PC SMS clients. On UNIX (as well as OpenVMS) systems, a background process periodically checks for newly arrived packages. When found, they are executed in the background, so there is no opportunity for specifying options at that time. Job execution times can be specified when the jobs are created in the SMS Administrator, but otherwise, there is no opportunity to ensure that jobs are executed at times convenient to the users. For this reason (as well as the fact that interaction is often required), operating system upgrades and other jobs that require reboots may not be appropriate for AssetWORKS jobs.

AssetWORKS's UNIX health monitoring facility (described in general later in this appendix) is one of the most valuable AssetWORKS features for many administrators. Many critical elements can be monitored to ensure they don't exceed thresholds, such as disk activity, memory usage, CPU load, loss (or activation) of processes, and so on. By monitoring these activities, the administrator can be alerted to problems before the users start calling.

OpenVMS Clients

OpenVMS is a nice operating system from Digital Equipment Corporation, providing a powerful, mature environment on which to run large-scale, critical applications on affordable minicomputers. As such, it is very valuable to many organizations, as AssetWORKS OpenVMS support will be. AssetWORKS's OpenVMS enterprise client components make it easier to manage these systems in much the same way as the UNIX client components.

Inventory collection for OpenVMS clients provides details in a variety of machine groups, as shown in Figure C.6. An example of the information in the OpenVMS machine group is shown in Figure C.7.

Figure C.6.
AssetWORKS's
OpenVMS
inventory groups.

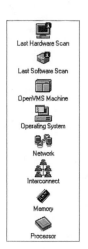

*Figure C.7.
Details of
AssetWORKS's
OpenVMS
machine group.*

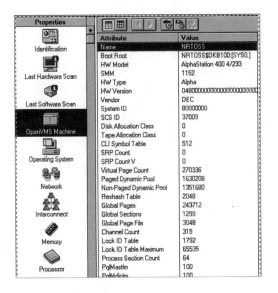

AssetWORKS OpenVMS client job execution facility is built on Digital's PolyCentre Software Distribution (PSD, formerly known as Remote System Management) client. PSD is a powerful and attractive facility in itself, but when used as part of AssetWORKS with SMS, it is much easier to use. The skills and tasks involved in PC management (other than package preparation) are much the same, simplifying management overall.

Packages for AssetWORKS's job execution facility must be prepared using the PolyCentre Software Distribution Trial Installation Procedure (SYS$UPDATE:RSM$TRIAL_ INSTALL.COM). This procedure records an "autoanswer" file for VMSINSTAL (or PolyCentre Software Install configuration file, as appropriate) and combines the installation files (while preserving the OpenVMS file attributes) into one container file.

REPORTING

AssetWORKS has two kinds of reports: tabular reports, called management reports, and graphical reports, which are all the others. The management reports provide various details about the SMS administrative functions—mainly job statuses but also software inventory and package details and a log of the reports produced. These reports have various options available in order to schedule when they are executed, limit them to various sites, and so on. However, you can only review these reports on paper. The management reports are bound to be useful to the SMS administrator to keep such information on file or to allow him to review system status away from the computer.

The non-management reports are graphical (as opposed to tabular, although the table is available if you want to see the details that the report is based on). A large number of predefined reports are available (see Figure C.8), some relating to standard SMS details, such as personal computers, packages, jobs, events, and history. Others relate to the new AssetWORKS options, such as Health Monitor, Metering, OpenVMS, and UNIX details. Some reports also cover both areas in the Cross Architecture group. Good examples of reports on standard details concern the average disk space used, package locations, Excel usage by site, machines with more than 8MB of memory, bad MIF events by system, and a weekly history of the number of software titles by site. Sample AssetWORKS-related reports include OpenVMS operating system versions, UNIX BIND servers, and audited software usage. Cross Architecture reports include total free disk space and network by type (and these are for all kinds of computers). This is just a small sampling of the reports that are available.

Figure C.8.
AssetWORKS's
provided reports.

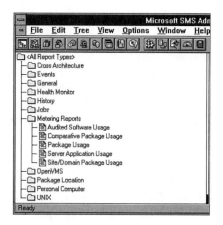

To be precise, AssetWORKS defines reports as output based on result sets collected on the basis of a report template. The report template tells the server what information the administrator is interested in and how he wants the output formatted. The result set is the result of a query based on that report template. The administrator selects a template from the appropriate template group and specifies any additional details if desired, including when to do the query. When the query is done, the result set is produced, and the result set can be viewed whenever convenient and as often as required. When scheduling the query, you can specify various details as may be appropriate to each report, including machines or sites to be included, what columns should be included, how they should be viewed, and so on.

METERING AND AUDITING

When checking with the Microsoft SMS third-party product Web pages or other sources, you see that various companies offer software metering features that integrate with SMS. Software metering usually involves keeping track of licenses and allowing users to use an application if sufficient licenses are available. AssetWORKS's approach to metering and auditing is a little different. AssetWORKS, if desired, will routinely check what programs are executing ("auditing") and how much specified programs are being used ("metering"). This is entirely passive; usage is not checked against predefined limits, the user is not stopped from using software or given a chance to go on a waiting list, and the user doesn't even have to be aware that this software is on the PC performing this function. Therefore, AssetWORKS's metering and auditing is a good mechanism to review how much applications are being used (and thus how many licenses are required) and to see exactly what programs are being run. However, it cannot be used to absolutely enforce concurrent licenses, and there is the danger of the Big Brother syndrome in which users are monitored to ensure they are working. For many sites, the AssetWORKS approach is the best. Other sites may prefer to consider an alternative, and some will need both.

AssetWORKS's metering and auditing involves a component (downloaded by means of a package) that sits on the client collecting the appropriate information and sends it back to SMS by using MIFs. The SMS Administrator can create reports to review what programs were run and whether application usage exceeds licensing limitations. (See Figure C.9, which is an example from Digital's documentation of metering reporting.)

Figure C.9.
A sample from
the AssetWORKS
documentation of
an auditing
report.

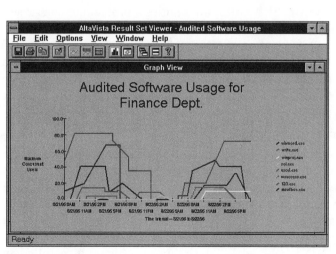

C

THIRD-PARTY INTEGRATION

With AssetWORKS installed, the SMS Administrator includes five extra buttons, one of which is for AssetWORKS Metering (and auditing). In that window, you can define new packages for metering. Metering packages include information to identify programs, such as program name, file size, checksums, and so on. This is much like the inventory details for SMS packages, but unfortunately, they are separate files. Digital provides various predefined packages, which are readily imported, and the SMS package can be associated with the metering package, but this is just for reference purposes. The package name is important because it is displayed on the metering reports that are produced. This window also includes a button to display the Software Audit Configuration dialog, which allows specification of the machines and platforms to be audited, if any.

HEALTH MONITOR

Health Monitor allows real-time monitoring for important system events. This is best implemented on Windows NT and UNIX machines, but these are the machines that are most likely to be significant, given that they are often servers. Health Monitor watches for a variety of critical events, such as insufficient disk space, excessive page faulting, system event logs that are growing too fast, excessive average system load, and so forth. On Windows NT and most versions of UNIX, it does all these things. On Windows 95, Health Monitor is limited to watching for low disk space, disk I/O failures, page file usage, and whether certain processes are running. On OS/2 and Macintoshes, Health Monitor is limited to just disk space and disk I/O failures, and Health Monitor isn't available at all for DOS or Windows 3.1x machines.

Once Health Monitor does notice a problem, it can execute a program locally, send an SMS event, send an SNMP event, or send e-mail to the root account (on UNIX machines). If the SNMP software is appropriately configured, it could page the administrator or take similar action to ensure that the problem is immediately rectified, perhaps before the users even notice that something is amiss. Health Monitor events can also be reported, using the appropriate AssetWORKS Reporting reports.

Health monitoring is configured through MONITOR.INI files, so it is best to set these up centrally, with some forethought, before installing the Health Monitor software on the clients. Unfortunately, there is no flexibility to add events that are monitored, but you can configure the different actions that are taken, the threshold levels at which they occur, and so forth. Once the MONITOR.INI files are set up, the client software is installed by means of packages (on Windows 95, Windows NT, OS/2, and Macintosh clients) or as part of the AssetWORKS for UNIX client installation on UNIX machines. When the client software is installed on Windows NT computers, it must also be configured to run as a service using an account with administrator privileges and the right to log on as a service.

APPLICATION LAUNCHING

When you view machine properties for a particular machine in the SMS Administrator, a few property groups allow executing a program with details relevant to that machine. The best example is the Help Desk group, which allows execution of the remote control functions, but the Network Monitor group also has similar functionality, and Windows NT machines have the Windows NT Administrative Tools group. Experienced system administrators know how to add property groups in order to display additional inventory details. How can action-oriented groups be added? AssetWORKS provides this functionality.

Adding such groups requires executing the AssetWORKS Application Launch Utility, which is added to the SMS Program Manager group when AssetWORKS is installed. This program connects to the SMS database and then makes it possible to work with the groups. For each group, it is possible to associate an icon with it, define how the application buttons are laid out, and add the applications to be executed (with icons associated with these as well). Any information contained in the SMS database for each machine can be provided to the application when it is started. For instance, if you want to make TCP/IP-oriented applications available, then you could give them each the address of the client when they are executed. A good example is that a button for FTP could be made available when you look at the machine's properties, and when the button is clicked, FTP is called up and directed to the client machine using the SMS database's record of its TCP/IP address.

DMI INFORMATION COLLECTION

Microsoft's syntax for MIF files, which are used to collect information for the SMS database, is based on the Desktop Management Interface standards but includes limitations that Microsoft says were necessary due to the way SQL Server works. Therefore, SMS cannot collect DMI-based MIFs created by DMI-compliant software. AssetWORKS solves this problem as well, by making available client software to make the appropriate adjustments.

The DMI client software is installed using SMS packages. When executed, the software collects the appropriate information from the DMI-compliant database and makes it available as an SMS-compliant MIF. The information can then be viewed using the SMS Administrator and the usual reporting tools.

PATHWORKS CLIENTS

PATHWORKS is a family of products available from Digital Equipment Corporation that provides PC networking solutions to traditionally DEC shops (although others could find it useful as well). OpenVMS or Digital UNIX computers are great systems to run a wide variety of powerful applications. If you have such a system, why also buy a NetWare or Windows NT server? Installing PATHWORKS client and server software will do the trick. PATHWORKS software is based on Microsoft's LAN Manager architecture, so it is highly compatible with solutions that work on such products. However, Digital has also extended this architecture to provide DECnet network protocol support, terminal emulation, messaging, and a variety of other features. Among these extensions is a special redirector for networking clients, providing additional security facilities and allowing the use of longer (and more meaningful) share names. Unfortunately, this redirector does not provide all the more sophisticated features of the Enhanced Redirector, which SMS requires. The AssetWORKS PC client software allows PATHWORKS sites to benefit from SMS while continuing to use this redirector. However, remote control, program group control, and Windows diagnostics are not supported, and domain logons must be enabled for these clients. Other, less significant, limitations exist for PATHWORKS clients, and the AssetWORKS documentation provides details about these.

Organizations with PATHWORKS servers distributed throughout their sites might also want to use those servers to support their SMS infrastructure. Using PATHWORKS (version 5 or higher) servers as logon servers is very straightforward, but the AssetWORKS documentation also points out that these servers can be used as package distribution servers as well. In so doing, the SMS administrator can avoid putting NT servers at all sites or can take some of the load off his Windows NT servers, but he'll have to be sure that PATHWORKS licensing is complete.

NetWare Support

Just as AssetWORKS allows use of a PATHWORKS server infrastructure for SMS, it can also allow use of a Novell NetWare infrastructure. This is provided by a component called the AssetWORKS Proxy Domain Client. This facility allows NetWare servers to be used as SMS distribution servers. Sites that only have a NetWare server can have full SMS services.

In addition, AssetWORKS allows collection of NetWare server information and delivery of packages through the use of a component called AssetWORKS NetWare Inventory Plus.

Summary

With the addition of third-party products, SMS can be an even more powerful system. Managing a computer infrastructure is often very complex, involving thousands of devices of various types. SMS is a great start to managing these devices in a useful fashion. Third-party products can enhance SMS's facilities by improving inventory collection, reporting, and software distribution. Third-party products can also use SMS as a base for their network management, help desk, license management, and other functions. We strongly encourage you to review the various possibilities in order to better solve your own problems.

+Plus Pack provides facilities to run the SMS Administrator and Security Manager on Windows 95, collect inventory based on Windows 95's and Windows NT's rich inventories, and include NetWare servers in the inventory and run jobs on them. AssetWORKS includes UNIX, OpenVMS, PATHWORKS clients and servers, and NetWare servers in the SMS client base and infrastructure. It also enhances reporting and adds health monitoring, DMI support, metering and auditing, and application launching. All these options can be very valuable when used with Systems Management Server. In fact, it is hard to imagine using SMS without such third-party products.

C

THIRD-PARTY INTEGRATION

- Architecture

- Object

- Group

- Attribute

- Common Keywords

APPENDIX D

Extending Inventory Collection

When the SMS Inventory Agent runs at an SMS client, it collects the inventory information and stores it as a binary file on the SMS logon servers. This file contains the computer's inventory in MIF (Management Information File) format. Microsoft's SMS uses an inventory process common to all the PC manufacturers.

The DMI (Desktop Management Interface) standard defined by the Desktop Management Task Force (DMTF) committee was adopted by all leading manufacturers of desktop computer systems. DMI is basically a set of rules on how to access information about your personal computer across different platforms.

SMS 1.2 uses six different .MIF files to provide information to the SMS database:

> Personal Computer MIF files (*.MIF)
> Custom architecture MIF files (*.MIF)
> SMSEvent MIF files (*.EMF)
> UserGroup MIF files (*.UMF)
> JobDetails MIF files (*.JMF)
> PackageLocation MIF files (*.PMF)

Note

In previous versions of SMS, all MIF files were named with the .MIF file extension. If you have any computers running a previous version of SMS, those computers continue to report all MIF files with the .MIF file extension.

For extending inventory, the focus is on custom architecture and personal computer .MIF files. Using .MIF files, you can add objects with custom architectures to the inventory, such as printers; add a new object to an existing architecture; and add groups (such as device driver information, hardware peripherals, and monitors) to computers already existing in the SMS database.

In an SMS site database, the inventory has a hierarchical structure. An architecture is the highest level in the SMS hierarchy, defining the structure for a set of objects. Each object is composed of one or more groups. Each group contains one or more attributes.

This hierarchy is reflected in the .MIF file format.

The SMS MIF Form Generator is automatically installed on site servers at primary sites. The SMS Setup program also creates the SMS MIF Form Generator program item for the MIF Form Generator window in the Systems Management Server program group.

Note

> The SMS MIF Form Generator runs only on the Windows NT operating system.

When you create a form, the SMS MIF Form Generator saves it as a file with an .XNF extension in the X86.BIN, MIPS.BIN, or ALPHA.BIN subdirectory. After creating a form, you must distribute it to users at clients so that they can use it to generate a .MIF file. On clients, the MIF Entry utility reads forms only with the .XNF extension and ignores those with other extensions.

Using the DMI interface, a local or remote application program can check what hardware and software components are installed on your computer, such as power management facilities. The following .MIF file detects the configuration of a Hewlett-Packard machine's power management configuration.

```
//-----------------------------------------------------------------
// Power Management group
//-----------------------------------------------------------------
 Start Group
  Name = "Power Management"
  ID = 39
  Class = "HP¦Power¦002"
  Description = "Advanced Power Management Group"

  Start Attribute
   Name = "Advanced Power Management Active?"
   ID = 1
   Description = "If TRUE, indicates that the Power Management is active"
   Access = Read-Only
   Storage = SPECIFIC
   Type=Integer
   Value = unsupported
  End Attribute
  Start Attribute
   Name = "Delay Before Stand-By mode"
   ID = 2
   Description = "this attribute specifies the time in minutes before the "
   "computer goes into standby mode.(low power consumption mode)"
   Access = Read-Write
   Storage = SPECIFIC
   Type=Integer
   Value = *"CPCODE"
  End Attribute
  Start Attribute
   Name = "Sleep Time"
   ID = 3
   Description = "Use this field to specify the time in 24-hour clock format "
   "(0:00 to 23:00) when your computer is to go into low power consumption "
   "mode. The screen is blanked, the hard disk drive stops spinning, "
   "and the processor stops."
```

```
 Access = Read-Write
 Storage = SPECIFIC
 Type=Integer
 Value = unsupported
End Attribute
Start Attribute
 Name = "Hard-Disk Power Management"
 ID = 4
 Description = "if True, the hard disk drive does not restart until the user"
 " password is entered"
 Access = Read-Only
 Storage = SPECIFIC
 Type= "BOOL"
 Value = *"CPCODE"
End Attribute
Start Attribute
 Name = "Sleep now"
 ID = 5
 Description = "if True, The screen is blanked, the hard disk drive stops "
 "spinning and the processor stops."
 Access = Read-Write
 Storage = SPECIFIC
 Type= "BOOL"
 Value = unsupported
End Attribute
```

The following keywords are used in .MIF files to describe computer components:

> Architecture
> Object
> Group
> Attribute

ARCHITECTURE

Every .MIF file added to the SMS database requires an architecture. A component's architecture describes a set of related objects.

An architecture is defined by the Architecture group, which specifies a unique architecture name. For example, the Personal Computer architecture has a structure for describing Intel x86, Alpha, MIPS, and Macintosh-based computers. Figure D.1 shows the properties of the Personal Computer architecture with the group Disk and the attribute Free Storage.

Figure D.1.
Example of
Personal Com-
puter architec-
ture.

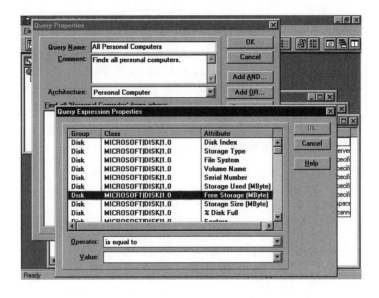

OBJECT

An object is a specific item within a specific architecture. DMTF standards refer to this as a component. For example, a specific Windows NT computer can be an object in the Personal Computer architecture. In an .MIF file, an object is equivalent to a component block.

For a specific object, the attributes of its Identification group combine to form a unique identifier for the object. The Identification group for Personal Computer objects contains six attributes that are used to uniquely identify a computer.

The following code segment is an example of an object definition:

```
Name = "Machine"
  Start Group
    Name = "User Information"
    ID = 1
    Class = "Your Corporation¦User Information¦1.0"
    Start Attribute
      Name = "Email"
      ID = 1
      Type = String(25)
      Storage = Specific
      Value = "Ric_Anderson@Stream.com"
    End Attribute
```

The `String(25)` entry specifies 25 characters for the `Email` field.

GROUP

A group is a structure for defining part or all of an object. A group combines a set of attributes into a single, identifiable entity. For example, Disk Drive, Network, and Operating System are some of the groups in the Personal Computer architecture.

A group is identified by its class and keyed attributes. This required string defines the class name for a group. In the following example, the administrative body is Microsoft, the product type is disk, and the version is 1.0:

```
Name = "Disk"
        ID = 6
        Class = "MICROSOFT¦DISK¦1.0"
        Pragma = "HardwareHistory"
        Key = 1
Start Attribute
            Name = "Free Storage (MByte)"
            ID = 1
            Access = READ-ONLY
            Storage = SPECIFIC
            Type = Int
            Value = 3
        End Attribute
```

In the Personal Computer architecture, groups can be used to store the properties of a hardware device such as a disk or a network adapter, a piece of software such as the operating system or extended BIOS information, or any user-defined entries such as asset tag or e-mail address through custom .MIF files. When the inventory for an object is displayed in the object's Properties window, all the groups for the object are displayed in the Query Expression Properties window. The attributes for the selected group are displayed in the right pane of the Query Expression Properties window.

Objects for every architecture must have an Identification group and an Architecture group.

A group starts with the line Start Group and ends with the line End Group. Objects for every architecture must have an Identification group. The Identification group can have any number of attributes. However, you should ensure that all attributes are included in all objects that are part of a single custom architecture.

ATTRIBUTE

An attribute is a property of a group. For example, a Disk group on a computer has attributes such as File System, Storage Type, Free Storage, and so on. Each attribute is assigned a value. For example, a File System attribute is assigned a value such as FAT, NTFS, and so on.

COMMON KEYWORDS

.MIF files are organized into blocks of code. The following are some of the most commonly used keywords:

◆ Name is a string enclosed by quotation marks that labels the group or attribute. When the group is displayed in the Query Expression Properties window (refer to Figure D.1), this string is used to label the group or attribute.

◆ ID is a number that identifies the group. The ID must be unique for each group within the object. ID is an integer value. Group IDs must be 1 or greater.

◆ Key applies only to multiple-instance groups. For example, an object such as a disk drive can have multiple instances on a computer. One or more keys are used to differentiate the instances. For example, the Disk Drive group has a key defined for the Drive Index attribute. The Key entry specifies one or more IDs for the attributes used to uniquely identify an instance of a group. If you have multiple keys, you must separate them with commas. If a group can have only a single instance, no key should be defined.

◆ Class is a required string that defines the class name for a group. The class name identifies the source and version of the group and should be unique within the SMS database. All groups sharing a class name must have exactly the same definition.

◆ Access determines the access type of the table where the attribute is stored. Values are READ-ONLY, READ-WRITE, and WRITE-ONLY. The Access statement is optional and defaults to READ-ONLY.

◆ Storage assists management applications to optimize storage requirements. Values can be common or specific. Common attributes are for properties that are likely to be common among many computers (for example, the processor name should be a common attribute). Specific attributes are for properties that are likely to have unique values on most computers (for example, the amount of free disk space should be a specific attribute). The Storage key is optional.

◆ Type is the data type used to store the value of the attribute. There are two data types. Counter is an integer. String is a character string. For strings, you must specify the maximum length for the string.

The SQL Server database has a limit of 255 characters for any attribute value. Any string longer than 255 characters is truncated. Also, any values longer than the originally defined length are truncated. For example, if attribute Email is defined as String(25), SMS adds only the first 25 characters for an Email value that is longer than 25 characters.

The SMS system uses the first definition of type. For example, if you first defined Email as String(25), the SMS system always uses that type. You cannot change the Type after you first define it.

◆ Value is the value assigned to the attribute. The value must be in the form specified by Type. Strings must be enclosed within quotation marks. Counters must be decimal integers. The Value statement is optional.

Listing D.1 is an example of a more complex .MIF file for extended video information.

LISTING D.1. EXTENDED INVENTORY MIF.

```
Start Group
   Name = "Video BIOS Characteristic"
   Class = "DMTF¦Video BIOS Characteristic¦001"
   Description = "This group defines the characteristics for the Video BIOS."
   Key = 1,2

   Start Attribute
   Name = "Video BIOS Characteristics Index"
   ID = 1
   Description = "This is an index into the Video BIOS Characteristics table."
   Access = Read-Only
   Storage = Common
   Type = Integer
   Value = 0
   End Attribute

   Start Attribute
   Name = "Video BIOS Number "
   ID = 2
   Description = "This is the Video BIOS numberwhich correlates to
the Video BIOS Index."
   Access = Read-Only
   Storage = Common
   Type = Integer
   Value = 1
   End Attribute

   Start Attribute
   Name = "Video BIOS Characteristics"
   ID = 3
   Description = "This field contains different attributes supported by this "
   "version of the Video BIOS"
   Access = Read-Only
   Storage = Common
   Type =Start Enum
      0x01 = "Other"
      0x02 = "Unknown"
      0x03 = "Unsupported"
      0x04 = "Standard Video BIOS"
      0x05 = "VESA BIOS Extension Supported "
      0x06 = "VESA Power Management Supported"
      0x07 = "VESA Display Data Channel Supported"
      0x08 = "Video BIOS Shadowing allowed"
      0x09 = "Video BIOS Upgradeable"
```

```
    End Enum
   Value = 0
  End Attribute

  Start Attribute
   Name = "Video BIOS Characteristics Description"
   ID = 4
   Description = "Expanded description on this Video BIOS characteristic"
   Access = Read-Only
   Storage = Specific
   Type = String(80)
   Value = ""
Name = "Video BIOS Table"
ID    22
Class    "DMTF¦Video BIOS Characteristic¦001"
   {1, 1, 4,""}
   {2, 1, 5,""}
   {3, 1, 8,""}
   {4, 1, 9,""}
   {5, 1, 6,""}
   {6, 1, 7,""}
```

For information about the Management Information Format (MIF), see the Desktop Management Interface Specification, which is provided on the SMS CD-ROM.

You can obtain the complete DMI specifications through the DMTF FTP server, `ftp.dmtf.org`, or through the DMTF Web page, `www.dmtf.org`.

D

SYMBOLS

A

Index

Q

queries
ad hoc, 355, 374-376
basing on existing, 375-376
creating, 374-375
query window, 374
alerts, 554
conditions, 554
architectures, 356-359
attributes, 357
groups, 357
inventories, 357
JobDetails, 359
PackageLocation, 359
Personal Computer, 358
SMNPTraps, 359
SMSEvent, 359
UserGroups, 359
associating with alerts, 610
attended, 355
background, 568
cancelling, 384
components, 356
contents, 354
creating, 372-374
wildcards, 373
deleting, 384-386
executing, 376-378
limiting, 377
expressions, 359-372
clauses, 360
group NOT, 370-371
groups, 360-371
nested groups, 371
operators, 362-372
precedence, 361-362
subclauses, 360
listing, 356
machine groups, 401
modifying, 387-393
expressions, 388-393
name/comment fields, 388

naming, 356
packages, 421
prefixes, 356
query window, 355-356
result formats, 378-384
creating, 378-380
deleting, 381-382
editing, 382-384
Identification, 378
saved, 355
denoting, 355
schemas, 528
site groups, 409
troubleshooting, 394-395
precedence, 394
unattended, 355
user groups (listing), 493
version 1.1, 24
viewing, 386-387
Queries window, 94
Query Expression Properties dialog, 436
Query Properties dialog, 357, 375, 387
Query Result Format Properties dialog, 380

R

RAID
hardware, 183
software, 183
RAS (Remote Access Server), 85
address properties, 453
clients, remote control, 178
encryption
MD4 algorithm, 166
settings, 165
support, 165
installing, 162
configuring client, 163
configuring server, 164
network configuration, 163

ports, 163
PPTP dependence on, 535
protocols
NetBEUI, 165
TCP/IP, 164
sender, 449, 453
installing, 453
phone book entry, 453
senders, 161, 261
addresses, 251-252
Async, 161
ISDN, 161
preparing for, 162-172
requirements, 161, 172
servers
location information, 167
phonebook entry, 167-172
receiving site configuration, 162
sending site configuration, 162
rate limits, 575
RAWCHECK.EXE program, 109
RC4, 166
rebooting, Remote Reboot utility, 345
records, deleting unused, 549
registration process, 284
registries, 52-54
editing, 54, 62
HKEY_LOCAL_MACHINE, 53
keys
HKEY_CURRENT_CONFIG, 54
SMS, 53
Registry, inventory, 621
relational databases, 57-59
relational operators, 362-366
changing, 392
date and time, 366
numeric, 362

Designing and Implementing Microsoft Index Server

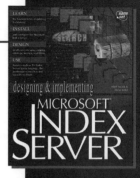

Mark Swank and Drew Kittel

Tripoli is an index server that allows companies to automate their indexing of crucial data. Its integration with Windows NT and Internet Information Server opens the doors to a large market of corporate NT and IIS users who will want to automate their indexing. This book shows readers how to use Tripoli. Everything from installation to implementation is discussed in detail.

Shows readers how to organize and maintain large amounts of information.

Teaches ways to integrate the server into existing systems.

Covers maintenance, administration, and security issues.

$39.99 USA/$56.95 CDN   *User Level: Accomplished*
1-57521-212-9   *350 pp.*
7 3/8 x 9 1/8   *12/01/96*
Internet—Networking/Servers

Designing and Implementing Microsoft Internet Information Server 2

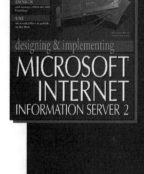

Arthur Knowles and Sanjaya Hettihewa

This book details the specific tasks to setting up and running a Microsoft Internet Information Server. Readers will learn troubleshooting, network design, security, and cross-platform integration procedures.

Teaches security issues and how to maintain an efficient, secure network.

Readers learn everything from planning to implementation.

Covers Microsoft Internet Information Server.

$39.99 USA/$56.95 CDN   *User Level: Casual–Expert*
1-57521-168-8   *336 pp.*
7 3/8 x 9 1/8   *07/01/96*
Internet—Communications/Online

Apache Server Survival Guide

Manuel Alberto Ricart

As one of the most popular servers on the Internet, Apache Server is an inexpensive, secure alternative to other Web servers. This book is an excellent resource that addresses diverse networking and configuration issues.

Provides all of the knowledge needed to build and manage an Apache Web site.

CD-ROM includes source code from the book, utilities, and demos.

Covers the latest version.

$49.99 USA/$70.95 CDN   *User Level: Accomplished*
1-57521-175-0   *650 pp.*
7 3/8 x 9 1/8   *11/01/96*
Internet—Networking/Servers

Netscape Server Survival Guide

David L. Gulbransen, Jr.

With the recent reduction in the price of its server technology, Netscape's marketability is increasing. Current and migrating Netscape administrators alike will need the comprehensive coverage found in this book.

Teaches the reader how to install, configure, and maintain a Netscape server.

Discusses third-party products, commonly used Netscape utilities, and extensive troubleshooting techniques.

CD-ROM contains software demonstrations, sample configuration files, and exotic logon scripts.

$49.99 USA/$70.95 CDN
1-57521-111-4
7 3/8 x 9 1/8
Internet—General/WWW Applications

User Level: Accomplished–Expert
800 pp.
10/01/96

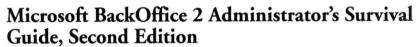

Microsoft BackOffice 2 Administrator's Survival Guide, Second Edition

Arthur Knowles

This all-in-one reference describes how to make the components of BackOffice version 2 work best together and with other networks. BackOffice is Microsoft's complete reference for networking, database, and system management products.

Contains the fundamental concepts required for daily maintenance, troubleshooting, and problem solving.

CD-ROM includes product demos, commercial and shareware utilities, and technical notes from Microsoft vendor technical support personnel.

Covers version 2.

$59.99 USA/$84.95 CDN
0-672-30977-7
7 3/8 x 9 1/8
Client/Server

User Level: Accomplished
1,200 pp.
11/01/96

Microsoft BackOffice 2 Unleashed

Joe Greene, et al.

An instrumental tool for anyone in charge of developing or managing BackOffice. It covers the individual pieces of BackOffice, as well as key phases in the development, integration, and administration of the BackOffice environment.

Covers using BackOffice as the infrastructure of an intranet or the Internet.

Instructs readers on integrating individual BackOffice products.

CD-ROM includes source code, third-party products, and utilities.

Covers BackOffice.

$59.99 USA/$84.95 CDN
0-672-30816-9
7 3/8 x 9 1/8
Client/Server

User Level: Accomplished–Expert
1,200 pp.
11/01/96

Microsoft SQL Server 6.5 Unleashed, Second Edition

David Solomon, Ray Rankins, et al.

This comprehensive reference details the steps needed to plan, design, install, administer, and tune large and small databases. In many cases, the reader will use the techniques in this book to create and manage his or her own complex environment.

CD-ROM includes source code, libraries, and administration tools.

Covers programming topics, including SQL, data structures, programming constructs, stored procedures, referential integrity, large table strategies, and more.

Includes updates to cover all new features of SQL Server 6.5, including the new transaction processing monitor and Internet/database connectivity through SQL Server's new Web wizard.

$59.99 USA/$84.95 CDN
0-672-30956-4
7 3/8 x 9 1/8
Databases

User Level: Accomplished–Expert
1,100 pp.
10/01/96

Microsoft Internet Information Server 2 Unleashed

Arthur Knowles, et al.

The power of Microsoft Internet Information Server 2 is meticulously detailed in this 800-page volume. Readers will learn how to create and maintain a Web server, integrate IIS with BackOffice, and create interactive databases that can be used on the Internet or a corporate intranet.

Readers learn how to set up and run IIS.

Teaches advanced security techniques and how to configure the server.

CD-ROM includes source code from the book and powerful utilities.

Covers Microsoft Internet Information Server 2.

$49.99 USA/$70.95 CDN
1-57521-109-2
7 3/8 x 9 1/8
Internet—Networking/Servers

User Level: Accomplished–Expert
800 pp.
09/01/96

Add to Your Sams Library Today with the Best Books for Programming, Operating Systems, and New Technologies

The easiest way to order is to pick up the phone and call
1-800-428-5331
between 9:00 a.m. and 5:00 p.m. EST.
For faster service, please have your credit card available.

ISBN	Quantity	Description of Item	Unit Cost	Total Cost
1-57521-212-9		Designing & Implementing Microsoft Index Server	$39.99	
1-57521-168-8		Designing & Implementing Microsoft Internet Information Server 2	$39.99	
1-57521-175-0		Apache Server Survival Guide (Book/CD-ROM)	$49.99	
1-57521-111-4		Netscape Server Survival Guide (Book/CD-ROM)	$49.99	
0-672-30977-7		Microsoft BackOffice 2 Administrator's Survival Guide, Second Edition (Book/CD-ROM)	$59.99	
0-672-30816-9		Microsoft BackOffice 2 Unleashed (Book/CD-ROM)	$59.99	
0-672-30956-4		Microsoft SQL Server 6.5 Unleashed, Second Edition (Book/CD-ROM)	$59.99	
1-57521-109-2		Microsoft Internet Information Server 2 Unleashed (Book/CD-ROM)	$49.99	
		Shipping and Handling: See information below.		
		TOTAL		

❏ 3 ½" Disk

❏ 5 ¼" Disk

Shipping and Handling: $4.00 for the first book, and $1.75 for each additional book. Floppy disk: add $1.75 for shipping and handling. If you need to have it NOW, we can ship product to you for an additional charge of approximately $18.00, and you will receive your item overnight or in two days. Overseas shipping and handling adds $2.00 per book and $8.00 for up to three disks. Prices subject to change. Call for availability and pricing information on latest editions.

201 W. 103rd Street, Indianapolis, Indiana 46290

1-800-428-5331 — Orders   1-800-835-3202 — FAX   1-800-858-7674 — Customer Service

Book ISBN 0-672-30984-x

MACMILLAN COMPUTER PUBLISHING USA
A VIACOM COMPANY

 **Technical** ---- **Support:**

If you need assistance with the information in this book or with a CD/Disk accompanying the book, please access the Knowledge Base on our Web site at **http://www.superlibrary.com/general/support**. Our most Frequently Asked Questions are answered there. If you do not find the answer to your questions on our Web site, you may contact Macmillan Technical Support **(317) 581-3833** or e-mail us at **support@mcp.com**.